Masculinities at School

RESEARCH ON MEN AND MASCULINITIES SERIES

Series Editor:
MICHAEL S. KIMMEL, SUNY Stony Brook

Contemporary research on men and masculinity, informed by recent feminist thought and intellectual breakthroughs of women's studies and the women's movement, treats masculinity not as a normative referent but as a problematic gender construct. This series of interdisciplinary, edited volumes attempts to understand men and masculinity through this lens, providing a comprehensive understanding of gender and gender relationships in the contemporary world. Published in cooperation with the Men's Studies Association, a Task Group of the National Organization for Men Against Sexism.

EDITORIAL ADVISORY BOARD

Volumes in this Series

Masculinities at School

Edited by
NANCY LESKO

RESEARCH ON MEN AND MASCULINITIES
Published in cooperation with the Men's Studies Association,
A Task Group of the National Organization for Men Against Sexism

Sage Publications, Inc.
International Educational and Professional Publisher
Thousand Oaks ■ London ■ New Delhi

For information:

Sage Publications, Inc.
2455 Teller Road
Thousand Oaks, California 91320
E-mail: order@sagepub.com

Sage Publications Ltd.
6 Bonhill Street
London EC2A 4PU
United Kingdom

Sage Publications India Pvt. Ltd.
M-32 Market
Greater Kailash I
New Delhi 110 048 India

Printed in the United States of America

Library of Congress Cataloging-in-Publication Data

Masculinities at school / [edited] by Nancy Lesko.
     p. cm.—(Research on men and masculinities series ; v. 11)
    Includes bibliographical references and index.
    ISBN 0-7619-1493-5 (cloth: acid-free paper)
    ISBN 0-7619-1494-3 (pbk: acid-free paper)
    1. Boys--Education--Social aspects. 2. Masculinity. 3. Sex differences in education--Social aspects. 4. Gender identity. I. Lesko, Nancy. II. Series: Research on men and masculinities series; 11.
    LC1390.M37 1999
    371.823'41—dc21   99-6785

This book is printed on acid-free paper.

00 01 02 03 04 05 06 7 6 5 4 3 2 1

Acquiring Editor:	Peter Labella
Editorial Assistant:	Brian Neumann
Production Editor:	Sanford Robinson
Editorial Assistant:	Patricia Zeman
Typesetter:	Marion Warren
Indexer:	Teri Greenberg

Contents

Series Editor's Foreword

Daily we're bombarded with pop advice books that proclaim an "interplanetary theory of gender"—that we come from different planets, speak different "genderlects," apply different moral standards, and know different things in different ways. On the other hand, we sit in the same classrooms, read the same books, listen to the same teachers, and have the same criteria used when we are graded. But are we having the same experience in those classes?

From our earliest classroom experiences we are becoming gendered. We learn more than our ABCs; more than spelling, math, and science; and more than physics and literature. We learn—and teach one another—what it means to be men and women. And we see it all around us in our schools—who teaches us, what they teach us, how they teach us, and how the schools are organized as institutions. Schools are like factories, and what they produce is gendered individuals. Both in the official curriculum itself—textbooks and the like—and in the parallel, "hidden curriculum" of our informal interactions with both teachers and other students, we become gendered, and what we learn is that gender difference is the justification for gender inequality. As law professor Deborah Rhode (1997) writes,

"What schools teach and tolerate reinforces inequalities that persist well beyond childhood" (p. 56).

For more than two decades, feminist campaigns have eroded some of the most glaring inequities, from overt classroom discrimination, curricular invisibility, tracking away from science and math, to equal access to sports and sexual harassment prevention programs. And though these problems have by no means been completely resolved, legal protections and heightened awareness have made the classroom a somewhat less "chilly climate" for girls.

So much so that the voices of backlash have grown to a chorus. Some new arguments suggest that boys, not girls, are the victims of gender discrimination in schools. After all, what happens to boys in schools? They have to sit quietly, take naps, raise their hands, be obedient—all of which does extraordinary violence to their "natural" testosterone-inspired rambunctious playfulness. "Schools for the most part are run by women for girls. To take a high spirited second or third grade boy and expect him to behave like a girl in school is asking too much," comments Christina Hoff Sommers (1994), author of *Who Stole Feminism?* The effect of education is "pathologizing boyhood," she claims. While we've been paying all this attention to girls' experiences—raising their self-esteem, enabling them to take science and math, deploring and preventing harassment and bullying—we've ignored the boys. "What about the boys?"

Well, what about them? Is the classroom the feminizing influence that critics once charged at the turn of the last century, just as they do today? In my classroom, women students dress in flannel shirts, blue jeans and T-shirts, baseball hats, leather bomber jackets, and athletic shoes. They call each other "guys" constantly, even if the group is entirely composed of women. The classroom, like the workplace, is a public sphere institution, and when women enter the public sphere, they often have to dress and act "masculine" in order to be taken seriously as competent and capable. A recent advertising campaign for Polo by Ralph Lauren children's clothing pictured young girls, aged about 5 or 6, in oxford button-down shirts, blazers, and neckties. Who's being feminized and who's being masculinized?

The virtue of the research collected in this volume is that the authors take seriously the question, "What about the boys?" but they do so within a framework that promotes greater gender equality, not the nostalgic return to some earlier model in which women knew their place and boys ran the show. What's more, they observe the social and psychological consequences for boys *and girls,* for men *and women,* of persistent gender inequality both in the classroom and outside. By tracking gender from elementary schools through secondary and postsecondary schools, these authors present a fascinating and much-needed elucidation of how the educational process reproduces gender difference and gender inequality.

This is Volume 11 in the **Sage Series on Men and Masculinities.** It is our goal in this series to gather the finest empirical research and theoretical explorations of the experience of men in contemporary society.

—MICHAEL S. KIMMEL
Series Editor

References

Rhode, D. (1997). *Speaking of sex.* Cambridge, MA: Harvard University Press.
Sommers, C. H. (1994). *Who stole feminism? How women have betrayed women.* New York: Simon & Schuster.

Introduction

NANCY LESKO

When CNN began its first reports from Littleton, Colorado, on April 20, 1999, the two members of the Trenchcoat Mafia responsible for the shootings were quickly and repeatedly described as having been taunted by jocks, as alienated geeks who took revenge on their oppressors. Yet they, like the school shooters from Pearl, Mississippi, to Springfield, Oregon, were white boys, although more affluent and successful in school than some of their compatriots. Given simple analyses of race, class, gender, and power, these boys and young men would seem to occupy privileged positions in and out of schools.

If one changed channels from CNN to *Oprah,* or browsed in bookstores, another story about boys like Dylan Klebold and Eric Harris emerged in which they are at risk, disadvantaged because they do not get sufficient "proper" attention; are unable to express their emotions; and suffer disproportionately from alcoholism, heart attacks, and other crippling physical and psychological ills. According to authors like Pollack (1998) and Kindlon and Thompson (1999), boys are an endangered group and must be rescued with gender-specific interventions, primary among them receiving help in expressing their true emotions.

These complex and contradictory images of white, middle-class boys as simultaneously predators and victims, social elites yet emotionally disadvantaged, powerful yet oppressed by their inability to express their anger in nondestructive ways, are emblematic of the multilayered representations, experiences, and social relations of masculinity that the authors of this volume address. Working against the conventional search for a single cause and a single cure, the contributors to this volume examine masculinities as historically contextualized, dynamic, and collectively produced. These scholars work against another tendency in the coverage of male violence, whether of school shootings, police profiling, or high school jock brutality, which is to report incidents as tragic, *one-time events,* unpredictable and inexplicable. While news reports portray male violence as without antecedents or patterns, the collected scholarship here inquires into the systematicity as well as the contradictory dimensions of masculinities, whether violent, heroic, or caring.

Reports of the Trenchcoat Mafia overlapped with the trial of Justin Volpe, a white, twentysomething New York City policeman who pleaded guilty to torturing Abner Louima, a young black man, in a fit of rage. Again, analyses of Volpe's behavior as dominant masculinity were absent, and his actions were attributed to individual pathology or temporary insanity. White male violence cannot be interpreted as simply isolated events, as one-time occurrences. How is it that white male rage against Others, which is everywhere chronicled, even sensationalized, is seldom named and dissected? Why are gruesome, violent crimes so easily juxtaposed and almost overshadowed by human interest stories of a disappointed father and neighbors who knew the brutalizers as "nice boys"? How does the discourse move so quickly toward empathy for the perpetrators? Part of the explanation is the elision of a sense of patterned, normative masculinity. These patterns of discursive visibility and invisibility suggest a broad and deep familiarity with and acceptance of the norm of righteous male anger and violence because public figures like Justin Volpe, Dylan Klebold, and Eric Harris are "our guys."[1] They are "our guys" not only because they are similar to and defended by real males in our families and workplaces, but because they are part of a broad and deep *social imaginary* (loosely defined as a potent complex of fears, desires, and fantasy) in which high-status guys are tough and hard, get angry and even, and do not talk about their feelings. We are simultaneously repulsed and thrilled by their feats, and the extensive coverage is an index of broad cultural investment (Acland, 1995). When "our guys" are hurting, we supporters and agents take care of their hurt feelings (Kenway & Willis, 1998), our mediated stories providing emotional protection for our guys who made bad decisions. In this light, U.S. Supreme Court Justice Kennedy's dissenting opinion from a recent ruling that holds schools liable for pervasive student-to-student harassment is a protection of our guys: "A teen-ager's romantic overtures to a classmate (even when persistent and unwelcome) are an inescapable part of adolescence" (cited in Greenhouse, 1999, p. A24). In this view, we may all partake of some emotional investments in, and a rapt attention to, narratives of violent men, and we must share the responsibility to move toward alternative interpretations. The Columbine Massacre may be "a politicizing moment" for geeks and nerds[2] (Dark, 1999, p. 62), and the beginning of a sea change in the cozy relations between elected officials and the National Rifle Association, despite Charlton Heston's full-tilt attempt to rescue and rationalize guns-and-masculinity. But the slaying of students and a teacher in Littleton, Colorado, hasn't led to a full-blown scrutinizing of masculinities and schooling by educators and policymakers, which would include attention to the institutional culture, as well as the relationships between high-status boys and girls and other boys; as noted above, the mediated response has been a narrative of repressed emotions of individual boys, which are amenable to therapeutic remedies. Despite our common transfixion with the images of and events at Columbine High School, masculinity as a problem remains largely unspeakable, invisible, and incredibly powerful, for we cannot yet collectively imagine things to be otherwise.

Recent events have a history, of course. Beginning in colonial New England, U.S. schools emphasized boys' education and significant opposition to the serious education of girls, to coeducation, and to women as teachers continued through the late 1800s (Bissell Brown, 1990; Kimmel, 1996; Tyack & Hansot, 1992). The creation of mass compulsory schooling in the United States occurred in the context of "nervous masculinity" and widespread worries about the emasculation of boys by women teachers (Filene, 1986; Macleod, 1983). Girls' presence in classrooms was met with substantial trivialization of academics and increasing emphasis on status through male-dominated extracurriculars.

Despite female students' and teachers' presence and sometimes numerical dominance, feminist philosophers of education have demonstrated how educational concepts are male centered; for example, how the "ideal of the educated person" relies upon masculinized traits of rationality and detachment (Martin, 1994). Classroom observers, such as Myra and David Sadker (1994), have documented that American schools cheat girls, for example, in allocating more classroom attention and probing questions to boys.[3] Examinations of the curriculum have identified how boys' interests, say in studying dinosaurs, are overly represented in elementary school practices (Clarricoates, 1987). Although feminist perspectives have been brought to bear on understanding historical, philosophical, curricular, and social dimensions of schooling, the expansion of feminist perspectives to examine masculinities as central to the process of being educated has occurred slowly. In addition, a problem with some gendered analyses of schooling is that the girls are declared deficient or deviant; for example, they lack sufficient self-esteem or achievement orientation (Bryson & de Castell, 1995), without companioning a critique of male-centeredness and dominance.

British and Australian researchers have led in studying masculinities and education.[4] R. W. Connell's (1989, 1995, 1996) studies of masculinities in and out of Australian schools have empirically investigated and theorized masculinities as collective social practices and as "body-reflexive practices." Máirtín Mac an Ghaill (1994) has proclaimed schools to be "intricate masculinizing agencies" (p. 31), and his empirical work examines intertwined conceptions of masculinity and sexuality among teachers and students in British schools. In Lois Weis's (1993) study of white male working-class youth, she linked U.S. school-based masculinity with economics, sexism, and racism. However, only in recent, dramatic scholarship on school violence have boys in the United States come out of the shadows.

The recent spotlight on U.S. masculinity seems to have begun in the streets with a focus, not surprisingly, on urban black boys, dubbed "teen-age time bombs" (Gest & Pope, 1996; Males & Docuyanan, 1996). The examination of violence moved inside schools, with Nan Stein's (1995) persuasive demonstration of the ubiquitousness of public verbal and physical teasing, bullying, and harassment of lower-status students, namely girls and not-sufficiently masculine boys, and Jackson Katz's (1995) work on violence prevention among athletes.[5] Bernard Lefkowitz (1997) traced the roots of a high-profile rape of a developmentally disabled young woman in Glen Ridge, New Jersey, and his portrait illustrates the dominance of the white jock culture and their affluent parents in the schools. When administrators are former athletes and coaches themselves, no one questions that boys will be boys and destroy school equipment, buy themselves out of criminal charges, and assault other students. Lefkowitz followed the trail of forgiving and forgetting attractive, wealthy, athletic, white boys' rampages, from elementary playgrounds to the justice system. Less than a year after Lefkowitz's book was released and prominently reviewed in the *New York Times Book Review,* a *Newsweek* cover story on the "crisis points" in boys' development announced that boys have been left behind in the recent educational and psychological focus on girls (Kantrowitz & Kolb, 1998). Alongside the analyses of boys and young men as bullyers and harassers, the boy as underdog is simultaneously being reinvented.[6]

Such multiple and contradictory representations of boys, men, masculinity, and schools are taken up by the contributors to this anthology. Just as there is nothing natural or inevitable about particular forms of dominant masculinity, there is nothing natural or inevitable about studying masculinities, even for feminists. My own interest in masculinities in schooling formed gradually across 8 years of teaching at a Big Ten University, the designation of which is synonymous with intercollegiate athletics and Greek organizations. I naively imagined that athletics and fraternities would have little to do with my undergraduate and graduate teaching. This fantasy was regularly challenged by the rows of visored fraternity guys who lined the edges of the classroom and glared at me in clear disapproval when discussion topics questioned the white, male underpinnings of school histories, values, and bureaucracies. Questioning the gender order of a Big Ten University was treacherous, both for female and male instructors and for students.[7] And fraternity members' disapproval had power over me and my curriculum—this was clear in my reactions to their silent stares, in their articulate defenses of "traditional" approaches to teaching U.S. history, and in their course evaluations. But the necessity of examining masculinities within educational theories and practices became clear during a research project with undergraduate teacher education students. One participant was a 20-year-old white student whose life had revolved around football and who was preparing to coach in high school and, eventually, in college. His narratives embodied athletic privilege and rage against suggestions of sexism and racism in schools and in other social settings. His metaphor of schools as "level playing fields" made a critical view impossible. I began to consider the shapes and effects of masculinities in the formal and informal curricula of schools.

Similar to mutable media constructions of boys, administrative, policy, and curricular emphases in schools are also fluid at all levels. Davies (1992) and Mac an Ghaill (1994) report processes of "remasculinization" of secondary schools; their analyses do not imply that schools haven't been dominated by men and male perspectives in the past, but emphasize, rather, the *nonstatic* quality of institutional gender relations; for example, technological innovations in education are a locale where men's expertise and predominance are accepted as natural, and male students are likely to be seen as rightful and inevitable leaders in this curricular area. Thus, the concept of remasculinizing pushes us to pay attention to the gender relations of economic and technological initiatives, new relations between white men and men of color, as well as with multiracial and ethnic women, and all children.[8] Davies's and Mac an Ghaill's work reminds us that masculinities are always under revision, in and out of schools.

Starting Points

A starting point for this volume is the understanding that gender is relational; "masculinity" must always be understood in relation to "femininity"; heterosexuality in relation to homosexuality; hypermasculinity in relation to effeminacy.[9] From this perspective, it is delusional to imagine changing the gender order of schooling by attending only to the girls (Kenway & Willis, 1998). Educators must examine girls' experiences and systems of meaning-making in relation to those of boys. But these relations are always in play and multidimensional, as Walkerdine (1990) demonstrated in her portrait of two young boys who escaped the power of a disciplining woman teacher by switching to a discourse that objectified her female body.

Furthermore, understanding masculinities involves conceptualizing them as "collective social practices" (Connell, 1995): Masculinities are not individualized psychologies but socially organized and meaningful actions in historical contexts. These collective social practices involve many different kinds of language, physical, sexual, and material actions. Feminist historian Joan Scott (1988) elaborates four levels of socially organized gender practices, which I find very helpful in thinking about how schools are masculinizing institutions:

1. *The level of divisions of labor and "kinship" networks.* At this level we would pay attention to who does different kinds of work (among students and among faculty and staff), with differentiated wages and support; what kinds of informal networks exist, for example, "old boys' networks" and/or "new boys drinking groups"; and the relations between both formal and informal affinities and resources.

2. *The level of symbols.* At this level we would examine how traits of hegemonic and subordinate masculinities (as well as femininities) were invoked in curriculum decision making, program planning, teacher-room discussions, or informal banter with students (Davies, 1989). The cartoon in Figure I.1 illustrates the gendered symbolic level of educational practice with one curricular approach portrayed as virile and macho and the competing approach as effeminate and ineffectual. The race and class dimensions are also significant. Similarly, symbols from school academic tracking, athletics, and competitive dimensions of school life are likely to

be widely invoked, and educators could trace which symbols are invoked in particular contexts.

3. *The level of normative concepts.* Normative concepts such as rationality, rigor, proper emotional display, being a team player, being a strict disciplinarian, or being a hard grader circulate endlessly and potently across many domains of school life. Norms often operate on the refusal or suppression of alternative possibilities; for example, the belief that school subjects must be constituted in traditional categories of math, science, and English, or that good teaching requires objective measures of achievement (Martin, 1994).

4. *The level of subjective identities.* At this level, we need to investigate how persons understand their own masculinity in relation to other masculinities and femininities and in fluid contexts. Obviously, subjectivities will utilize available concepts and representations from these other three levels, but we must also pay attention to the "feeling rules" of various masculinities, that is, the emotional investments of boys and young men in adopting and adhering to particular politics and identities, such as the antigovernment Rambo or the heterosexist Don Juan.

These four levels of the operation of gender categories are useful to understand how masculinity works as an unspoken standard, as a style, as well as a division of labor, process of resource allotment, and informal networking. The chapters in this volume utilize and develop analyses on all four of Scott's levels.

Masculinities must also be understood as profoundly intertextual: That is, masculinities are constructed, performed, and revised across knowledges, symbols, styles, subjectivities, and norms including distinctive racial, ethnic, and sexuality components. Masculinities are composed as much by knowledge as by willed ignorances (Sedgwick, 1990). In addition, particular masculinities may draw from popular cultural texts or political movements, and position themselves in relation to current controversies or crises. To understand the multiple political and social aspects of masculinities, it is important to interpret them within particular historical, gender, sexuality, and political contexts (Davies, 1992; Kimmel, 1996; Mac an Ghaill, 1994; Uebel, 1997).

Finally, a critical pedagogical and policy perspective informs this edited collection. If educators are to intervene in masculinities in ethical and counterhegemonic ways, we need to understand students' and faculty members' prior semiotic processes regarding masculinities (Whitson, 1991). That is, we need a familiarity with the structuring symbols, norms, subjectivities, divisions of labor, and kinship networks of different masculine modes if we are to work to reshape masculinities (and femininities) in school. And we need an ethical perspective on masculinities: Following Harpham (1992), I propose a dynamic ethical perspective that connects that which is to that which will be in the future. The authors of this volume are concerned with examining what is, in order to imagine and elaborate on what ought to be.

Studying Masculinities at School

Although there may be agreement that schools are key social arenas for the normalization, surveillance, and control of sex/gender identities, there are not universal gender representations and relations. Kessler, Ashenden, Connell, and Dowsett (1985) argue that each school has a particular "gender regime":

> This may be defined as the pattern of practices that constructs various kinds of masculinity and femininity among staff and students, orders them in terms of prestige and power, and constructs a sexual division of labor within the institution. The gender regime is a state of play rather than a permanent condition. It can be changed deliberately or otherwise, but it is no less powerful in its effects on pupils for that. It confronts them as a social fact, which they have to come to terms with somehow. (p. 42)

Among the various masculinities and femininities of a particular gender regime, there will be a dominant, or hegemonic, masculinity and an emphasized femininity. In U.S. public schools, the hegemonic masculinity will likely be that of the jocks—young men skilled in athletics, especially high-status athletics, usually football and basketball, at least in many public schools. In addition to sports, the "boys' subjects," (i.e., informal gender segregation in courses) and discipline are two additional schooling dimensions with high salience for masculinity-making (Connell, 1996).

If we acknowledge, as Lynne Segal (1990) does, that it may be difficult "to grasp the institutional dimensions of 'masculinity' " (p. 295), how and where do we locate and interrogate masculinities (i.e., the divisions of labor, symbols, norms, and subjectivities) in schools? The groundbreaking work from Australia and England provides some approaches. Mac an Ghaill (1994), for one, has investigated "the transmission of official sex/gender codes through *systems of management, instruments of discipline, and institutional values and rituals*" (emphasis added; p. 16). His

Figure I.1. A cartoonist's view of the competition between the liberal, classical tradition and emerging egalitarian utilitarianism in education.
SOURCE: Reprinted from Joncich, 1968, p. 247.

study of Parnell School investigated three teacher subgroups and educational ideologies, with distinctive masculinities and emphases on particular curricular domains, school discipline, and views of the purpose of education. According to Connell (1989), schools exert their strongest effects on the construction of masculinities through the *indirect effects of tracking and failure, patterns of authority, the academic curriculum, and definitions of knowledge* (emphasis added; p. 297). Paul Willis's (1977) heralded study, *Learning to Labour,* demonstrated the relationship among curricular tracks, class backgrounds, and styles of masculinity. The "lads" dueled with the teachers and the "ear'oles" largely on the terrain of style—clothing, smoking, drinking, and sexual exploits—and demeaned academic success as feminine.

The cartoon from the early 1900s in the United States (Figure I.1; reprinted from Joncich, 1968, p. 247) portrays a similar class and masculinity struggle over the focus of the school curriculum, with the forces akin to Willis's "lads" clearly getting the marks for virile masculinity and the proper curricular focus.

Other scholars have examined how concepts such as reason and rationality, concepts at the very core of education, are masculinized (Broughton, 1987; Martin, 1994; Walkerdine, 1988, 1990), as are ideas of success and knowledge (Kenway & Willis, 1998). Martin (1994) also discusses how analytical philosophy of education has offered a definition of teaching as "an initiation into open rational discussion" (p. 43) and equates an educated person with an educated mind. Martin argues that an adequate ideal of an educated person must "join thought to action and reason to feeling and emotion" (p. 48), an idea still alien to most schools despite efforts to implement community service requirements.

The division of labor continues to attract and keep women teaching in the earlier grades, while men tend to move up into administration and teaching of older students. However, subject area cleavages also remain, with more women in traditional "feminine" subjects like English and counseling, while the durable image of the high school teacher of the "hard sciences" remains male, as does the science student, given the push of girls out of classes with a highly competitive "shark tank" ethos (Sadker & Sadker, 1994). Cafeterias may be even more dangerous than high-level science classes, according to Donna Eder (1995), who examined patterns of middle school talk at lunch and reported the nonstop, withering castigations of lower-status students as "wimps" and "fags." Bronwyn Davies (1989) demonstrated how a heterosexist and homophobic discourse between teachers and students produces sanctions against muddying clearly differentiated masculine and feminine activities, narratives, and relationships.

Extracurricular activities must also be taken into account as influencing both the formal curricular areas and the informal school learnings. Bissinger's (1990) study of football in West Texas and Lefkowitz's (1997) study of athletes in New Jersey demonstrate the centrality of successful interscholastic athletics in making men and communities (see Corrigan, 1985, on the physical costs of success). Foley's (1990) study of a South Texas high school further demonstrates the relationship between football and hegemonic masculinity, while Gruneau and Whitson (1993), Walker (1988), and Robins and Cohen (1978) describe similar processes in Canada, Australia, and England, respectively.

My aim here has not been to provide a comprehensive review, but rather to illustrate a range of approaches to examining empirically the production of masculinities in educational settings. Masculinities are associated with most of the categories through which schools have been studied, as indicated by the following (provisional) list:

1. systems of management
2. instruments of discipline
3. institutional values and rituals
4. tracking and failure
5. patterns of authority
6. academic curriculum
7. definitions of knowledge
8. "style"
9. normative concepts of reason, rationality, and rigor
10. distinctive control/release of bodies and emotions
11. race and ethnicity
12. definitions of good teaching
13. patterns of talk
14. public performances of teasing, bullying, and harassment
15. compulsory heterosexuality and homophobia
16. sports and other extracurriculars
17. distinctive uses of space and time

This list must be considered unfinished, for it does not include topics such as language and masculinities, which is likely to be important in multilingual societies with largely monolingual schools. Nevertheless, this listing demonstrates the range of approaches to examining schools as masculinizing institutions and how masculinity is interwoven with nearly every aspect of schooling. The contributors to this volume demonstrate the ways in which masculinities are part and parcel of what we know as schooling.

This Volume

As I have indicated, the topic of masculinities and schooling encompasses an enormous range of topics and issues; the authors in this volume engage with and represent scholarship in this huge, disparate arena.

James R. King looks at elementary males—men teachers in kindergarten through third grade—within the context of the commodification of the male body, and calls for more men in early childhood education. He finds that when his research participants entered elementary education, they monitored and regulated their teaching to correspond with preconfigured images of masculinity and the (feminine) teacher. The teachers in his study scrupulously evaluated their touch, dress, and relationships with children and other teachers. King closes with an evaluation of these Herculean monitorial tasks.

From ethnographic research with 9-, 10-, and 11-year-olds, *Jan Nespor* problematizes "the body" by looking at bodies as they extend beyond the skin, that is, through networks of technologies and locations in spatial and temporal networks of practice. His stimulating work reads boys' takeover of spaces in exclusive ways as technologies of power. He also suggests that masculinities (and femininities) can take various spatial forms, although the properties of different forms are still unclear to him. Certainly, issues of space and time are central to daily school life and Nespor's theoretically informed analysis provides a provocative perspective.

Khaula Murtadha-Watts examines teacher expectations in a mostly male African-centered elementary school in Detroit, Michigan, and also emphasizes masculinity in relation to physical space. She reads the strict control over students' bodies and minds as a direct response to images of urban spaces as "jungles" and images of black male bodies as dangerous. Even alternative schools may replicate this sense of urban danger, thereby cutting off young African American boys from critically engaging with popular culture and their racial histories within school curricula.

Laurie Mandel and *Charol Shakeshaft* focus on conceptions of masculinity and femininity utilized by middle school students. In their examination of subjective identities, norms of heterosexism and homophobia dominate images of masculinity and femininity; although girls produce a range of feminine modes, boys produce only one version of high-status masculinity, which holds as axiomatic the domination of girls and nonmasculine boys. Mandel and Shakeshaft find these norms oppressive for both girls and boys and make recommendations for how schools might respond.

Jeffrey J. Kuzmic reads high school U.S. history texts for what is left in (rather than what is left out). He sees masculine privilege as invisible, while male historical actors form a primer on hegemonic masculinity: exploring, making, winning, and building. Male historical figures are always public and define that realm; women always exist in the private realm and must become public persons. For example, "Mother" Jones became a labor leader after her husband and children died of yellow fever, whereas Eugene Debs was always already public. Kuzmic concludes that despite more inclusive appearances, textbooks support and help reproduce patriarchy.

In order to understand peer relations as sources and influences of connection and alienation in shaping and reshaping racial masculine identities, *Jeremy N. Price* utilizes the perspectives of two African American male high school students. There are relatively few accounts that reflect the range of experiences of young African American men and their relationship with school, particularly through a race, class, and gender lens. Price traces how these two young men created their masculinities differently in particular social contexts: For example, in one context, a participant represented himself through a sexual relationship and as a father, while in a second social context, he portrayed himself primarily through academic and economic aspirations. This chapter helps us see the variations in active, conscious construction of racialized masculinities.

Máirtín Mac an Ghaill talks with young gay black men in order to grasp what is occurring in British schools in relation to sexual identity formation. He argues that sexual/gender relations can be seen as a crucial point of intersection of different forms of power, stratification, desire, and subjective identity formation. And he notes that identifying sexuality as part of a wider schooling process reconceptualizes it as a key element of a public agenda. His work explores the range of heterosexualities in schools and their intersections with school arrangements and with different groups of students. His participants also portray extraordinary insight into the dynamics and effects of exclusionary human thinking and feeling, insights grounded in their experiences with both racism and homophobia.

Nancy Lesko explores the "harnessing of affect to political life" (Stoler, 1995, p. 136) in the logic of competitive athletics, specifically football, in U.S. secondary schools. The life history narratives of one white male student who was preparing to teach and coach are situated in post-Persian Gulf War remasculinization, when nationalistic aggression was valorized and articulated via brutality, the language of football, and spectacle, and coaches were touted as exemplary teachers. Lesko elaborates connections between the discourse of competitive athletics and intolerant attitudes toward girls, multicultural education, and critiques of the status quo in education.

Melody J. Shank critically examines the history and lineage of "rigor" in education as interwoven with masculine privilege. She describes its current popularity in secondary school reform and its seeming inclusiveness; but in tracing its history, she claims strong connections between rigor and technical, objective, and measurable approaches to teaching, which push teachers toward certain curricular areas and kinds of knowledge and away from others. As she notes, rigor does not pertain to pursuits of creativity or imagination, the heart, or human interaction; thus, rigor calls forth a traditional, technical- or rational-centered, measurable curriculum.

Male military academies have grabbed headlines for their opposition to accepting women. *Diane Diamond, Michael S. Kimmel,* and *Kirby Schroeder* compare and contrast the opposition to women at Virginia Military Academy (VMI) and The Citadel with the voluntary inclusion of women at Norwich University and West Point. The authors describe the central dilemma for women at historically male military academies as negotiating the problems of sameness and difference: Women cadets must aim to be traditional cadets, but in doing so simultaneously accentuate their femaleness, their difference. Cadets who were interviewed navigated these institutional waters by strategically emphasizing sameness, overcompensating in achievement, establishing informal networks of support, and emphasizing conventional femininity in social situations. The authors highlight the ways these female cadets can inform us about the creation of equality grounded on difference, rather than on sameness.

After sports, computers may be the second most masculinized school arena. *John Willinsky* begins with an understanding of the masculinity of computer technology and the boys' club atmosphere that surrounds its school presence. Assuming that emphasizing the social relevance of computing would increase girls' interest, Willinsky describes a computer curriculum that challenges the usual pedagogy, as well as the institutional social relations of computers. The Information Technology Management (ITM) program has been piloted in high schools in British Columbia, and its innovations involved self-directed learning, team projects in which male and female students rotated through positions from project manager to systems architect, and a broadening of computer topics. Willinsky argues that this tempering of the masculinities of technology is not complete, but there was change: Some boys gained greatly in their cooperative capacities; girls' presence was increased; and some girls valued the freedom to explore their own interests.

Why are relatively few men in K-12 educational institutions actively involved in leading gender-based violence prevention efforts with girls and boys? In answering the question, *Jackson Katz* draws upon his work as an activist and argues that male educators must begin by breaking the customary silence among men about violence against women. He also suggests that violence prevention work should be framed as "leadership," male and female teachers ought to work together and model collaborative relationships, and male educators must acknowledge their own experiences with hegemonic masculinity.

After substantial efforts toward gender reform, educators and politicians now ask the seemingly inevitable question, What about the boys? *Lyn Yates* reviews some aspects of why and how boys and masculinity have moved to center stage. She investigates the discursive construction of the "popular" views that, first, boys are now losing out and, second, Australia (or the United Kingdom or United States) needs to respond by adapting the policies that have been successful with girls for use with boys. She reports that when schooling is connected to labor market employment, the impact of school gender reforms is mixed; that is, while women seem to have improved in some areas (e.g., more enter medicine and law), there is almost no change in women's access to a wider range of jobs and senior ranks. Yates raises a compelling issue: How do researchers and policymakers maintain an equitable focus on girls (the "old news" of gender equity issues) as they turn to the important work of documenting masculinities?

What kinds of masculine subjects will feminism make? *Brian Carr* begins with feminist theorists' claim that feminism is about *dis*identification, about remapping commonsense categories of "male" and "female," and then moves to question how feminism and pedagogy might disorient "masculinity," at the same time wondering whether "women" will stop being a question when masculinities share the analytical space. Carr raises serious questions for theory and pedagogy, and he pushes toward pedagogies that disorient "masculine" and "feminine," emphasizing that politics ground affinity, not vice versa.

Next Steps

The chapters in this volume are intended to contribute substantive understandings of gender relations and representations in school (especially U.S. schools, where fewer gender initiatives have occurred), as well as to incite further work. Read together, they do not promote one or another approach to teaching the boys, teaching the girls, or to incorporating feminist perspectives in school programs or policies. These remain open, debatable, and formidable issues, as Kenway and Willis's (1998) important report on the contradictory effects of gender equity programs in Australia attests. In closing this introduction, I want at least to raise some central issues in teaching the boys and the girls differently.[10]

I began this introduction within recent media stories of white male violence that absent references to normative masculinity and toughness. I emphasized the position of hegemonic masculinity in the *social imaginary:* men being cool, tough, and eventually violent is "the dominant plot" (White, cited in Denborough, 1996, p. 103). Working to create and sustain "counterplots" (p. 104) becomes the aim of transformative gender education.

I support three general principles for working toward fairer gender relations in schools. First, we need alternative constructions of masculinity and male-female relations to be "available," that is, to be reasonable, possible, and desirable by boys and girls, and by men and women teachers. Of course, broad critique of gender relations must occur, as well as the pointing out and creating of alternative images, stories, and patterns of emotions. These efforts cannot be done from an authoritative teacher-telling stance, nor will they emerge from getting boys to express their true feelings. David Denborough (1996) provides a clear and insightful curricular model for analysis and critique of the dominant plot.

A second principle is that schools must help boys and girls negotiate their ways through alternative masculinities and femininities, which means addressing the charged emotional investments in particular gendered identities and positions, and thereby the related power of distinctive masculinities and femininities. Various authors note the contradictions of mandating students' participation in these efforts, which suggests that students' participation is optimally voluntary (but recruitment and incentives strategies need to be developed) and must involve good pedagogy (Denborough, 1996; Kenway & Willis, 1998). Maxine Greene's (1995) emphasis on developing social imagination through the arts—visual, literary, musical, and performative—can be utilized as part of creative and enjoyable transformative gender education.

Third, teaching the boys and girls must be accompanied by teaching the men and women in the school; that is, the culture of the school as a whole and its masculinizing dimensions must be scrutinized and a process of change begun. School reformers for the past 100 years have found educational institutions resistant to change; however, committed administrators, teachers, students, and parents can have an impact.

Of course, I imply neither assurances in these approaches nor innocence, for each reform will affect new power arrangements. Nevertheless, my responsibility to teach toward a transformative gender regime in all schools is sustained by the collective commitment of the scholars in and out of this volume who help me imagine and negotiate counterplots of masculinity and femininity.

Notes

1. I borrow this evocative phrase from Bernard Lefkowitz's (1997) book by that title.

2. Cliff Cheng (1996) notes that the attribution "nerd" participates in the dominant masculinist gaze with its Eurocentric, heterosexist, patriarchal, and sporting values (p. 193).

3. See also the American Association of University Women (1992) report, *How Schools Shortchange Girls*.

4. In addition to the work of Connell and Mac an Ghaill, see Askew and Ross (1988), Heward (1988), Lee (1993), and Skeggs (1991) for explications of masculinities and education.

5. See also Eder (1995) and Miedzian (1991).

6. On the topic of men as victims, see Farrell (1993) and Browne and Fletcher (1995).

7. See Peter Lyman's (1987) portrait of fraternity joking and gender relations.

8. Jeffords (1989) provides a useful and compelling analysis of the remasculinization of the United States after the Vietnam War via film and memoirs; she emphasizes the realignments between white men and men and women of color, as well as white men's relationships to the U.S. government.

9. Barrie Thorne (1993) presents a detailed portrait of the development of these necessarily linked boy-girl relations in two elementary schools, which she terms a sense of "opposite sides."

10. I cannot review all the scholarship on transformative gender strategies in schooling, but I rely heavily on the ideas of Connell (1996), Denborough (1996), Kenway and Willis (1998), McLean (1996), and Salisbury and Jackson (1996).

References

Acland, C. R. (1995). *Youth, murder, spectacle: The cultural politics of "youth in crisis."* Boulder, CO: Westview Press.

American Association of University Women. (1992). *How schools shortchange girls—The AAUW Report.* New York: Marlowe & Company.

Askew, S., & Ross, C. (1988). *Boys don't cry.* Philadelphia: Open University Press.

Bissell Brown, V. (1990). The fear of feminization: Los Angeles high schools in the Progressive Era. *Feminist Studies, 16*(3), 493-518.

Bissinger, H. G. (1990). *Friday night lights: A town, a team, a dream.* New York: HarperCollins.

Broughton, J. (1987). The masculine authority of the cognitive. In B. Inhelder, D. de Caprona, & A. Cornu-Wells (Eds.), *Piaget today* (pp. 111-124). London: Lawrence Erlbaum.

Browne, R., & Fletcher, R. (1995). *Boys in schools: Addressing the real issues—Behaviour, values and relationships.* Sydney: Finch.

Bryson, M., & de Castell, S. (1995). So we've got a chip on our shoulder! Sexing the texts of "educational technology." In J. Gaskell & J. Willinsky (Eds.), *Gender in/forms curriculum: From enrichment to transformation* (pp. 21-42). New York: Teachers College Press.

Cheng, C. (1996). "We choose not to compete": The "merit" discourse in the selection process, and Asian and Asian American men and their masculinity. In C. Cheng (Ed.), *Masculinities in organizations* (pp. 177-200). Thousand Oaks, CA: Sage.

Clarricoates, K. (1987). Dinosaurs in the classroom—The "hidden" curriculum in primary schools. In M. Arnot & G. Weiner (Eds.), *Gender and the politics of schooling* (pp. 155-165). London: Hutchinson.

Connell, R. W. (1989). Cool guys, swots and wimps: The interplay of masculinity and education. *Oxford Review of Education, 15*(3), 291-303.

Connell, R. W. (1995). *Masculinities.* Berkeley: University of California Press.

Connell, R. W. (1996). Teaching the boys: New research on masculinity, and gender strategies for schools. *Teachers College Record, 98*(2), 206-235.

Corrigan, P. (1985). The making of the boy: Meditations on what grammar school did with, to, and for my body. *Journal of Education, 170*(3), 142-161.

Dark, J. (1999, June 1). Suffer the (white, middle-class) children. *The Village Voice,* pp. 61-62.

Davies, B. (1989). The discursive production of the male/female dualism in school settings. *Oxford Review of Education, 15*(3), 229-241.

Davies, L. (1992). School power cultures under economic constraint. *Educational Review, 43*(2), 127-136.

Denborough, D. (1996). Step by step: Developing respectful and effective ways of working with young men to reduce violence. In C. McLean, M. Carey, & C. White (Eds.), *Men's ways of being* (pp. 91-116). Boulder, CO: Westview.

Eder, D., with Evans, C. C., & Parker, S. (1995). *School talk: Gender and adolescent culture.* New Brunswick, NJ: Rutgers University Press.

Farrell, W. (1993). *The myth of male power: Why men are the disposable sex.* New York: Simon & Shuster.

Filene, P. G. (1986). *Him/her/self: Sex roles in modern America* (2nd ed.). Baltimore, MD: Johns Hopkins University Press.

Foley, D. E. (1990). *Learning capitalist culture: Deep in the heart of Tejas.* Philadelphia: University of Pennsylvania Press.

Gest, T., & Pope, V. (1996, March 26). Crime time bomb. *U.S. News & World Report,* pp. 28-30, 32, 36.

Greene, M. (1995). *Releasing the imagination: Essays on education, the arts, and social change.* San Francisco: Jossey-Bass.

Greenhouse, L. (1999, May 25). Sex harassment in class is ruled schools' liability. *New York Times,* pp. A1, A24.

Gruneau, R., & Whitson, D. (1993). *Hockey night in Canada: Sport, identities and cultural politics.* Toronto: Garamond.

Harpham, G. G. (1992). *Getting it right: Language, literature, and ethics.* Chicago: University of Chicago Press.

Heward, C. (1988). *Making a man of him.* London: Routledge & Kegan Paul.

Jeffords, S. (1989). *The remasculinization of America: Gender and the Vietnam War.* Bloomington: Indiana University Press.

Joncich, G. (1968). *The sane positivist: A biography of Edward L. Thorndike.* Middletown, CT: Wesleyan University Press.

Kantrowitz, B., & Kolb, C. (1998, May 11). Boys will be boys. *Newsweek,* pp. 54-60.

Katz, J. (1995). Reconstructing masculinity in the locker room: The Mentors in Violence Prevention Project. *Harvard Educational Review, 65*(2), 163-170.

Kenway, J., & Willis, S., with Blackmore, J., & Rennie, L. (1998). *Answering back: Girls, boys and feminism in schools.* London & New York: Routledge.

Kessler, S., Ashenden, D. J., Connell, R. W., & Dowsett, G. W. (1985). Gender relations in secondary schooling. *Sociology of Education, 58*(January), 34-48.

Kimmel, M. (1996). *Manhood in America: A cultural history.* New York: Free Press.

Kindlon, D., & Thompson, M. (1999). *Raising Cain: Protecting the emotional life of boys.* New York: Ballantine Books.

Lee, C. (1993). *Talking tough: The fight for masculinity.* London: Arrow.

Lefkowitz, B. (1997). *Our guys: The Glen Ridge rape and the secret life of the perfect suburb.* Berkeley: University of California Press.

Lyman, P. (1987). The fraternal bond as a joking relationship: A case study of the role of sexist jokes in male group bonding. In M. Kimmel (Ed.), *Changing men: New directions in research on men and masculinity* (pp. 148-164). Newbury Park, CA: Sage.

Mac an Ghaill, M. (1994). *The making of men: Masculinities, sexualities, and schooling.* Philadelphia: Open University Press.

Macleod, D. (1983). *Building character in the American boy: The Boy Scouts, the YMCA and their forerunners.* Madison: University of Wisconsin Press.

Males, M., & Docuyanan, F. (1996, February). Crackdown on kids: Giving up on the young. *The Progressive, 60*(2), 24-26.

Martin, J. R. (1994). *Changing the educational landscape: Philosophy, women, and currriculum.* New York: Routledge.

McLean, C. (1996). The politics of men's pain. In C. McLean, M. Carey, & C. White (Eds.), *Men's ways of being* (pp. 11-28). Boulder, CO: Westview.

Miedzian, M. (1991). *Boys will be boys: Breaking the link between masculinity and volence.* Garden City, NY: Anchor Books.

Pollack, W. (1998). *Real boys: Rescuing our sons from the myths of boyhood.* New York: Henry Holt & Co.

Robins, D., & Cohen, P. (1978). *Knuckle sandwich: Growing up in the working-class city.* Harmondsworth, UK: Penguin.

Sadker, M., & Sadker, D. (1994). *Failing at fairness: How our schools cheat girls.* New York: Touchstone Books.

Salisbury, J., & Jackson, D. (1996). *Challenging macho values: Practical ways of working with adolescent boys.* London: Falmer.

Scott, J. W. (1988). *Gender and the politics of history.* New York: Columbia University Press.

Sedgwick, E. K. (1990). *The epistemology of the closet.* Berkeley: University of California Press.

Segal, L. (1990). *Slow motion: Changing masculinities, changing men.* New Brunswick, NJ: Rutgers University Press.

Skeggs, B. (1991). Challenging masculinity and using sexuality. *British Journal of Sociology of Education, 12*(1), 127-140.

Stein, N. (1995). Sexual harassment in school: The public performance of gendered violence. *Harvard Educational Review, 65*(2), 145-162.

Stoler, A. L. (1995). *Race and the education of desire: Foucault's* History of Sexuality *and the colonial order of things.* Durham, NC: Duke University Press.

Thorne, B. (1993). *Gender play: Boys and girls in school.* New Brunswick, NJ: Rutgers University Press.

Tyack, D., & Hansot, E. (1992). *Learning together: A history of coeducation in American public schools.* New York: Russell Sage.

Uebel, M. (1997). Men in color: Introducing race and the subject of masculinities. In H. Stecopoulos & M. Uebel (Eds.), *Race and the subject of masculinities* (pp. 1-16). Durham, NC: Duke University Press.

Walker, J. C. (1988). *Louts and legends: Male youth culture in an inner-city school.* Sydney: Allen & Unwin.

Walkerdine, V. (1988). *The mastery of reason: Cognitive development and the production of rationality.* New York: Routledge.

Walkerdine, V. (1990). *Schoolgirl fictions.* London: Verso.

Weis, L. (1993). White male working-class youth: An exploration of relative privilege and loss. In L. Weis & M. Fine (Eds.), *Beyond silenced voices: Class, race, and gender in United States schools* (pp. 237-258). Albany, NY: State University of New York Press.

Whitson, J. A. (1991). Post-structuralist pedagogy as counter-hegemonic praxis (Can we find the baby in the bathwater?). *Education and Society, 9*(1), 73-86.

Willis, P. (1977). *Learning to labour: How working class kids get working class jobs.* Westmead, UK: Saxon House.

PART ONE

ELEMENTARY SCHOOLS

1

The Problem(s) of Men
in Early Education

JAMES R. KING

Men are staying out of primary grade classrooms in droves. Despite calls
for "more men teaching young children," and despite claims that men as
teachers in the early grades might repair the disintegrating family, and perhaps because of the inherent problems embedded in these claims, problems this chapter addresses, men continue to ignore this work niche. The
relationships between the socially constructed categories of "men" and
"teacher" are troubled ones. In many ways the culture views these two
categories in opposition. In particular, males who teach in the primary
grades, or primary males, face the task of eroding the multiple layers of os-
sified popular beliefs about "those men who teach children." Yet, the
voices of men who teach young children have not been part of the discussion about "those men." In this chapter, I have described primary teaching
from the perspectives of men who teach there. Synthesized from their collective experiences, five themes frame the discussion.

This chapter is an outgrowth of a study shared by nine men who, at the
time of the study, were teaching in kindergarten through third grade. I began the study with observations, interviews, and written journal ex-
changes. When several of the members of this group expressed a desire to
meet the other participating teachers, we became a study group that met
periodically to discuss our teaching and lives. Finally, we became a writing group that exchanged written accounts of our teaching, particularly
with regard to issues of gender and teaching. The understandings in this
current writing are drawn from data sources that include personal life his-

tory narratives written by the participants, transcripts of several interviews with the participants, and field notes from observations. All of the writing, from data to report stages, has been member checked among the participants. A more complete description of the study can be found in King (1998).

When I examined the transcripts of the early interviews and compared them with the narratives that the men wrote, several themes became clear because of their repetition across participants, and also because of their prominence within individual participants' talk and writing. I have used five of these themes as an organizing frame for this chapter. The themes center on primary grades teaching as an act of care, men working in women's roles, the use of discipline in classrooms, men's touch as part of their teaching, and primary teachers who are gay. For each of the themes, I provide a description from the men's perspectives and then interpret each issue from several external frames. The examples and quotes used in this chapter to illustrate the five themes are all from transcripts of interviews with Steve, who was a first-grade teacher in his third year of teaching during the time of the study. Consistent use of Steve's words opens the possibility of assembling a "case study" of his experience. In addition, I have used quotes from Ken to illustrate his experiences as a gay primary teacher. The two vignettes that appear in italics in this chapter were written by Richard Chisolm as he struggled through both preservice course work and his first year of teaching in a second-grade class. Richard's perspectives, first recorded as a 36-year-old undergraduate male, and then as a first-year teacher, offer a comparative look between coming to know about education from the outside, and coming to know teaching from the inside. Steve, Ken, and Richard were all participants in the larger study.

Primary Teaching as Care

A first theme or issue that was reported by the primary males is the prominence of care in their teaching. In many discussions with Steve about his teaching, he emerged as a young teacher who was committed to his kids, who was always looking to learn, and was ready to talk about it all:

In primary education, you become someone other than your person on the street. But it doesn't stop when we leave the classroom. It transforms people in good ways. (2-11)[1]

Later in the interview Steve discussed his coming to know the ways of primary education:

> I did a lot of observing of peers in college about hugging. The girls always gave a hug, and guys, if they did give a hug, it was like [makes small pats on his back] real standoffish. I did a lot of watching at first. Even in the early childhood lab, I did a lot of observing. . . . I would watch them first and then try to. . . . It felt awkward at first. I didn't do any mess ups or anything embarrassing, and then I did a few hugs and pats. (2-11)

Steve's comments reveal his awareness that elementary teaching, particularly in the primary grades, is a context of caring. As he presents it, caring is manifested in touch, or hugging. As a "nontoucher" he saw himself as deficient for teaching in a caring role and proceeded to learn what he didn't know. Steve's formulations of teaching are supported by philosophies and descriptions of teaching that rely on teachers' care.

Noddings (1984, 1992) makes the case that acts of caring are special instances of moral and ethical relationships. While these caring acts between the one-caring (teacher) and the one-cared-for (student) are not exclusively attributed by Noddings to teachers, it is significant that most of her discussion is related to student-teacher relationships and interactions where the center is the student. According to Noddings (1984), teachers accomplish their focus on students by "be[ing] totally and nonselectively present to the student—each student—as he [sic] addresses me" (p. 180). In a similar vein, Noddings (1992) suggests that the "soul" of the one-caring (teacher) "empties itself of its own content in order to receive the other" (p. 16). It is clear from Noddings that students' needs are not only cognitive or academic ones, but would also include interpersonal, spiritual, and moral needs as well. To me, this stance toward teaching requires that we are able to reconstruct ourselves in response to each instantiation of "their needs." Being a "being there/their teacher" is a taxing path. Teachers' abilities to "be there" are at least related to, if not determined by, their comfort levels with first being themselves in the classroom. Therefore, any discomfort with self-as-teacher can be seen as a distraction from being available for students. Of course such selflessness or self-denial is a potential problem for both men and women who teach. These acts of selection are common to all teachers. However, choosing how to care as a male teacher adds yet more complexity.

Another source of complexity is the existence of other models of caring that predate Noddings's. Looking at caring behavior, or the intent to care, from these perspectives suggests that caring may be a challenge for men. Gilligan's (1982) argument that women (teachers) live "a life in response, guided by the perception of others' needs" (p. 143) offers primary males a paradox. Being connected with the lives of others through relationships, through caring, concomitantly requires the suppression of teachers' personal needs. While Gilligan is careful to maintain that caring is not essentially feminine, she does suggest that a morality of care tends to be realized socially as a feminine attribute. Following Gilligan's reasoning, it is possible that these men, as well as countless other men, are able to care for and about others. However, it may also be that acts of care may be constructed by individual men in opposition to a morality of justice and individualism, which tends to be male (Kohlberg, 1981).

In her description of British elementary teachers' views of their profession, Nias (1985, 1989) describes teaching lives that are lived in paradox, ambiguity, and contradiction. Nias (1989) suggests that "throughout their professional education and socialization, teachers are led to believe that they are capable of 'knowing' not just one child, but all the pupils in their care" (p. 15). Of course, to know even one other person is intense and complex work. To know 19 to 29 others, let alone the interactive effects of their knowing each other, seems a formidable task. In my mind, it requires a selflessness that gives over personal agenda to others' (students') concerns. Nias's teachers saw themselves as people with strong concerns for others' welfare.

The question here is not so simple as, "Should or could men care?" Intense concern for others' welfare is certainly possible for males. Yet, the following vignette from Richard's experiences illustrates that representing oneself socially as a primary teacher exacts personal costs. Resources that we draw from a social system with set limits are ones unavailable for other purposes, such as attending to the needs of children. The vignette suggests that others may look at men's work with children differently, and that their perspectives about our work are part of our identity, even outside of our classrooms.

The Turnoff

During my final semester as a 36-year-old bachelor's degree student, I took an undergraduate course in International Relations. One of the guest lecturers was a noted feminist banker, who had headed a project providing starter loans to women seeking to start their own small businesses. Since these loans were made available only in underdeveloped nations, some time was spent addressing the difficulties these women had in overcoming cultural barriers to female participation in traditional male occupational roles.

Curious about her background and wishing to know more about her experience, I approached her after the lecture. As we discussed a number of details related to the project, we discovered that we had mutual acquaintances in the international banking community. We talked briefly about my own experiences as a consultant on Wall Street in the 1980s. It was an animated and enjoyable discussion for me. Then the inevitable happened:

"So, what are you doing here?" She had asked with a tonal downstroke on the "here," politely inferring that I might be underutilizing my talents and experience.

"You must be taking courses in International Finance, or something like that, right?" She had answered her own question and was waiting for confirmation with unbreaking eye contact, head slightly tilted to one side in the characteristic pose of an interested listener.

"Actually, I'm taking a second degree in Elementary Education."

"Oh." In that moment, the turnoff happened, as it so frequently does. Her eyes glazed and shifted their focus to some suddenly fascinating spot on the wall beyond my left shoulder. Her conversational reflexes continued to function, even if her interest had moved on to some more engaging subject:

"That's good, we need more men in education . . ." She began to collect her things, clearly dismissing me.

I felt angry at her for all the underlying assumptions this type of response usually indicates, and sadness at the discontinuity of the communication. Unwilling to be so summarily dismissed, rejected as a functional intellectual being capable of having diverse interests, and wanting to jolt her a little, I asked the loaded follow-up question:

"Really? Why do you think so?" modulating the sarcasm in my voice, fixing a wry smile in my eyes, and hoping to let her know as gently as possible that I didn't appreciate the turnoff, but that I had caught her at it.

I was disappointed that someone who I viewed as insightful to the nature of challenging gender barriers in the workplace would be so insensitive. Of course, this also exposes my own assumptions about women as sensitive and considerate of others' issues. This expecta-

*tion has led me down the path of disappointment and frustration
more than once.*

*"Well, don't we need more male role models for kids who haven't
got fathers around?" This, delivered in a blurt, as she attempted to
shift gears and re-engage the conversation, seeking a graceful exit.*

*She'd already lost me. Now it was my turn to turn her off; as I
thought about all the research results which tell us that the one thing
teachers DON'T do well is teach values. This kind of statement implies a lot of things, which are less than complimentary of either my
female colleagues or male teachers. I'd like to think that I have more
to offer than merely my gender, but most of the time it seems to be
such an obstacle* (Chisolm, 1996).

At this point one might ask Richard what is it like to engage in this process of self-denial for the benefit of "being there" for students. Further,
what is it he perceives as the payoff when others clearly do not value his
"sacrifices"? On a first gloss, I am tempted to reason that the biological sex
and the socially constructed gender of the caring teacher matter very little.
This reasoning would be in agreement with both Noddings and Gilligan. It
is arguable that, in fact, men can provide the kind of selfless caring that is
suggested in both of these models when they are applied to elementary
teaching. Yet, the situated act of "moving over" psychologically for the
emergence of a child seems a different act for a male, who is socially constructed by self and others as an individual (Chodorow, 1978). As a stake-
holder in patriarchal culture, accommodating the child can be heroic, or
suspicious. Child centering can be heroic when the adult male temporarily
surrenders a dominant position framed by both male and adult privileges.
These are not uncommon occurrences in either education or in the larger
culture. Such surrender may seem less heroic, or less of a relative loss for
an already marginalized adult female. It is important to point out that acknowledging such differential privilege is not the same as accepting it. It
is, therefore, productive to examine the effects "making way for children"
may have, when this intention is performed by male and by female teachers. This behavior can be framed by multiple interpretations. It can be seen
as a "female attribute," as a "male performing a female attribute," a "male
choosing to perform a female attribute," wherein the intention to care can
be understood as "compulsory care that traps women," to name only a few
of the interpretive refractions that ripple from the center.

Accommodation to children by males who are not family members has
also been marked with suspicion. Adult males who do make this space for

kids are often thought to have ulterior motives, too frequently construed as pedophilia. This theme will be explored in a later section. For now, suffice it to say that responses of suspicion and praise toward men's use of care are interactive phenomena.

Men in Women's Roles

A second theme addressed men's occupation of women's professional roles. In spite of resistance or recasting the tasks, the men who participated in this study often saw themselves as "doing women's work." But such a gloss misses most of the complexity of how this work was deployed. First, it is important that most of their talk about women's work was in resistance to the label. Of course, resisting accusations of "women's work" in a context that is female-identified is tricky work. The men used strategies such as "denial" and "redefinition of the task." Denial happened when the primary males did not accept or own some aspect of teaching as their own. Steve reported that he neither asked other teachers for help nor felt compelled to come to others' assistance. Yet, observations and other stories confirm that he is highly involved in the teaching and lives of his colleagues. His denial was made in the context of an observation that women were overly concerned about others' teaching. In redefining the tasks of teaching, the men consistently reported their awareness that others might belittle or devalue their work as women's tasks. But then following their recognition of the risk of ridicule, they made a case for their more legitimate definition of the behavior as "good teaching" in contrast to something done by women. Steve's discussion of touch in teaching touch, which occurs later in the chapter, is an example of redefinition.

Steve's strategy, unique in this study, was to legitimize his use of what would normally be construed as female as something that he did better than the women who also teach young children. He viewed the assumed differences between men and women who teach young children as a challenge. "I can do it better" seemed to be his motto. The "better" often set him apart, a target for the resentment of these other, female teachers. He saw teaching as a series of "merit badges" and proudly wore each accomplishment:

> When I make a [stenciled T-shirt], or make brownies and bring them in, I'll get comments like "Oh, did your wife make that?" And I always say, "No, if my wife wasn't even there, I still would have made it myself." (2-11)

When Steve dramatized the role of the doubting teacher, he raised the pitch of his voice. I interpreted a "whine" and realized that while he was pointing out the inaccuracy of his colleagues' assumptions, he was also interrogating the underlying purposes of their questions. With his high-pitched whine, he dismissed his female interrogators with what I heard as misogynistic mockery. Seemingly unaware of the effects of such dismissal, he later examined the communication problems that are played out in these conversations that embed a subtext of gender-appropriate teaching behaviors. Steve reflected on his terse ownership of the T-shirt and brownies and continued:

> Everyone assumes my wife made it [the stenciled T-shirt]. She doesn't even know anything about the Ellison machine [cuts stenciled shapes]. I made it myself. I made the cake. I made the brownies. I made the shirt. I made the cookies. I *can* bake! And I don't want them to assume that because I am married, that my wife does all my baking, all my sewing, and all my T-shirts, and stuff. (3-7)

Steve crosses stereotyped gender expectations when he owns the value of his knowledge despite the interrogation of his female colleagues. He is proud to be doing "women's things." For him, competence with these skills is an important part of what others construct as an image about him. He wants credit for his acquired skills, even if the risk is possible discredit to his masculinity. To minimize this risk, he has already contained the discredit by owning the task as a "teacher's task," not a "woman's task." This maneuver seemingly legitimized his effort and disarmed the possible attack of his colleagues, and it was consistent with redefinition.

There is at least one other way of looking at this. Steve's use of "things female" and his demonstration of expertise, or to be "the best," is an ethical issue. In effect, he appropriates the skill, or the ability, and uses it to make himself "the best." Female teachers' interrogations, likewise, might not be about "who" baked the brownies, but a way to remind Steve that indeed he is a male who continues as an apprentice in a female social context. One can imagine the scene as it was portrayed by Steve having very different lessons when a female colleague later recreates it for an exclusively female group.

Gilligan (1982) describes female morality in terms of connectedness, equality, and a lack of individualism and self-promotion. In fact, Gilligan, as well as Belenky, Clinchy, Goldberger, and Tarule (1986), reported that women they interviewed saw individualism and self-promotion as morally dangerous, socially risky behaviors. By investing in a competition for female attributes, Steve is unable to ask about the competition he constructs. Rather, he is trapped in a series of judgments about what is, and what is not, permissible for male teachers. Jewelry is not OK, but shorts and, conceivably, sleeveless shirts are. Baking food for children and their parents is fine, but eating lunch with other teachers who are women is not. Thus, shorts are justified as more comfortable and, therefore, appropriate for teaching attire in an active teaching approach. Artistic expression must always have a functional analog. Jewelry presumably has no function in teaching. His decisions about what is appropriate behavior center on his functional relationship with his students. Regardless of the gender inscription on a particular behavior, it is used or not used in his teaching in relation to how it will impact his work with children. To me, this seems like an example of "doing it for the kids." Centering on children and on the impact of behavior or strategies on them is only one aspect of the complexities of caring for and teaching young children. It is the use of "child centering" as a default morality that masks other, more politically charged or personal reasons for this gender work.

The past two decades have textualized women's ways of doing morality (Gilligan, 1982), reading (Christian-Smith, 1993; Gilbert, 1988; Long, 1986), and teaching (Nias, 1989; Walkerdine, 1990; Weiler, 1988). These perspectives on women's potential for unique epistemologies are particularly relevant to early education. Such potential has created the possibility that there are indeed other ways of looking at the social phenomena (as well as others) that are parts of teaching. And, it is productive to see a set of practices, grouped as a way of knowing, that is explicitly related to the fact that females are doing them. However, using that set of categorized behavior as stuff that women do, because they are women, also creates an essentialized "female way" that can be devalued and dismissed. In the case of this study, it opens the possibility that men, these particular men and others, can appropriate women's ways of teaching young children and claim to "do it better."

The fact that Steve is competing in women's ways of teaching is interesting. First, that he recognizes that these are "feminine" marked behaviors is noteworthy. One might even categorize him as "liberated" (Farrell, 1974). Relative to others, he can indeed be seen as such. Second, that he chooses to apprentice himself to these behaviors (and to female colleagues?) is important to recognize. Choosing to become skilled at what he needs in order to be a teacher, regardless of gender, or gender-expected, coding (Butler, 1990), seems a productive, progressive choice. However, that he competes to be better than the women at "women's skills" is problematic. From an individualist perspective, Steve's self-constructed "I'll show them" attitude could indicate a variety of personal characteristics that inform his teaching decisions. In this regard, he would be no different from any other teacher. However, from a feminist perspective, "I'll show them" may be seen as a privileged intention of one who presumes to show. The intention to show them sets Steve off from a culture he attempts to join, and places him outside the very relationship dynamics that have been described by Gilligan (1982). Further, in this particular social context, Steve intends to compete in an environment that is scripted on connectedness and self-effacement for the emerging child (Walkerdine, 1990). It is, therefore, especially problematic for individualists, who can see themselves as "winning" but do not really understand the rules around them.

Steve's appropriation of things female may also be understood as parody, as attempts to control the value through definitions of "high quality." Finally, Steve's self-positioning as the definer for what is good female practice can be productively understood as patriarchal manipulation. The behavior is objectified, commodified, and appropriated as the skill. And having pushed this analysis as far as it seems productive (maybe too far), it is also important to recognize Steve's fluidity, centeredness, and comfort with his students. In my observations of his teaching, Steve's use of acquired teaching behaviors appears as a coherent, productive approach to his students. Further, for the most part, he reports collegial relationships with other teachers. But to some degree, the preceding analysis may shed light on his loner status in a culture of women's work.

Making Them Mind

A third theme has to do with discipline and how it is understood in primary grade teaching contexts. For the male teachers in the study, discipline was preconfigured for them as male, authority based, and threatening (to others). The underlying assumption, which was usually unexamined, was that men as teachers were somehow better able to provide "problem" students with their needed discipline. By default, female teachers were less able to provide appropriate discipline. In this reasoning, discipline is an object. In contrast, disciplining can also be seen more subjectively as an internalized process of self-regulation. The assumptions made by the primary males and by their colleagues do not examine what is meant by discipline, and what kind of teaching behaviors would more likely facilitate productive discipline. Rather, the common wisdom that *was* monitored and critiqued by the primary males was that their female colleagues often asked them to use authoritarian, external approaches to discipline. The school's version of "Wait until your Dad gets home!" was reported as part of the schools' social context where these men taught and was presumably considered appropriate for their classrooms. The men also consistently reported resisting the call to discipline. Steve was told he was given a certain child as a student because he was a man, and the child needed a male figure. He understood this placement as an implied request for a stricter, harsher discipline. His dramatized response was:

> "Why did you give him to me? Why don't you give him to her or to her?" I don't think I'm any different from a neighbor[ing] teacher in discipline techniques. I thought it was sexist. (2-7)

For me, the call to discipline is related to the privilege primary males experience as the in situ representatives of the patriarchy. Often with a female principal, the (frequently) lone male in the elementary school is the only professional male in the building. In loco parentis must apparently be enacted by the gender-appropriate "parent." Other males may work in the building, but their lower social status as custodians or groundskeepers prohibits them from disciplining. Discipline is a male teacher's "privilege" that is further stratified by social class within the school culture.

These primary males' refusal to discipline reneges on the patriarchal bargain struck in the larger culture. At its most extreme, discipline is about physically hurting children to establish consequences for their undesirable (or lack of desirable) behavior. In their refusal to dispense discipline for others, the primary males refuse to "be masculine." Their refusal constitutes a reversal at several levels. Most immediately, the men are refusing to perform their gendex, or gender expected, behavior (Butler, 1990). Second, their refusal in a female context of care constitutes a second reverse that functionally situates them with their female colleagues. Understanding primary education as a child-centered enterprise, self-control, rational social behavior, and the development of the student self are the overriding objectives of our work with children. We must, therefore, examine the deployment of discipline by teachers in general.

Another perspective on discipline or classroom structure that was shared by the men in the study was that it results from close meaningful relationships between children and adults. Viewing discipline as an outcome of a relationship is in line with Walkerdine (1990), who reasons that teachers in the early grades produce rationality within their students by systematically moving over to make way for the decisions of the emerging child. Walkerdine sees this giving over of self as a potentially problematic condition that prompts her to label teachers as the "containers of irrationality." While the culture outside the classroom, including the children's homes, may be suffused with neglect, indulgence, competition, and aggression, in classrooms the intention is that the children take turns, are listened to, and are required to solve conflict rationally. Therefore, effective child-centered primary teachers' instantiation of discipline is to induce children's self-regulation. In the following vignette, Richard points out the complexities in establishing these caring and meaningful relationships with students and their parents. In the vignette, Richard refers to discipline by its isomorph, structure. Yet, none of the participants in the following vignette appear to want the structures they wish for.

The Placement

He had been placed in my class at the mother's request. Both the administration and his mother thought the placement was appropriate, primarily because the student would "benefit from my more structured environment." Puck, the student, was clearly aching for some attention, and used his considerable dramatic skills to obtain it in the first few weeks. We had begun to understand together some appropriate ways to get attention without disrupting the class. His major obstacle was task initiation. Consequently, despite his obvious intellectual gifts and command of language, he proved unable to complete any task which needed to be done within the same class day. Conversely, every assignment he took home was returned, completed and with immaculate handwriting. He had previously been home-schooled by his mother, and it was clear to me that he depended on her for "inspiration" to the task. Without her support, he was unable to be successful. Several conferences which involved the mother, the principal, and myself took place. In our final conference, we began with a discussion of Puck's need for opportunities to initiate and complete assignments. This led the mother to insist that I was failing to challenge Puck's intellectual abilities. The mother continued to find fault, and insisted that he be placed in another class or she would withdraw him from the school.

In the aftermath, the principal told me that Puck was moved because I had reminded the mother of her soon-to-be ex-husband. The "structure" that her child needed turned out to be the perception that the boy would benefit somehow from my maleness. What about my qualifications as a teacher? What about the pattern of forming and breaking connections with male figures that the mother was perpetuating?

Puck continues to fail at task completion. He is now in another class where he receives even less attention from the teacher, who is beset with an even higher student-teacher ratio than mine. He stops me in the hallway daily to hug me and asks to have lunch with me and my class frequently. The mother is happy, though. She can come and go freely from her son's new classroom, enabling him with his own personal task initiator (Chisolm, 1996).

Men who refuse invitations to enact harsh, threatening discipline, and instead attempt to engage children in self-monitoring, are consistent with a child-centered, caring approach, which characterizes much primary education philosophy. Female teachers who ask males to discipline their children can be seen as inconsistent. From a third perspective, it seems problematic also to recognize that this same production of rationality will, if push comes to shove, ask and expect adult males to threaten children on behalf of the female teachers. And while physically harming children is generally an unacceptable way to treat them, there is something that the primary males (and the rest of us) feared even more. Spanking or hitting children is still safer for male teachers than is touching children in caring ways, as the next section details.

Men Without Hands

A fourth theme that emerged as the primary males discussed their teaching was the hysteria surrounding touch. Men who teach in primary grades are perhaps caught in a no-win situation. They likely chose to enter a female identified professional context in response to the promise of relating to other humans in more caring ways, and for relationship-oriented work lives. Yet, as unusual or marginal participants in women's culture, men in early education contexts are scrupulously monitored by others and by ourselves. Paradoxically, the target of all the monitoring is our enactments of care.

Steve understands touching as part of his teaching behavior, and since he grew up in a family that did not regularly touch each other, he considers it a learned behavior. In a preceding quote, Steve detailed his desensitization to, and eventual acquisition of, touch. His apprenticeship in touch was undertaken with his tacit knowledge that it marked his learning with risk:

> [I was] uncomfortable in day care. All I did was walk around. Walk around. I couldn't sit down. I was afraid that they [the students] would sit on my lap. When I did flop down on the floor, I had about thirty kids sitting on me. After awhile, I got used to it. (4-12)

As I watched him move around his classroom of first graders, it appeared that he was comfortable in his physical relationship to his teaching and his students. His hands rested on shoulders. He hunkered down next to his first graders as they worked and reached around their backs to help them with their work on their desks. Is it his touch of children that he's gotten "used to," or the suspicion he believes others to have about his touch? Steve takes the analysis to a larger cultural frame:

> Society allows men to hug children at home. But outside of home, men don't hug children or other men. They will hug women. (4-12)

Steve's shift from what society allows and what men do is an interesting one. It seems to allow him the space to admit that certain expectations do exist, but that he has some degree of choice in how he will respond to those expectations. From one perspective, a historical legacy of in loco parentis would suggest that home and school sites share much. Indeed, we might expect that hugging, as well as other family-based touching, would occur in both contexts. The tacit and ubiquitous belief that male teachers should not hug or touch children adds weight to Steve's concerns. If men's public hugging is only for women, Steve's parameters for hugging include an implicit argument that hugging is sexually informed touch for men. The argument essentializes all intimacy between genders as sexual, and all physical contact as overture to sexual activity. And while these are certainly overgeneralizations, I suspect that the implicit deployment of "reasoning" like this is part of the touch panic that has invaded classrooms.

Pronger (1990) argues that "gender is the myth that justifies, expresses, and supports the power of men over women" (p. 52). He maintains that gender polarizes the sexes and implicates minor physical difference between men and women as the site for creating opposites, a prerequisite for the dominance of patriarchy. One fallout of patriarchal culture is men's possession of an autonomous sexuality. In contrast, women's socially constructed sexual identities have been absent, repressed, possessed, and controlled (Fine, 1993). A "privilege" such as autonomous sexuality can also be construed as predatory, and it becomes more visible in contexts that are constructed as "asexual" (McWilliam, 1994, 1995). Whereas teaching, particularly with young children, may still be seen as virginal work (Waller, 1932), men are viewed as sexualized in predatory ways. It is difficult negotiating a place in this "sacred trust" of caring in desexualized ways for desexualized children (Kincaid, 1992) when the caregiver is seen as a sexual suspect.

Steve's solution for his paradox of care is to frame his touch inside a restrictive set of rules. Since he is afraid, and aware of his fear "that the kids will go home and say 'Mr. Norris touched me' and all that," he predetermines how his touch is given as well as where and when it is appropriate. He reasons:

> My hugs are side hugs. I stand next to them. I do want to [hug them]. I also pat them on the head, pat them on the back. (4-12)

Steve's hugs and pats are in safe zones. Patting kids' heads is not the same as touching their faces. Side, or hip-to-hip, hugs circumvent the possibility of any contact with Steve's genitals. He also uses "hug substitutes. . . . I also use positive feedback. You know, 'nice job. I like the way you are thinking.' " After he learned to hug as part of his teaching, Steve had to rethink and reschedule how his learned behavior was to be used as part of his teaching. His first graders heard:

> I let them [his first graders] know I was very open. I said "If you want to give Mr. Norris a hug, it's OK. Mr. Norris will hug you back. If you don't want to, Mr. Norris understands." You know, I just let them know it was OK either way. (4-12)

It is interesting that his monitoring of his touch has effectively put the students in charge of the rules and their deployment. Because students must initiate the contact, Steve has vacated his professional agency. His learned teaching behavior (touch can teach) can only occur at the point of need, and only at the students' request.

Hugs, as *the* manifestation of teacher touch, are available at certain times and occur with certain ritualized behaviors:

I don't hug them when they come in early. They sharpen pencils, get a book, use the rest room . . . hugs happen when leaving, arriving. I hug them as a group during the day. Less often, I hug them before special subject, when they leave for or return from lunch, or on the way to the bus. In the morning, I greet them by name. (4-12)

Like his use of women's ways of teaching, Steve's use of hugging is situationally specified and functionally grounded. He understands how and when hugging is acceptable. Steve also understands that some primary teachers, male and female, are not huggers. That Steve even talks about hugging is noteworthy. It is a marked discourse for males. Steve's specificity of rules suggests that he has thought much about this, and that what he does and how he thinks about it are both important to him. Steve's rules, while more clearly articulated than touch rules for other primary males, are a prototype. Checking on doors that need to be open, arranging conference settings so that another adult is able to "see in," and close monitoring of appropriate touch are ubiquitous strategies. I do not mean to suggest that men should work differently in primary classrooms. However, it is critical to realize what a pervasive influence this thinking plays in our daily decisions about children and our work with them. Further, the suspicious nature of touch has also impacted women's work with children (Johnson, 1997).

The "circumstances" are also worthy of commentary. Our understanding of the rules of touch is that we deploy them in anticipation of others' judgments that teachers, particularly male teachers, have the potential for inappropriate, sexually intended touch with our students. I am neither capable of nor interested in debating which acts of touch are permissible, which are objectionable, and which are suspect. Each observed behavior is an open opportunity for limitless interpretation. But because we are male (or, more important, perceived as such) our touch carries extra weight, our hands are prejudged as guilty. To be a male in a primary classroom is to be presumed guilty of the very thing that attracted us to the field, the opportunity to touch (teach) young children.

One way we manage these difference is to blame it all on someone else. Steve's critical imitation of such blame discourse sounded like: "Harry, he's a good first-grade teacher, but those ones who go into teaching just to get at some little child . . ." Steve is aware that we use "pedophile" to be responsible for our anxieties over touch, over children's appropriate handling, over our clumsiness in reasoning about something that we are embarrassed to speak, let alone analyze. While the pedophile has a high utility in our discourses on touch and desire in early classrooms (King, 1997), we scarcely mention it and seldom interrogate it.

Kincaid (1992) reasons that "the pedophile" is a construction of the Victorian era and related to the co-temporaneous construction of "the child." Prior to Victorian normalizing, children were routinely used in a variety of positions that benefited adults. They were used in factories, as chimney sweeps, and as sex partners by adults, all with apparent impunity. These heretofore undifferentiated young humans became a bargaining chip in normalizing adult social patterns and "the child" was invented. Protecting and providing for innocent children (at times to their very misfortune) became the hallmark of civilized society (not to mention the continued colonialization of women's lives). Yet, the formation of the innocent and vacuous child, made to be filled with adult intentions, could not also be misconstrued as waiting to be filled with adult desires (as had previously existed). Now, desire, in its displacement, could never attain its object. When the production of desire is exactly not about object attainment, deferral or transfer only enhances it. It does not go away. The desire, both sexual and asexual, that compelled adults into relations with children, "normal" and "illicit" alike, remains. Accordingly, desire for children, now totalized as unhealthy, is transferred to the waiting pedophile. Rather than responsibly analyzing what is and is not moral, healthy, and productive for children *and* adults, all desire between adults and children becomes suspect. To enjoy a hug or a caress with your students is unthinkable. Men's laps are for accusations, not for sitting. It is complex. We say, "Better safe than sorry."

Kincaid (1992) dares us to take a closer look at how we perpetuate mythologies surrounding a constructed pedophilic monster, and then appropriate the monster to hold our own projected desires. For teachers, all teachers, the paradox is immediate. We choose to teach because we care about and for children. Our enactments of care are idiosyncratic, context situated, and built upon the relationships that teachers as people have with children as people. What parts of our relationships with our students, of any age, are related to our desire? What kinds of desire, if any, are permissible, appropriate, professional? And if our mission is to be an influence on children's lives, to mold them, what then is the shape of the one who molds? That such desire is mapped onto teachers, male teachers, is related to resentment over our sexual "privileging." This mapping is also used as a strategy to keep men away from teaching for reasons other than our desire, our behavior, or its instances of performance, as the next theme illustrates.

Primary Teachers Are Gay

A fifth theme repeatedly mentioned by the primary males was others' speculation about the males' sexual orientations. One way to keep men out of primary education is to accuse them of being gay. Accusations of being gay are used against men who choose to teach in primary grades. That such accusations are effective in a homophobic culture, and that they are successfully deployed in this context, deserves some attention. But, the material fact is that many men who choose to teach in elementary, and especially in the primary, grades *are* homosexual. My reasoning, as a gay, frequently returning primary teacher, is that being gay is a strength that I bring to my teaching. Both of these stances, homophobic extortion and gay giftedness, were considered by the gay-identified participants in this study. But first, it is important to realize that this accusation is leveled at *all* men, gay and straight, with the heterosexist assumption that we all are, or should be, straight. That way, "What are you, a fag?" works to manage male behavior in teaching as well as in other social and professional contexts.

In the following excerpt, Steve recreates a conversation from his undergraduate days and reflects on its impact:

"People think you're gay because you're in education."
"Who said that?"
"Oh, just some people. And I told them that you were."
"Oh, thank you" [with heavy sarcasm]. I don't know, I guess hanging around with a bunch of women and doing artsy craftsy things . . . (3-7)

Steve resists the notion that he is gay, but not the underlying assumptions that put him "at risk." He does not directly interrogate the belief that gay men characteristically do "female things." He does, however, argue in several places for the right of men to do things that are identified as female; or that the right to do so is one that should not carry social criticism. He continues his recollections:

I was fine in college. I was in a fraternity and all that. It's just the snide little comments. . . . I don't know. Maybe people think that only women can teach, be caregivers. And if you are acting like that maybe you're gay. (3-7)

For Steve, the demonstration of caring is acting like a woman; and acting like a woman signifies him as being gay. Given this reasoning, all male teachers in the primary grades are gay. This time, however, it is others who are making the connection, perhaps mistakenly from Steve's perspective. He does think that some men are dissuaded from elementary, and especially the primary, grades because "they are afraid of their feminine side." As we talked, he assumed the character role of the ambivalent male, who was trying to decide whether or not to be a teacher. "Maybe they'll think I'm weird or maybe they'll think I'm gay." Now, feminine, weird, and gay are all brought to the same side of the analysis. In occupying a character while he performed this discussion, Steve did not own these values, but projected them onto others. Steve's fears were not unique. His awareness and ability to articulate his beliefs were. Steve reasoned:

> Had I not been married and had begun teaching, there would be questions. That's the mentality . . . when I started teaching, I carefully placed a picture of my wife on my desk. What difference does it make? When I was single and interning, the parents came to check me out. I think what they're afraid of is that I'm gay . . . [and] that if someone is gay they're a child molester. (4-12)

Steve didn't believe in the chain of logic he had just created in the quote above, but he knew it existed. He summarized:

> What difference does it make? Women can be gay. Men can be gay. But as long as they are providing care for kids . . . (4-12)

I agree. But living under the threat that men shouldn't be gay, shouldn't be like women if we are men, is oppression that exacts costs. For Steve it was enacted in purposeful behavior, not unlike his purposeful and strategic use of female behaviors that are functionally related to this teaching. Placing a picture of his wife on his desk is a gesture. The fact that he connected it with a purpose makes it a strategy for fending off others' speculations about his sexual orientation. This is accommodating to oppression. Steve's deployment of herterosexism makes his wife part of his strategic resistance.

But how does this silliness acquire its teeth, and why use such a despicable, manipulative ploy? Malicious character assassination is hard work, so I reason it has a payoff. So does Owens (1992). In paraphrasing Sedgwick (1985), Owens reasons that homosexuality is used as a category to control the behavior of men. Working from the assumption of compulsory heterosexual norms, difference is constructed as deviance (Foucault, 1978) and then accusations of deviance can be used to bully men back to appropriate heterosexual norms, however those norms may be constituted in a given situation. For primary teachers, semantic features of the category "gay" are entailed in connotations for "primary male" and are intended to keep the job prestige at a minimum and thereby dissuade men from participating. Reskin (1991) reminds us that job differentiation is a necessary condition for unequal wages for men and women. Related to the low prestige of primary education, the previously mentioned attributions of caring and nurturing to females as naturally occurring phenomena work to maintain the "naturalness" of these attributes. Constructed as natural, caring and nurturing are not related to technical expertise and therefore do not require remuneration. To continue this exploitative, false economy, we must ensure men do not participate. If we can remain convinced that primary men are gay, then few males, gay or straight, will be enticed. And finally, this use of homosexuality as a social tool requires that it be criminalized and recriminalized. Of course, all of this has little to do with real individuals with same-sex orientation who choose to live as "gay men" and work as primary teachers.

For self-identified gay men who teach young children, the stakes are much higher. At this time in Florida, "family-oriented" political groups are exerting pressure to "out" gay and lesbian teachers so that we can be forced from our teaching positions. The gay teachers in this study may lose their jobs. The internal binary of self-worth and pride contrasted with hiding and secrecy are everyday realities for gay primary teachers. While Steve is not gay, another teacher in the study was: Ken, a gay kindergarten teacher for 17 years. Because he feared reprisal, Ken claimed he simply couldn't talk explicitly about his life partner at school. Yet, he consciously pushed himself to be as open as he could in each social circumstance.

> Usually when I do talk about Jack [Ken's partner], I say "we" and I never really define the other part of "we." I feel as though my coworkers must feel as though they've walked in on the middle of a movie. (3-13)

Ken claimed a relationship between his gayness, his childhood, and his teaching. He maintained that primary education is a highly verbal and female context and that he sought to be a practicing member of the local norms. In talking about gay men, he said, "We're verbal because we hung out in the kitchen." This makes sense to me, because I hung out in the kitchen. It fits, in a glib way, how I understand coming to know what I know about women's ways of talking. But I am also aware of many gay friends, some primary teachers, whom I would consider quiet and reserved.

Ken continued with a stylized remembrance of collective holiday experiences to reinforce his point. He remembered that the men sat in the living room watching football while he was in the kitchen listening to wonderful stories. Because of these and similar repeated experiences, Ken is comfortable working with women and comfortable in rich linguistic contexts, like primary classrooms. He suggested that "men [gay and nongay] who choose to work in a female context and not work within women's ways [of knowing] do so with some costs." However, Ken did not see these choices along lines of gender or lines of sexual orientation. Rather, it is the ability, however acquired, however understood, to work with children and other teachers within women's ways of knowing. Ken related that he has worked with several men who identified themselves as heterosexual, and who were also very effeminate. Ken suggested that these are "straight men who know women's ways." Ken concluded:

> The men who do a real good job in primary teaching identify with women. They relate to women, and they relate to women's tasks. Whereas, the men who are the lone wolves, are trapped between both worlds. They're uncomfortable being in this socializing, nurturing situation. But their economic situation is dependent on being there. . . . A friend of mine said, "The male [primary] teachers who are good are gay. The mediocre ones are straight." It seems like a stereotype, but . . . (3-13)

Ken understood his own positioning in line with this statement, and personalized it:

> I think I'm good because I overcompensate. I know people will be looking at me. . . . Number one, because I'm male. Number two, because they suspect that I'm gay. And if they are going to be looking, they're going to be looking at something good. (3-13)

Indeed, Ken's gambit seems to be working. He is consistently profiled in the local newspaper ("the gentle giant") whenever a "good example" of a male teacher of young children is desirable. True to form, he was aware of the "use" potential, and turns it to his advantage. "At least if they're the [newspaper] stories they talk about, it gives them something positive."

Reframing the Issues

People who claim to be masculine are caught in a bind. A history of wide-ranging sexual privilege has finally been harnessed in the discovery of the "male body." A free-floating sexual signification has found a frame in the configurations of the male body, which is now manufactured in queer gyms, appropriated to move products (Pronger, 1990), and marketed materially (Simpson, 1994), like any other commodity. What then are the features attributed to this new site? How do these acquired features align with the expectations of what we call teachers?

If the underlying motive in primary males' strategies for "being teachers" is to preserve the masculine while they apprentice in a feminine context, then critique of that goal is certainly productive. It seems reasonable that the more centered, or vested, an individual is on self, the less he will be aware of (let alone critique) the privilege of individualism. Therefore, it makes some sense to look at male teachers from a feminine/feminist deconstruction of "elementary male."

Systematic use of feminist perspective in the analysis of male primary teachers creates yet another platform or stance that must itself undergo some critical analysis. If descriptions of "teachers" include people engaged in compulsory caring, trapped in self-denial, then teacher is again problematic. Early education is a rich context, not without its own conflicts and points of resistance. For a male-identified man to enter this arena is a choice. Another choice for that man, these men, is choosing what "man" means in this feminine context, for certainly the meaning is being formulated by others for him. Giroux (1992) has called this purposeful maneuvering of selves "border crossing." Likewise, Gergen (1991) has commented on the situated reconstruction of our different selves as characteristic of postmodern identity shifting.

When these primary males entered elementary education, they monitored and regulated their teaching so as to correspond with preconfigured images of masculinity *and* teacher (as female). They scrupulously monitored their touch, dress, and relationships with children and other teachers. This is the work of Sisyphus. Within an oppositional binary of male/female, the primary males ricochet between identity platforms. Any resolution is unlikely, as stasis, or a stable sense of self, necessitates a shared sense of what is masculine, while the concept itself remains undefined. Masculine has been realized in patriarchy as not feminine. Early education, as a culture that is quietly not masculine, offers males opportunities to analyze what it means to be both male and teacher in a critical way. Or the occupation of early education by males offers the chance to dismiss the whole enterprise of early education as something simply female.

Note

1. Interview excerpts are identified with the month and date on which they occurred.

References

Belenky, M., Clinchy, B., Goldberger, N., & Tarule, J. (1986). *Women's ways of knowing*. New York: Basic Books.

Butler, J. (1990). *Gender trouble: Feminism and the subversion of identity*. New York: Routledge.

Chisolm, R. (1996, May). *Thoughts on courses and students*. Unpublished manuscript, University of South Florida, Tampa.

Chodorow, N. (1978). *The reproduction of mothering: Psychoanalysis and the sociology of gender*. Berkeley: University of California Press.

Christian-Smith, L. (1993). *Texts of desire*. Washington, DC: Falmer.

Farrell, W. (1974). *The liberated man: Beyond masculinity; freeing men and their relationships with women*. New York: Random House.

Fine, M. (1993). Sexuality, schooling, and adolescent females: The missing discourse of desire. In L. Weis & M. Fine (Eds.), *Beyond silenced voices: Class, race, and gender in United States schools* (pp. 75-100). Albany: State University of New York Press.

Foucault, M. (1978). *The history of sexuality: Vol 1*. New York: Pantheon.

Gergen, K. (1991). *The saturated self: Dilemmas of identity in contemporary life*. New York: Basic Books.

Gilbert, P. (1988). Student text as pedagogical text. In S. de Castell, A. Luke, & C. Luke (Eds.), *Language authority and criticism: Readings in the school textbook* (pp. 234-250). Washington, DC: Falmer.

Gilligan, C. (1982). *In a different voice*. Cambridge, MA: Harvard University Press.

Giroux, H. (1992). *Border crossings: Cultural workers and the politics of education*. New York: Routledge.

Johnson, R. (1997). The "no touch" policy. In J. Tobin (Ed.), *Making a place for pleasure in early childhood education* (pp. 101-118). New Haven, CT: Yale University Press.

Kincaid, J. (1992). *Child-loving: The erotic child and Victorian culture*. New York: Routledge.

King, J. (1997). Keeping it quiet: Silence, desire and gay teachers in the primary grades. In J. Tobin (Ed.), *Making a place for pleasure in early childhood education* (pp. 235-250). New Haven, CT: Yale University Press.

King, J. (1998). *Primary males: Learning from men who teach young children.* New York: Teachers College Press.

Kohlberg, L. (1981). *The philosophy of moral development.* San Francisco: Harper & Row.

Long, E. (1986). Women reading and cultural authority: Some implications of audience perspective in cultural studies. *American Quarterly, 38,* 591-612.

McWilliam, E. (1994). *In broken images: Feminist tales for a different teacher education.* New York: Teachers College Press.

McWilliam, E. (1995, April). *Touchy subjects: Pedagogy, performativity, and sexuality.* Paper presented at the annual meeting of the American Educational Research Association, San Francisco.

Nias, J. (1985). Reference groups in primary teaching: Talking, listening, and identity. In S. Ball & I. Goodson (Eds.), *Teachers' lives and careers* (pp. 105-119). London: Falmer.

Nias, J. (1989). *Primary teachers talking.* New York: Routledge.

Noddings, N. (1984). *Caring: A feminine approach to ethics and moral education.* Berkeley: University of California Press.

Noddings, N. (1992). *The challenge to care in schools: An alternative approach to education.* New York: Teachers College Press.

Owens, C. (1992). Outlaws: Gay men in feminism. In S. Bryson, B. Kruger, & J. Weinstock (Eds.), *Beyond recognition: Representation, power, and culture: Craig Owens* (pp. 218-255). Berkeley: University of California Press.

Pronger, B. (1990). *The arena of masculinity: Sports, homosexuality and the meaning of sex.* New York: St. Martin's.

Reskin, B. (1991). Bring the men back in: Sex differentiation and the devaluation of women's work. In J. Lorber & S. Farrell (Eds.), *The social construction of gender* (pp. 141-161). Newbury Park, CA: Sage.

Sedgwick, E. (1985). *Between men: English literature and male homosocial desire.* New York: Columbia University Press.

Simpson, M. (1994). *Male impersonators: Men performing masculinity.* New York: Routledge.

Walkerdine, V. (1990). *Schoolgirl fictions.* London: Verso.

Waller, W. (1932). *The sociology of teaching.* New York: Russell and Russell.

Weiler, C. (1988). *Women teaching for change: Gender, class, and power.* South Hadley, MA: Bergen & Garvey.

2

Topologies of Masculinity

Gendered Spatialities of Preadolescent Boys

JAN NESPOR

Connell (1995, 1996) has argued that masculinities and femininities are produced in "body-reflexive practices" that articulate sensuous experiences with discursive constructions of the body. Bodies are thus "both agents and objects of practice":

> Particular versions of femininity and masculinity are constituted in [body-reflexive practices] as meaningful bodies and embodied meanings. Through body-reflexive practices, more than individual lives are formed: a social world is formed. Through body-reflexive practices, bodies are addressed by social process and drawn into history, without ceasing to be bodies. (Connell, 1996, p. 159)

This view of gender as a "social practice that refers to bodies and what bodies do" (Connell, 1996, p. 159) raises the question of just what a "body" is (cf. Stone, 1995; Turner, 1995). Connell's insistence on the centrality of the body leads him to treat it as a well-bounded physical entity that can be disciplined, trained, liberated, or variously imbricated in different interpretive frames. But bodies are not necessarily well-defined physical regions: They move, occupy, produce, negotiate, and transgress spaces beyond the skin. Bodies, as Lefebvre (1991) puts it, "generate spaces" (p. 216) and are, in important senses, constituted by their spatiality. As Leigh Star (1995) argues, we can think of

human beings as *locations* in space time. We are relatively localized for many
bodily functions and for some kinds of tasks we perform alone. But for many
other kinds of tasks we are highly distributed—remembering for example (Middleton & Edwards, 1990). . . . Parts of our selves extend beyond the skin in every
imaginable way, convenient as it is to bound ourselves that way in conversational shorthand. Our memories are in families and libraries as well as inside our
skins; our perceptions are extended and fragmented by technologies of every
sort.

All the matter in our body can be thought of this way, including the brain. . . .
The brain is not a lump of meat with a few electric channels strung through it.
The body/brain of any person is a location of dense arrangements, nested in
like others. When we use the shorthand "individual" or "individual cognition,"
we are thus only pointing to a *density*. (pp. 19-20)

If we treat bodies as spatio-temporal locations of variably dense articulations of practice, we can amend Connell's (1996) notion of gender as a
temporal "project." Instead of focusing on "dynamic processes of config-
uring practice through time" (p. 160), we need to look at gender *trajectories*[1] unfolding in time and *space*. From this perspective, genders are the
effects of performative accomplishments of particular articulations of
space and time (cf. Butler, 1990). These articulations are enacted in material landscapes (e.g., Lefebvre's, 1991, comments on "phallic vertical-
ity"), semiotic landscapes (e.g., Appadurai's, 1996, "mediascapes" and
"ethnoscapes"), and in social practices regulating the way people assert
versions of gender through the orchestrations of their movements.

In this chapter I examine some of these issues by looking at the spatialities of masculinity among 9-, 10-, and 11-year-olds in an urban American
elementary school where I spent 2 years doing ethnography (Nespor,
1997). Preadolescent boys have been relatively neglected by theorists of
gender practice—Connell's (1995) comprehensive account of masculinities, for example, takes adolescence as a starting point. My aim is not to fill
this gap by making generalizations about characteristic spatial realiza-
tions of masculinity among preadolescent boys. Instead, I want to pry
open some theoretical issues related to the variety of spatial forms within
which and by means of which masculinities can be assembled. If we think
of the body as a distributed system, an arrangement of densities in space
and time, then the body-reflexive practices of masculinity can be seen to
unfold well before puberty. Body-reflexive practices concern not only the
biological body, but the spatially and temporally extended body, which is
best spoken of in terms of *topographical* and *topological* spaces.

Gender Topographies

Topographies locate entities—boys and masculinities as well as cities and mountains—in the "abstract" three-dimensional space (Lefebvre, 1991) of mapmakers and planners. Topographies of gender look at differences in the kinds of spaces boys and girls (or men and women) occupy, and differences in how they move through those spaces. A wealth of studies,[2] for example, demonstrate that by ages 9 or 10 boys have greater "environmental ranges" than girls, that is, whether because of fears for girls' safety (Katz, 1993; Valentine, 1997) or because girls are disproportionately saddled with housework and child care responsibilities (Lynch, 1977; Ward, 1978),[3] boys are allowed to go farther from home and stay out longer and with less supervision than girls (Hart, 1979; Katz, 1993; Lynch, 1977, 1979; Matthews, 1992; Valentine, 1996, 1997; Ward, 1978). Boys seize control of public spaces within buildings like schools (Shilling, 1991) and on the street, and command spaces within the home (McNamee, 1998).

These studies recount what, following Lefebvre (1991), we could call the distributions of gendered "bodies in space," the ways bodies categorized and gendered by dominant social institutions are organized in the abstract, administrative-bureaucratic spaces of the modern world. These distributions have consequences for children's development. Katz (1993) argues that "the erosion of children's autonomy and outdoor experience in industrialized Western cities marks not only a deterioration in the quality of children's lives, but an arena of deskilling with long-term implications both for the children and for the society as a whole" (p. 100). Kids' analytical and spatial abilities, for example, seem to be constricted by this "erosion" of spaces and spatial experience for children and youth, with girls being especially hard hit (Katz, 1993, 1998).

Although the physical distribution of boys and girls is thus an important channel for the production of gendered meanings of public and private space generally, the topographies of childhood may be more complex than such accounts suggest. As most writers on these subjects acknowledge (but do not often pursue), gender spacings are torqued by age, class, region, and race.

Consider, to begin with, a pair of white, working-class fourth-grade classmates, Felix and Carol[4] (see Nespor, 1997), whose experiences seem generally consistent with the literature just cited. That is, Felix got around much more than Carol, who wasn't allowed out of her yard without an adult accompanying her (cf. Valentine, 1997). When I asked Carol if she ever walked around the neighborhood, she replied:

Well, we only took the dog out once. We took him out on his leash. But there was other dogs out there. And we didn't take him out no more. So we only did it that one time.

Carol's mobility (and that of her dog) was restricted to her fenced-in backyard, where she rode her bike and played with the friends her parents allowed over. When I asked if there were dangerous places in the neighborhood, wondering if she could identify particular areas, her answer suggested that the neighborhood in general was dangerous, including the homes of friends who didn't appreciate the risks:

Well, my friend Hetty she's bossy, but she also asks if I can spend the night, and my mom says no, because one night, at 9:00, I was in bed, 'cause I have to go to bed at 9:00, sometimes 9:30 sometimes 10:00. And my dad, he was outside switching the cars around, for work. And Hetty she was outside, and she's seven—but now she's eight—and she was walking her dog outside, outside in our street at 9:00. And someone could have grabbed her. And my mom and dad won't let me go over there because, because, you know, she might, you know, her parents don't even, her parents didn't even know she went out. And dad goes, "someone's going to pick her up, and that dog ain't gonna save her."

In contrast to this enactment of public spaces as areas of high danger, Felix rode his bike all around the same area. Here he described an idealized weekend routine:

I go into my friend's yard. I stop. I really should get him first, but for some reason I like riding back and forth. Then we go to Buddy's house. Then we ride our bikes through here, go to Aphex Park to the swing set, we play, then after we're tired, we ride our bikes all the way down here. Actually, the second park is in another neighborhood. But there's a little chain right here.[5] So we go into somebody's yard, cross to the second park. Play. Go up here. Get Brenda. Stop. Go up, go up to a real big hill. . . . Aphex Hill is a real big hill. So we go down again. We never get done. And sometimes we go to Tony's house. Sometimes Troy's nice to me. And then we stop. And go to my house for my sisters. Go to Janie's house. And then we do that all over again riding through the neighborhood. . . . There's like, 20 houses separating our house from [Brenda's]. And then you've got to go down here, and then there's 20 more houses. And then turn up, and that's her house. So we ride about a mile just to get to Brenda's house . . . from my house, two miles. From Aphex Park, a mile.[6]

These accounts illustrate the familiar topography of enclosed females and mobile males. What is interesting is that this pattern did *not* hold on the whole for their classmates. A classmate of Felix's and Carol's, Cicily, for example, had a solitary bike-riding routine that rivaled Felix's. An African American girl who lived in a different area of the city and was bused to the school Carol and Felix attended, Cicily biked all around her neighborhood, and unlike Felix even rode down a very busy street by herself to a strip mall to buy candy at a drugstore. Is race the warping factor here? In general, the independent mobility of African American children is restricted compared to European Americans, just as girls' is compared to boys' (Matthews, 1992), and Cicily's routines were much more extensive than those of other African American girls living close by (Nespor, 1997). But if we see gender and race as woven together with class and biography, the patterns begin to make more sense. Cicily's African American classmates lived in a low-income apartment complex surrounded by a four-lane road, an interstate highway extension, and open fields (zoned commercial). Cut off from the rest of the city by these physical barriers, the apartments were fashioned to work as self-contained islands—with their own playgrounds, for example—to contain their black residents spatially (this physical enclosure of African American communities, along with deteriorating mass transit systems and the spatialization of violence in poor urban neighborhoods, may explain why their children are less mobile than European Americans). Cicily, by contrast, lived in a house set among an older isolated cluster of black-owned residences, giving her easier access to connecting streets through which she could ride her bike (when I asked her if there were dangerous places in the neighborhood, she said there were not).

If, as Valentine (1996) insists, "the production of space, like gender, [is] a performative act, naturalized through repetition" (p. 206), then more attention to how boundaries are performatively created is required (cf. Thorne, 1993). Race, class, neighborhood organization, and residence form, as well as the length of time one has lived in the area (Nespor, 1997), all play roles, along with gender, in shaping kids' spatial practices. We should also note, the emphases of geographers on kids' solitary movements notwithstanding, that there are no good reasons to ignore kids' *collective* movements through areas, their mobility as members of youth organizations (Adler & Adler, 1994; Heath & McLaughlin, 1994), as participants in organizational outings (e.g., school field trips, outings organized by youth groups or churches), or even their family-mediated mobility.[7]

My point is not that we need ever finer matrices of generalizations to represent kids' topographies. On the contrary, the attempt to identify the spatial practices or representations that differentiate boys and girls is problematic in itself. Aside from relying, at least implicitly, on categorical theories of gender (as well as of race and class), such a project *assumes* a certain kind of gender topology in which boys' and girls' domains can be conceptualized as clearly defined regions across which individual actors, in bounded bodies, can be tracked (see Rose, 1993a, for a critique of Hagerstraand's "time-geography" along these lines).

Instead of looking for such unique spatialities of masculinity and femininity, I want to consider now the possibility that along with complex gender topographies there are multiple "gender topologies"—multiple masculine and feminine spaces. Examining how the 9-, 10-, and 11-year-olds I worked with constructed themselves as gendered beings, I want to suggest that, at least at this age, gendered identities can be organized as *regions, networks,* or perhaps, as *fluid* spaces.

Gender Topologies

Unlike topography, the mapping of objects in a Euclidean space, *topology,* as Mol and Law (1994) define it, is a mathematics of spatial form that "doesn't localize objects in terms of a given set of coordinates. Instead, it articulates *different rules for localizing* in a *variety of coordinate systems*" (emphasis in original; p. 643).

A topological approach to masculinities would ask what kinds or forms of spaces constitute and are constituted by masculinities and masculinist practices. Mol and Law's (1994) analysis of medical classification systems as kinds of spaces provides a useful preliminary framework. For Mol and Law, the key questions concern the boundaries of entities. Boundaries can be relatively impermeable and rigid or porous and malleable; practices can be linked across space and time by networks circulating immutable mediating artifacts (Latour, 1987) or they can be relatively localized and situated. These dimensions produce three kinds of topologies:

> There are *regions* in which objects are clustered together and boundaries are drawn around each cluster. Second, there are *networks* in which distance is a function of relations between the elements and difference a matter of relational variety. . . . [Third,] sometimes . . . neither boundaries nor relations mark the difference between one place and another. Instead, sometimes boundaries come and go, allow leakage or disappear altogether, while relations transform themselves without fracture . . . social space behaves like a *fluid.* (p. 643)

These topologies are not exclusive of one another (indeed, they are closely related). People may be constructed (in the sense that institutions and activity systems organize the space and time of their experience) or may strategically construct themselves and their situations as complexly textured landscapes, with some areas being dense and continuous, others lattice-like, and still others viscous and ill defined. If the body, as Star (1995) suggested, is a location, a set of densities, then its production in terms of these forms is always tenuous, the result of ongoing struggle. Instead of arguing that masculinities assume a particular topology, I want to suggest that multiple masculinities are constructed, on differing scales, sometimes in reinforcing layers and other times in tension, within all three topologies. Body-reflexive practices take different forms in the context of different topologies.

Masculinity as a Region

The most common mapping of masculinity portrays it as a bounded space, a region. Kirby (1996), for example, asserts that "masculine" and "feminine" identities are "the effects of qualitatively different forms of space, with the masculine occupying a securely bounded and expansive space, and the feminine taking a porous, flexible form" (p. 9). This perspective is shared by analysts of gender spatialities influenced by object relations theory (e.g., Sibley, 1995b), and can also be linked to characterizations of the masculine body in terms of what Bakhtin (1968) described as the canon of the closed-off, "civilized" body, which "presents an entirely finished, completed, strictly limited body, which is shown from the outside as something individual. That which protrudes, bulges, sprouts, or branches off . . . is eliminated, hidden, or moderated. All orifices of the body are closed" (Bakhtin, 1968, p. 320).

Rose (1993b) argues that this classical body is one that has lost its "vulgar and feminine orifices and excretions" and replaced them with an "enlightened masculine mind . . . clearly separate from and untainted by its body" (p. 77).

This bounded body and its role as the simple container of rationality both contribute to the idea that we are socialized by internalizing lessons which the "outside" world teaches us when we act in it, and also produce a lack of interest in the unconscious, in dreams and fantasies. (p. 77)

And, one might add, the bounded masculine body is stereotypically portrayed as avoiding emotional openness and vulnerability as well as intense, caring relationships. One problem with such accounts is that, in a curious reflection of the perspectives they critique, they center on the biological body bounded by the skin rather than the body as a distributed, material-semiotic network of heterogeneous elements (Haraway, 1991; Star, 1995). Instead of essentializing masculine spatialities in this fashion, it might be more useful to think of regionalized masculinities as topologies constructed to deal with those parts of public space fashioned into sharply demarcated regions. The corollary spaces for such bodies are the partitioned, functionally specific settings described by Foucault (1979). Massey (1996), for example, explains that high-tech workplaces

> are not merely spaces where things may happen but spaces which in the nature of their construction (as specialized, as closed-off from intrusion, and in the nature of things in which they are specialized) themselves have effects—in the structuring of the daily lives and the identities of the scientists who work within them. Most particularly, in their boundedness and in their dedication to abstract thought to the exclusion of other things, these workplaces both reflect and provide a material basis for the particular form of masculinity which hegemonizes this form of employment. (p. 121)

Although the logic of an "abstract space" (Lefebvre, 1991) that organizes experience into homogenized, fragmented regions may be spreading to a very wide range of institutions (including the home), regions are still only one spatialization of masculinity, reflecting the topology of affluent professional men who do well in spaces like schools and go on to get jobs in similarly organized corporate settings.

But if schools are regionalized, the control of those regions is continuously contested by kids who struggle to appropriate them and teachers determined to manage them, and gender is often at the crux of these struggles. As Henley (1977) points out, preadolescent children's bodies are spatially and temporally controlled much as women's bodies are. Preadolescent kids, male and female alike, are in some senses spatially "feminized" within regions defined by masculinist logics and controlled by women. For young boys this creates the problem of how to construct masculinities in spatial regimes that deny them such identities. One response is to try to carve out controllable regions within classroom space.

For example in the fourth-grade classroom that Felix, Carol, and Cicily belonged to, the teacher one day in mid-year rearranged desks. The kids had been complaining about the previous arrangement, but seemed particularly dismayed by the new plan. Glenn, who'd been telling me just a few days earlier how much he disliked the old seating arrangement, said, "This is terrible!" "But you didn't like the way it was," I reminded him. "This is worse," he replied, "I can't work with Lila and Kerri!", the two African American girls he was now to be clustered with.

Cindy, who was good friends with Kerri, heard Glenn and responded with her own complaint when she realized she was facing Karl and Doug. "I can't work with boys!" she cried, "boys are stupid, I don't want to sit with boys." She punctuated her comments by giving Karl a couple of kicks to the shin.

In fact, the kids' desks had been arranged in mixed gender clusters throughout the year. What their teacher had done in this redeployment was break up several groups of boys who'd been sitting near one another. The boys responded by trying to regionalize their new settings. First, they cut cardboard strips to a size they could wedge into their desk openings to create doors with "Warning Keep Out" written on them. Mel and Glenn then tried to set up a bounded social space by starting a kind of club. Each had little cardboard badges that said "MMD" ("Mel's Mad Dogs") and a little card that said "That is the Question." If someone gave the group's password—"to be or not to be"—members were to show the card in response rather than answering verbally.

My point is that the gendering of spaces like classrooms was not a simple function of the physical distribution of boys and girls. The spatial organization of the elementary school as a whole—regions controlled by female teachers where boys and girls alike had little control over their movements and bodies—played a role as well. Even more important, the meanings of physical arrangements depended on particular performances of spatial gendering. As Moore (1994) points out, following Bourdieu (1977), "symbolic meanings are not inherent in the organization of space, but have to be invoked through the activities of social actors" (p. 76). For boys it was critical, at least in certain contexts, to perform exclusions of girls. Boys who failed to do this—Felix, for example, who rode his bike with female classmates and liked to interact with girls he openly had crushes on—were ostracized by other boys attempting hegemonic spatial exclusions. When he first saw the new arrangements of desks, Mel tried to find a pattern: "I bet it's two boys and two girls at each table," he told me. When I pointed out that one cluster of desks had three boys, including Felix, Mel replied: "Felix doesn't count" as a boy. Mel informed me, "Felix messes with his sister's dolls."

In fact, Felix's relations with his sister illustrate a different facet of regionalization. Along with neighborhood space and school, the home is a third arena of gender regionalization (McNamee, 1998; Sibley, 1995a). Unlike school, where the boys seemed to be simply claiming control of spaces, houses got carved into regions when boys bounded spaces for *activities* they defined as exclusively theirs. When I asked Felix if he read much at home, he responded that he read only when grounded, and that he got grounded

> [w]hen I'm bad in school, when I back-talk to my mom, when I hit my sister. I can get grounded really easy. 'Cause that's what, that's mostly what I do. . . . But only if I back-talk her real bad. And I hit my sister like taps, but when she gets me real mad I'll really punch her. . . . She gets on my nerves, like she sings these baby songs and I might say "Sis, stop it," and she keeps on bugging me while I'm playing Nintendo, SuperNintendo. 'Cause we, I made a rule in the house: Anybody that goes upstairs and bothers me or talks near me when I'm playing Nintendo, they will pay the price.

McNamee (1998) describes similar patterns of exclusion surrounding video gaming in Britain, and argues that,

> The physical ownership of computer and video games, and the physical control of space which arises from it, are also of *symbolic* importance to teenage boys in the domestic sphere. Young men are controlling and policing their sisters' access to computer and video games in the expression of their masculine identity. (p. 204)

Battles over video games and the spaces of privacy needed to practice them are not merely *expressions* of masculinity, however; they are means of constructing a certain kind of masculine topology. "The home" is not a given, a well-bounded region (as Mcnamee seems to assume). There are connections between battles over things like video games within the home and gender spatializations *outside* the home. I want to suggest that video games are "mediating artifacts" (Latour, 1994) allowing boys to orient themselves within network topologies of masculinity, and they are vehicles for organizing embodied interaction with other boys around these new topologies.

Masculinity as a Network

The concept of "mediation" is crucial for understanding what I mean by network topologies of masculinity. The association of people across space and time requires standardized, reproducible artifacts that can move and be circulated while remaining relatively stable in form and content. The artifacts themselves crystallize the complex practices and beliefs that went into their creation. "Think of technology as congealed labour," Latour (1994, p. 40) suggests. Elements of past actions from physically distant sites are mobilized or carried into each encounter or use of technology. A campus speed bump "is not made of matter, ultimately, it is full of engineers and chancellors and lawmakers, commingling their wills and their story lines with those of gravel, concrete, paint, and standard calculation" (Latour, 1994, p. 41). Agency is a property of these entanglements of people and objects:

> There is no sense in which humans may be said to exist as humans without entering into commerce with what authorizes and enables them to exist (i.e., to act). . . . Purposeful action and intentionality may not be properties of objects, but they are not properties of humans either. They are the properties of institutions, *dispositifs*. Only corporate bodies are able to absorb the proliferation of mediators, to regulate their expression, to redistribute skills, to require boxes to blacken and close. Boeing 747s do not fly, airlines fly. (p. 46)

Similarly, certain forms of masculinity may be said to be properties of institutional networks (and distributed bodies that extend beyond the skin) rather than individuals. Popular culture provides a familiar illustration. Milkie (1994), for example, describes boys slightly older than the kids I worked with who recited lines and mimicked actions from movies, usually scenes that portrayed gender-stereotyped or aggressively masculinist activities. She analyzes such mimicry as a process of social reproduction: Boys learn stereotypical masculinist attitudes by literally reproducing them for each other. As many have pointed out, however, this kind of interpretation is a problematic: It portrays kids from the standpoint of expected adult roles, introducing a teleology that explains kids' behaviors solely as preparation for adulthood. As Thorne (1993) and others stress, kids' practices need to be examined in their own right as elements of an alternative cultural sphere. The appropriation of phrases, metaphors, and imagery from popular media is not so much a way of learning adult perspectives as a means of articulating masculinities across space and time—of creating masculinities in the form of network topologies.

Boys who lack control of physical regions and whose embodied activities are tightly constrained by adults can perform masculinities by associating themselves with distant representations of manhood available in the form of stable, transportable representations. One example comes from a conversation with two fourth graders that took place in the classroom after school one day as the buses were delayed by a heavy thunderstorm. As we waited for an announcement, kids from the other fourth grade next door wandered in and out, games broke out, some little girls practiced their religious cheerleading ("Jesus Jesus he's our man; If he can't help you no one can"), and we all got progressively antsy and hungry. I decided to use the time for an extemporaneous "interview" with Mel and Doug about an upcoming standardized test, and after answering a few of my questions the boys began to exploit the carnival-like atmosphere to generate this little rant:

Mel: I hate homework!!

Doug: School sucks!

Mel: And one thing, one thing I hate more than homework, more than school!

[Together]: More than anything, GIRLS!

Jan: Why?

Doug: They get on my nerves. One sitting right there (Lauren) gets on our nerves.

Mel: [said almost whispering] And girls, they admit things to boys, like they like them and stuff, and that makes some boys upset and stuff. But not me: I just make fun of them and stuff.

Doug: Me too.

Mel: Call them names.

Doug: Me too . . .

Mel: And then when I get like into high school, I'll go skiing and see these ski bunnies, ask them out for a date or something.

Jan: Ski bunnies? What?

Mel: Ski bunnies, I'll ask one out for a date.

Doug: Yeah, they're girls!

Mel: Oh man! Whooo!

Jan: What's a ski bunny?

Doug: It's girls dressed like in a skin suit.

Mel: And bunny ears and a cotton tail, skiing down mountains and stuff. And they walk around in the snow and stuff. Wooo! That's when I'm gonna get big in college. I mean, not college but high school.

Doug: The other thing we hate in school, is school! School sucks. But you can make it fun by going into detention.

Mel: That's not fun.

Doug: Noo!! Like—on *Saved by the Bell*—

Mel: You try to get your girlfriend in trouble then you get in trouble and you're all alone!

Doug: Then you go to detention and lock it and cut off the lights.

Mel: [slaps hands together] Oh baby!!

In this dense strip of discourse the boys attach masculinities to particular networked locations—high school, college, detention hall—within which they anticipate performing as fully sexualized men. They draw gender imagery from a variety of sources—the bunny women (presumably of *Playboy* magazine) materialize somehow in the Blue Ridge mountains, and the boys then construct a brief "collaborative narrative" (Eder, 1995) based on a script of adolescent masculinity within a school context taken from the television show *Saved by the Bell*.[8] In the television show, boys apparently combined misbehavior (getting sent to detention) with spatial regionalization and control (locking the door) to produce a heterosexual masculinity.[9] This masculinity is produced in body-reflexive practices, but not in bodies bounded by a simple skin. It is a masculinity distributed across space and time in a network associating movable and repeatable representations (from both print and broadcast media) with an architecturally standardized and widely distributed structural form (the school detention hall)—elements creatively brought together (not merely reproduced, as in Milkie's, 1994, example) in a joint performance with me, an adult male, and perhaps also Lauren (who wasn't that far away), as audience.

Appadurai (1996) describes such networks as "mediascapes" that offer viewers

> a series of elements (such as characters, plots, and textual forms) out of which scripts can be formed of imagined lives, their own as well as those of others living in other places. These scripts can and do get disaggregated into complex sets of metaphors by which people live . . . as they help to constitute narratives of the Other and protonarratives of possible lives, fantasies that could become prolegomena to the desire for acquisition and movement. (pp. 35-36)

In one sense, bodies (and body-reflexive practices) organized across such mediascapes (or networks circulating other kinds of mediating artifacts) are no longer the bodies-as-bounded-region that are self-contained and uninterested in "dreams and fantasies" (Rose, 1993b). On the contrary, they extend far beyond the skin and link a heterogeneous ensemble of elements. In another sense, however, such networks may well be linked to regionalized masculinities. The difficulties boys have establishing materialized regions at school and home may contribute to their attention to media imagery (while the prevalence of masculinist fantasy in artifacts like video games may reflect the abilities of male designers to monopolize control of the material spaces of image production).

This connection between regions and networks provides one explanation for why "bounded," regionalized bodies and spaces should be defined as "masculine" in the first place. Impermeable borders are tools of separation and exclusion (e.g., Sibley, 1995b), but in addition to keeping things in and out, they have another useful property: They allow the entities they define to move (or be moved) across great distances without undergoing fundamental change (cf. Latour, 1987). This makes possible the production of spatially extensive networks of power tied together through the circulation of standardized and relatively stable forms (see Law, 1987, on Portuguese sailors, and Nespor, 1994, on management students). Bounded and networked masculinities thus complement one another: The creation of sharply defined regions (e.g., bounded bodies) allows the creation of networks linking such regions. Felix and his video games provide a humble example. Recall that Felix kept his games in his room, fiercely monopolized their use, and threatened anyone who transgressed his space of play. In many respects, however, this highly regionalized activity makes sense only when viewed as a network phenomenon:

Jan: When you're playing SuperNintendo, do you have to read instructions to learn how to play them, or do you just start playing them?

Felix: Well, when I first get the game, I've learned how to play them. 'Cause they're out in the malls, and you get to play them, and then I'll learn all of the moves. Like, in Allstars? The only time when I learned how to erase was like a couple of days ago and I've had that since January. So I learn by myself.

Jan: You learn by yourself just through trial and error.

Felix: Uh-huh, except in Mortal Kombat, that I learned from Michael and Bob. 'Cause they rented it a couple of times. They're pretty good at games. When they get 'em, they beat 'em—well, not the first time, but they beat 'em when they rent 'em. And then they teach me how to play, and I buy them, and they buy them.

Jan: So you play them sometimes at the mall, at the video arcades.

Felix: Yeah, that's how I learned how to play—well, not the video arcades. Video arcades it's harder because you have different controllers.

Jan: So where do you play them at the mall?

Felix: Like, in KB Toy Stores and stuff, they have sort of like a TV now, they set up a game, and then you get to play them. At Toys "R" Us they do that. At Toys "R" Us they do that with the *new* Nintendo, not the old ones. The new Nintendo, Sega Genesis, Gameboy, and SuperNintendo.

The regionalization of masculinities in commercial establishments (patterned spaces such as Toys "R" Us and the mall arcades that are reproduced throughout the country) and Felix's and his friends' tenuous successes in creating bounded regions within their homes allowed the creation of networks linking the boys to each other (video games became mediating artifacts linking the boys socially) and to networks through which globally produced representations of hegemonic masculinities could circulate. It's not that there's something intrinsically "masculine" about separation, boundedness, or networking (there are likely regionalized and networked topologies of femininity as well). Rather, regionalization, boundedness, and networking are technologies of power by means of which men constitute masculinities to secure a "patriarchical dividend" (Connell, 1996).

Masculinity as Fluid Space?

Is there a third topology of masculinity? Mol and Law's (1994) third category, "fluid" space, is commonly framed as the antithesis of bounded masculine space:

> In fluid spaces there are often, perhaps usually, no clear *boundaries*. Typically, the objects generated inside them—the objects that generate them—aren't well-defined. . . . In a fluid space normality is a gradient rather than a cut off point. . . . [Fluid spaces] are better seen as being composed of various more or less viscous combinations. Which means that it may or may not be possible to separate a fluid into its component parts. And it may or may not be possible to mix these in with the components of another fluid. (pp. 659-660)

Critiquing what she sees as a masculinist imaginary underlying the distinction between "real" and "nonreal" spaces, Rose (1996) comments on geographers'

> horror of imaged, non-real space as fluid, "that opaque world of supposedly unfathomable differences" (Harvey, 1993: 5). The horror of the ephemeral, specular, eclectic, fragmented, chaotic, schizoid, fascistic, fetishistic, fluids, veiling, titillating, enveloping, wallowing, swamping. Fluid and fusing. . . . The object of desire itself, for geographers, would be the transformation of fluid to solid (cf. Irigaray, 1985: 113). (p. 71)

Mol and Law (1994) themselves suggest that "fluids are the 'others' of regions: that their elements are the noise, the unconscious, the deviance suppressed by regional order" (p. 663). Fluid topologies are constantly shifting and reconfiguring. Unlike regions that partition time into schedules and calendars (Foucault, 1979), or networks, which signal the "annihilation of space through time" (Harvey, 1989) by making physically distant things quickly available through commodity circuits or high-speed transportation, fluid topologies map localized enactments of space in which boundaries are dissolved or transgressed and networks are cut or condensed (cf. de Certeau, 1984).

Masculinities can be made "fluid," for example, by the disruption of bounded regions. One boy in a fourth-grade classroom I observed, Bob, had been labeled "learning disabled," which meant among other things that a special education teacher came into the room to work with him one-on-one while the rest of the class was otherwise engaged. By itself, this direct surveillance weakened Bob's boundaries around himself, and the teacher periodically tried to erase them altogether, publicly humiliating Bob by forcing him to empty the entire contents of his desk onto the floor (ostensibly to find missing homework assignments, though these never materialized). Denied his desk as a bounded region, Bob reconstructed his skin-bounded body as a region: dropping affect, refusing to meet the teacher's eyes, disattending, slumping at his seat, and remaining passive in response to her demands and threats.

One aspect of the illustration I've just used that sets it off from previous data extracts is that instead of being based on one-on-one interviews or conversations with groups of boys, it involves "border work" between a male and female (Thorne, 1993). I suspect that fluid masculinities, when they emerge at all, are likely to be produced in such encounters. In the exchange below, Helen, a fifth grader, teases her classmate Earl about forgetting to get his "girlfriend" a birthday present. Helen suggests he send the girl something "romantic," and what ensues is a brief border war about the construction of gender:

Earl: I was going to but I said, no, that's not boy's stuff.

Jan: Not what?

Earl: Not boy stuff yet.

Jan: When does it get to be?

Helen: Please! I've had—Earl—I've had more romantic *dogs* than you.

Jan: When does it get to be?

Earl: Uh, 15 years old.

Helen: Earl! I've had more romantic dogs than you. [laughter]

Earl: You are really mean Helen!

Helen: Well, excuse me!

Earl: The bathroom's right down the hallway.

Helen: I could throw you from here to the bathroom.

Earl: [sarcastically] Oh! Wow!

Helen: Earl, let's put it this way, I've had dogs that were more romantic than you; I've had *fish* that were more romantic than you.

Earl: I've had *pigs* more romantic than you.

Helen: You wouldn't know, you've never been my boyfriend.

Earl: And never would be!

Helen: Yeah, I know. I never want you to be either. I like older guys, not younger guys. More experienced older guys.

Such examples suggest that fluid topologies are localized in emergent interactions (including mediated interactions articulated across electronic or technical interfaces; see Stone, 1995). Fluid masculinities may be difficult to *represent* inasmuch as they are, by definition, unbounded, ill defined, and transitory, but they may in fact be quite common in everyday situations where males and females interact on an equal footing (as in the interactions between Helen and Earl), or where women hold power (as in the special education teacher's humiliations of Bob).

Conclusions

This chapter boils down to a set of suggestions for studies of gender and for the analysis of masculinity in particular. Building on Connell's (1995) notion of body-reflexive practice, I argue that we must problematize "the body" and begin to look at bodies as they extend beyond the skin—both in terms of extensions and prosthetics, and in terms of their imbrication in spatially and temporally extensive networks of practice. One result of such a focus is that preadolescent boys (and girls), generally neglected in the literature on gender practice, can now move to the foreground. The fourth and fifth graders I studied were already deeply enmeshed in mediascapes full of gender imagery and in networks that connected them with spaces of adult masculinist practice.

More generally, I argue that looking at bodies as distributed systems focuses our attention on spatializations of embodied practice. Here, along with the established studies of gender topographies that tell us how moral and physical boundaries regulate the mobilities of boys and girls, we need to look at gender topologies as well. I have suggested that masculinities (and femininities) can take various spatial forms: They can be constructed as regions, networks, or fluids. These forms are clearly related—networks depend on regionalized, bounded entities that can be circulated and connected, regions and fluids are dialectically linked—but much of the logic of their relations remains unclear.

For example, how are types of masculine regions standardized across social space (e.g., in the case of video gaming), and how are the local, potentially fluid spaces of arenas such as the home linked to global networks of masculinity? How do boys first get connected to network spaces of masculinity, and do their points of entry (e.g., video games vs. television shows vs. sports) have implications for later gender practice? Are the kinds of spaces of fluid masculinity boys encounter linked to their strategies of regionalization or to the kinds of masculinist networks in which they become imbricated? As these questions suggest, there are methodological implications to the perspective adopted here. My emphasis on spatiality (and the nature of my ethnographic case study material) may have slighted the temporal dimension (space and time, after all, cannot be legitimately separated; see Massey, 1994). And while ethnography tends to focus on regions and relatively short time spans, a reliance on life history interviews (e.g., Connell, 1995) obscures the fluid spaces that emerge in interaction. The answer, if there is one, may lie in long-term collaborative studies linking academics and activists committed to rethinking gender as a "project" unfolding in time—and space.

Notes

1. People, settings, and organizations are bundles of multiple trajectories that can constrict into knots or fray apart over time. Only in very special cases would it make sense to speak of someone moving along a single trajectory, nor should "trajectory" be thought of as a two-dimensional path (cf. de Certeau's, 1984, critical comments). See Strauss (1993) for a formal discussion of the concept and Nespor (1994) for an empirical study.

2. I am restricting my attention to American, British, and Australian work. There is a small but interesting body of cross-cultural literature (e.g., Shire, 1994) that space does not allow me to examine.

3. As Valentine (1997) points out, many parents are now equally concerned for their sons' safety in public spaces (although for different reasons than they worry about girls).

4. All of the kids' names are pseudonyms.

5. Felix explained elsewhere that this "park" was actually the playground of an apartment complex that was meant to be used only by residents. He and his friends ignored this restriction.

6. It's worth emphasizing that there were girls included in Felix's bicycle treks—although they didn't initiate the jaunts and, according to Felix, were not allowed to ride around on their own. I'll suggest later, however, that Felix was unusual, among boys in his class, in including girls in his play groups.

7. Carol, for example, while on her own virtually imprisoned in her house and fenced-in yard, had a much greater environmental range *in the company of her parents*—that is, went

more places with her parents, saw more of the city, interacted more with adults—than the other kids in the study.

8. Girls, too, drew on masculine imagery from the media in arguments and struggles with other girls; see Nespor (1997, pp. 188-189) for an example.

9. The contrast with Felix, whose masculinity Mel had questioned in the context of the desk arrangements, is interesting. Felix was almost alone among the fourth graders in openly showing his attraction to girls, a kind of embodied, (regionalized) performative heterosexuality. The vast majority of the other boys in the class rejected this in favor of the kind of (networked) mediated heterosexuality exemplified in the exchange just quoted.

References

Adler, P., & Adler, P. (1994). Social reproduction and the corporate other: The institutionalization of afterschool activities. *The Sociological Quarterly, 35,* 309-328.

Appadurai, A. (1996). Disjuncture and difference in the global cultural economy. In A. Appadurai, *Modernity at large* (pp. 27-47). Minneapolis: University of Minnesota Press.

Bakhtin, M. (1968). *Rabelais and his world.* Cambridge: MIT Press.

Bourdieu, P. (1977). *Outline of a theory of practice.* Cambridge, UK: Cambridge University Press.

Butler, J. (1990). *Gender trouble.* New York: Routledge.

Connell, R. W. (1995). *Masculinities.* Berkeley: University of California Press.

Connell, R. W. (1996). New directions in gender theory: Masculinity research, and gender politics. *Ethnos, 61,* 157-176.

De Certeau, M. (1984). *The practice of everyday life.* Berkeley: University of California Press.

Eder, D., with Evans, C., & Parker, S. (1995). *School talk: Gender and adolescent culture.* New Brunswick, NJ: Rutgers University Press.

Foucault, M. (1979). *Discipline and punish.* New York: Vintage.

Haraway, D. (1991). *Simians, cyborgs, and women: The reinvention of nature.* New York: Routledge.

Hart, R. (1979). *Children's experience of place.* New York: Irvington.

Harvey, D. (1989). *The condition of postmodernity.* Cambridge, MA: Blackwell.

Harvey, D. (1993). From space to place and back again: Reflections on the condition of post-modernity. In J. Bird, B. Curtis, G. Robertson, & L. Tickner (Eds.), *Mapping the futures: Local cultures, global change* (pp. 3-29). London: Routledge & Kegan Paul.

Heath, S. B., & McLaughlin, M. (1994). Learning for anything everyday. *Journal of Curriculum Studies, 26,* 471-489.

Henley, N. (1977). *Body politics: Power, sex, and nonverbal communication.* Englewood Cliffs, NJ: Prentice Hall.

Irigaray, L. (1985). *This sex which is not one* (C. Porter, Trans.). Ithaca, NY: Cornell University Press.

Katz, C. (1993). Growing girls/closing circles: Limits on the spaces of knowing in rural Sudan and U.S. cities. In C. Katz & J. Monk (Eds.), *Full circles: Geographies of women over the life course* (pp. 88-106). New York: Routledge.

Katz, C. (1998). Disintegrating developments: Global economic restructuring and the eroding of ecologies of youth. In T. Skelton & G. Valentine (Eds.), *Cool places: Geographies of youth cultures* (pp. 130-144). New York: Routledge.

Kirby, K. (1996). *Indifferent boundaries: Spatial concepts of human subjectivity.* New York: Guilford.

Latour, B. (1987). *Science in action.* Cambridge, MA: Harvard University Press.

Latour, B. (1994). On technical mediation—Philosophy, sociology, genealogy. *Common Knowledge, 3*(2), 29-64.

Law, J. (1987). On the social explanation of technical change: The case of the Portuguese maritime expansion. *Technology and Culture, 28,* 227-252.

Lefebvre, H. (1991). *The production of space.* Oxford, UK: Basil Blackwell.

Lynch, K. (Ed.). (1977). *Growing up in cities.* Cambridge: MIT Press.

Lynch, K. (1979). The spatial world of the child. In K. Lynch, *The child in the city: Today and tomorrow* (pp. 102-127). Toronto: University of Toronto Press.

Massey, D. (1994). Politics and space/time. In D. Massey, *Space, place, and gender* (pp. 249-272). Minneapolis: University of Minnesota Press.

Massey, D. (1996). Masculinity, dualisms and high technology. In N. Duncan (Ed.), *BodySpace: Destabilizing geographies of gender and sexuality* (pp. 109-126). New York: Routledge.

Matthews, M. (1992). *Making sense of place: Children's understanding of the large-scale environment.* Savage, MD: Barnes and Noble.

McNamee, S. (1998). The home: Young, gender and video games: Power and control in the home. In T. Skelton & G. Valentine (Eds.), *Cool places: Geographies of youth cultures* (pp. 195-206). New York: Routledge.

Middleton, D., & Edwards, D. (Eds.). (1990). *Collective remembering.* London: Sage.

Milkie, M. (1994). Social world approach to cultural studies: Mass media and gender in the adolescent peer group. *Journal of Contemporary Ethnography, 23,* 354-380.

Mol, A., & Law, J. (1994). Regions, networks, and fluids: Anaemia and social topology. *Social Studies of Science, 24,* 641-671.

Moore, H. (1994). *A passion for difference: Essays in anthropology and gender.* Bloomington: Indiana University Press.

Nespor, J. (1994). *Knowledge in motion.* Philadelphia: Falmer.

Nespor, J. (1997). *Tangled up in school.* Mahwah, NJ: Lawrence Erlbaum.

Rose, G. (1993a). *Feminism and geography.* Minneapolis: University of Minnesota Press.

Rose, G. (1993b). Some notes towards thinking about the spaces of the future. In J. Bird, B. Curtis, T. Putnam, G. Robertson, & L. Tickner (Eds.), *Mapping the futures: Local cultures, global changes* (pp. 70-83). New York: Routledge.

Rose, G. (1996). As if the mirrors had bled: Masculine dwelling, masculinist theory and feminist masquerade. In N. Duncan (Ed.), *BodySpace: Destabilizing geographics of gender and sexuality* (pp. 56-74). New York: Routledge.

Shilling, C. (1991). Social space, gender inequalities and educational differentiation. *British Journal of Sociology of Education, 12*(1), 23-44.

Shire, C. (1994). Men don't go to the moon: Language, space and masculinities in Zimbabwe. In A. Cornwall & N. Lindisfarne (Eds.), *Dislocating masculinity: Comparative ethnographies* (pp. 147-158). London and New York: Falmer.

Sibley, D. (1995a). Families and domestic routines: Constructing the boundaries of childhood. In S. Pile & N. Thrift (Eds.), *Mapping the subject: Geographies of cultural transformation* (pp. 123-137). New York: Routledge.

Sibley, D. (1995b). *Geographies of exclusion: Society and difference in the West.* New York: Routledge.

Star, S. L. (1995). Introduction. In S. L. Star (Ed.), *Ecologies of knowledge* (pp. 1-35). Albany: State University of New York Press.

Stone, A. (1995). *The war of desire and technology at the close of the mechanical age.* Cambridge: MIT Press.

Strauss, A. (1993). *Continual permutations of action.* New York: Aldine De Gruyter.

Thorne, B. (1993). *Gender play: Girls and boys in school.* New Brunswick, NJ: Rutgers University Press.

Turner, T. (1995). Social body and embodied subjects: Bodiliness, subjectivity, and sociality among the Kayapo. *Cultural Anthropology, 10*(2), 143-170.

Valentine, G. (1996). Children should be seen and not heard: The production and transgression of adults' public space. *Urban Geography, 17,* 205-220.

Valentine, G. (1997). "My son's a bit dizzy." "My wife's a bit soft": Gender, children and cultures of parenting. *Gender, Place and Culture, 4*(1), 37-62.

Ward, C. (1978). *The child in the city.* New York: Pantheon.

3

Theorizing Urban Black Masculinity Construction in an African-Centered School

KHAULA MURTADHA-WATTS

born in challenge, created by ancestors and their enemies relations.
now my interactions with self, peers, elders and youths are all distinct.
who views me in the black light . . . the lost soul radiating anger and hatred
the robber rapist? i must calm that view to attain any honesty until i am
truly seen. so i fight premonitions to show i am more than a dark
exoskeleton. i accept the challenge to portray the million piece puzzle
that is me.

Abdul-Haleem Young, 1999

The complexities of everyday life, of racialized and gendered constructions resound in the hip hop lyrics of Abdul Haleem, exhorting young people to take on both the very personal and social challenges of prejudice and
bigotry. But many argue that African American males are losing ground in
a difficult battle for their lives on the streets in most U.S. cities. Statistics
abound citing problems that include lack of educational achievement,
drugs, high crime involvement, and black-on-black homicide. Of course,
the question of how best to deal with these life-threatening issues is debated in circles of educators, religious leaders, community activists, as
well as social and political scientists. The black male is labeled violent,
deviant, predatory, "endangered," and "lost" (Bowser, 1991; Monroe,
1987). Some groups clamor that there is a need to lock most young black
males on our city streets into the lucrative penal institution marketplace.

Nevertheless, there are those who on a day-to-day basis hold forth hope beyond this nihilistic cacophony. Among those who respond with specific long-term strategies are African-centered thinkers not only raising questions about Euro-American culture, its social, political, and economic structures, but suggesting that Eurocentrism, capitalism, and white supremacy are leading contributors to a malaise that destroys the health of African American and other marginalized American communities.

In this chapter I seek first to draw attention to social and popular cultural theorists on constructions of black masculinities. The works of Dyson, Haymes, Franklin, and Lemelle provide a conceptual and analytical framework as well as a lens to the second part of the chapter where I present an overview of African-centered education and describe an African-centered school as it worked and struggled to create an alternative school educating black male youth. The school is contextualized amid the setting of urban community, social, economic, and political life.[1]

The specificity of African American masculinity construction in an urban school setting means several perspectives are necessarily linked in this chapter. As noted by Massey and Denton (1993) in *American Apartheid,* urban areas represent spatially racialized concentrations of poverty. The black family in the city has developed different forms of relationships from the white, middle-class, mythological ideal. Urban poverty, underemployment, and unemployment has led to a higher proportion of both female-headed and other alternative household forms for African American families. At issue here is the profound racialized, gendered nature of poverty in the city. The daily life of many urban residents "becomes a continuous problematic, an unresolvable set of dilemmas which confronts everyone" (Yeo, 1997, p. 9). Urban schools, therefore, present a unique context for the construction and deconstruction of black masculinities because these are the educational sites for the highest concentrations of blacks and poverty. In 1992, Coontz noted,

> The experience of black families has been qualitatively different from that of white, or even minorities, all along the line. . . . More than other minorities, blacks encountered periodic increases in discrimination and segregation. . . . No other minority got so few payoffs for sending their children to school, and no other immigrants ran into such a low job ceiling that college graduates had to become Pullman porters. No other minority was saddled with such unfavorable demographics during early migration . . . or was so completely excluded from industrial work . . . during its expansion. (cited in Clatterbaugh, 1997, pp. 164-165)

Much of black life, and hence black masculinity constructions, has been and will continue to be located in the harshest regions of American economic, cultural, and political reality. Al-Hajj Malik Shabazz (Malcolm X) put it succinctly when he noted, "We didn't land on Plymouth Rock, Plymouth Rock landed on us." This systematic exploitation of African descendants became so deeply entrenched in American culture that today, nearly a century and a half after the period of chattel slavery, racism and discrimination still plague this society and are most evident in the culturally diverse hubs of this nation's cities. The texture of contemporary urban life is woven into a cultural fabric that is as hopeful as it is fatalistic, as spirited as nihilistic, and as promising as it is jeopardous. These real, not minimized, homogenized, or essentialized dynamics of culture in the contemporary urban U.S. context are elements with which any theorist on contemporary black masculinity construction in schools must ultimately grapple and understand.

Second in this chapter, I attempt to show the nexus of urban life, urban pedagogies, and racialized gendered constructions. Focusing on one school site, I look at: how teachers and administrators view black males and the construction of male identities; how teachers explicitly and implicitly engage them as students through curriculum and instruction; and the role of school rituals in the context of everyday events, informing, shaping, impacting masculinities.

This chapter necessarily includes a discussion of black popular and hip hop cultures with an emphasis on rap music to draw attention to the tensions and conflict with black masculinity constructions within urban educational structures. It is *against* much of this culture that many teachers create an assaultive anti-hip hop offensive. Graffiti art, rap music, style of dress, attitude, verbal language, body language, and "urban-influenced lifestyles" are all aspects of hip hop culture contributing to notions of black masculinity (Kitwana, 1994) that many administrators, teachers, and policymakers attempt to contain or oppose. The trend of commodification of various black cultural forms, but particularly rap music, has been toward manipulation in the form of stereotypes of black urban street life, crime, sexuality, and sexual violence. For some educators this imagery represents an affront not merely to their sense of appropriate school attire but an overall malevolent assault on the traditional values and beliefs that the black community needs to survive (for a discussion of this perspective see Bowser's, 1991, work on black male adolescents).

Historically, patriarchal, racist ideology has taken the black male body, or rather its fantasied version, and attempted to reduce it to a singular identity, an essentialized stereotype fixed on physicality and physical strength, one that is inhuman, dangerous, athletic, and virile. Indeed, rather than perceiving black males as individuals, as social agents, negotiating multiple discourses, oppositional binarisms are constructed that also reduce black females to mammies, bitches, and matriarchs. Finally, I link these ideas about the control of black male bodies, a curriculum devoid of popular cultural critique, and schools in central cities as places of racialized masculinity negotiation.

Theorists on Constructions of Black Masculinities: Identity, Consumerism, and Agency

What shapes the social, political and cultural realities for African American males in central cities? What factors define and maintain these realities and how do they contribute to the construction of masculinities that are different for white, middle-class males in schools? There are many responses as cultural critics and activists struggle with these issues, yet there is usually agreement that poverty and the racist structuring of urban spaces has a dramatic impact on day-to-day existence. In many urban, poverty-ridden neighborhoods, the collapse of structures of meaning and feeling can be seen in the "sense of community" breakdown. To Marable (1992), this discontinuity is striking. Young blacks act as competitors within a culture of consumption, often relating to each other out of mistrust and fear. Cultural and religious critic Michael Dyson draws attention to how many inner-city communities (code words for poor, black, and brown) live under what may be called a "juvenocracy": the economic rule and illegal tyranny exercised by young black men over significant urban territory. His point is that in addition to being detached from the recognition and rewards of the dominant society, inner-city communities are continually devastated and cut off from sources of moral authority and legitimate work, as underground political economies reward both young children and teens with quick cash.

Dyson (1993) explores not only the cultural expressions, but the material conditions and social problems associated with rap music. His work is useful in this chapter about the constructions of black masculinities because, as he points out, rap culture represents to a great extent "the voice and vision of a significant segment of young black culture" (p. 281).

Rap also mirrors the varieties of sexism that persist in many poor black communities, themselves reflections of the patriarchal tendencies that are dispersed throughout our culture. Only by confronting the powerful social criticism that rap culture articulates can we hope to understand its appeal.... And by examining its weaknesses and blindnesses, we are encouraged to critically confront our similar shortcomings, which do not often receive the controversial media coverage given to rap culture. (p. 281)

Kitwana (1994) points out that what is in part problematic about many rap artists' message is that black women and men are objectified and dehumanized with distorted images bought and sold by black youth who lack an understanding of African American culture and historical struggles. For this reason I draw attention to rap's impact on constructions of masculinity in schools. Children do not leave their socially constructed knowledges at the school door. Not to examine the cultural forms that greatly impact their lives is to miss the engagement of black youth culture's values, attitudes, and concerns. For the most part, black males do not limit or confine themselves to the representations and images of white cultural productions, particularly television, film, and advertising. This is an issue of agency. Nevertheless, dominant white representations of black males may socialize black males to see themselves as always inadequate, as always "subordinated to more powerful white males whose approval they need to survive" (hooks, 1994, p. 103). The existing popular dominant representations of black masculinity are continuously reproduced, serving to reinforce and sustain particular power relationships.

In response to young listeners and others defending rap with an insistence that words such as "bytch, hoe, and nigga" are being reclaimed and redefined, cultural critic Madhubuti (cited in Kitwana, 1994) argues,

There are certain words . . . that are debilitating to us, no matter how often they are used. Such a word is nigger. . . . A nigger which is a pitiful and shameful invention of Europeans, cannot be de-stereotyped by using it in another context, even if the users are black and supposedly politically correct (they are mostly young and unaware). (p. 27)

The "gangsta" rap word/world that dehumanizes women subsists within violence and is a master teacher of the very young. Visually stimulating music videos, appealing to the joy of rhythms and rhyme, powerfully suggest values that inform what it means to be masculine and to act in ways that are unquestioned or rethought as to their usefulness.

Stephen Haymes (1995) creates a different context for exploring the pedagogy of place in the urban environment by exploring how socially constructed mythologies about black people are

> realized in the material landscapes of the city, in its racialization of black residential space through the imagery of racial segregation. This imagery along with the racialization of crime portrays black residential space as natural "spaces of pathology," and in need of social control through policing and residential dispersion and displacement. (back cover)

For Haymes, black popular cultural forms act as points of resistance. His work draws attention to black masculinity construction as a response to geo-political manipulation and commodification of culture. His views are worth quoting at length:

> What is important about the concepts of decolonization, emancipation, and hooks' notion of "radical black subjectivity" is that they provide us with a way to talk about black public spaces in the city not simply as "spaces of opposition" but as "spaces of self actualization." In this way, defining black public spaces as "spaces of self actualization" is understanding the centrality of black popular urban culture in constructing such places . . . it is through black popular culture that black people in the city resist mainstream white culture's racializing and therefore biologization of their spaces, bodies, and personalities. (p. 138)

Representational politics, the struggle over identity, and the fashioning of images is at issue here. Madhubuti's and Haymes's differing points give rise to questions about the usefulness of rap for naming who we are in the black community and the problematics of reclaiming a language used to degrade and oppress women and people of color. The narrative complexity and vitality of "hip hop," "gangsta," and "righteous teaching" rap on the one hand represents desires and shifting attitudes, values, and definitions of social relationships that black youth claim for themselves. At the same time, it represents historical amnesia, a lack of political and pedagogical insight. Haymes (1995) argues,

> This is important in the early twentieth-century construction of the city as jungle—an image that preceded the emergence of large-scale black urban settlements—is now connoted with black people's dark skin. In other words, the urban has become a metaphor for race, and in white supremacist culture, like ours, race does not mean white, but black. So, in the city, urban problems, such as poverty, homelessness, joblessness, crime, violence, single-parent house-

holds, and drugs, are seen as racial problems, the problems of blacks, not of whites. And in a white supremacist culture, where race is biologized, racial problems are reduced to black people's bodies. (p. 138)

Both Haymes's and Madhubuti's points raise questions about the significance of rap to black communities' ability to name who they are and how they relate to the larger society and across gendered discourses. I would argue that, even within black communities, the association of "blackness" and urban problems has been uncritically accepted, particularly by the black middle classes (a pool from which, in conjunction with commuting whites, most inner-city teachers are drawn). Because they identify themselves as being black, everything in black culture is not seen as horrible and bad. Therefore, a tension exists that pits a desire to impart positive role modeling (and save individuals) against the terrifying menace of the urban "jungle." The perception—commercially manipulated and promoted—of black males as dangerous should not be dismissed easily. Prejudged by many, there is a fear that potentially wild animals, violent destructive gangsters, or sexual deviants lurk in the young bodies of black males who, if left alone in their environments, would endanger the safety of American culture. It is important to recognize that this view of the urban context suggests a typology of black youthful masculinities that, early on, must be tamed and trained in elementary schools. A culture and implicit curriculum of physical restriction permeates many urban schools, and the explicit curriculum disassociates student learning from engaging black urban cultures and any possible constructivist notion of a culturally responsive pedagogy.[2]

Franklin's (1994) work identifies at least five distinct categories of black masculinity construction: *conforming, ritualistic, innovative, retreatist,* and *rebellious black masculinity. Conforming* masculinity is the acceptance of "mainstream society's prescriptions and proscriptions for heterosexual males." Black males follow the rules, according to Franklin, despite the fact that when society teaches men to work hard, set high goals, and strive for success, it does not teach black men that their probability of failure is high because glass ceilings and limited opportunities for them are endemic to U.S. society. Resembling conforming masculinity, *ritualistic* masculinity for blacks is following the prescriptions and rules but not really believing one will win—it's playing without really believing, without purpose or commitment. *Innovative* black masculinity distances itself from conforming or ritualistic by exaggerating traits of hegemonic masculinity in that the pursuit of material success leads to black-on-black crime and debases women, as a means of making money (as do some forms of rap music). *Retreatist* black masculinity reflects a giving up of all hope and may be seen in those men who are alcoholics, drug addicts, or who have given up looking for a meaningful existence. Franklin further suggests that a *rebellious* black masculinity is exhibited by those who work in organizations committed to black liberation.

Franklin's work is not about black boys in schools. However, I use his framework, taking into consideration that black masculinities are more accurately understood in terms of complex associations on more than one level of social arrangement. Thus we begin to recognize the differences between older black masculine identities—middle class, middle age, and single—on impoverished youth in cities. Schooling after the elementary level is highly ambivalent and much less hopeful about the outcomes for secondary black students. White males can be educationally and therefore socially hopeful. They can get back on track if they temporarily get out of line. Black masculinities are seen as determined and set at a very early stage. This complexity of associations is conspicuous in the case of schools.

In his study of African American males, Lemelle (1995) is concerned with what he calls a teacher's role to make black male students conform to the hegemonic vision of people of color: "the students are on the scene to establish an improved quality of life for themselves and their families" (p. 53). Black males become "bad" to express individual autonomy in the school in much the same way that slaves became "criminals" through lying, cheating, and "stealing away" to obtain freedom. In his discussion of urbanization, Lemelle points out that black males are labeled as "unprepared for education, good jobs and promotions. Because of their deviance, they are in need of reform and rehabilitation." Thus, teachers, many of whom live outside of urban, predominantly black, low-income or impoverished communities, act as diplomats of prevailing values and become the means by which dominant white, middle-class values are supported and unquestioned.

African-Centered Scholarship

Clearly, long-term strategies are required that address the myriad socioeconomic, political, spatial, and other constructs that continue to impact the lives of our urban youth. African-centered thinkers not only raise questions about Eurocentrism and white supremacy, but question education's role in perpetuating the miseducation and disempowerment of black males. For Ani (1994), African-centered thought as part of a politics of difference reveals what have been canonized distortions of Eurocentric historical narratives, unmasking the significance of Africa and its peoples as central to the development of civilization. African-centered learning is important as a means of developing a culturally centered identity that, as outlined by Nobles (1989), includes: (a) a sense of self that is collective or extended, (b) an attitude wherein one understands and respects the sameness in oneself and others, (c) a clear sense of one's spiritual connection to the universe, (d) a sense of mutual responsibility, and (e) a conscious understanding that human abnormality or deviancy is any act that is in opposition to oneself. This represents, in theory, a pedagogical shift from a focus on individuality and competition to an emphasis on communitarianism, cooperation, and a leveling of male/female hierarchies.

There are scholars who are uncomfortable with the "African-centered" worldview and have written criticism ranging from Cornell West's (1993) "a gallant yet misguided attempt to define an African identity" (p. 4), to Edward Said's comment naming Afrocentric, Islamocentric, or Eurocentric proclamations as a "disturbing eruption of separatist and chauvinist discourse" (Said, 1993, p. xx). Nevertheless, by arguing the case for examining not only an African-centered discourse but by also calling for the recognition of others to speak their cultural truths, I agree with Keto (1989), who suggests that nonhegemonic, culturally centered perspectives can contribute to the world's multicultural knowledges. Educators, across the board, must learn to recognize, evaluate, and work with culturally responsive pedagogies.

A Male, African-Centered Experiment in Detroit

A number of studies done on the history and condition of Detroit's black population have revealed what is now described as the classic pattern of migration, congestion, adaptation, hope, and despair that characterizes so much of contemporary life. The downward spiral of failures of schools and in schools is equally well documented.

In 1960, the Detroit High School Study Commission reported that the high schools of Detroit were appallingly inadequate, a disgrace to the community, and a tragedy to the thousands of young men and women who were compelled to attend them. In the nearly three decades since, conditions for many in Detroit have scarcely improved. The homicide rate has tripled, and the rate of teenage pregnancies and single-parent households has also increased. Independent schools, summer workshops, and religious or secular community-based education initiatives have, in varying degrees, been considered by the black citizens of Detroit as viable possibilities to give black children not only some added sense of self-worth, but to allow them the hope of economic viability. Perhaps the latest and most controversial institutions established in this mode are public, male-dominated, African-centered schools, of which the "Academy" in this study is prominent.[3]

The Academy

Planned to be an all-male school, the "Academy" is different from most other public educational institutions because it is explicit in its articulation of an ideology of African-centeredness (for a thoughtful exploration of African-centered education see the work of Shujaa & Lomotey, 1994). Initial plans for the school designated it as a school of choice with a mandate to "provide high-quality educational experiences which result in a certainty of opportunity for target students in employment and advanced education" and to develop "competencies demonstrated through performance required for a job or entrance into college or the military. A marketable skill is also any vehicle that provides a legitimate source of employment or income resulting in a productive citizen" (Murtadha-Watts, 1994).

The school was further directed to stress ethnic pride and self-esteem. "The program will stress, emphatically the development of a proud sense of self, high expectations, appropriate levels of demand, and multiple opportunities for success. Students will be encouraged to . . . prepare for careers in areas where minorities are under represented" (Murtadha-Watts, 1994).

The principal, an African American male, a former elementary school science and math teacher, taught for 14 years and served 9 years as a principal. The assistant principal, an African American female, taught for 24 years before her appointment as an administrator. The 21-member teaching staff was unusual for an elementary school because almost half the number were male. These teachers at the time of the study ranged from new, recent graduates of schools of education, to those with 20 and more years of teaching experience; in age from early twenties to late fifties. A full-time language teacher from Tanzania taught the children in Kiswahili, and a paraprofessional taught Spanish. Computer technicians, other para-professionals, and noon-hour aides assisted primary teachers with their classes, made copies, monitored the lunchroom and outdoor play, and tutored students. Compared to many other schools in the system, the Academy was well supplied and staffed. The cultural constructions observed at the site, however, represented much more than funding and planning could anticipate or control.

Rituals, Room Arrangements, and Rules
of Classroom Control

Ritual can be thought of as an aspect of nearly "all social action rather than as a categorical type of social act. When we think of ritual as an aspect of social action, the most ordinary and mundane of activities have within them the potential for achieving the various effects that are attributed to ritual" (Quantz & Magolda, 1998, p. 218). The rituals that were established as part of the Academy's everyday program reflected teachers' beliefs about black males and the need for control. A problem exists in many low-income, predominantly black, urban schools wherein more emphasis is put on containment than on dynamic inquiry, problem-solving, teaching, and learning. When "containment" is emphasized, the school's contribution to constructing black masculinities becomes a reinforcement of society's deviance and at-risk labels assigned most often to children of color and those who are poor.

The following excerpts from field notes include many examples of the school's rituals:

The school day began as the Academy's 550 students (95% male and 5% female) disembarked from numerous cars and public school buses since few of the children lived in the community. They were met either in the auditorium (K-3rd grades) or the gymnasium (4th-7th grades) by staff who directed them to be seated and to remain seated until the 9:30 bell indicating the beginning of the day. When recognized by the teacher in charge of monitoring the students, their class was told to get on line and was escorted to the "conference classes."

The upper grade students formed a continuous long line around the walls of the gymnasium and when quiet, released to pass to their conference rooms. A uniform (white shirt and blue pants with girls wearing blue skirts or pants) "check" was occasionally done at that time. Regular uniforms were worn four days of the week with Friday set aside for wearing clothes that were Afrocentric, i.e., made of African fabric and stylistically cut in African designs.

Once in the conference rooms, the students would begin to do "bell work." Designed to immediately engage student attention, the seat work assignment varied from locating word definitions to multiplication drills. At 9:45, school announcements were given, preceded by the Kiswahili language, greetings of "Jambo!" and the Academy school song or pledge:

> We at the [name of school] Academy will strive for excellence
> in our quest to be the best. We'll rise above every challenge with our
> heads held high. We'll always keep the faith when others say die.
> March on till victory is ours. Amandla!

The dynamics of the relationships within three observed classrooms—one fourth grade, one fifth, and one sixth—were unique. Each room had its own sounds, colors, and character. The fourth-grade space decor brought to mind Franklin's (1994) *conforming* masculinities where males must be taught to work hard, set high goals, and strive for success, while not being taught that glass ceilings and limited opportunities for them are endemic to U.S. society. Images of the successful—Adam Clayton Powell, Shirley Chisolm, Colin Powell, Oprah Winfrey, Whoopi Goldberg, Bill Cosby, Michael Jackson, Douglass Wilder, and Harriet Tubman—look down from high positions on the walls of the fifth-grade classroom. A large yellow, red, and brown-tone portrait of Malcolm X completely covered a bulletin board encaptioned, "Malcolm X, the Man, the Enigma." The teacher in this classroom believed her students generically had low self-esteem that needed to be challenged:

> What I think increases the self-esteem is when they really understand who they are and what they are capable of. . . . These children don't see themselves as really being able to accomplish. They don't really see themselves in college, in my opinion. They don't *really* see themselves in a hundred thousand dollar house.

There appeared to be, with this teacher and others, an unquestioning hopefulness that the building of self-esteem would lead to economic and job security—that if black boys knew the history of African Americans and believed in their worth that they would be able to achieve the American dream.

The fifth graders lined up rather quietly outside of the math classroom to begin their set of rituals. The teacher issued directions to enter the room, put homework assignments on desks, raise hands to speak, and to begin "bell work." Pausing only for public address announcements, the teacher directed the students to have all homework corrected and signed by parents. A heavy silence permeated the room as the teacher walked from student to student commenting on the absence of parent signatures on completed homework assignments. After "bell work," the students completed drills from the math textbooks. On those inevitable occasions when the students were "acting up," the teacher used the class behavior grade as both a motivation to do better and a threat to lose school privileges, typically referring to recess.

Room arrangements were also linked to the perceived need to control behaviors rigidly and to maintain order. An example was the same math classroom. Sparse in comparison to other classrooms, all the desks were arranged in symmetrical rows facing a center aisle—conducive to the teacher's continuous movement. New math textbooks were only briefly stored under the desks because they served as the primary source of the day's lessons. The page numbers of the day's assignment were always written on the blackboard prior to the students' entry, as well as homework page assignments, serving the purpose of placing the children immediately on task through seatwork. Students remained in their seats except for times at the pencil sharpener or when told to come up front where the teacher's desk was centrally positioned.

A very different list of rules and approaches was used by the music teacher. Her serious manner, however, reflected in unwavering tones, seemed to inhibit any resistance to her authority, though there were times when the students would try her. She, too, used the class behavior grade as both a motivation and a warning. Once the students were settled in, music textbooks were passed out and students began to sing the lyrics of the printed text, accompanied by the teacher poised at the piano. Their voices rose and easily merged in unison and at times harmonies that were rewarded with generous smiles and encouraging gestures indicating her approval. Her room rules were the following:

1. To receive the best grade, students must participate in class, not chew in class, and not talk freely.
2. The best music students sit up tall, hold their books properly, and smile.
3. When you look good, you sound good and when you look ugly, you sound ugly.

With decades of experience, another fifth-grade teacher discussed her rules for classroom conduct with both visiting parents and children, clearly establishing her relationship to the students:

This is an Academy. I'm a strict disciplinarian . . . expect children to cooperate. The foolishness stops at the door. When I say bring in homework, bring it in. When I say sit down, sit down. Who is a strong black person? Who can master fifth grade? We are going to master fifth grade. . . . Every eye on me.

She proceeded with rapid-fire comments about the mayoral campaign and her favorite (the incumbent), youth gangs, and former students. Her posture was authoritative, upright. She sat either at her paper-covered desk in a rear corner of the room or on a chair up front. She never sat in the center, but positioned herself to the left, where she could easily point to the blackboard and see the students.

The 34 children, all males, were successfully quieted. A reading survey ensued. The students had a wide range of abilities that were most apparent when asked to read aloud. For some, two-syllable words produced scowling faces and verbal corrections from other class members. After the completion of the morning work, the class, directed to line up, was escorted to the rest room by the teacher.

Over the next 6 weeks, the spaces and rhythms of the school day became more ordered as school-wide routines became a part of the students' and teachers' habitual tasks. As they filed upstairs from the multipurpose room, the children, some talking, some playing, were met in the hallways by paraprofessionals who reminded them to stop talking and not to stop at their lockers. Standing outside the classroom door, the students awaited the teacher's greeting and permission to enter.

Their assignments included silent reading in the science textbook and correcting sentences that were written on the board containing grammatical errors. When students' voices rose, an occasional exhortation of "heads down" coupled with a lecture-like admonition maintained order:

Don't be a coward, have some courage about yourself. . . . If you don't get an education your life will be a disaster. We need to be attending to our business of learning. [Dr. King] would turn over in his grave if he could see what black boys are doing now, drive-by shootings . . . it starts from right where you are now. Thirty thousand men are in Jackson prison and some of you are running to join them.

The teacher's words demonstrate a passionate concern for urban problems; however, they also reflect Franklin's typology. Black boys are told what they will be like if they don't conform—follow the prescriptions or rules; if they don't find a meaningful existence, then they are confronted with visions of joblessness, hopelessness, and uselessness if they are drug addicts or alcoholics. This is the work of schools in the elementary or primary years. Haymes's (1995) point is significant here. Problems of poverty, joblessness, crime, violence, and drugs are seen as racial problems, as belonging to the black community and perpetuated by black males. In this case a black teacher is mirroring some of the same beliefs as many white educators: Prison is in the future of uneducated black males. Students are also reminded that they will receive a class behavior grade. Recorded on a small slip of paper, carried to all classes every day, this is an "A, B, C, D, or E" grade given by each teacher after evaluating the class's performance. Poor grades result in losing the privileges of playground time, attending school social events, or shopping at the school store.

During the periodic teacher-designated break times, given because they've "worked hard," the boys enthusiastically drew. On one occasion they sketched their versions of "X-Men" comics. Some played a hand-slapping game, while others talked. A very brief visit from an administrator served as both a spot check to see if students were "on task" and to question whether the students had permission to play the game.

Implicit Curricula of Redirection,
Explicit Curricula of Black Content

One aspect of the Academy's curriculum suggested a focus on goals, values, and beliefs, a directing of student convictions and life purposes. On a bulletin board in the sixth-/seventh-grade classroom are the following words in black and red colors:

I Am Black
Set Goals

Serious	Attitude
Love	The Future
Victory	Ownership
Knowledge	Pressure
Dedication	Faith
Dignity	Consistency

The teacher's concerns for student racial identity was evident along with the message of routing the student toward an ethical purposefulness in life.

Later in the school semester the fifth-grade children were told to have five people, that is, people like their parents or a pastor, sign the following room pledge:

> I believe that education is the key to my future. Once it is earned, it is something that no one can take away. My education depends on my efforts and commitment with the assistance of my family, my community and my school.

The new sixth- and seventh-grade English teacher's daily journal writing assignment served as an example of how one teacher approached lessons that were to surface student's understandings about their day-to-day existences and the possibilities for their future. It was structured around the use of three suggested topics written on the front blackboard:

1. Who is Rosa Parks and how has she helped make life better for blacks?
2. Write about what you think your life will be like when you are old.
3. If you could make one wish, what would it be and why?

Another day the questions were:

1. Who is Coretta Scott King and what role did she play in the civil rights movement?
2. Write about the differences between living in the city, country, and the suburbs.
3. What are your plans for your day off tomorrow?

The overt intentional focus on goals and the future contribute to a hopefulness in shaping the intentions of the black male students outside of the school environment. Yet the students' perceptions about the school and why it was structured in particular ways is just as telling and provides insight about their personal beliefs linked to identity. One sixth-grade boy voiced a certain savvy about the school's educational purposes:

> It's supposed to be a discipline school and they're suppose to teach you more than at the other schools. [At the other] schools you can do what you want to.

Another response to my question, "What makes this school different from others?" revealed that the emphasis on black culture offered choices that were unavailable in other schools:

> One thing different [than my previous school] is . . . with history. That's different because at my old school for Black History Week—this was every year—Dr. Martin Luther King, Jr., Dr. Martin Luther King, Jr., Dr. Martin Luther King, Jr. [he laughs] and all those years I would think, "What was so special about a guy that would go out and nearly get his brains beat out for freedom" . . . that was a difference right there, he was a non-violent, peaceful, warrior. . . . I just don't care too much for his way of thinking. . . . Marcus Garvey, now I really admire him for the "Back to Africa Movement." Now, I thought that was a good idea right there 'cause Dr. Martin Luther King, Jr., his main focus was to gain freedom for all. On the other hand, Marcus Garvey, he was working on a lot of things. Not only did he want to gain freedom, he wanted us—he wanted to take us back to Africa. So really he was trying to do two things at one time.

Given choices about what kind of role model he chose, this young man valued alternative knowledges more than the ideas considered acceptable to the dominant culture.

Control of the Male Body

Racism and white supremacist discourse have created fear of the black male body and attempted to contain it. Inhuman physicality, both dangerous and virile, located in a school must be rule bound and limited in its freedom. Questions should be raised about how much of this white mythology black educators have bought into or how much the pedagogy results from knowledge that blacks have about home cultures and the most effective ways to teach African American children.

In a fourth-grade class I asked the students what rules they had to follow. They responded in writing,

[Student #1] [* without correction]

> I know that if you act good you'll receive a very nice award. I act very normal. And if you act bad you face the consequences . . . All the teachers are not the same. They have different rules to. Mr. R——- rules are No lying, No tatelling . . . The board of education makes rules like no weapons, no guns and so on.

Most of the rules come from [the principal]. And some of the rules come from the teachers.

[Student #2 *]

No, runnin, No stealing, No lying, No telling, No play, No horseplay, No shoot, Always rise Your hand, Always think, No eating or gum choming, No drinking, No jonig, respiet each ohe, No takeing, No yelling

The Consequences for good is free time,

prizes, gym, outside playing, cards, pazzi

The Consequences for bad is writing 1,000 words, No gym, and suffer, and go to detention

These lists, while hinting at differing teaching strategies employed in classrooms, also reflect educators' and communities' concerns for developing respect for authority, adherence to rules, and strict discipline. Many liberal educators hold that the primary goal of education is that children become autonomous without having arbitrary, outside standards forced upon them. This approach makes numerous assumptions that have come under the critical scrutiny of several black educators. Lisa Delpit (1988) points out that the liberal view is a goal for people whose children "are already participants in the culture of power and who have already internalized its codes. . . . However, students must be encouraged to understand the value of the codes they already possess as well as understand the power realities. Otherwise they will be unable to work to change these realities" (p. 97).

Delpit and many other black educators recognize that students should learn to read and write in meaningful contexts—with a critical (not unquestioning) acceptance of white, middle-class oral and written orientation—but they also defend the perspective that the teaching of skills in a quiet, controlled environment is absolutely essential to black students' survival.

Implications of a Racialized Masculinity Negotiation

Young African American males have to negotiate among expected roles from families, messages that they hear in music and other mediated knowledges, interactions with their peers, expectations from teachers—an array of social/cultural messages. *Negotiation* refers to the idea that individual or personal masculine (and other gendered) constructions hinge on choices and constraints of various social contexts. For black males and black females, the historical marginalization of their importance and significance to this society suggests that they have to negotiate across the power line as well. They have to look at the lack of just treatment and social equity, and define and redefine themselves (Madhubuti, 1994). They begin to see themselves as not having the same kinds of options, for example, of living wherever they choose and establishing a home there; or obtaining positions they want in the workplace. Self-defined goals that are considered mainstream masculine privileges are only partially available to black youth. My point here is that while mainstream masculinities are privileged and expected, racialized constructions must be negotiated by black males, and that this continually occurs *within* black communities as well as in contact with whites. I call the ways in which black males must traverse these multiple levels of identity construction racialized *masculinity negotiation.*

An African-centered view, its histories, cultures, and values, are an alternative to self-deprecating choices. The deconstruction of negative stereotypes serves as a viable method to begin exploring reconstructive values in education. Conversely, more "traditional" African American educators would argue that the Civil Rights Movement effectively opened the doors to equal opportunity, and all that has to be done is to motivate and empower students with skills in the mainstream explicit curriculum of math, language arts, science, and foreign language infused with a clearly identifiable emphasis on racial identity, historical recovery, and a focus on the black community. Both these views share, implicitly, the view that "successful" black masculinity negotiation can occur in the school context.

A seemingly contradictory if not paradoxical position develops. The efforts to create learning environments that strongly encourage discipline, self-control, and orderliness contrast with the effort to give voice to liberating African American codes, values, and creativity. This duality becomes a major preoccupation of conscious black educators, and certainly manifested at the Academy, where it was felt that black males required this bodily control and a curriculum of what might be called acceptable black content.

The black child's masculinity in schools is formed in part as a response to rituals of purposing and rituals of control; to implicit curricula of redirection from black hip hop cultural forms and explicit curricula of black mainstream acceptable content. At the Academy, exhortations from teachers functioned to point students toward career tracks, and extracurricular clubs (the synergy club, the air and flight club, the future engineers) organized to focus on professional career choices. There were ever-present reminders to get educated and to become a success in the job market. During the time of this study, no direct instruction was observed at the Academy as *critical* of the aforementioned beliefs. Nor was there critical engagement of the capitalist economic structure. They had not begun to question or teach how a racist society, fractured with beliefs of white supremacy, undermines the myth of economic security for all and results in contradictory experiences of power for African American males. The Academy staff, however, did challenge the retreatist notion of "life without meaning." They were anxious for the young people to see themselves as involved with their communities, knowledgeable about both modern and ancient histories of black people.

Strengthening self-discipline and control, building self-esteem, and developing a sense of responsibility were the reasons most teachers and parents stated in interviews for sending their children to the Academy. Ritualized school-wide practices were constant reminders of the common goals that parents and school staff shared for the students. Through minilectures given in the auditorium and on the playground, through classroom rules and procedures, the children were consistently reminded of the goal of becoming self-disciplined, to control the body and its possible loss of direction.

Conclusions

The idea of the Academy as originally formulated was to have a radically different educational setting, an all-male school taught principally by black males. It was an educational institution explicitly designed to address themes of masculinity in a racist society. Perhaps the teachers and administrators in the Academy felt that they were helping their students' life chances and clarifying the youths' perspectives on "success" by containing and restraining the body for their students' sake—that they were *protecting* their lives by creating an alternative urban space. This would suggest that a pedagogy of recontextualization was being developed that named this city school not as place of hopelessness and failure but a site of success and achievement within complex urban life. A notion of "safe place making" is useful here because it suggests that in the context of urban communities, an oppositional public space, a school, can be created that is caring or nurturing of black children, where self-definition or identity formation develops and where black masculinity construction is not limited to racialized notions of criminality, wildness, and deviance. Nevertheless, this study also suggests that there are limitations to this kind of thinking and a pressing need for black empowerment pedagogies that deconstruct and critique earlier modernist strategies about identity formation. The challenge to demystify sexist, racist, and classist power relations continues, as well as to construct more multidimensional responses that articulate the complexity of urban life.

Several recent studies in urban high schools (Fine, 1993; McQuillan, 1998) use a deconstructive framework to examine identity and student behaviors in school. Cohen (1993) suggests that black children cut up and act out to express anger and frustration with a curriculum devoid of meaningful content. Within the realm of day-to-day life and struggle, students challenge at times and buy into at times the school dominant codes and cultural norms of dress, behavior, and relationships. This resistance and assimilation interplay creates a space from which alternative gendered constructions may find validation.

Notes

1. This study was conducted over a period of 6 months, from August to January, 1993-1994. I "attended" school with the fourth, fifth, and sixth graders, going from class to class with them, standing out on the playground during recess, eating lunch with the students, and attending all of their after-school functions. I was present at all staff meetings and in-service trainings during the 6-month period as well. In-depth interviews were conducted with the principal and assistant principal, the coach, six teachers, the head of the parents' organization, and three students.

2. A number of texts theorize African American constructions of masculinity outside of the African-centered framework. See, for example, *Black Men Speaking* by Charles Johnson and John McCluskey (1997). Popular culture is significant and insightfully taken up in the analysis offered by Michael Dyson (1993) in *Reflecting Black: African American Cultural Criticism.*

3. One year after the opening of the "Academy," the American Civil Liberties Union brought suit and the courts ruled that girls must attend the school. At the time of this study, 5% of the student population was female.

References

Ani, M. (1994). *Yurugu: An African-centered critique of European cultural thought and behavior.* Trenton, NJ: Africa World Press.

Bowser, B. P. (1991). *Black male adolescents: Parenting and education in community context.* Lanham, MD: University Press of America.

Clatterbaugh, K. (1997). *Contemporary perspectives on masculinity.* Boulder, CO: Westview.

Cohen, J. (1993). Constructing race at an urban high school: In their minds, their mouths, their hearts. In L. Weis & M. Fine (Eds.), *Beyond silenced voices: Class, race, and gender in Unites States schools.* Albany: State University of New York Press.

Coontz, S. (1992). *The way we never were: American families and the nostalgia trap.* New York: Basic Books.

Delpit, L. (1988). The silenced dialogue: Power and pedagogy in educating other people's children. In L. Weis & M. Fine (Eds.), *Beyond silenced voices: Class, race, and gender in United States schools.* Albany: State University of New York Press.

Dyson, M. (1993). *Reflecting black: African American cultural criticism.* Minneapolis: University of Minnesota Press.

Fine, M. (1993). *Beyond silenced voices: Class, race, and gender in United States schools.* Albany: State University of New York Press.

Franklin, C. W. (1994). Men's studies, the men's movement, and the study of black masculinities in the 1990s. In R. G. Majors & J. U. Gordon (Eds.), *The American black male: His present status and his future* (pp. 271-283). Chicago: Nelson-Hall.

Haymes, S. (1995). *Race, culture and the city: A pedagogy for urban black struggle.* Albany: State University of New York Press.

hooks, b. (1994, February). Sexism and misogyny: Who takes the rap? Misogyny, gangsta rap and the piano. *Z Magazine.*

Johnson, C., & McCluskey, J. (1997). *Black men speaking.* Bloomington: Indiana University Press.

Keto, T. (1989). *The Africa centered perspective of history and social sciences in the twenty-first century.* Blackwood, NJ: K. A. Publications.

Kitwana, B. (1994). *The rap on gangsta rap.* Chicago: Third World Press.

Lemelle, A. (1995). *Black male deviance.* Westport, CT: Praeger.

Madhubuti, H. (1994). *Claiming earth: Race, rage, rape, redemption: Blacks seeking a culture of enlightened empowerment.* Chicago: Third World Press.

Marable, M. (1992, November). Black America in search of itself. *Progressive Magazine,* pp. 18-23.

Massey, D., & Denton, N. (1993). *American apartheid: Segregation and the making of the underclass.* Cambridge, MA: Harvard University Press.

McQuillan, P. (1998). *Educational opportunity in an urban American high school.* Albany: State University of New York Press.

Monroe, S. (1987, March 23). Brothers. *Newsweek,* p. 55.

Murtadha-Watts, K. (1994). *A case study: Communitarian ethical challenges confronting the developers of an African-centered school.* Unpublished doctoral dissertation, Miami University, Oxford, OH.

Nobles, W. (1989). Psychological nigrescence: An Afrocentric review. *The Counseling Psychologist.*

Quantz, R., & Magolda, P. (1998). Nonrational classroom performance: Ritual as an aspect of action. *Urban Review, 29*(4), pp. 221-238.

Said, E. (1993). *Culture and imperialism.* New York: Knopf.

Shujaa, M., & Lomotey, K. (1994). *Afrocentrism and Afrocentric education.* A paper submitted to the Encyclopedia of African-American Education Project.

West, C. (1993). The new cultural politics of difference. In C. McCarthy & W. Critchlow (Eds.), *Race identity and representation in education.* New York: Routledge.

Yeo, F. (1997). *Inner-city schools, multiculturalism, and teacher education: A professional journey.* New York: Garland.

PART TWO

SECONDARY SCHOOLS

4

Heterosexism in Middle Schools

LAURIE MANDEL
CHAROL SHAKESHAFT

This chapter addresses the complex ways in which heterosexism underlies adolescents' ideologies of masculinity and femininity—in their self-concepts, in their relationships, and within gender relations in school. We explore girls' and boys' descriptions of their gender identity and the role assumptions about heterosexuality play not only in their conceptions but in the social culture of school. The form of heterosexism we are seeing is misogynistic, where boys exert (exploit?) their masculinity in ways that are antifemale and homophobic and where girls both exploit and down-play their femininity largely to attract attention from boys. It is important to point out that the particular sexual orientation of individual students is not the focus, rather the heterosexist ideology that underpins students' conceptions of what it means to be female and male. What is addressed is the presence of a male dominated, misogynist form of heterosexism that is pervasive in middle school and its effects on adolescents. Thus this chapter explores the heterosexist ideology that largely informs adolescents' notions of gender identity.

Schooling is one of the most important socializers in our society. Societies presumably engage schools to educate and socialize young people for the roles they are expected to take as adults. During the middle school years adolescents are expected to forge an identity, often in the face of overwhelming peer pressure and scripts by which to conform. They must deal with sexual feelings that may not only be overpowering, but also have taboos (especially against female sexuality) and proscriptions attached to them. These years are critical because, neither child nor adult, adolescents must tackle two major tasks, usually on their own: identity formation and the development of self-worth. While schools are primarily focused on what students learn from the formal curriculum, much of what students learn in school is from the "informal curriculum," particularly in the social culture of school.

Adolescence is not only a time when friendship, social acceptance by peers, and a sense of belonging grow in importance; but it is a time when physical, sexual, cognitive, and emotional changes significantly alter the way young adolescents think about themselves and each other. The middle/junior high school years are pivotal in the construction of an adolescent's gender identity. The transition from the relatively asexual gender system of childhood to the overtly sexualized gender system of adolescence not only involves dramatic bodily change, but also entails complex shifts in adolescent gender relations and systems of meaning (Thorne, 1994). By middle/junior high school the formation of identity occurs in a gender system organized around the "institution of heterosexuality" (Blumenfeld & Raymond, 1988; Rich, 1980; Thorne, 1994) whereby fairly rigid adherence to gender roles becomes the norm, and peer cultures take on an active role in enforcing these roles.

There exists today a real confusion between gender role behavior and sexual orientation among theorists (Blumenfeld, 1992). Conventional studies of gender socialization "fail to explain the issue of gender identity and its relationship, if any, to sexual identity" (Sears, 1992b, p. 140). A major reason for this confusion may be that the binary relation between genders is restricted. Judith Butler (1990) argues that the concepts of girls and boys and women and men are troubling because they conform to a heterosexual matrix. Thus the "heterosexualization of desire requires and institutes the production of asymmetrical oppositions between 'feminine' and 'masculine' as expressive attributes of female and male" (p. 17). In this view, the cultural matrix through which gender identity is constructed requires that certain identities cannot exist. Thus, only recently have researchers, particularly queer theorists (see, for example, Butler, 1990; Devor, 1989; Sears, 1992b), begun to challenge conceptually and politically the institution of heterosexuality.

The impact of the institution of heterosexuality is crucial to understand, particularly during adolescence when gender and sexuality norms are piqued in pubertal middle school adolescents. As Janice Irvine (1994) points out, "gender scripts underpin virtually all social relations, including norms and ideas about sexuality" (p. 12).

Although numerous studies on gender socialization have been conducted in the past two decades, research had overlooked the complex nature of peer socialization on gender identity; in particular, the extent to which heterosexism plays a part. We not only question how heterosexual assumptions inform the discourses on adolescent gender identity, but argue that along with the pressures in middle school to adhere to conventional gender roles is the culturation of homophobia, misogyny, and male dominance. Through adolescents' voices we demonstrate how these forces become status quo for compulsory heterosexuality and gender identity in their beliefs, attitudes, and behaviors. This chapter intends to shed light on the complexity and implications of heterosexism in schools and to provide an increased understanding of the developmental challenges of early adolescence in schools.

Conceptual Framework

In spite of societal changes promulgated by the feminist and gay movements, stereotypic gendered norms and expectations remain prominent in our culture. In adolescence, gender roles and expectations for what are considered appropriately male and female become central (Thorne, 1994). Adolescent notions of masculinity and femininity, compartments still buttressed by gender-appropriate stereotypes, are fraught with internal and external pressures in school. It is argued here that the requirements for young adults to conform to heterosexually defined gender roles for femininity and masculinity are harmful to adolescents in at least four ways:

1. Boys learn that masculinity means to reject feminine behaviors and attributes, contributing to misogyny and homophobia (Devor, 1989; Kimmel, 1994; Koegel, 1994; Mandel, 1996; Thorne, 1994).

2. Girls continue to face pressures to be beautiful, attractive, and sexy (American Association of University Women [AAUW], 1991; Bush & Simmons, 1987; Davies & Furnham, 1986; Eder, 1995; Fabian & Thompson, 1989; Fine & MacPherson, 1993; Ornstein, 1994; Pipher, 1994; Sadker & Sadker, 1994) and thus grow into young adulthood believing appearance is their primary (or only) attribute.

3. Large numbers of girls literally struggle to identify positive aspects of being female; few boys struggle to identify positive aspects of being male (AAUW, 1991; Baumgartner-Papageorgiou, 1982; Brown & Gilligan, 1992; Mee, 1995; Riley, 1993; Sadker & Sadker, 1994).

4. Adolescents must contend with being "straight" in junior high school, the assumption that one is presumed to be heterosexual unless demonstrated

otherwise (Herdt, 1989; Savin-Williams & Rodriquez, 1993). Studies consistently report that gay and lesbian youth who depart from traditional norms of masculinity and femininity are often targets of violence and harassment in school because they do not conform to cultural ideals of what is considered "appropriately" male or female (see, for example, Governor's Commission on Gay and Lesbian Youth, 1993; Herek & Berrill, 1992; Hetrick & Martin, 1987; Hunter & Schaecher, 1987; McManus et al., 1991; Seattle Commission on Adolescent Youth, 1989).

Heterosexism

We situate this work on adolescent gender identity within a larger framework of heterosexist ideology. This ideology typically underlies the dual ways we think about and categorize masculinity and femininity. We argue that cultural heterosexist roots organize our system of beliefs, experiences, and attitudes about gender and sexual identity. Heterosexism, as defined by Audre Lorde (1984), is the "belief in the inherent superiority of one pattern of loving and thereby its right to dominance" (p. 45). It is a belief system that dictates compulsory heterosexuality or heterosexuality as the norm. Heterosexist ideology thus socializes individuals to conform to binary gender roles and traits associated with heterosexuality. Though not always direct or overt, heterosexism, like homophobia, is a form of discrimination. Its subtlety is even more insidious because it is harder to define and combat. Though "heterosexism is discrimination by neglect, omission, and/or distortion, homophobia is discrimination by intent and design" (Blumenfeld & Raymond, 1988, p. 245). Perhaps the omission of the term *heterosexism* from most dictionaries further indicates the lack of attention to the presence of heterosexism in Western culture.

Further, homophobia, a central component of heterosexism, is "a weapon of sexism" in that heterosexism creates the climate for homophobia with its assumption that the world is and must be heterosexual and its display of power and privilege as the norm (Pharr, 1992). Heterosexism is the systemic display of homophobia in the institution of society. Heterosexism and homophobia work together to enforce compulsory heterosexuality.

Of the relatively few studies related to heterosexism, one study examined the nature and the effects of heterosexist silencing in high school (Friend, 1993). Each of these literatures, however, addresses heterosexism and homophobia as they affect or are related to gay, lesbian, and bisexual individuals, predominantly adults. We explored how the forces of hetero-sexism impact all female and male teens, without regard to their sexual identity.

Methodology

To understand how adolescent gender identity is mediated by assumptions about heterosexuality—or heterosexism—this study drew on data from a total of 200 interviews and observations from 75 field visits with seventh-, eighth-, and ninth-grade adolescents in two schools on Long Island. The two sites for this study, which were part of a larger study of nine sites on peer interactions (Shakeshaft, Barber, Hergenrother, Johnson, Mandel, & Sawyer, 1995, 1997), took place in a middle school and a junior high school between 1993 and 1995. Both were medium-sized suburban schools in middle- to upper-middle-class, white communities. The sample consisted of 144 self-selected students (100 girls and 44 boys) in seventh, eighth, and ninth grades. To understand the students and the social culture in one school setting, 22 key informants (15 girls and 7 boys) from one school were selected and interviewed three times each. Individuals from different social groups were selected; for example, those who are considered athletic, smart, freaky, popular, and unpopular.

Observations of students' interactions and interviews were conducted in the cafeteria, in extracurricular activities, and in the hallways. Interviews took several forms, from one-on-one, to small groups of 3 or 4, to large groups of 12 students.

After the study began we addressed a methodological issue that we did not anticipate. When we asked students how they define their masculinity and femininity, girls were rather quick to respond (i.e., I can wear dresses and I like sports); boys nearly choked in response to the question. They were either offended or became hostile over this question. Thus, we devised a pencil and paper informal survey to better ascertain students' notions of both their own masculinity and femininity. The survey, given to 60 of the students, consisted of two horizontal lines drawn on the paper; one line represented femininity and the other line masculinity. Students were asked to mark an X on each line where they perceived their femininity and masculinity to be. Then students were asked to give each X a numeric value from 1 to 10, according to how masculine and feminine they perceived themselves to be. We then asked students to write a description about what aspects they saw in themselves as masculine and feminine.

We also had a unique opportunity, provided by the school social worker, to sit in on discussion groups she facilitated: five coed and three all-girl groups.

Findings

Describing Femininity

The pressures in middle schools are daunting. Girls talked about the importance of being popular, having a boyfriend, being accepted, looking good, and being liked; boys talked about the importance of being built, being athletic, and having a girl.

We opened many interviews with students with, "How do you describe/define femininity/masculinity?" Although students' initial descriptions of femininity were traditional and focused on appearance and affiliations with boys as measures of femininity, deeper interviews by and large suggested that there were complex, contradictory, and confusing notions about the term *femininity*. Three models of femininity, which are not mutually exclusive, emerged from students' descriptions of what it means to be feminine. The most common description was the *unidimensional model* of femininity in which girls and boys largely associated femininity with a girl's appearance and the extent to which she was affiliated with, liked by, or hung around boys; the second description was the *mascufemininity model*, an expanded model of conventional femininity by which girls identified themselves as both feminine and masculine; and the third description was the *independent model* of femininity, a category by which girls countered rigid ideals of conventional femininity and gender stereotypes.

Unidimensional Model of Femininity: Appearance and Boys

In the unidimensional model, descriptions of the term *femininity* by both girls and boys were laden with stereotypic feminine characteristics, such as a feminine girl wears skirts and dresses, is prissy (a girl perceived as stuck-up), brags about herself, hangs out with boys, flirts with or flaunts over boys, talks on the phone, shops, acts squeamish, is chatty, is insecure, and is nonathletic. Although it would *appear* that girls in these communities may have more leeway to develop feminine and masculine attributes, many girls (and boys) embraced stereotypical notions about femininity, putting tremendous emphasis on and energy into their popularity, appearance, and relationships with boys. Cassie, an eighth grader, talked about how important looks are in order to be noticed by boys:

> You always have to worry about what you say, wear, how you act, how you dress ... for the most part I think it's just your looks. I think it's hard to constantly hear guys say all these things about girls who are pretty. I'm not one of the prettiest girls in the school. (143, Cassie, eighth)

In the lunchroom I (Mandel) asked Julia, a ninth grader, "Who in this room is considered feminine?" She replied, "the group that all they talk about is this hot guy they saw in the mall or on TV, or what they are going to wear or what lipstick they are going to wear" (149, Julia, 398, ninth). Similarly, Jahmalia responded, "[A feminine girl] wears skirts once in a while, she does her hair, puts it in a pony tail. . . . She acts, like, a normal person, I guess, she doesn't talk about video games and stuff, she'll talk about guys and stuff" (92, Jahmalia, ninth).

Boys also described very conventional notions about the term femininity: "Femininity is being really sensitive, crying over and over" (122, Bently, eighth). "[Feminine girls] bake, go to the mall" (121, Budd, ninth). "A feminine girl? (long pause) A feminine girl would be more restrictive, maybe not as loud. Someone who's laid back. Someone who's more kept, who worries about what someone thinks of her" (94, Bradley, eighth).

One heterosexist assumption was that if a girl had a boyfriend, she earned popularity and social status. The extent to which girls talked about the importance of popularity and having a boyfriend in middle school was daunting. Girls focused so much on what boys thought of them:

> A lot of boys and girls go out with each other but I think it's more of an image thing, not a romantic thing. . . . I think girls are too focused on boys. I think girls worry too much about their looks, their image, their hair. (40, Jillian, eighth)

Joy recalled how Gabrielle became popular because she was the talk of the boys' locker room. A girl who was beautiful, defined here as physically well developed, tended to get a lot of sexual attention from boys.

> Every guy thinks she's so beautiful—basically it's emphasized on her chest. She has a really big chest size compared to us. She could have any guy she wanted. (179, Joy, ninth)

Jessie, a seventh grader, also explained that girls became popular when they were seen with a boy:

Laurie: How do you become popular?

Jessie: Like if you go out with someone or if a popular boy likes you. If you go out to the movies and then you hold hands in school people notice you more. You get like ten more friends. His friends become your friends. People notice you more. (137, Jessie, seventh)

Relate to #5

A second heterosexist assumption is that if a girl appears sexual she is perceived as a slut. Although attention from males or affiliation with boys largely determined a girl's popularity, it was also an indication of the complex heterosexist expectations or messages about what it means to be female. Socially, girls are expected to have boyfriends and are encouraged to be sexy, but they are not expected to be sexual. This assumption perpetuates the perception that when a girl displayed her (hetero)sexuality, she was perceived to be a slut. For example, Mercedes, a ninth grader, was called a slut by boys after having sex with her boyfriend and her boyfriend bragged to his friends about his sexual experience:

> Guys see me mostly as outgoing and as a slut because everyone knows the guy I went out with last year . . . we had sex over the summer and he came back to school this year and told everyone. He said, "Listen to this, I got screwed over the summer and you [his friends] didn't." Now they call me "slut." (175, Mercedes, ninth)

Stereotypic, heterosexist notions of young women were further described by a group of eight boys in the eighth grade. The boys sat on top of the lunch table while others huddled around me. They were asked, "What kinds of things do you see girls doing after high school?" Eager to talk, they shouted out their responses:

"Girls should be in *Playboy*." (boys hysterically laugh)

"They should be a loving and caring wife."

"She should be in a nice big bed."

"They should have a job but not a job that is as hard or as tough as a man's job."

"They should be loyal in a relationship."

"She should have to be able to cook."

[handwritten: △ in beh. relates to performance theory]

The strong influence of the male culture in these face-to-face interactions with this group of eighth-grade boys was quite apparent. A wave of sexist remarks began to take hold among the boys in the group environment, even from boys who individually were more shy and less forthcoming. The male culture created among the group elicited attitudes that might have sounded or been quite different if this question were asked in a dyadic interview. Two exceptions to these stereotypic, sexist comments included, "I would want it [marriage] to be equal, we should not be dependent on each other," and "They [girls] should be able to stand up for themselves."

The contrast between how these boys viewed the roles of girls and women as compared to the roles of boys and men became apparent when I asked, "What kinds of things do you see yourselves doing after high school?" In a more serious tone the boys responded: "I want to be a veterinarian," "I'm going to be in my family's business," "An athlete," "I want to be a lawyer," "Me too, I want to be a lawyer" (171, Aaron and 11 friends, seventh). The boys viewed themselves in more serious-minded ways and with a sense of a career plan, unlike the ways in which they viewed young women, as sex objects and as nonprofessional (i.e., in domestic roles).

MascuFemininity: Girls Who Embraced
Femininity and Masculinity

It appeared that whereas feminine traits have expanded, feminine ideology has not. There was incongruence between feminine ideologies and girls' actual behaviors. Although both boys' and girls' conceptions of girls were largely conventional, girls were actually less conventional than the descriptions. For instance, some girls realized that they either did not fit into such narrow notions of femininity or were uncomfortable with such definitions when they looked more closely at themselves. Girls who were athletic, for example, found femininity to be quite restrictive; in actuality they didn't like to wear makeup and dresses and preferred acting "tough" and "hard" to "acting like a girl." The girls who were comfortable being and doing things considered masculine tended to view themselves as being both masculine and feminine. Such girls located themselves in the middle or somewhere along a masculine-feminine continuum. One girl even suggested that "there shouldn't be separate categories of femininity and masculinity but rather something like 'mascufemininity' so you can be both" (thus we named the expansion of femininity, a combination feminine and masculine traits, mascufemininity). A ninth-grade girl, for example, resisted a unidimensional notion of femininity. With a tone of aggression, she said,

> I'm a tomboy. I never act like a girl. I act tough and hard. I act like a guy. I hate acting like a girl. I yell a lot and I like to beat up people. Masculine is active, sporty. A girl can do the same thing. To me, acting like a girl is acting polite, cute. I don't like acting like a girl. (survey, female, ninth)

Similarly, Lani, a ninth-grade girl, commented on how she doesn't think of herself as very feminine: "I don't wear skirts. I'm not too much of one or the other. I'm in the middle" (109, Lani, ninth). She situated herself along a continuum of both feminine and masculine identities. Another ninth-grade girl articulated her way of conceptualizing feminine that is more masculine than feminine:

> I'm more masculine but I'm feminine. I don't care much about nails or hair. Sometimes I think I'm more of a guy. I still have features of a girl, I like to wear makeup. I still like to act female. (survey, female, ninth)

Carman, also a ninth grader, ultimately deconstructed the either/or gender constructs and brought the feminine and the masculine together. "I think masculinity and femininity are both equal in all people. Some people may show one side more but in my opinion they are equal qualities" (survey).

Bryan alone saw himself as influenced by femininity. He says, "I'm close to the feminine side. I live with three sisters and a mom so I get a lot of that female culture. I have a lot of guy friends so I'm masculine too, I guess. A guy can be feminine. He doesn't have to wear dresses" (Bryan, eighth).

In contrast to the unidimensional model of femininity, these girls describe their femininity in ways that are more fluid rather than fixed; they can be athletic, aggressive, and tough and also be assertive and soft-spoken. Essentially, they feel they can play soccer by day and wear a prom dress by night.

Independent Model: Girls Who Rejected Traditional Femininity

Still, there were other girls who either largely rejected femininity or who were perceived as unfeminine. Such girls were considered to have one or a combination of characteristics: athletic, muscular, independent, tough, butchy, anti-makeup, unromantic or asexual, confident. Rather than perceiving feminine girls as independent, for example, nonconventional girls were described as unfeminine. "Non-feminine girls," according to Justine, a seventh grader, "are confident, they are not afraid of other people, they don't care about nails or hair. They do things for themselves" (105, Justine, seventh). Her perception also indicated that to be confident, self-assured, and less focused on appearance meant that one is unfeminine, and as one male student concluded, "Unfeminine girls are not seen as attractive or as potential girlfriends."

Some girls and boys couldn't even think of or point out any girls who are feminine. "I don't think there is such a thing [as feminine]. Some are too feminine, like those who brag about themselves or break a nail. Some are not feminine at all" (105, Justine, seventh). "There isn't a girl who's really feminine. Some play sports, some don't. I can't think of any real feminine girls" (93, Natalie, eighth).

We listened as girls struggled with what they perceived the term *unfeminine* meant in a discussion among 12 ninth-grade girls lead by the social worker. For example, Caren recognized unfeminine girls as girls whose "voice is deeper, or who are into sports. The butchy look. Like if you wear work boots." Stella disagreed. "No, it's not what your wear . . . it's how you act." Rhea said, "It has to do with voice." In each of their descriptions these girls intertwined notions of femininity with notions about sexuality. It appears that Caren's, Rhea's, and Stella's references to a butchy look, either in looks, voice, or appearance, was equated with being lesbian. In a peer culture where "boys think about sports and girls think about guys," there were several girls who saw themselves as exceptions. Charmika worried over her lack of interest in boys: "I feel I have to 'hide' that I'm not really into boys in front of my friends" (4, Charmika, seventh).

Rhea, a ninth-grade key informant, was more interested in her friends and her work than in boys. Rhea spoke not only for herself but for her friends:

> We don't like the guys in this school. They're immature and annoying. We don't find any attractive. We're becoming more independent so we look to our friends more. Friendships are important. We're looking to connect with people. Even just one close person you can talk to. We're trying to find ourselves. It's helpful to find people that are like you. I don't think boys think about it. We talk about everything. (172, Rhea, ninth)

In a confident tone she added, "I feel like I'm a strong person. I think more ahead than some of my friends." At 14 years of age, she understood the association between gender and power when she summarized:

I'm happy being female but it's a man's world and it's always going to be like that. You kind of have a challenge to try to become better. In some ways it's worse, it's harder to get things and to earn respect. You hear guys talk about girls. That's the way society raises women, to be self-conscious and to worry about what people think of us. (135, Rhea, ninth)

Similarly, a seventh-grade girl, Erica, illustrated what seemed be an independent model of femininity. She expressed an interest in girls' rights:

I think about boys but not very much. They [boys] are a lot different than girls. They don't care what they look like. . . . I want to preach for girls' rights or something . . . even though they aren't treated equally they should do the best they can because they will be treated equally one day. (138, Erica, seventh)

Anna Lee also believed that girls needed to work harder to get a point across. With strength and conviction, she said,

I think it's important for girls not to give up and to succeed at what we want. I don't think girls should give up but we have to try harder than boys do because people think boys can do all this stuff better but if girls want to get a point across they have to try harder than boys. (134, Anna Lee, seventh)

These independent girls appeared to be noticeably more aware of being treated fairly, and were less interested in boys. Signs of feminist thinking are apparent in their thoughts (though only a few girls used the term *feminist* to describe themselves), particularly in the way they spoke about wanting respect and rights for girls and women.

Thus, we assert there is the presence of three models of femininity that are not mutually exclusive. The unidimensional model of femininity is one that many girls don't challenge. This model, promulgated by images of and notions about beauty and appearance, greatly contributes to overwhelming numbers of girls who are consumed by worry, fear, and insecurity about their appearance and image, especially in front of boys—but in front of other girls as well. The mascufemininity model refers to an expansion of girls' perceptions of femininity and an acquisition of the concept that their identities are along a continuum and are not fixed. Such girls embrace both feminine and masculine aspects of themselves. The independent model of femininity is one by which girls challenged rigid heterosexist ideals of femininity associated with beauty and heterosexuality. Such girls are considered nonconventional and, interestingly, were often perceived as unfeminine because they exhibited one or a combination of characteristics: confidence, self-assuredness, toughness, athletic ability, disinterest in romantic relationships with boys, independence, and were not focused on their looks. Many girls articulated an understanding of the association between gender and power.

Describing Masculinity

In contrast to the varied and rather complex meanings of femininity, masculinity was described by girls and boys with ease, clarity, and agreement. Masculinity was largely antifeminine and characterized by the extent of a boy's machismo, athletic, and (hetero)sexual statuses.

Antifeminine

Boys in these schools vigorously embraced masculinity. An antifeminine norm strongly defined male behavior parameters. Whereas girls could embrace masculine attributes, boys refused to embrace anything feminine. The avoidance of typically feminine behaviors by boys is central to students' notions of masculinity. For example, boys are vehemently opposed to having feelings.

Feminine is when you have feelings for other things. I don't have feelings. I'm not a woman and I don't want to be one. I'm not feminine. That's when you like guys. I'm not gay. (survey, male, seventh)

A regular guy is, you know, someone who likes girls and plays sports. When you're more feminine you're more sensitive. When you're more masculine you're not as sensitive. I am sensitive but not too much. (122, Chad, eighth)

Many boys shared statements like, "I don't cry in front of other people. I am not emotional and I'm only a little sensitive."

A boy was perceived as unmasculine if he was sensitive, nonathletic, had too close a friendship with another boy, was not interested in girls, and if he was not tough, built, and/or strong. In particular, a boy is considered unmasculine or gay if he looks, acts, appears, sounds, or shows feminine attributes. As this eighth-grade boy reports, "Masculine is 'acting normal' . . . not strength . . . but like normal. Feminine is like gay, I don't consider myself gay" (survey, male, eighth).

The antifeminine norm encouraged boys to define themselves in opposition to girls. Boys worked hard not to show any feminine behaviors; boys could not be both masculine and feminine.

Machismo (Attitude/Appearance)

Looking or acting macho was also central to many boys' definitions of masculine identity in these schools. Descriptions of machismo attitudes and behaviors by both girls and boys included: thinking they [boys] rule; thinking they are "the man"; being confident, built, arrogant, "tough and buff"; and being "up on themselves." In addition, some described boys as "wearing armor." As these ninth-grade girls said about boys:

> They look like they've got to kick your butt. They think they're so manly. (88, Julia, ninth)

> I can't stand most of the guys in this school. [She smiles wide and clenches her teeth and makes fists with her hands.] They're, like, fake. They always have to act tough. They can't let anyone get close to them. Like they have to be "tough and buff." (88, Sandra, ninth)

Two boys discussed how boys need to be macho not only in front of girls, but in front of other boys. Mark says, "Guys talk differently to other guys [than they do with girls]."
   Adds Jahosef:

Jahosef: They talk about what they've done with whomever even though they didn't. Guys lie a lot.

Laurie: Why do they lie?

Jahosef: They lie to feel good about themselves. They're macho to impress girls and they're always macho in front of each other. (110, Jahosef and Mark, eighth)

Budd and Scott also talked about how boys acted more macho with their friends:

Budd: At home I'm regular, you don't try to act big or anything, with your friends you want to be more macho.

Scott: Unless you're pretty comfortable around your friends, then you can act more natural.

Budd: I guess a guy is macho if he beats people up.

Scott: If you're not macho it doesn't mean you're a wimp though.

Budd: I feel I have to put on an act when I'm threatened by a guy. (121, Budd and Scott, ninth)

Machismo was considered a shield of toughness and confidence—particularly when boys felt vulnerable or intimidated by other boys or girls.

Jacob was an exception in that he didn't believe that masculinity was about machismo or how tough one is; rather, he believed masculinity was more about being able to have freedom of thought or being able to stand one's ground:

> How would I describe masculinity? I don't know, it's a hard question. Different people ask different things. I don't think it's how strong you are or who you beat up. It's being able to say what you want to say and not letting others interfere or change your views. I see a lot do other things so that they look more masculine. Their meaning of masculinity is different than mine. I think they think being tough is being bad, rebellious. I think it's a big thing in this grade. (159, Jacob, ninth)

Athletic Status

Athletic status was a key definitional factor of a boy's masculinity. Boys indicated they felt pressure to be known for their athletic skill, to impress others, and to stand out among their peers. Physical aggression, competition, and winning—determinants of one's athletic status—are themes that undergirded masculine identity. The competitiveness and roughness of the sport matter, as Roman and Brendan illustrated:

Roman: My vision of a guy who isn't really masculine is a guy who doesn't really do anything, like play sports, they're just into their work or something.

Brendan: I agree. I could probably be a much better student if I didn't play sports.

Roman: It also depends on what sports you play. If they play, like, tennis we would say they're fags.

homosexuality = unmasculine

Brendan: But then you turn on the TV and they're guys making millions of dollars. Usually we play contact sports. Tennis is like golf, it's relaxing. I wouldn't play tennis because there are so many sports I'd rather play. I wouldn't want to hear it.

Laurie: Hear what?

Brendan: Oh, he's a fag. Look at those short shorts.

Roman perceived tennis as a masculine sport only when men were professional and earned lots of money. Otherwise, wearing "short" shorts is synonymous with looking like a girl—a fag—thus, he cast tennis aside as a less-than-masculine sport. The tougher and more competitive the sport, the more masculine a boy was considered to be.

Hetero/Sexual Status

A male's heterosexual status was core to his masculinity. The more sexual a boy acted or showed, the more masculine he was perceived to be. Boys got "points" for sexual experiences and conquests and were teased as being gay for not showing interest in girls.

A third heterosexist assumption, then, was that if a boy did not have a girlfriend, he was perceived as gay. For a boy to be considered masculine, he must have either a girlfriend or show interest in a girl. A girlfriend earned a boy masculine status (heterosexual status), particularly if the girl was pretty:

> Overall I think it's better that you're not alone. If you don't have a girlfriend people purposely say "how is your girlfriend" even though they know you don't have one. They say stupid things like that. (148, Matthew, ninth)

Being heterosexual is so important to a boy's masculinity, that if one isn't overtly or obviously heterosexual, students believe there is something wrong with him. Even in seventh grade a boy needs to display a heterosexual identity to not be perceived as a gay male. In an observation of a table of seventh-grade boys in the cafeteria, all but one of the six boys was talking about girls. A boy at the table turned to this one boy and asked, "What's wrong with you, man? Don't you want to do it with any girls?" Boys are expected to have girlfriends and, as in this case, when one does not he is teased. As Cherrie affirms, "If a guy doesn't have a girlfriend then they tease him for not having one" (73, Cherrie, eighth).

A fourth heterosexism assumption, which arguably drove most boys' beliefs about gender identity, was that if a boy is heterosexually active, he is perceived as manly. Boys who had girlfriends were perceived as being "manly" or macho. Dating a girl not only affirmed a boy's social status, but his (hetero)sexual status as well. As Budd said,

> Dating a good looking girl is very important. I have a friend in eighth who isn't looking for personality, they're [he's] just looking for looks. In eighth grade boys look for girls who have good looks and who are popular. You look good if you're with some popular or good looking. (121, Budd, ninth)

Nathan added, "a typical 15-year-old male likes sports, likes ladies, likes to spend a lot of time with girls. Guys want to have sex. In ninth grade a lot of people start dating, including me."

Thus we found masculinity to be largely antifemale and characterized by a boy's machismo, athletic, and heterosexual statuses. The norm of masculinity fervently dictates that boys develop a protection of armor (from each other) that consists of appearing tough, arrogant, insensitive, physically buff, and (hetero)sexual. Boys must—according to this norm—eradicate from themselves any emotional feelings.

How Heterosexism Limits Girls' and Boys' Identities

This section further details how students' underlying heterosexist notions about gender identity play out, particularly in the ways boys felt pressured to prove their manhood and girls felt pressured to be popular. Gender relations in middle school, as described by and observed in students, are at best disrespectful and at worst abusive, as evident in the presence of

1. sexually harassing and disrespectful language;
2. homophobic attitudes toward students perceived to be or who are gay or lesbian; and
3. sexually intensive gender relations.

Sexually Harassing and Disrespectful Language

The extent of peer sexual harassment in middle and junior high school is pervasive. Boys appear to define and demonstrate their masculinity through abusive, embarrassing, or humiliating language toward girls, such as bitch, slut, and whore, and homophobic language toward other boys such as faggot, homo (Shakeshaft et al., 1995, 1997).

Lynette's rage, expressed here, is testimony of the depth of emotional and psychological hurt she feels being called slut and thus the dilemma she feels toward boys:

> They [boys] call girls sluts. Even if you are a slut it's your business—they call them ho's, they're really mean. I hate them [boys] all so much. It repulses me that they can lie. It's costing me not to be friends with guys. You don't want to be around them but you do. Guys hang around my friends and I hate them. I'm so angry. I do not even want to talk to them. I think at this age people's feelings about us is really important. You can really hurt someone. Why should I care about what people say about me, but I do. I wish I could say, "you don't realize what you are doing." They call my friend "cow." I can defend my friends but I can't defend myself. What am I going to say, stop? I feel if I say something it's not going to do anything.

When asked if she had talked to a guidance counselor, Lynette replied,

> It's just going to make it worse for me. Even detention or suspension will make it worse for me. School used to be such a joy. Now it's like, great, I have to go to school. (36, Lynette, eighth)

Lynette described a feeling of sheer powerlessness in that she felt she couldn't defend herself from the boys' comments. She talked about how mean boys were; she struggled between not wanting to be around boys and wanting to be with them. Ultimately, Lynette did not even want to go to school.

Rhonda believed boys know it hurts when they call a girl "whore." "One time I got called that, not that I was, but they [boys] knew I'd be defensive. I went through a whole big fight with them. I feel they didn't think I was really a whore, they just knew it would hurt" (87, Rhonda, ninth).

Sexual harassment occurred on a daily basis in school. Girls collectively expressed that boys made them feel body-conscious, humiliated, embarrassed, frustrated, disrespected, voiceless, discriminated against, and powerless. Cassie, for example, described how boys humiliated girls in the middle of class when they had their periods:

> When a girl takes her school bag to the bathroom guys call her "red." Or if a girl is in a bad mood guys say "oh, I bet it's her time of the month." It's so stupid. . . .

We just laugh. What do you say? You feel really embarrassed. (143, Cassie, eighth)

As reflected in Cassie's statement, boys stereotypically blame a girl's hormones for her bad mood. Sadly, it is as if Cassie apologizes for being a girl when she says, "You want to say 'leave me alone I can't help it.' You want to say something to get back at them, but what do you say? There's nothing you can say."

Lauren, a ninth grader, talked about the vulgar language from boys. "Guys say things like 'Are you going to fuck her?' This guy said this to someone on the bus. They were eighth graders! And I said, 'Oh you're so immature.' I think they disrespect girls. Not all guys, but some guys definitely just want sex" (85, Lauren, ninth).

Natalie expressed how boys talk about girls' bodies in very sexual and judgmental ways. For example, "if your chest is too small they'll say 'you're flat.' If you're too big they'll say 'Oh that's so much to handle.' They're not my friends so I don't care. They criticize you for how you look. That's how they are" (144, Natalie, eighth). Natalie excused the comment since they are "not her friends," a justification heard several times. If a friend made a comment, then no matter how hurtful it might feel it was not taken as badly as when it was from someone who was not considered a friend.

The following boys agreed that boys notice, talk about, leer at, and sexualize girls' bodies; a girl's looks or appearance was perhaps more important than any other attribute. Jason, for instance, revealed: "We talk about their bodies, how hot they are, if she's easy. Sometimes we'll say a girl's cool but it's not much about her personality. It's more about her face and body" (93, Jason, eighth). Johnathan added:

> Boys talk about girls' bodies. I think a guy might like a girl for her personality or because she's pretty hot. Then they'll brag to their friends. Guys talk about how they [girls] act, how they look, how they dress . . . how much clothes they have on . . . or off. (107, Johnathan, eighth)

Austin, too, commented: "I think guys talk about a girl's looks, like if they're fat. Oh, they [boys] say things like 'she has such a nice butt, nice breasts, and stuff' " (90, Austin, eighth).

According to Dana, boys influenced the way many girls felt about themselves and their bodies, particularly if a boy sensed a girl had low self-esteem:

It depends on who you are. If a guy senses you have low self-esteem then he says things to you. They [boys] say a lot about their [girls'] physical appearance. It makes me wonder a little what they might be saying about my body. Sometimes when a girl walks by they'll make comments. They write about what they want to do with who on the weekend. (84, Dana, ninth)

Girls repeatedly said that they didn't know how to respond to boys' remarks, gestures, or expectations, nor did they know how *not* to be passive; thus they most often accepted the way boys treated them.

Homophobic Attitudes

Homophobic beliefs and attitudes permeated male students' beliefs about what it means to be a boy. In particular, boys' comments revealed disdain for hypomasculine and gay males. Boys expressed fear of being looked at, touched by, liked by, or associated with another boy. Students unanimously agreed that a student who is gay would be made fun of, would have to hide, would not be treated very well, and would need to find his or her own people to hang out with.

Unequivocally, students believed school was not a safe place for gay students to reveal their identities. An overwhelming number of students believed that there were probably no gay students in the school, but if there were, then "they wouldn't be able to tell anyone." I asked Jahosef, an eighth-grade boy, "How do you think it would be if a guy didn't feel for girls but for boys?" Jahosef's comment reflected a pathological view of homosexuality. He said, "I don't know. I guess at first he'd try to figure out what was wrong with him and then hopefully he'd accept it" (157, Jahosef, eighth).

The terms *fag* and *faggot* were directed with hostility by boys toward other boys to hurt or put down those considered hypomasculine or gay. "I don't talk to faggots. I saw two faggots holding hands at Friendly's. If a gay guy ever touched me I'd beat the shit out of him" (161, eighth-grade boy).

Students—even among those who claimed to be accepting of different people—believed gay or lesbian students would have to cover up who they were. As one seventh-grade girl said, "I don't think they'd ever bring it up. They'd be made fun of" (12, Marianne, seventh). Kiera, a seventh-grade girl, agreed that if a student was gay, he or she wouldn't be able to show it:

I don't think there are any gay students. Well, someone might be, maybe they are covering it up. Maybe they [boys] have a girlfriend. You hardly see girls who are gay, but you see a lot of guys who are gay.

Kiera, who lived near a gay club, would sometimes see gay men and lesbians outside the club. She commented on how she didn't expect such a club would be in the open, so close to her house.

> There is a gay bar near my house. I don't think about it. I don't really know any gay people. But I always see a guy with his hand in the other guy's pocket going into the bar. I never really see two girls. I thought it would be located in a place very far away in a dark and secretive place. I didn't know a bar like that would be right near my house. (33, Kiera, seventh)

Students consistently remarked how difficult it would be to be gay or lesbian in middle school. When a student is different, she or he becomes a target. For homosexual students the climate is hostile and unwelcoming:

> If there was a homosexual in this school I don't think they'd be treated very well. They would need to form a group of their own to find their own identity to say "we're people too." I think it would take too much time and I think it would be hard for them. (40, Jillian, eighth)

Though students didn't really know for sure if they could tell if there were any gay students in school, they agreed that school "would not be a good place. Kids call each other faggot all the time" (198, Jared, eighth).

Justin, an insightful ninth grader, believed society influences us to believe that being gay is a bad thing. He suggested that teens really need to talk about their sexuality:

> Society projects to us that being gay is not a good thing. I think it [faggot] means geek, nerd. I think people in this grade—a lot of people—have questions about their sexuality. It's a subject many people are embarrassed about. (159, Justin, ninth)

Sexually Intensive Gender Relations

The interactions between girls and boys in the adolescent social culture of school were highly sexualized. In these schools—in the hallways, at the lockers, in the cafeteria, and at social events—students openly made out (French-kissed), held hands, flirted, and displayed other heterosexually romantic behaviors. There was a consistency, not only in the flirtatious behaviors, but in the intensity with which 12-, 13-, 14-, and 15-year-old students displayed heterosexuality. Rita, for example, a seventh-grade girl who was labeled by other girls as "sexually advanced" and "popular," talked about the sexual pressure she felt in the relationship with her boyfriend. Worried about sexually pleasing her boyfriend and afraid of being dumped by him for not moving at his sexual pace, Rita responded in this way to the question, "What is it like being a female in seventh grade?"

Rita: It's hard . . . how everybody has relationships . . . like everybody goes out with each other and it's hard when you break up. Everybody's dating someone.

Laurie: What concerns do you have?

Rita: Fitting in, rumors spreading that aren't true, jealousy of other people. Worrying if you're going too fast or too slow with a boyfriend.

Laurie: How do you know if you're going too fast or too slow?

Rita: You'll know you're going too slow because they'll go faster but when you go faster they don't care. If you go too slow they'll tell their friends "she's going too slow," then they'll dump you.

Rita was particularly nervous because it's the first time she has asked a boy out. Her statements illustrated how much sexual power her boyfriend has, or how much sexual power she has given him. She felt incredible pressure to "be like an eighth grader," which meant, as she perceived, to be willing to please her boyfriend sexually.

Rita: He's in eighth grade and really popular. You just want to do everything right so they don't break up with you. Since he's in eighth I feel pressured because I feel I should be like an eighth grader. A lot of my friends in eighth grade already did it, most of the popular ones. I feel like if I don't do it I'll be like fading away.

Laurie: Fading away?

Rita: Once people say something about you it's over. So the pressure is on. They want blow jobs and stuff like that and if you don't give it soon they'll dump you. They'll say "You know you want me." And if you say "no" they think you mean "yes." (120, Rita, seventh)

In response to the question, "What is it like being female in eighth grade?" Eileen, an eighth grader and key informant, talked about the sexual attention she gets (and expects) from boys:

It's, like, good because some of the guys are like "oh, look at her." You expect them to do that, like, you don't think it's sexual harassment, that's ridiculous, but they say things like "nice outfit" or they stare at you in the hallway. They look you up and down. Sometimes it's flattering. Sometimes it's annoying. It's something that's going to happen. I know they won't grab my butt or anything. We're good friends. (164, Eileen, eighth)

Though girls learned to expect sexual attention from boys, most often they did not know what to do with such remarks. Jenny believed, for example, girls "tolerated" boys and overlooked their behaviors: "Girls who are good friends with guys, it's not that they respect the guys, it's that they overlook things they do" (25, Jenny, eighth). It is as if these girls believe they're supposed to accept this kind of behavior.

Seventh-grader Leeza commented that both

boys and girls have one thing on their mind. Sex . . . that's all they think about. They talk about it. You can hear it during class and in the hallway all the time. There are boys and girls kissing all the time in the hallways. When I'm hanging out with my friends they talk about it, too. (178, Leeza, seventh)

We have illustrated how heterosexism limits ALL girls' and boys' identities. Sexual harassment, gender disrespect and violence, and hypersexualization are ubiquitous in the peer culture of middle school. We have found that the norms of heterosexism and homophobia dominate images of femininity and masculinity and that these norms are oppressive for both girls and boys. And yet, these students' stories, we believe, are but a small testimony to the crisis they face brought about by these norms in the social construction of their identities.

Conclusion

The "hidden curriculum of sexuality in schools remains a generally unaddressed phenomenon" (Sears, 1992a, p. 13). We've asked students questions about gender identity that actually reflected their gendered and sexual beliefs, feelings, and values (and experiences). Questions such as: "What is it like to be 'female' and 'male'?" "How do you describe 'femininity' and 'masculinity'?" and "How do kids treat each other in school?" has lead us to understand, we believe, a relationship between notions of gender and sexuality and the heterosexist beliefs at the root of these notions. Central to girls' and boys' descriptions about being female and male is the requirement to be heterosexual or to display heterosexual behaviors.

Our study suggests that in middle and junior high school heterosexuality is a culturally defined norm, or what Richard Friend (1993) calls an "assumption of universal heterosexuality in schools." In addition, the peer culture teaches that popularity is important and to be popular one must be physically attractive, heterosexual, and conform largely to gender expectations. We argue that adolescents' assumptions about heterosexuality embedded in school social norms promote homophobia and sexual harassment, promulgate gender inequality, and foster limited expressions of identity.

Youth is becoming increasingly complex. Teenagers in the average middle and high school are learning not only powerful messages about their gender and sexuality from the hidden sexuality curriculum, but that in order to be popular one has to be attractive, physically fit, heterosexual, conform to gender role expectations, and dress according to school norms. While the spectrum of "acceptable" gender behaviors has expanded for girls, female sexuality and desire are still downplayed and undervalued. Similarly, yet conversely, the spectrum of "acceptable" gender behaviors for boys has not expanded, and while male heterosexuality is encouraged, acceptable, and valued, homosexuality is not.

Similar to the way sexual harassment is about bullying rather than about sex (Bordo, 1998; Stein, 1995), we recognize heterosexism is about power rather than about sexual orientation. We problematize the power dynamics brought about by heterosexism in the school setting in order to understand how adolescent gender identity is conceptualized. We've documented how heterosexist ideology is counterproductive and harmful for four reasons:

1. Heterosexism teaches limited conceptions of cross-gender and same-gender relationships. It socializes adolescents into a narrow, simplistic understanding of gender and sexuality.
2. Heterosexism reproduces social and sexual asymmetry (inequality) by which masculine norms dominate girls and less-masculine boys. It leads to

divisive and disrespectful gender relations among peers and does not question misogynist language or behaviors.

3. It creates intense pressures for all students, and even more so for gay and lesbian students, because heterosexism essentially dictates one acceptable pattern of relating and loving.

4. Ultimately, heterosexism limits girls' and boys' self-expression, gender identity, and patterns of relating. While it requires strict conformity to hypermasculinity, it victimizes girls and less-masculine boys, thereby victimizing everyone.

In adolescence, gender identity is one of the most central aspects of developing a sense of self. Sexual orientation, though not the primary issue here, gets tied in with the effects of heterosexism because those who violate traditional gender role expectations are often equated with also violating traditional heterosexual expectations. As Richard Friend (1993) asserts:

> Boys who are "too sensitive" and girls who are "too independent" not only violate traditional gender-role expectations, but are also negatively stigmatized as homosexual. In this way, a homophobic label is used to enforce a sexist arrangement and functions to try to keep all students, heterosexual and homosexual alike, from violating what is expected of them in terms of gender-role behaviors. (p. 232)

Next Steps

If we are to be successful in promoting social change in schools, we need to understand how daily practices in schools and other institutions affect the construction of beliefs about gender definitions and gender inequality (Eder, 1995). By not allowing any variation of sexuality or gender to coexist, schools continue to reinforce heterosexuality (Elia, 1994) and conventional gender roles. Since junior high school is the time when social control is at its peak, it is during these years that the force of society's pressure to conform to heterosexuality is brought to bear (Pharr, 1992). One way to address these practices is to begin challenging the norm of masculinity in school. In an effort to expand how individuals view themselves and each other, we need to understand better the link between the norm of masculinity and the language and behaviors toward girls and boys that are disrespectful, demeaning, inappropriate, and/or sexually harassing. Michael Kimmel (1994) has argued that homophobia, men's fear of other men, is the dominant definition of masculinity in America. Thus, "the reigning definition of masculinity is a defensive effort to prevent being emasculated" (p. 135). In boys' efforts to suppress or overcome these fears, those who are deemed less than fully manly become targets: girls and gay males (or those perceived to be).

We need to challenge administrators', educators', and students' beliefs and behaviors about what it means to be male and female, which often go unquestioned. In addition, the climate of male sexual aggression needs to be explored. We believe it is important to ask: Do contemporary school practices prepare adolescent girls to recognize expanded ways of being female? Do they prepare girls to resist male aggression and misogyny in male culture? Do contemporary school practices prepare adolescent boys with expanded ways of being male? Do they prepare boys to resist aggression and competition and misogyny in male culture? Do they help boys to believe it's okay to be masculine *and* to express feelings?

Further, we suggest taking a critical look at adolescent culture and language. Donna Eder (1995) stresses the importance of understanding how language becomes the basis for maintaining power differences between males and females: "A general knowledge of male and female school culture provides an important background for understanding the nature and construction of sexuality and gender relations" (p. 4).

We hope the findings of this study will call into question the normative labeling of femininity, masculinity, and sexuality and will illustrate the impact of such labeling on adolescents. Whereas Eder's (1995) study was among the first to draw attention to the construction of masculinity as a dominating and potentially sexist practice that results in the subordination of other boys as well as of girls, our study points to the critical role that heterosexist ideology plays in limiting the construction of male and female gender identity.

Finally, we believe we must help girls and boys to develop their personal, emotional, and intellectual strength and abilities. We must teach girls to focus on themselves, rather than gaining a false sense of worth through their affiliations with boys. We must teach boys to develop and value attributes of caring, compassion, and sensitivity, rather than focusing on toughness and aggression. We can and must address the unspoken heterosexist culture to build a school environment that is less abusive, less sexualized, and more supportive and growth producing for girls and boys.

Understanding that the heterosexist or overtly hidden curriculum is not intended and is transmitted through everyday interactions in school, schools must become deeply thoughtful about the developmental stage that adolescents are in and consider how the peer social climate in the school itself contributes to or hinders a positive experience for diverse students. As Ianni (1989) points out, "Adolescents generate their own norms and rules, but this process does not and cannot develop in isolation from the institutional context of the communities in which they live and learn" (p. 679). Administrators and teachers as well as students must critically analyze the social and sexual aspects of the school system. We must question the politics of the unspoken curriculum, call for one that is held together by contemporary social issues, and develop the ability to take on these issues.

References

American Association of University Women. (1991). *How schools shortchange girls: A study of major findings on girls and education.* Washington, DC: AAUW Educational Foundation.

Baumgartner-Papageorgiou, A. (1982). *"My daddy might have loved me": Student perceptions of differences between being male and being female.* Denver, CO: Institute for Equality in Education.

Blumenfeld, W. J. (1992). Squeezed into gender envelopes. In W. J. Blumenfeld (Ed.), *Homophobia: How we all pay the price* (pp. 23-38). Boston, MA: Beacon.

Blumenfeld, W. J., & Raymond, D. (1988). *Looking at gay and lesbian life.* Boston: Beacon.

Bordo, S. (1998, May 1). Sexual harassment is about bullying, not sex. *Chronicle of Higher Education,* p. B6.

Brown, L. M., & Gilligan, C. (1992). *Meeting at the crossroads.* New York: Ballantine.

Bush, D., & Simmons, R. (1987). Gender and coping with the entry into early adolescence. In R. Barnett, L. Biener, & G. Baruch (Eds.), *Gender and stress.* New York: Free Press.

Butler, J. (1990). *Gender trouble: Feminism and the subversion of identity.* New York: Routledge.

Davies, E., & Furnham, A. (1986). Body satisfaction in adolescent girls. *British Journal of Medical Psychology, 59,* 279-287.

Devor, H. (1989). *Gender blending: Confronting the limits of duality.* Bloomington: Indiana University Press.

Eder, D., with Evans, C. C., & Parker, S. (1995). *School talk: Gender and adolescent culture.* New Brunswick, NJ: Rutgers University Press.

Elia, J. P. (1994). Homophobia in the high school: A problem in need of a resolution. *The High School Journal: The Gay Teenager* (University of North Carolina, School of Education), *77*(1 & 2), 177-185.

Fabian, L. J., & Thompson, J. K. (1989). Body image and eating disturbance in young females. *International Journal of Eating Disorders, 8*(1), 63-74.

Fine, M., & MacPherson, P. (1993). Gender at work among adolescents and adults. In S. K. Biklen & D. Pollard (Eds.), *Gender and education: Ninety-second yearbook of the National Society for the Study of Education* (pp. 126-154). Chicago: University of Chicago Press.

Friend, R. A. (1993). Choices, not closets: Heterosexism and homophobia in schools. In L. Weis & M. Fine (Eds.), *Beyond silenced voices: Class, race, and gender in United States schools* (pp. 209-235). Albany: State University of New York Press.

Governor's Commission on Gay and Lesbian Youth. (1993). *Making schools safe for gay and lesbian youth: Breaking the silence in schools and in families.* Education Report. Boston, MA.

Herdt, G. (1989). Introduction: Gay and lesbian youth, emergent identities, and cultural scenes at home and abroad. *Journal of Homosexuality, 17*(1/2), 1-42.

Herek, G. M., & Berrill, K. T. (Eds.). (1992). *Hate crimes: Confronting violence against lesbians and gay men.* Newbury Park, CA: Sage.

Hetrick, E. S., & Martin, A. D. (1987). The stigmatization of the gay and lesbian adolescent. *Journal of Homosexuality, 15*(1/2), 163-183.

Hunter, J., & Schaecher, R. (1987, Spring). Stresses on lesbian and gay adolescents in schools. *Social Work in Education, 9*(3), 180-189.

Ianni, F. A. J. (1989). Providing structure for adolescent development. *Phi Delta Kappan,* (70), 673-682.

Irvine, J. M. (1994). Cultural differences and adolescent sexualities. In J. M. Irvine (Ed.), *Sexual cultures and the construction of adolescent sexualities* (pp. 3-28). Philadelphia: Temple University Press.

Kimmel, M. S. (1994). Masculinity as homophobia. In H. Brod & M. Kaufman (Eds.), *Theorizing masculinities* (pp. 119-141). Thousand Oaks, CA: Sage.

Koegel, R. (1994, March). Healing the wounds of masculinity. *Holistic Education Review,* pp. 1-9.

Lorde, A. (1984). *Sister outsider.* Freedom, CA: Crossing Press.

Mandel, L. S. (1996). *Heterosexism, sexual harassment, and adolescent gender identity: A social and sexual curriculum in junior high school.* Unpublished doctoral dissertation, Hofstra University, New York.

McManus, M. C., Asher, G., Bloodworth, R., Chambers, J., Fulmer, S., Goldberg, E., Hinds, E. A., Holloway, M. S., & Stutesman, D. (1991). *Oregon's sexual minority youth: An at-risk population.* Lesbian, gay and bisexual youth. Portland, OR: Task Force on Sexual Minority Youth.

Mee, C. S. (1995, March). Middle school voices on gender identity. *Women's Educational Equity Act Publishing Center Digest,* pp. 1-2, 5-6.

Ornstein, P. (and the American Association of University Women). (1994). *Schoolgirls: Young women, self esteem, and the confidence gap.* Garden City, NY: Doubleday.

Pharr, S. (1992). Homophobia as a weapon of sexism. In P. S. Rothenberg (Ed.), *Race, class, & gender in the United States: An integrated study* (pp. 431-440). New York: St. Martin's.

Pipher, M. (1994). *Reviving Ophelia: Saving the selves of adolescent girls.* New York: Ballantine.

Rich, A. (1980). Compulsory heterosexuality and lesbian existence. *Signs: Journal of Women in Culture and Society, 5,* 631-660.

Riley, L. (1993). *"My Worst Nightmare . . . " Wisconsin students' perceptions of being the other gender: A statewide study to document current gender perceptions of Wisconsin students.* Menomonie, WI: Center for Vocational, Technical and Adult Education.

Sadker M., & Sadker, D. (1994). *Failing at fairness: How America's schools cheat girls.* New York: Macmillan.

Savin-Williams, R. C., & Rodriquez, R. G. (1993). A developmental, clinical perspective on lesbian, gay male, and bisexual youths. In T. P. Gullota, G. R. Adams, & R. Montemayor (Eds.), *Adolescent sexuality* (pp. 77-102). Newbury Park, CA: Sage.

Sears, J. T. (1992a). Dilemmas and possibilities of sexuality education: Reproducing the body politic. In J. T. Sears (Ed.), *Sexuality and the curriculum: The politics and practices of sexuality education* (pp. 7-33). New York: Teachers College Press.

Sears, J. T. (1992b). The impact of culture and ideology on the construction of gender and sexual identities: Developing a critically based sexuality curriculum. In J. T. Sears (Ed.), *Sexuality and the curriculum: The politics and practices of sexuality education* (pp. 139-156). New York: Teachers College Press.

Seattle Commission on Adolescent Youth. (1989). Report on gay and lesbian youth in Seattle. *Guide Magazine,* pp. 15-25.

Shakeshaft, C., Barber, E., Hergenrother, M. A., Johnson, Y., Mandel, L., & Sawyer, J. (1995). Peer harassment in schools. In J. L. Curcio & P. F. First (Eds.), *Journal for a just and caring education* (pp. 30-44). Thousand Oaks, CA: Corwin Press.

Shakeshaft, C., Barber, E., Hergenrother, M. A., Johnson, Y., Mandel, L., & Sawyer, J. (1997, October). Boys call me cow. *Educational Leadership, 55*(2), 22-25.

Simon, R. W., Eder, D., & Evans, C. (1992). The development of feeling norms underlying romantic love among adolescent females. *Social Psychology Quarterly, 55*(1), 29-46.

Stein, N. (1995). Sexual harassment in schools: The public performance of gendered violence. *Harvard Educational Review, 65*(2), 145-162.

Thorne, B. (1994). *Gender play: Girls and boys in school.* New Brunswick, NJ: Rutgers University Press.

5

Textbooks, Knowledge, and Masculinity

Examining Patriarchy From Within

JEFFREY J. KUZMIC

What will be maintained throughout this chapter is that while textbooks may appear to be (indeed they are) more representative and inclusive of women, the construction of curricular knowledge continues to define masculinity in ways that support and reproduce patriarchy. The curriculum more generally, and textbooks in particular, of course, do not determine what is taught and learned in/through schools in and of themselves. However, their failure to provide a curricular foundation for examining the significance of gender, the gender order, or the power of men over women leaves an opportunity to question the orientation of the school, the curriculum, and indeed patriarchy, unexamined.

This chapter, then, seeks to examine the relationship between curricular manifestations of masculinity and the construction and reproduction of patriarchy in/through high school history textbooks. Specifically, this chapter provides a framework for examining how textbooks, as curricular and cultural texts, construct and define masculinity in particular ways. The focus for such an analysis is embedded in concerns for the ways in which schools serve as social, political, and cultural sites where patriarchy is not only manifested and maintained, but may also be contested. Toward this end, the chapter is organized around two interrelated sections. The focus of the first section takes up the relationship among patriarchy, masculinity, and schooling. The second section, drawing on the previous section, examines how masculinity is portrayed and constructed in a selected group of high school history textbooks.

Schooling, Textbooks, and Patriarchy: Why Study Masculinity?

> Yet textbooks are surely important in and of themselves. They signify—particularly through their content and form—particular constructions of reality, particular ways of selecting and organizing that vast universe of possible knowledge. (Apple & Christian-Smith, 1991, p. 3)

Reading and deconstructing high school United States history textbooks from the perspective of masculinity involves an examination of the portrayal of men in/as history in a way that seeks to illuminate gender as a socially constructed pattern of practices and relationships. From the perspective of masculinity, history can be viewed as an interpretive account of men by men in the sense that it is both a reflection and a product of patriarchy. The social studies curriculum, as represented in United States history textbooks, can be viewed as a cultural terrain where patriarchy is both produced and reproduced through schooling.

At the core of my analysis are a number of fundamental assumptions about the centrality of gender as a social, political, cultural, and educational construct. First among these is the need to understand social reality as the complicated interaction between structural/material conditions and human agency. Second, central to this is the recognition that social reality, as currently constructed (or as constructed in the past), is characterized by a complex set of historically situated social, political, cultural, material, and institutional practices that privilege particular groups over others. Third, while these inequities are in themselves complex and interrelated, cutting across, through, and against class, race, and gender divisions, one of the central and most conspicuous of these is the privileged position of men in society. Feminist scholarship and the women's movement have illuminated these inequities and sought redress through both political action and theoretical analysis. Fourth, the perspective taken here acknowledges that the role of men, in seeking to support these political and theoretical developments, is not unproblematic. However, while problematic, given men's privileged position in public and scholarly discourse, it is important that men not only support such efforts, but engage in the political and theoretical struggle to decenter men and masculinity. Finally, it is important to note at the outset, as feminist theory has pointed out through its analysis of women's experience, that the relationship between masculinity and patriarchy is not just about men, but about the juxtaposition of men in relation to women, of how men's power relative to women is constructed, negotiated, and maintained. The social construction of gender, of masculinity and femininity, is not about men or women in isolation, but the way in which inequality is structured to privilege men over women. This chapter seeks to examine the ways in which the curricular knowledge embedded in textbooks reflects particular constructions of reality and particular constructions of femininity and masculinity.

Schooling, Patriarchy, and Masculinity

As Connell (1996) suggests, schools do serve as "sites" where the social construction of masculinity gets played out. As such, the role of schools can be examined in two primary ways: as *agents* of the process where the structures and practices of schooling serve to define masculinity for students and teachers and as the *setting* where other agencies are in play, particularly the agency of students and teachers. By focusing on curricular issues, specifically the representation and production of masculinity in social studies/history[1] textbooks, the emphasis here is on schools as agents. This is neither to deny nor to devalue the importance of schools as settings where teachers and students act as critical agents in the construction of masculinities and patriarchies (e.g., Connell, 1987; Fine, Weis, Addleston, & Matusza, 1997; Kessler, Ashenden, Connell, & Dowsett, 1985; Mac an Ghaill, 1994), but only to acknowledge the scope of this chapter.

Equally as important is the need to recognize, examine, and interrogate how schools contribute to the construction of masculinity in relation to modern constructions of patriarchy. As Hearn (1992) suggests, "Patriarchy isn't reducible to one societal system or process; instead there are effectively lots of patriarchies, dominated by different types of men, operating simultaneously, overlapping, interrelating, contradicting" (p. 3). An additional characteristic of these patriarchies is that they have changed their fundamental character over the past century, moving from private or family patriarchy to a form of patriarchy now dominant and characterized as public or social patriarchy (Ehrenreich, 1995; Hearn, 1992). Inherent in the definitions, practices, and understandings of such public patriarchies are the institutionalization of men's privileged role in society, the development of gendered identities (both male and female), and what Connell (1995) has referred to as gender regimes. This chapter takes up how and in what ways schools in general and the high school social studies curriculum in particular serve as one possible site where these patriarchies are produced, negotiated, and, potentially, contested.

Patriarchy, Masculinity, and Textbooks

Emerging from the same social and historical dynamic that has informed the scholarship on gender, race, class, and, more recently, masculinity, the past 10 to 15 years have witnessed a large number of critiques of the social studies curriculum and textbooks. Because of the dominance of textbooks not only as curricular tools, but as the foundation for much of the instructional practice in high school social studies classrooms (Cole & Sticht, 1981; Goldstein, 1978), these critiques have served as a foundation for rethinking the nature of what is taught and learned. Many of the critiques of high school history textbooks and curriculum have approached the task from the perspective of what's missing or misrepresented, focusing on issues of gender (Bloom & Ochoa, 1996; Christian-Smith, 1991; Sleeter & Grant, 1991; Tetreault, 1987; Zinn, 1994), race (Loewen, 1995; Sleeter & Grant, 1991; Zinn, 1994), and class (Loewen, 1995; Marshall, 1991; Zinn, 1994). The impact of these critiques, while not completely tangible, suggests several things. First, the social studies curriculum—and textbooks as the primary way in which this is expressed and put into practice—is contested terrain influenced in part by larger social and political struggles. The conflicts surrounding national "standards," for example, reflect this struggle (Ross, 1997). Second, the emergence of these critiques has had little impact at the level of classroom practice (Loewen, 1995). Third, despite efforts to be more inclusive of ideas, groups, and individuals consistently absent from American history textbooks, the curricular knowledge and ideological focus of textbooks remains little changed.[2]

The starting point for the following analysis of high school history textbooks, building on the above critiques, seeks to explore what's left in as opposed to what's left out. The analyses mentioned above have contributed a great deal to our understanding of the relationship between the social construction of curricular knowledge, power, and practice, and the gendered, raced, and classed landscape of textbooks. Still, there has been little attention focused on how an examination of masculinities might contribute to an understanding of curricula as agents in the creation of public spaces where the social construction of patriarchy is played out.

Hegemony, Knowledge, and Power: Masculinity (and Patriarchy) in Textbooks

In the remaining portion of this chapter I provide an analysis of how masculinity is represented in selected textbooks:[3] *The Americans* (TA), *Triumph of the American Nation* (TAN), *A History of the United States* (HUS), *A Proud Nation* (PN), and *The American People* (AP). In order to analyze the textbooks, I draw from four theoretical perspectives that give insight into the complexity of masculinity and how this is played out within the context of curricular knowledge. The first of these examines what Kimmel (1996) and Hanke (1992) have referred to as the invisibility of men and masculinity within social, historical, scientific, and cultural narratives. The second theme explores the subtle and complex ways in which masculinity is defined and how particular representations of masculinity are privileged, what Connell (1996) refers to as "hegemonic masculinity." The third centers around the construct of power itself and how notions of "power over" as opposed to "power with" (Kreisberg, 1992) serve to differentiate and privilege constructions of masculinity and men in the historical narratives. The fourth addresses the construction of masculinity within the public sphere, a theme taken up by both feminist theory (Elshtain, 1981) and studies of masculinity (Hearn, 1992).

The Invisibility of Men, Masculinity, and Patriarchy

"Masculinity," like "whiteness" does not appear to be a cultural/historical category at all, thus rendering invisible the privileged position from which (white) men in general are able to articulate their interests to the exclusion of the interests of women, men and women of color, and children. (Hanke, 1992, p. 186)

The invisibility of masculinity referred to by Hanke also speaks to the ways in which masculinity, and therefore patriarchy, as a socially constructed system of power and gender relationships, is ignored within the historical narrative of middle and high school history textbooks. This is not surprising given the conservative and conserving function of the curriculum more generally and textbooks specifically (Apple & Christian-Smith, 1991). Keeping masculinity and patriarchy invisible in textbooks supports this conserving function.[4]

Kimmel (1996), in the introduction to his *Manhood in America,* acknowledges that American men—as men—have no history. Men and masculinity are made invisible, ironically, through the visibility of women as marginalized characters in history. One way that the textbooks I analyzed kept men, masculinity, and patriarchy invisible was not to "name" them as conceptual categories. An example of this is readily visible in all of the indexes of the textbooks examined. In none of the indexes for these books were the terms *masculinity, men,* or *patriarchy* mentioned. However, in each of the six textbooks there was a separate heading for "women." In one of the texts, TAN, there was a separate heading for feminism, and it was mentioned as a subheading under women in TA. In addition, each of the texts had a separate heading for "the Women's Rights Movement" or "women's suffrage." Under the general heading of women, there were a variety of subheadings, the most common of which were the following: in abolitionist movements, as business leaders, in the Civil War, education of, employment, health reform, in the labor movement, social work, suffrage for, World War I, and World War II. In the most recent text, TA, subheadings direct more of a political nod to the impact of feminism with areas such as: in America, historical theme of, political office, political power, in public life, and social activism. In the best light, the former could be viewed as a means of more inclusively acknowledging the contributions of women within the context of American history. The latter, particularly in light of its inclusion in the most recent text, could be viewed as an acknowledgment of the significance of women as a political force in the shaping of the historical and political fabric of society and illustrative of the impact of the modern women's movement and feminism on social and curricular discourse. This, however, is illusionary, even misleading. An analysis of these indexes shows that women must be named as women, whereas men do not have to be named as men. While the "naming" of women suggests the need to acknowledge a previously oppressed or disenfranchised group, the lack of categories for naming men as well as the social and political processes responsible for this suggests the invisibility not only of patriarchy, but of men and masculinity.

Just as these books' indexes tell us what needs to be made visible and what is best left invisible, book introductions can do the same. In *The Americans* (1998), "Women in America" is included as one of the stated "themes of United States history" found in the introduction to the book. Other themes—"The American Dream," "Science and Technology," "Economic Opportunity," "Cultural Diversity," "Immigration and Migration," "Constitutional Concerns," "Expanding Democracy," and "Civil Rights"—have no reference to gender, masculinity, or femininity. TA (1998) explains why the recognition of women is important in the following manner:

Half of all Americans are women. But only recently have their contributions and concerns found their way into history books. American women have helped shape the social and political history of every era. In their private roles as wives and mothers, they have strengthened families and raised America's children. In their more public roles as workers, reformers, and crusaders for equal rights, they have attacked the nation's worst social ills and challenged barriers to women's full participation in American life. (p. xxxii)

As Tetreault (1987) suggests, acknowledgments such as the above may represent a movement from "male-defined" history to "contribution" history, where the absence of women is noted (but still essentialized), or to "bifocal" history, where human experience is conceptualized primarily in dualist categories: male/female, public/private, and agency/communion. Once again such treatment is misleading. Women's role and place in have to be acknowledged whereas men's are taken for granted. Not only does this mask men and their role as men, it masks patriarchy as well.

Another way in which men are made invisible, even though they carry a greater presence in the historical narrative, is through the individualization of history. Thus, when discussions of men are taken up in all of these texts, for example Abraham Lincoln in TA, the complexity of who he was as a politician, a policymaker, his views on slavery, his speeches, and his relationships with others (mostly male politicians) are dealt with in detail and at multiple points throughout the text. Just in terms of the amount of coverage, men are given a privileged presence in TA: George Washington (mentioned on 27 pages), John Adams (9 pages), John Quincy Adams (6 pages), William Jennings Bryan (9 pages), George Bush (15 pages), Jimmy Carter (12 pages), Bill Clinton (15 pages), Dwight D. Eisenhower (13 pages), Gerald Ford (9 pages), Adolf Hitler (21 pages), Andrew Jackson (19 pages), Thomas Jefferson (22 pages), John Kennedy (16 pages), Abraham Lincoln (19 pages), and Richard M. Nixon (21 pages). While this suggests that more coverage is given to political leaders, specifically presidents, within the context of the argument being made here this also serves as a powerful statement not only about men, but about masculinity. The extensive coverage given to individual men provides a norm for thinking about history as the action of individuals, but not about masculinity. That their significance, their importance, and, indeed, their power as historical actors is somehow embedded in and connected to their gendered identity as men is made invisible through the focus on individual men rather than on the privileged position that men as men occupy.

Whereas men are acknowledged and noted as individuals—for their individual achievements, efforts, and contributions—women bear a collective sameness and identity that serves to deny their individuality, what Tetreault (1984) refers to as "clustering." Women never receive the allotted space given to men, nor are their stories told in a way that provides insight into the complexity of their views or their lives. In TA, for example, under a five-page section titled "Women and Reform," the following topics are dealt with: "Women's Roles in the Mid-1800s," "Women Mobilize for Reform" (with the subheadings: "Women Abolitionists," "Working for Temperance," "Education and Women," and "Women and Health Reform"), and "Women's Rights Movement Emerges." In this section the following women are mentioned: Elizabeth Cady Stanton, Lucretia Mott, Sarah and Angelina Grimke, Lucy Stone, Mary C. Vaughan, Emma Willard, Prudence Crandall, Elizabeth Blackwell, Catherine Beecher, Amelia Bloomer, Margaret Fuller, Isabella Baumfree, and Sojourner Truth. On average, the contributions and impact of these women is covered in two sentences. While this section does seek to acknowledge the importance of women in social reform, making connections between different historical movements (abolitionist, women's suffrage, and women's rights), it does so in a way that collectively depersonalizes (and trivializes) both their contributions and their involvement. This is particularly true when compared to the amount of coverage and the way in which individual men are represented.

By making women visible, men are made even less visible, but more central. It is precisely this invisibility of men and masculinity that serves to perpetuate ideological messages and perspectives that mask patriarchy. Take, for example, the following section on women abolitionists in TA (1998):

Some men supported women's efforts [for abolition]. William Lloyd Garrison, for example, voluntarily joined the women who had been denied participation in the World's Anti-Slavery Convention in 1840. Garrison said, "After battling so many long years for the liberties of African slaves, I can not take part in a convention that strikes down the most sacred rights of all women." Many men, however, denounced the female abolitionists. The Massachusetts clergy criticized the Grimke sisters for assuming "the place and tone of man as public reformers."

Opposition only served to make women reformers more determined. The abolitionist cause became a powerful spur to other reform causes, as well as the women's rights movement. In the 1840s, Lucy Stone, who retained her own name when she was married, became the first female abolitionist speaker to give lectures solely devoted to the problem of women's rights. (p. 236)

This section conveys how women are used as contextual filler. Even here, under a section on women abolitionists, a man, William Lloyd Garrison, is not only centrally located textually, but given a moral position and a "voice" that is denied the Grimke sisters or Lucy Stone. It also represents a missed opportunity to explore the reasons or possibilities for men's resistance; a place where "patriarchy" could have been named, even included in the index, and thus acknowledged. Rather, what seems important here is that when there is a positive male presence it is as a man, an individual. Garrison is pictured in a positive light (a role we now approve of); in this context he demonstrates a heightened sensitivity to women's activism. As an individual, when we see him he does good, but the role of patriarchy is made invisible in sentences such as: "Many men however, denounced the female abolitionists" and "Opposition only served to make women reformers more determined." Masculinity is defined through individuals in a positive light, while patriarchy is not, indeed cannot, be named.

TA is also interesting in that it spends a significant amount of space (nine chapters) discussing recent history (post-World War II). In the section of Chapter 31, "An Era of Social Change," the subsection, "Women Fight for Equality" is covered in five pages focusing primarily on the Equal Rights Amendment. Sections such as this could be taken as what Apple and Christian-Smith (1991) call "progressive echoes." Such echoes represent a curricular victory in the politics of official knowledge and representation. These point to the contradictory character of knowledge as constructed in textbooks and, for Apple and Christian-Smith, create possibilities for challenging the dominant ideological tenor of textbook knowledge. However, while this seems promising at first, both the content and its ideological character serve to neutralize any critical discussion of gender politics. Once again, following the line of argument here, women are provided with a collective rather than an individual identity. Indeed, the text "names" three women of significance: Betty Friedan, Gloria Steinem, and Phyllis Schlafly. While these texts provide individual identities and a fairly complex understanding of prominent men (at least those mentioned in the text), women are merely mentioned. Betty Friedan is noted for being one of several women who created the National Organization for Women; Gloria Steinem for the creation of the National Women's Political Caucus and *Ms.* magazine; and Phyllis Schlafly as the national chairman of the Stop-ERA campaign. Political differences aside, each of these women is connected to a larger group or association. In seeking to address the women's movement and the fight for equality (an admirable goal), the text limits the discussion to women. While noting the increased number of women entering the workforce from the 1950s through the 1990s and the income disparities between men and women, "the glass ceiling," and the lack of opportunities for women in education, employment, and politics, the text "mentions" the existence of inequity based on gender. Still, by emphasizing the changes that have occurred—less of a income disparity, more opportunities in education, employment, and politics—this text leaves the reader with the feeling the struggle was not only a success, but that it is over. By focusing on women, the power men have in society, the power men have over women, is lost in a haze of information that masks not only patriarchy, but the privileged status of men and masculinity. Without such a context, the significance of the women's movement itself, feminism, and the persistence of patriarchy remain hidden. In itself, such limited representations of women in history suggest an ideological position that seeks to marginalize rather than meaningfully integrate. When seen in a relational politics of representation, men and masculinity can only be viewed as coming out on top in these textbooks.

Hegemonic Masculinity, Patriarchy, and the Legacy of Columbus

> What counts as knowledge, that is public knowledge, is so bound up with men, and men's public power, that it is necessary to deconstruct "men," "public men," and "men's power." (Hearn, 1992, p. 5)

The history and social studies curriculum in schools reflects the concerns of Hearn. As the previous section demonstrated, masculinity is not only implicit in the curricular knowledge of textbooks, but made invisible. Investigating the taken-for-granted malestream requires that masculinity be explored as a material and social process; as the relationships through which men develop and negotiate their gendered identities and lives. This section seeks to examine the ways in which masculinity, even though invisible, is defined and constructed. Because of the complex ways in which gender is negotiated and embedded in social practices and institutions, it is important to recognize that there is no one masculinity, but rather socially constructed masculinities (Connell, 1995; Hearn, 1992).

Connell (1995) uses the constructs of hegemonic, conservative, and subordinate masculinities in capturing these complexities. Connell asserts that hegemonic masculinity can be defined as "the configuration of gender practice which embodies the currently accepted answer to the problem of the legitimacy of patriarchy, which guarantees (or is taken to guarantee) the dominant position of men and the subordination of women" (1995, p. 77). For Connell, this means that hegemonic masculinity maintains a privileged existence while other forms are marginalized. Therefore, hegemonic masculinity needs to be understood not only in relation to other masculinities (conservative and subordinate), but in relation to the gender order as a whole; it is an expression of the privilege men collectively have over women as a whole.

I want to argue in this section that masculinity, while absent from the texts themselves in terms of overt curricular content, is present as a primer on hegemonic masculinity. In other words, what is not directly stated, but embedded in the ideological character of these texts, is a historical record of hegemonic masculinity that serves as a curricular foundation for not only reproducing and validating hegemonic masculinity, but that mediates against resistance and challenges to it. The historical account of Columbus, as a man, is the first encountered by students through textbooks and is therefore a significant introduction to the ideological construction of masculinity. Second, the portrayal of Columbus illustrates, initially for students, and ideally for my purposes here, the herofication of history (Loewen, 1995). Such a process illustrates how the complexity of historical events tends to be defined in and through a single individual (with few exceptions, white men) and, as such, makes history appear to be the accomplishment of selected individuals (again, mostly men) rather than a complex social, political, and cultural interaction among individuals and between groups. It also emphasizes particular characteristics of these individuals viewed as positive (courage, leadership, the ability to overcome adversity, vision, and commitment), while downplaying or neglecting altogether characteristics viewed as negative (greed, selfishness, ruthlessness, arrogance, dependency on others, violence, and control). This serves, then, not only to privilege men in the historical record, but to define masculinity in particular ways.

While each of the textbooks examined spends some time discussing the "first Americans" or the pre-Columbian indigenous population, the historical narrative, the defining of history in/through men and the ideological character of masculinity of these textbooks, could be said to begin with Columbus. Columbus, along with other early explorers, is the primary focus for what in more enlightened texts (TA) is described as the "meeting of three worlds" and in other texts as "exploring the Americas" (TAN) and "the making of the Americas" (HUS). While TA addresses many of Loewen's (1995) concerns in his critique of textbooks' treatment of Columbus, the meeting of three worlds is still contextualized around the date associated with Christopher Columbus in section titles: "Native American Societies around 1492," "West African Societies Around 1492," and "European Societies Around 1492." It is important to understand these discussions of Columbus and their portrayal of hegemonic masculinity by beginning with the end—that is, by beginning with those statements in the textbook that summarize the impact of Columbus. In TA (1998), for instance, this is captured in the following manner:

> Neither Columbus nor anyone else could have foreseen the long chain of events that his voyages set in motion. In time, settlers from England and other European countries would transplant their cultures to the colonies in North America. From within these colonies a new nation would emerge a new society—and a new nation—based on the ideas of representative government and religious tolerance.
>
> The story of the United States of America thus begins with a meeting of peoples and cultures that radically transformed the North American, African, and European worlds. The upheaval threw unfamiliar peoples and customs together on a grand scale. The Europeans would impose their ways on North America, but never completely. Their need to borrow from the peoples they sought to dominate proved too strong. Furthermore, the Native Americans and Africans resisted giving up their cultural identities. The new nation that emerged would bear the touch of these three worlds, as well as others, in a distinctly multicultural society. Throughout the history of the United States, this multiculturalism would be one of its greatest challenges and also one of its greatest assets. (pp. 32-33)

It is important to recognize at the outset that the story here, even though ostensibly about the "meeting of peoples and cultures," is told through the historical lens of Columbus. Indeed, these paragraphs come only at the end of the seven-page section on Columbus. While this personalization of history is designed to create a more interesting and engaging story (Loewen, 1995), it also represents how history has come to be told through individuals. In so doing, even though he is supposedly only used as a vehicle, history inextricably becomes linked to "a" man. This inverting of history, using individuals to tell history, rather than focusing on the significance of history—in this case, the collision of three worlds, peoples, and cultures—gets us to focus on the individual, not the significance of history. To the extent that this is repeated throughout the one thousand plus pages in TA, and that the overwhelming majority of these individuals are men, not only contributes to a privileging of men in history, but of men as history.

As a man, Columbus is not portrayed in TA as only a heroic explorer who died "a poor, lonely, heartbroken man" not "knowing that his explorations would, in time, have more influence on Europe than all the riches of Asia" (TAN, 1990, p. 12). Rather, TA seeks to present in its seven pages of coverage of Columbus his impact on a wider scale, discussing his relations with (but not his brutality toward) the indigenous population, the beginnings of and Columbus's efforts at colonization and slavery, the effects of disease, and the long-term impact on Europeans (the Columbian Exchange). Even though such portrayals depict a more complex picture of Columbus the man, they also serve to decontextualize and mystify the larger social, cultural, and historical influences. And since we are portraying an individual, a hero, even if he is a hero with a dark side, it is difficult to take a critique of Columbus too far. In the end, Columbus remains a true hero, even if brought a little closer to the rest of us. What stands out are his courage, conviction, and determination and his contribution to the development of a new nation and our heritage of democracy and multiculturalism. This is the picture of hegemonic masculinity portrayed in textbooks, not his brutality, his legacy of genocide, cruelty, and slavery. In focusing on a man rather than on men (and women), in focusing on the outcome of his activities decontextualized from the context in which these took place, Columbus, in spite of his flaws and mistakes, becomes a hero, and masculinity is located in the characteristics that define his positive contributions, rather than his negative traits.

In this sense, high school history textbooks can be seen as texts on and a portrait of hegemonic masculinity. Given the dominance of textbooks and their singular presence in the curriculum and classroom practice, they assert a powerful (if hidden) statement about who men are and what they do. To the extent that these texts, as curricular manifestations of masculinity, remain unquestioned as cultural texts, they construct and reproduce hegemonic masculinity and, therefore, patriarchy.

What history textbooks do, without the historical, cultural, and gendered critique offered by Connell and Kimmell, is to reproduce the historical evolution of hegemonic masculinity. In doing so, modern conceptualizations of hegemonic masculinity are provided with a historical and ideological, if unexamined, justification. In other words, through the uncritical (or, if critical, superficial and decontextualized) experiences of early explorers like Columbus, Cortes, and Ponce de Leon, the stage is set for defining masculinity (through the actions of these men) as the ability to take action, to justify the imposition of their (or others') will on "the Other," to act bravely, to exercise power, and to situate men in the public sphere.

Seeing textbooks and the curriculum as a site where hegemonic masculinity, as the culturally dominant form of masculinity, gets played out involves a reading of the subtext of textbooks as cultural texts. This involves looking at the ways in which men (and women) are defined and portrayed not only as political actors and historical figures, but the ways in which their motivations, both public and private, are embedded in gendered identities. Exploring the relationship between masculinity and patriarchy, as Kimmell suggests, would seem to require two things: to chart how the definition of masculinity has changed over time and to explore how the experience of manhood has shaped the activities of American men. Neither of these would seem to be present within the historical narrative present in these textbooks.

Power as Power Over

> If authority is defined as legitimate power, then we can say that the main axis of the power structure of gender is the general connection of authority with masculinity. (Connell, 1987, p. 109)

Central to the definition and the very existence of patriarchy is the notion of power. It is clear from much of the literature on masculinity that the use and experiences of power by men, as well as men's relationship to power, is problematic (Connell, 1987, 1995; Seidler, 1991, 1994). The issue of power and how it is defined and justified is central to understanding the hegemonic character of masculinity as defined in high school history textbooks. If, as suggested in the previous sections, textbooks make men invisible and reify hegemonic masculinity, then power must also play a central role in defining what it means to be a man and be foundational to how men are portrayed. Quite simply, to be a man is to posses and exercise power. But what does this mean with regard to masculinity? Seth Kreisberg (1992), in his analysis of power, notes the nonmonolithic character of power, recognizing that power can be understood in terms of relationships in multiple ways. Central to his account is the distinction between notions of "power over" and "power with" (Follett, 1924, 1942; Starhawk, 1987). For Kreisberg, the dominant (read socially predominant and accepted definition) of power is "power over" rather than "power with." Power over is something that is done to others and is embedded in a configuration of unequal relations between those who hold power and those who don't.

> Power is embedded in images of the father, the teacher, the political leader, the policeman, the soldier, and the businessman. In a world of domination and subordination, the ability to control others, for men in particular, is seen as an archetypical expression of identity, a confirmation of meaningful existence. It not only says "I am," but "I am on top," "I am special," "I have power." (Kreisberg, 1992, pp. 46-47)

One of the primary ways in which masculinity gets defined through prominent individuals in textbooks has to do with power, and because this is about their power as individuals—to "discover" a new world (Columbus), to create a new nation (Washington), to end slavery (Lincoln), to create social policy and declare war (Franklin Roosevelt)—this tends to privilege a particular conceptualization of power: power over, rather than power with. While older texts tend to portray power in a primarily patriotic context and in a positive light, TA, for example, provides a more complex notion of power over, one that is not always viewed in a positive light. Such is the case when discussing Columbus and his interactions with indigenous populations, Woodrow Wilson and his lack of commitment to civil rights, or Richard Nixon and Watergate:

> The effects of Watergate have endured long after Nixon's resignation. Along with the divisive war in Vietnam, Watergate produced deep disillusionment with the "imperial" presidency. A poll taken in 1974 showed that 43 percent of Americans had "hardly any" faith in the executive branch of government. In the years following Vietnam and Watergate, the American public developed a general cynicism about many public officials that still exists today. (TA, 1998, p. 957)

However, even though the use of power is not always justified from the standpoint of historical hindsight, this does not necessarily challenge the association among men, masculinity, and power. Men are still the primary lens for history, and masculinity is still defined in terms of the exercise of power, as power over. If such power can have negative as well as positive effects, this is to be viewed as part of human nature. The glorification of this through men and men's lives in the historical narrative of history textbooks not only provides an ideological justification for power as power over, but directly links this to what it means to be a man. The naming of history of/by men carries with it a conception that to be an important historical figure (i.e., a man) is to exercise power over; to create, to change, to make happen, and to control. Men do things, and what they do is to wield power to make things happen. This is the true significance here: Masculinity as defined in and through the activities of historical figures is about the exercise and use of power over.

Defining Public and Private Spheres: Reifying Patriarchy

In textbooks I examined, men seem to be neither limited by nor characterized by a gendered identity, an identity that influences what they do, what they value, what they are motivated to accomplish. They are given an identity that is defined, in part, by the public sphere. Men are not identified primarily as gendered beings and therefore do not succumb to the "limitations" of their individual experiences as a man. Men are not portrayed as gendered creatures: They are rational beings. Our image and understanding of them is defined in terms of their presence and significance as public figures. This is in sharp contrast to the dominant representations of women as gendered beings whose actions and motivations are always reduced to a narrowly defined essentialized femininity always connected to the private sphere, what Connell (1987) has referred to as "emphasized femininity." By dichotomizing private and public spheres associated with gendered identities, patriarchy remains solidly unacknowledged and unchallenged.

A good example of how men's and women's roles and identities are defined in the public and private spheres is found in TA (1998) in a chapter titled "Workers of the Nation Unite." Focusing on the labor movement, this chapter examines the exploitation of workers, the emerging solidarity and militancy of unions, and strikes by workers and the government's response to these. In the middle of the chapter are found two side boxes positioned next to each other noting "key players" in the labor movement: Eugene Debs and "Mother" Jones.

The chapter acknowledges the labor movement in general, and two individuals specifically who struggled on its behalf, in ways not previously acknowledged by earlier texts. Indeed, the positioning of Mother Jones alongside Eugene Debs even suggests a certain equality. Still, the narratives themselves suggest not only different motivations, but different locations from which these individuals struggled; situating Debs clearly within the public sphere through his political activities and Jones in the private sphere, the motivation for her being maternally linked to and defined in ways that emphasize her role as mother and wife. Hearn (1992)

Eugene V. Debs
1855-1926

Eugene V. Debs realized his true calling while he was in prison following the Pullman strike in 1894. The failure of the strike and Debs's disillusionment with the conditions of workers under capitalism turned him into a fervent socialist. He became a spokesperson for the Socialist Party of America and was its candidate for president five times. In 1912, he won 900,000 votes—an amazing six percent of the totals. "I say now," Debs vowed, "that while there is a lower class, I am in it; while there is a criminal element, I am of it; while there is a soul in prison, I am not free."

"Mother" Jones
1830-1930

Mary Harris "Mother" Jones–born in Ireland and raised in Canada—became a leading figure in the American labor movement after husband and children died of yellow fever in 1867. According to a reporter who followed "the mother of the laboring class" on her children's march in 1903, "She fights their battles with a Mother's Love—and she continued fighting them until her death at age 100." Maternal as she was, Mother Jones was definitely not the kind of woman admired by John D. Rockefeller and other industrialists: "God almighty made woman," she protested, "and the Rockefeller gang of thieves made ladies." (*The Americans,* 1998, p. 432)

suggests that the dominant tradition in the social sciences on the relation between public and private domains is an unquestioned naturalism where public and private are viewed as separate, dichotomized realms. In particular, political and social philosophy have reinforced this through the dualistic distinctions between passion and reason, knowledge and desire, and mind and body. The paralleling of Debs and Jones reinforces such distinctions, clearly associating Debs with the public sphere, emphasizing his activism, sense of conviction, political ambitions, and his struggle for the disenfranchised. "Mother" Jones, as her nickname implies, is directly situated within the private sphere, focusing on her role as mother and wife, entering the labor movement after her husband and children died, and characterizing her role in the public sphere in terms of her maternal experiences. As suggested in previous sections of this chapter, political life, men, and the public sphere are closely associated and dominate the historical narrative of these textbooks. Defining the public life of Mother Jones in terms of her identity as a woman, mother, and wife in the private sphere serves to reproduce the significance and importance of men while maintaining the gendered dichotomy between public and private.

If the research and scholarship on masculinity has tried to make the private more public and the public more private through an analysis of men as men, such arguments are lost on the writers of textbooks (mostly men themselves). Consistently throughout the coverage of American history in these textbooks, men remain the primary, if not sole, occupants of the public sphere. Textbooks are about men. If there has been an attempt to incorporate women, the result has been to replace exclusion with marginalization.

If these texts do focus on men and men's activities, what, then, is it that men do? Anyone having attended almost any elementary or secondary school in the United States is aware of the military, political, and economic focus of these texts. Even with the attempts by the contemporary publishing industry (and this includes textbook publishers) to be more inclusive, Connell (1987) concludes that, "The main narrative of the public world—wars, rockets, governments falling, profits rising—carries on as before" (p. 248). And the main narrative in these high school social studies textbooks is about the public world. In addition, it is through men's activities, actions, and character that the public world gets defined.

Conclusions: Contesting Patriarchy

The analysis of textbooks undertaken in this chapter has shown how critical scholarship on men and masculinity can provide a theoretical lens further to deconstruct and challenge patriarchy. The power of patriarchy, as a system of socially constructed meanings about gender identity, lies in its ability to create the ideological conditions that support the institutionalization (social, cultural, political, educational, familial) of a gender regime that privileges men (Connell, 1995). As noted at the outset, critiques of history textbooks and social studies curricula have illuminated their gendered character, and efforts have been made to be more representative and inclusive of women, persons of color, and other marginalized groups. That these changes have provided little in the way of a curricular foundation for examining or critiquing patriarchy seems symbolic of the resiliency and adaptability of patriarchy in the face of such challenges. Textbooks, through the absence of gender as a critical and significant lens through which to view and understand history, the privileging of notions of "power over" rather than "power with," the emphasis on the public sphere over that of the private, and the close linking of these to men and masculinity, serve to make not only men, but patriarchy, invisible.

As noted at the outset, the focus throughout this chapter was to understand how schools serve as agents—in this case, through the structuring of curricular knowledge found in history textbooks—to define masculinity in particular ways for teachers and students. When it comes to contesting patriarchy, the picture painted here is less than positive. However, as noted by Connell (1996), schools also serve as settings where other agencies—particularly those of teachers and students—are at play. While this point is taken up in other chapters throughout this book, this chapter reinforces the need to understand better and more clearly the ways in which teachers and students address issues surrounding men and masculinity in relation to the curriculum; how the curriculum itself might provide a forum about men, masculinity, and patriarchy in light of teaching for equity and justice; and in what ways teacher education and teacher educators might assist prospective teachers in thinking about patriarchy, men, and masculinity with regard to a gendered politics of teaching.

Connell (1995) suggests that schools in general, and the curriculum in particular, are a significant site in the politics of challenging and transforming the gender order, power relations, and men's privilege. Toward this end, Connell suggests, as others have (Apple & Christian-Smith, 1991; Bernard-Powers, 1997; Loewen, 1995; Noddings, 1997; Zinn, 1994), the need for "curricular justice," the organization of knowledge from the point of view of the least advantaged and marginalized, reversing the current social practice of organizing knowledge from the point of view of the privileged. In doing so, he emphasizes that we "not abandon existing knowledge, but reconfigure it, to open up possibilities that current social inequalities conceal" (1995, p. 239). At a more concrete level, the ways in which masculinity is constructed in and through textbooks would suggest the need critically to examine and interrogate gender as a significant lens through which we "read" history. While certainly not the only means through which patriarchy can be contested at a curricular level, this chapter would suggest the need for teachers and students to examine history critically in the light of the role of men as men, the portrayal of masculinity, and their relationship to the perpetuation of patriarchy. If we have sought to be more inclusive and representative of those who have been marginalized, it is also time to be more critical of those who have marginalized and the ways in which they have been able to maintain their power to marginalize.

Notes

1. Technically, the textbooks examined in this chapter are used in history courses, but these are courses that are taught under the rubric of social studies. Social studies as a field of studies within education and as an area of curriculum in elementary, middle, and high school education is in itself contested terrain. Debates surround the discourse in social education over the purpose and practice of social studies, its scope and sequence across the grades, and the balance/integration between the various social sciences and history to be covered in and through the curriculum (e.g., Hertzberg, 1981; Ross, 1997; Saxe, 1991, 1997; Whelan, 1997). The tenor and nature of this discourse is beyond the scope of this chapter; however, I mention it here to acknowledge that while throughout this chapter I refer to the textbooks as history textbooks (not social studies textbooks), this is because of my focus on the texts used in United States history courses.

2. A number of scholars have explored the ways in which the politics of the curriculum is influenced by a variety of formal and informal social institutions; most notably textbook publishers (Apple & Christian-Smith, 1991; Loewen, 1995) and conservative educational and political groups (Aronowitz & Giroux, 1991), but also state and local textbook adoption committees (Fitzgerald, 1979; Loewen, 1995; Marshall, 1991). While such work recognizes the political and ideological dimensions of curricular decisions, focusing on issues of class, race, and gender, such discussions have failed to examine curriculum politics in light of its potential implications for a gender politics that seeks to challenge patriarchy.

3. This should not be viewed as a comprehensive or exhaustive reading or analysis, but rather as a representative critique. The analysis in this chapter has focused primarily on the most recent textbook, seeing it as the most current construction and manifestation of the high school United States history curriculum. The texts selected for this analysis were texts currently in use within middle and high schools in the Chicago metropolitan area and were "loaned" to me by practitioners working with me on a different research project. Loewen (1995) as well as others (i.e., Sleeter & Grant, Apple) have provided extensive critiques of recent high school history textbooks and while these certainly differ by publisher, the relative similarity of these textbooks is one of their most observable features. The texts examined were: *The Americans* (TA), McDougal Littell, 1998; *Triumph of the American Nation* (TAN), Harcourt Brace Jovanovich, 1986; *A History of the United States* (HUS), Ginn, 1981; *A Proud Nation* (PN), McDougal Littell, 1989; and *The American People* (AP), McDougal Littell, 1986.

4. Loewen (1995) points out how textbooks mask or make invisible other important relationships as well: the cultural conflicts surrounding the "discovery of the new world" and early relationships between Europeans and Native Americas, the invisibility of racism and antiracism, the myth of opportunity and the reality of poverty, the disappearance of the recent past, and the lack of critical discussions surrounding the portrayal of the pervasive power of progress and the glorification of government.

References

Apple, M. W., & Christian-Smith, L. K. (1991). The politics of the textbook. In M. W. Apple & L. K. Christian-Smith (Eds.), *The politics of the textbook* (pp. 1-21). New York: Routledge.

Aronowitz, S., & Giroux, H. (1991). Textual authority, culture, and the politics of literacy. In M. Apple & L. Christian-Smith (Eds.), *The politics of the textbook* (pp. 213-241). New York: Routledge.

Bernard-Powers, J. (1997). Gender in social education. In E. Ross (Ed.), *The social studies curriculum: Purposes, problems, and possibilities* (pp. 71-89). Albany: State University of New York Press.

Bloom, L. R., & Ochoa, A. (1996). Responding to gender equity in the social studies curriculum. In R. Allen & B. Massiales (Eds.), *Crucial issues in teaching social studies* (pp. 309-339). Belmont, CA: Wadsworth.

Christian-Smith, L. K. (1991). Texts and high tech: Computers, gender, and book publishing. In M. W. Apple & L. K. Christian-Smith (Eds.), *The politics of the textbook* (pp. 41-55). New York: Routledge.

Cole, J. Y., & Sticht, T. G. (Eds.). (1981). *The textbook in American society*. Washington, DC: Library of Congress.

Connell, R. W. (1987). *Gender and power: Society, the person, and sexual politics*. Stanford, CA: Stanford University Press.

Connell, R. W. (1995). *Masculinities*. Berkeley: University of California Press.

Connell, R. W. (1996). Teaching the boys: New research on masculinity, and gender strategies for schools. *Teachers College Record, 98*(2), 206-235.

Ehrenreich, B. (1995). The decline of patriarchy. In M. Berger, B. Wallis, & S. Watson (Eds.), *Constructing masculinity* (pp. 284-290). New York: Routledge.

Elshtain, J. (1981). *Public man, private woman*. Princeton, NJ: Princeton University Press.

Fine, M., Weis, L., Addleston, J., & Matusza, J. (1997). (In)secure times: Constructing white working-class masculinities in the late 20th century. *Gender & Society, 11*(1), 52-68.

Fitzgerald, F. (1979). *America revised*. New York: Vintage.

Follett, M. P. (1924). *Creative experience*. New York: Longmans, Green.

Follett, M. P. (1942). *Dynamic administration*. New York: Harper & Brothers.

Goldstein, P. (1978). *Changing the American schoolbook*. Lexington, MA: D. C. Heath.

Hanke, R. (1992). Redesigning men: Hegemonic masculinity in transition. In S. Craig (Ed.), *Men, masculinity, and the media* (pp. 185-198). London: Sage.

Hearn, J. (1992). *Men in the public eye*. New York: Routledge.

Hertzberg, H. W. (1981). *Social studies reform 1880-1980*. Boulder, CO: Social Science Consortium.

Kessler, S., Ashenden, D. J., Connell, R. W., & Dowsett, G. W. (1985). Gender relations in secondary schooling. *Sociology of Education, 58*(January), 34-48.

Kimmel, M. (1996). *Manhood in America: A cultural history*. New York: Free Press.

Kreisberg, S. (1992). *Transforming power: Domination, empowerment, and education* (SUNY Series, Teacher Empowerment and School Reform). Albany: State University of New York Press.

Loewen, J. (1995). *Lies my teacher told me: Everything your American history textbook got wrong*. New York: New Press.

Mac an Ghaill, M. (1994). *The making of men: Masculinities, sexualities and schooling*. Philadelphia: Open University Press.

Marshall, J. D. (1991). With a little help from some friends: Publishers, protesters, and Texas textbook decisions. In M. W. Apple & L. K. Christian-Smith (Eds.), *The politics of the textbook* (pp. 56-77). New York: Routledge.

Noddings, N. (1997). Social studies and feminism. In E. Ross (Ed.), *The social studies curriculum: Purposes, problems, and possibilities* (pp. 59-70). Albany: State University of New York Press.

Ross, E. W. (1997). The struggle for the social studies curriculum. In E. W. Ross (Ed.), *The social studies curriculum: Purposes, problems, and possibilities* (pp. 3-20). Albany: State University of New York Press.

Saxe, D. W. (1991). *Social studies in schools: A history of the early years*. Albany: State University of New York Press.

Saxe, D. W. (1997). The unique mission of the social studies. In E. W. Ross (Ed.), *The social studies curriculum: Purposes, problems, and possibilities* (pp. 39-55). Albany: State University of New York Press.

Seidler, V. (1991). *Recreating sexual politics: Men, feminism, and politics*. New York: Routledge.

Seidler, V. (1994). *Unreasonable men: Masculinity and social theory*. New York: Routledge.

Sleeter, C., & Grant, C. (1991). Race, class, gender, and disability in current textbooks. In M. W. Apple & L. K. Christian-Smith (Eds.), *The politics of the textbook* (pp. 78-110). New York: Routledge.

Starhawk. (1987). *Truth or dare*. San Francisco: Harper & Row.

Tetreault, M. K. Thompson. (1984, November/December). Notable American women: The case of United States history textbooks. *Social Education*, pp. 546-550.

Tetreault, M. K. Thompson. (1987, March). Rethinking women, gender, and the social studies. *Social Education*, pp. 170-178.

Whelan, M. (1997). History as the core of social studies education. In E. W. Ross (Ed.), *The social studies curriculum: Purposes, problems, and possibilities* (pp. 21-38). Albany: State University of New York Press.

Zinn, H. (1994). *A people's history of the United States* (2nd ed.). New York: Harper & Row.

6

Peer (Dis)Connections, School, and African American Masculinities

JEREMY N. PRICE

Through those guys, I discovered the strength and solace in camaraderie. It was a confidence booster, a steady support for my fragile self-esteem. Alone, I was afraid of the world and insecure. But I felt cockier and surer of myself when hanging with my boys. I think we all felt more courageous when we hung together. We did things in groups that we'd never try alone. The group also gave me a sense of belonging that I'd never known before. With those guys, I could hide in the crowd and feel like the accepted norm. There was no fear of standing out, feeling vulnerable, exiled, and exposed. There was a comfort even my family couldn't provide.

McCall, 1994, p. 33

McCall (1994) provides a powerful image of the meanings of friendships in *Makes Me Wanna Holler,* his autobiographical account of his life growing up as a black man in the United States. This image lies in stark contrast to many of the representations of African American peer groups and of the role of peer groups in the lives of adolescents.

This chapter takes up the question of meanings of peer relationships in the lives of two working-class African American young men, Jeff Davidson and Marcus Williams, both in tenth grade and attending school. While some attention has been given to the experiences of young black men in schools, in the main, much of this work tends to represent only *some* of the visible strands of *one version* of black masculinity. Seldom explained are the multilayered dimensions of an array of masculinities in relation to the experiences of African American men. Furthermore, there has been little attention given to an examination of the formation of African American masculinities in relation to peer groups in school. This chapter attempts to contribute toward understanding peer relations as sources and influences of connection and alienation in the shaping and reshaping of the racial masculine identities of two young African American men attending school. Drawing from a larger study, I examine the meanings that two working-class young men gave to the relationships they experienced in various peer groups, and how these relationships were simultaneously shaped by their images of themselves as African American men and by their racialized and gendered images of their peers. I situate their meanings within institutional and social practices that seemed to perpetuate racial and gender divisions through privileging some images, representations, and social practices, and subordinating others.

At the outset, I want to note that the stories I share about these two young men's experiences in schools are not intended to reify images of working-class African American men. Rather, the stories provide glimpses of the complexity of individual circumstance of two African American men that allow us to consider these circumstances dynamically in relation to larger social, cultural, and political contexts. In this chapter, I provide a glimpse into one cultural arena: relationships with peers that they experienced and the gendered and racialized meanings that seemed interwoven through these relationships.

Representations of African American Men

Recent discussions about African American men's experiences have suggested that they are placed at risk in society (Gibbs, 1988; Madhubuti, 1990; Staples, 1987) not only because of structural factors such as racism, unemployment, and poverty (Glasgow, 1980; West, 1993a, 1993b; Wilson, 1987), but also because of cultural factors (Franklin, 1984; Oliver, 1988; Staples, 1982, 1986) such as "cool pose" (Majors & Billson, 1992), or what is sometimes referred to as the expressive rage of the African American men, which is often portrayed as "hypermasculinity." Collectively, these accounts contribute toward some of the understandings of African American men's experiences in the United States. However, such accounts tend to represent only *some* of the visible strands of *one version* of black masculinity. Seldom explained are the multilayered dimensions of an *array* of racial masculinities in relation to the experiences of African American men. This issue of representation bears particular significance for teachers, teacher educators, and scholars committed to unraveling and addressing the persistent inequalities that pervade educational institutions and institutions in our larger society. Granted, there have been a few studies that have focused on young black men and their relationship with school; for instance, Mac an Ghaill's (1988) study in England, MacLeod's (1987) study in the United States, and Solomon's (1992) study in Canada each attempted to blend stories of young black men's relationship with school with larger issues of inequality and oppression. Notwithstanding, there are relatively few accounts that reflect the range of experiences of young African American men and their relationship with school, particularly through a race, class, and gender lens.

This issue of representation has been influenced by recent scholarship (Collins, 1990; Connell, 1987; Dill & Baca Zinn, 1990; Harding, 1987; hooks, 1992; Kimmel & Messner, 1992; Marriott, 1996; Smith, 1987; Weis, 1988) that has challenged essential constructs of gender and considered the dynamic ways in which social processes of race, class, and gender are interwoven through experience. Through examining biographies and the complexities of individual experiences in the context of the interconnections of race, gender, and social class we learn how the relations of domination and oppression often lead to the marginalization of some groups and provide "unacknowledged benefits for those who are at the top of these hierarchies—Whites, members of the upper classes, and males. The privileges of those at the top are dependent on the exploitation of those at the bottom" (Baca Zinn & Dill, 1994, p. 5). This work fundamentally challenges universal constructs of masculinity and femininity that have been guided by sex role theory, whereby particular behaviors, attitudes, and attributes are associated with and seen as appropriate for men and others for women, and instead generates lenses that consider relational and oppositional dynamics at play in the making of gendered identities.

Emerging from these discussions has been research (Carrigan, Connell, & Lee, 1985; Connell, 1987, 1995; Kimmel, 1987; Hearn, 1987; Mac an Ghaill, 1994) on men and masculinity that argues there are multiple masculinities where "the meaning of masculinity is neither transhistorical nor culturally universal, but rather varies from culture to culture and within any one culture over time" (Kimmel & Messner, 1992, p. 9). These advances have dramatically influenced constructs of gender and masculinity. As Baron (1994) argues, "studying masculinity transformed the question of sexual difference from asking how women are different from men, to investigating how men are constituted by gender" (p. 150).

Although there has been increasing attention to understanding the gendered identities of men, there has been little focus on understanding the complexity and multidimensional nature of African American youths' lives, particularly in relation to school. Broader studies about African American men have been conducted by Franklin (1991), Hunter and Davis (1994), and Majors and Billson (1992) who, among others, point to the contradictory nature of the emergence of black masculinity, where African American men are seen simultaneously as agents and victims of their destruction. McCall (1994) writes about the hardships facing some African American men:

> Sometimes I get mad at the brothers, especially those hanging idly on street corners, thinking they were bad. At the same time, I understand why they were having such a hard time getting it together. I know why many young brothers, and black people in general, were losing their minds. They look up and see that they're catching hell from the cradle to the grave, and that the whole fucking country is pointing fingers at them and saying it's black people's own fault that they're catching hell. They're beating the pavement, trying to find work, and nobody will hire them, and white folks cite them as examples of people who are trifling and don't want to work. And those blacks who have jobs are catching hell, trying to move up the ladder, like everybody else, and the same white folks who hold them back accuse them of being lazy and unambitious. Times for brothers were getting rougher when it seemed things couldn't get any worse. When I think of all that the brothers have to go through in this country, I am reminded of something I once heard someone say: "If we ain't in hell, we sure see it from here." (p. 362)

McCall's (1994) portrait of the complex circumstance of African American men in the inner city points to the complexities of racial and economic oppression in the shaping of the lives of black men. Franklin (1991) and Staples (1986) note that African American men are visible figures in the United States, yet their lives and everyday experiences are little understood. In particular, Staples (1987) argues that dominant ideas about African American men as "deviant," "socially disorganized," and "sexual" seem to disregard the systemic racism most African American men confront daily. Furthermore, as Roberts (1994) argues, "rarely, if ever, is the issue raised concerning the possibility of healthy and constructive relationships among African American boys and young men" (p. 381).

There have been a growing number of studies that have focused on explanations for emerging masculinities in relation to schooling. For example, Willis's (1977) *Learning to Labor* argued that two patterns of masculinity emerged in his study about the high school experiences of white working-class young men where the "lads" developed an oppositional masculinity that ushered them into jobs in factories, while boys from the same group, the "ear'oles," conformed to the school's requirements and competitive fervor through academic work. In later work, Mac an Ghaill (1988, 1994) showed different kinds of masculinities within race-class groups of young men. These studies significantly point to the construction of different kinds of masculinities—ways of becoming and being men—within social groups in relation to schooling. What is glaringly absent from most studies about schooling is not only a focus on the making of masculinities, but the perspectives of black men themselves. This is particularly notable in relation to youths and their peer groups.

Peer Groups Explored

There have been many approaches to studies about adolescents and the role of peer groups in their lives. In the main, this research has not attended to understanding the gendered or racialized meanings of peer relationships, but rather has situated peer groups and peer pressure in the context of paths to adulthood. Peer groups are framed as generating positive or negative influences in the lives of youths. Not only has research undermined the significance and value of peer groups, but the work has chiefly ignored complex representations of peer groups, particularly historically marginalized youth. Certainly overlooked in this work has been the intersection of race, class, and gender and the ways in which relations of power come to play in the making of peer groups and the *meanings* of these relationships to adolescents. For example, an important study and theoretical perspective that has come to influence understanding of peer culture is that of Coleman (1961), *The Adolescent Society,* who argued that being popular was much more significant to high school students than attaining good grades. This approach, albeit critiqued, had been found to be a pattern in subsequent work (Cusick, 1973; Hammersley & Woods, 1984; Willis, 1977). Adolescents' succumbing to peer pressure is seen as problematic. As Lesko (1996) argues, "The linking of uniformity and conformity among adolescents in relation to strong peer orientation persists in research, with some modifications. This conceptualization established teenagers as dangerous *others,* not as individuating adults" (p. 154). In essence, peer pressure is seen as a fundamental barrier to adolescents' embracing an individualism that is seen as instrumental to becoming successful adults in the larger society. But whose vision of success is embedded in such perspectives? What are the representations of masculinity embedded in such visions?

Absent from many studies about adolescent relationships are not only the range of experiences among various race-class-gender groups, but the variations within particular groups. For example, overwhelmingly, accounts of peer group relationships among African American men have been accounts of the experiences of black men from the inner city, and have not always been conducted in relation to school. Taylor (1991) considered the significance of the peer group and noted that, "For boys, the peer group is the all-important tribunal, in which identity is shaped and validated by the 'brothers' on the streets. . . . In short, 'being cool' involves emotional toughness, even callousness and indifference towards many of the problems people and the adolescent encounters" (p. 151). This image painted by Taylor has been further examined by Majors and Billson (1992), who argue that, "Cool pose gives the black male his greatest sense of pride and masculinity" (p. 34). They build upon Oliver's (1988) notion of "compulsive masculine behavior," and maintain that compulsive masculinity emerges as an alternative to "traditional definitions of manhood, compensating for feelings of shame, powerlessness, and frustration. Being a man becomes redefined in terms that lead to destruction of self and others. Staying cool ensures that destruction remains palatable" (pp. 34-35). Majors and Billson suggest that many young African American men may reject those "brothers" who reject the standards of being "cool." These perspectives situate the making of black masculinity within the context of societal racism and economic oppression and suggest the peer group becomes a refuge.

This image of African Americans presented by Taylor (1991) and Majors and Billson (1992) explains the behavior and cultural patterns of some African American youths. I wonder to what extent these studies may lead to an essentialism of the experiences of young black men. Do all black men adopt a view of black male peer groups as a refuge? Are particular versions of black masculinities and sexualities dominant? Might there be variation among and within social class groups? Franklin (1992) addresses some of these question in his examination of the form of relationships among African American men from different social class positions. He argues that many working-class men engage in close, caring relationships much more frequently than middle-class men:

> when black men accept and begin to display societal definitions of masculinity, many of the traits thought to be essential for the development of close friendships are lost. Basically, what happens is that expectation for these males begins to change. Empathy, compassion, trust, cooperation, and other such traits are eschewed in favor of ones such as aggression, competitiveness, stoicism, rational thinking, and independence. (pp. 209-210)

Franklin (1992) suggests that embrace of a hegemonic white masculinity sees some African American men, particularly "upwardly mobile" black men, suppressing other forms of masculinity. His proposition suggests different forms of masculinity emerging among African American men where social class is influential. His argument is significant for it brings into sharp relief the construction of different forms of masculinity in relation to one another. In my larger study (Price, 1995), I examined the meanings of peer relationships among six black young men from different social class locations who attended different schools and overwhelmingly found that their desire to be connected with *African American* peers was central to the formal and informal networks they associated with. Forging such relationships was not easy and, in most cases, was contradictory. The ways in which the contradictions manifested in these relationships were influenced by a variety of processes, shaped by experiences in and out of school, for high schools are not organized around students' trusted relationships, but rather around meritocratic impulses embedded in and organized through school curriculum. None of the young men talked about forming or sustaining connected relationships in classrooms. All the relationships they valued were ones forged outside of the classroom and, more than often, outside the boundaries of school. These six young men persevered, with varying degrees of success, to sustain their friendships in spite of the disengaging pedagogy that many had to encounter, and in spite of the institutional racism they each confronted. But it wasn't just the structure or nature of the relationship that I was interested in, it was also the very meanings of gender and race that infiltrated their relationships. In this process, the young men were learning about and experiencing different representations of masculinities and femininities, through pedagogical practices, curriculum representations, and other relationships in the school. Thus there became numerous ways in which these six young men interacted with others in various cultural spaces in the school. I learned not only about the similarities and differences in their representations of social identities, but the different ways in which these identities were shifting from context to context, from relationship to relationship. Jeff and Marcus, both working class, both living in the same neighborhood, and who had attended the same school for much of their lives, reveal the complexities of going to school and of the shifting and complex meanings of their masculine identities.

Methodology

My discussion of the lives of Jeff Davidson and Marcus Williams is drawn from a larger study (Price, 1995) in which I examined, over the period from August 1992 to April 1993, the lives of six young African American men of different social class locations, who had decided to stay in school. In this larger study, I focused on different dimensions of school experience through examining the meanings the young men construct of the high school diploma, their relationship with teachers and peers, and the racialized and gendered images of their own and others' identities.

I learned about the young men through interviews that were conversational and relatively unstructured. Also, field notes were kept that documented interview situations. The interviews were conducted outside of the context of school, in places selected by participants because I did not want to be associated with the authority structure of schooling, as I thought it would hinder my opportunities to be open with the young men, and with their willingness to connect with me. My social identity as a white middle-class male in relation to their social identities as young African American men was very much in the forefront of my mind in making this decision. Although, through sharing my history as a white activist in South Africa, I learned that they didn't quite always see me as an "American," they certainly did see me as a white person. They were interested in learning about my involvement in youth, community, and educational organizations and my role as a teacher in a so-called Colored high school, as I worked with others committed to fundamental social change in South Africa. However, while I believe that the initial decision to interview them outside of school and my sharing aspects of my experiences in South Africa certainly lessened the social distance between us (see Andersen, 1993), we were certainly not equal partners in this study in that our differences in age, social class, race, and nationality all were at play in the making of our relationships.

From the various data I began to develop more focused conversations with the young men that attended to the relationships with peers, family members, and teachers. These areas of focus became increasingly important as I learned that while they were committed to acquiring their high school diplomas, it was the day-to-day relationships that seemed significant to them sustaining their commitment to acquire a high school diploma. Furthermore, it was through these relationships that I learned about their meanings of friendships and the intermingling of raced and gendered meanings in their current and previous relationships. This became an important theme in my analysis.

Meanings of School

Jeff Davidson and Marcus Williams were each 17 years old and lived in the same predominantly working-class neighborhood. They attended different schools in Allerton, a medium-sized Midwestern city. Up until tenth grade, they attended the same high school, Central High School, where 46% of the student population at the high school was African American. Jeff moved to another school, Allerton Christian School (ACS), as a consequence of his embroilment with the criminal justice system. Hence, although Marcus and Jeff could be viewed as occupying similar positions in a race, class, and gender hierarchy of power and privilege, the ways in which they experienced the world saw them responding to school in very different ways. Jeff moved from almost rejecting to zealously embracing school, while Marcus resented what he learned in school and provided a strong racial critique of school, yet he remained committed to the acquisition of a high school diploma.

Jeff Davidson

In January 1993, Jeff decided to move from Central High School to a private parochial school in Allerton, Allerton Christian School, a predominantly white school with an African American student population of 3%. Although this move was encouraged by his parents, Jeff said that the decision represented a huge financial burden to his parents. The move symbolized his commitment to go to school regularly and a concerted attempt to acquire a high school diploma as a consequence of his arrest, a month in a juvenile detention center, and a conviction on charges on robbery and assisting in the theft of a vehicle. Prior to this encounter with the criminal justice system, Jeff had attended school sporadically. In the midst of his disengagement with school and his ongoing quarrels with his parents, Jeff also fathered a baby girl, Cheranne, who was born in August 1992. Sharon, the white mother of the baby girl and Jeff's current girlfriend, was 15 years old and an honors student at Central High School. During Sharon's pregnancy and after the birth of Cheranne, Jeff continued to attend school sporadically. However, in December 1992, 6 months after Cheranne was born, and after his experience in the juvenile detention center, acquiring a high school diploma became a central goal for Jeff. At one point he told me, "[Cheranne] kind of helps me, because she makes me want her to be proud of me. . . . I wanna give her a good life. I wanna have something in my past that she can be proud of." Jeff was so scared by his ordeal with the criminal justice system, and even more scared by the thought of actually receiving a prison sentence, that he tried to alter the direction of his life dramatically. Jeff told me that he did not commit the crimes for which he pleaded guilty:

> I got on armed robbery, assisted stolen car . . . to cut it all down, I was in this car, some people had got into trouble, so I went to jail also. Somebody else did, and they try to blame it on me . . . I guess the police officers, 'cause the guy that I got caught with, he was Mexican, and I guess the police officer said we probably know it was the black guy you know, if you tell us such and such, he probably, you know. I was just riding and stuff, and all this other stuff. . . . What it was, they had robbed somebody and stolen a car.

The incident shook the foundations of Jeff's existence and deepened his sense that the criminal justice system does not seem to serve the interests of African Americans. As Jeff spoke about his encounter with the criminal justice system, he began to tell me how school, and ACS in particular, suddenly began to play a different role in his life:

Jeff: It's a big part now.

JP: It wasn't before though?

Jeff: No, 'cause you know you get the attitude that [the teachers] don't care, they are just in it for the money. . . . What made me take that turn was juvenile. Like I was telling Mr. Chisholm [a teacher] today, you go for so many years, not worried about getting locked up or anything, being the goodest guy I could, one hundred percent

American, and then you know, just recently, everything starts running down, get locked up. There goes my freedom right there. And for me, if you wanna hurt me, take away my freedom.

Although Jeff claimed that teachers "don't care," school became more central in his life as a consequence of his experience of the "hurt" emerging from his encounter with the criminal justice system. School thus emerged as playing a contradictory role in his life. For a time he felt disconnected from school, yet it was a predominantly white and middle-class school he utilized to build his dignity and pride.

Marcus Williams

Although Marcus lived in the same neighborhood as Jeff, and attended Central High School, the school that Jeff attended until his transfer to ACS, they had very different orientations toward school. Marcus was particularly critical of a Eurocentric curriculum he had to endure at school. He spoke to me about his commitment to generating unity among members of the African American community and talked about the centrality and importance of the African American woman as the strength that binds the African American community. He was a member of a study group that read the work of Farrakhan and other African American leaders.

Marcus said he went to school because he felt as though he wanted "to make something out of himself," although he admitted that school was "not a big part of his day." School became almost a ritual that he had to endure.

> Because I don't really acknowledge it really, it just something I have to do. . . . Just to survive, just have to do it, just to survive. Because basically what I feel is this. 'Cause what I've been learning now I'm understanding what they're doing, they're really taking us back. So basically I don't have a feel for school. I won't drop out . . . I have to do it, I wanna to get my education, you know I want to hurry up and get out of here.

Marcus's rationale for going to school was linked to his sense of "survival," and to establishing economic security through a job that the diploma might yield. His primary commitment after school was to enter the food service industry as a chef. He also said he would like to own his own restaurant. "Lord knows we need more black businesses around here," he said.

Even though Marcus wanted to acquire a high school diploma so he could become a caterer, he provided a scathing critique of school. In particular, he was critical of a Eurocentric perspective that dominated the curriculum. At one point he told me,

> they ain't teachin' you nothin'. 'Cause if they was teachin' you somethin', they would be teaching you somethin' about your black African culture, instead of teaching you white is superior. Because that is all they are teaching you, white is so superior, they dominate everything.

In spite of his disdain for the content of the curriculum, he continued to go to school, not only because he wanted the diploma to get a job, but also because the very act of going to school was an important stance to take in his tenuous relationship with his parents. During the course of the year, his relationship with his parents became so strained that he moved out of the home. He stayed with his cousin in the neighborhood, and continued to work at the restaurant in order to support himself. At one point he said, "My parents gonna think I can't do it. They think I gonna slack off because I ain't in the house now." Despite the strained relationships with his parents, despite his critique of school, he continued to go to school because doing so became one of the ways that he could prove to his parents that he could be "successful."

Both Jeff and Marcus gave meaning to the diploma that was tied to their experiences of the social, political, and economic worlds in which they lived. Going to school, and making meaning of that process, was intimately tied to their different versions of success and their different ideas about what it means to be a successful man. Although they each generated different rationales for going to school, engaging in this process meant being involved in a system that promotes a version of academic success that is achieved through intense competition and individualism. The process of schooling selectively ushers credentialed students into the world of professional work—a system that primarily benefits white, middle-class men. It is in relation to dominant constructs of masculinity that they forge their racial masculine identities and meanings of school success and acquire resources that may or may not allow them to achieve their goals.

Understanding these young men's experiences of school, and relationship to school, helps situate the making of friendships and peer relationships that emerged not only because they attended school, but because of what they experienced in school.

Peer Connections

Although Marcus and Jeff may have sought the intense peer group that McCall (1994) and Taylor (1991) described, it was only Marcus who had a group of friends he could rely on. Marcus connected with peers, solely African American young men and women, inside and outside of school. Jeff, on the other hand, was someone who had few friends at school, at Central or at ACS. The only friend he said he had was Sharon, a white young woman and mother of Cheranne. Through the different individuals and groups they connected with and separated themselves from, they were able to display and live out versions of their racialized masculine identities. The concept of connection seems important to understanding the relationships that Jeff and Marcus experienced. A connected relationship was not a relationship with just anybody. First and foremost, a connected relationship for these young men was a person they could trust and share their thoughts and their feelings with. Stern (1990) writes about the importance of connection in young adolescent girls' relationships. She argues that as girls develop their sense of femininity, their "relationships provide the support one needs to push one's own further development" (p. 85). There are parallels between the need for connection in the lives of young girls (see Gilligan, Lyons, & Hanmer, 1990) and the desire for connection in these young African American men's relationships. Connection seemed important to these young men's sense of self, their sustenance, and their version of masculinity. Ward (1990) argues that in the case of black adolescents, "Integration of the individual's personal identity with one's racial identity is a necessary and inevitable developmental task of growing up black in white America" (p. 218). For these two young African American men, developing solid, trusting, caring, and understanding relationships with others, particularly other young African American men, seemed not only paramount but crucial in their lives. The kinds of relationships they sought and the kinds of relationships they experienced tell us a lot about these young men and their experiences as African American young men.

Marcus: "They will stand by me"

Marcus formed relationships with students with whom he shared or developed common values and interests, and who were thereby able to sustain him in school. Because he felt alienated from relationships in classrooms, the relationships with peers outside of the classroom seemed to take on great significance. Spending time with school friends during the recesses of the school day became an important activity in his experience of schooling. There was a particular area in their school that he hung out in, where mostly African American students hung out. Outside of school, Marcus was involved in what he called a "brotherhood," an organization closely connected to a college-based fraternity. He attended weekly meetings with other young African American men of varying social class backgrounds, and they talked about issues and ideas affecting African Americans. They also planned social get-togethers. In addition, Marcus was involved in a college-based group that met to discuss ideas around Afrocentrism and attempted both to understand the plight of African Americans in the United States and to develop strategies to build and strengthen solidarity within the African American community. Many of the members of the groups he belonged to lived in working-class and middle-class neighborhoods, which suggests that racial identity was more significant than social class in memberships of these organizations. The peer relationships became significant to his identity as African American because they served as a context to define himself—his racial masculine identity—in relation to the meanings of the insiders and outsiders of his peer groups. What is significant about the organizations, formal and informal, that Marcus belonged to is that they were organizations that were composed almost exclusively of African Americans and were mostly male.

Amid these many peer groups that Marcus was involved with, Marcus simultaneously had a core group of friends. His relationships with these particular friends seemed to be defined by mutual support, respect, and care. Marcus described his connections with these friends:

> Basically they grew up with me, they know me real good. They will stand by me. If I ever got into any trouble where I was going to get to beat up by a whole group of people, they would help me. Because that's how we are, that's how me and my best friends are. If somethin' happened to them, I would happen to stick up for them, I will stick up for them and stand by them, if somethin' happened to them. And they're goin' to stand by me. It's not like we are a big ole gang.

There is no doubt that these friends were important to Marcus, and it was his friends to whom he turned for support and connection. The group was maintained through "sticking up" for each other, "standing by" each other.

Marcus: I hang around Tyrone a lot. He likes me. He make time to see me. Anyway. 'Cause that's how close we is.

JP: How long have you known him?

Marcus: Ever since middle school. I've got about five best friends that I can deeply talk to.

JP: What kind of things do you talk about?

Marcus: Like, you know, my parents and everything. 'Cause them was the only people that was there for me when I had problems with my parents. They know more about that than my relatives do. They are the only person I can talk to. I can't go nowhere.

The significance of the support of friends in Marcus's life as he went about interacting with his family, going to school, or going to work, cannot be overstated. Their solace and comfort helped him sustain himself in the face of the challenges he encountered as a young black man. Through his particular experiences in family, school, or work, he developed a close emotional bond with his five friends that reflected a strand of his version of masculinity that he lived out. Intermingled with Marcus's sense of a strong network of friends was also a wide network of friends.

Marcus: I've got lots of friends. I'm very well known. I try to make myself have no enemies. Don't want none. 'Cause I ain't the type that goes around . . . I have a lot of friends but I have five best friends, that I basically grew up with ever since I came up to Allerton. Well, we sort of split up after middle school. But we still keep in touch. I have all their numbers. Just this weekend we was all together. Down at the river front, walking around. I have three that go to Central. Two that go to Western . . .

JP: Who do you hang around with most then?

Marcus: Well, I don't hang around the same people all the time. I have my best friends, but I don't hang around them constantly.

Marcus talked about the different kinds of conversations he had with different friends and acquaintances. He was selective in what he talked about with the peers outside of his "close friends" network. "I don't like people to know too much about me. I always been like that. To me they can hurt me in the long run," he said. But to his close friends, he talks about "family and things. We always talk the same things. Basically talk about problems we have." Thus the various kinds of relationships provided Marcus with opportunities to talk about different dimensions of his life. He selectively shared aspects of his emotional and personal self, which suggests the significance of maintaining an image of emotional control in the eyes of others. This can be seen as reflective of his masculine identity in the making, in that emotional control, while seen as a way of protecting himself against hurt, also suggests a barrier or the limit of the way he interacted with men outside of his "best friends" circle. In part, the form and content of the relationships, is also shaped by the history, nature, and contexts of his various relationships.

As I explored the extent to which the peer group became a source of affiliation for these young men, I asked them to talk about the important people in their lives. It was significant that neither Marcus nor Jeff named a teacher or an adult connected to their school as someone they could talk with. This is an important point and illuminates the significance of friendships as they went to school.

Jeff: "I have many associates," not friends

Jeff's experiences of friendships lie in contrast to those of Marcus. Common to both these young men, however, was the extent to which "trust" became a defining dimension of friendship. This theme, together with how they had been "let down" by friends, continually resurfaced during our many conversations. While the theme in itself is an interesting topic, the vital significance of having strong and connected relationships with peers in their lives was the overarching issue in many of their conversations with me about relationships with friends and peers.

That "trust" in friendship was a central topic of discussion is not surprising. But these particular young men's concern about trust in their relationships also told me something about the kind of men they wanted to be. Talk about trust in friendships was not just about what they hoped for. It also emerged from what they had experienced with others as they were growing up. Most centrally, they wanted connection, community, belonging, and sharing with others. Their discontent about the lack of trust in their friendships perhaps reveals the values they embraced and attempted to live out.

Jeff argued that there were few people that he could trust or depend upon. He said, "I think there's a few people who I can depend on maybe, but not really. Well, there is one person who I know is behind me one hundred percent, Sharon." In fact, Jeff didn't even use the word *friend* to describe the people he connected to. He called them *associates*.

Jeff: Well you get people talking about you, you know.

JP: What do they say?

Jeff: Basically like "Jeff want to be white. He don't have so many friends." So that's why I don't say I have friends. I have *associates.* You might catch me once in a while saying friend, but don't take it to mind. I have *associates*

Jeff distanced himself from other people through using a different term to label the people he connected with. Jeff's image of a friend seemed to reflect the kind of connections that Marcus talked about. For Jeff a friend was "somebody that is always there for you. No matter what you do to them. No matter what happened between you and him." This issue of trust was very important to Jeff: "I tend not to trust too many people anymore, because those that I did trust, turned on me . . . basically 'cause of Sharon, spending too much time with Sharon," he said.

Intermingled with Jeff's conception of a good friendship—going "the extra mile," "trust," "somebody you can tell anything"—are certain codes of conduct. I discovered from Latasha (Sharon's best friend) that some of Jeff's friends were not happy with Jeff, not because he was dating Sharon or because he made her pregnant, but because he had liaisons with other young women while he was dating Sharon, and he did this without Sharon's knowledge. But more significantly, I learned from Jeff that as he began to act "white," his childhood circle of friends slowly disintegrated. Jeff seemed to develop ways of being that were in part in conflict with those sanctioned by his group of friends. Part of this conflict seemed to be centered on his embrace of "acting white." Significant in the changed relationship with his boyhood friends was that the friendships themselves became part of a process of racial identity construction.

This process was partly linked to the differing values that Jeff and his boyhood friends embraced. When at Central, his peers teased him because, he said, "they say, I talk funny, talk too proper." They called him a "sell-out." For Jeff, talking "proper" meant talking like "white people." "Acting white" to Jeff was seemingly part of his strategy to get ahead. At one point he said,

> If it takes me to change my culture, to change my speech, to get ahead of life to get that big house with that white picket fence, I'm going to do it. As long as it ain't hurting nobody else. Don't hate me because I speak more proper, be happy

for me, and in return, I'll be there for you. A lot of people don't want to see you achieve.

Jeff believed that a recipe for success included embracing talk and ways of being that he associated with white people. But for Jeff, who spent 2 years as a sophomore and struggled to get good grades, "acting white" was not just about getting ahead through getting good grades and acquiring a diploma; "acting white" in itself was synonymous with being a "proper person." His commitment to believing in the importance of "acting white" in order to get ahead seemed to intensify after his entanglement with the criminal justice system and as he moved to the private school. But Jeff was not always like this:

> I was brought up where I used to be around a whole lot of black people and stuff, but [now] I more relate . . . to more proper people. And at Central, you find people like with slang and stuff. I used to talk slang a lot. . . . For another reason, when we came up here, we went to a proper school, Miller Street, and we mostly associated with younger white kids.

Being "proper" was important to Jeff. This was not just about the way he talked or dressed. It was also his connectedness to symbols of "whiteness" such as school, or *being* with white people. Ironically, although Jeff may have attended a predominantly white elementary school, his friends were predominantly African American, not white, throughout elementary and middle school. And it was during this time he acknowledged that he "used to talk slang a lot." He had a group of friends that he used to spend most of his recreational time with.

Jeff: . . . we used to do everything together, they used to come over and spend the night. There wouldn't be a day that I wouldn't go over to their house, go to movies and stuff.

JP: Was it like a group of three or four people?

Jeff: Oh yeah, it was two brothers, and two others.

JP: About four people then.

Jeff: About four or five of us.

JP: And were they black or white?

Jeff: Black.

But Jeff no longer was connected to these friends. In fact, he had few friends. He said that he wasn't "hurting anybody" by talking "proper." But many of his peers were not enamored with Jeff's ways of being and talking. In fact, Jeff said that a lot of people at school said things such as, "Jeff want to be white. He don't have so many friends." It seemed that Jeff's way of being that his African American peers criticized cost him his friendships. Jeff elaborated further on his understanding of "being proper":

Jeff: Like you know, they talk more proper, and you can kind of relate to them.

JP: You have to break it down for me now, what does it mean to talk proper?

Jeff: Basically, not to talk in slang. Like "hello" instead of "yo." I might joke around with my friends and stuff and say "watsup (inaudible)"

JP: What about dressing?

Jeff: You can say I dress kind of preppie.

JP: Is it a conscious effort for you, or does it seem natural?

Jeff: It seem natural, regardless. I used to say to a lot of black people too, "Oh you just want to be white," and all this other stuff.

JP: You used to say that?

Jeff: Well I used to think that. It's just a process, you know. . . . Another reason, 'cause I talk too properly, they say "Oh you just want to be a white person." . . . You might get a few of them, like "you act white" and stuff, they don't want to be involved with you.

It is interesting that Jeff's move to a new predominantly, and almost exclusively, white private school saw him feeling better able to "relate" to his peers. Most significant is his account of moving to a stance of "acting white" as "just a process." While he admitted that he used to say to some African Americans, "Oh you just wanna be white," he later began to live out the kind of identity he criticized.

The question becomes, How do we account for such a change? To argue that the change of schools or his entanglement with the criminal justice system was the influence upon Jeff's new ways of being would be to discount his prior experiences in school and in the larger society where he had constantly learned about "proper" people. As he grew up, he learned about the value placed on symbols he associated with white people, and it seems that over time these symbols became part of his identity. Earlier, I noted that Jeff believed that it was harder for an African American person to get ahead than a white person, and he acknowledged that being "proper" was related to "whiteness," which suggests that he recognized some barriers ahead of him. Consequently, despite Jeff's "acting white" and resisting and rejecting connections with his friends and peers, his identity reflected a hegemonic culture and simultaneously acknowledged structural inequality. Hence, the need and desire to appropriate the symbols has to be understood within a context of what Jeff thought he needed to do and be in relation to the dominant symbols and images of "whiteness." In the meantime, the friends he grew up with became disconnected from him, and it was students with whom he shared no personal history, but a common way of "acting," that he chose to associate with. Jeff suggested that the way he talked, acted, and dressed may have been the reason some African American students disassociated themselves from him. The cost for Jeff of "acting white," however, was the loss of his boyhood African American friends and connections.

Although Jeff seemed to resist the pressures of his African American peers to conform to certain behaviors and ways of talking that they sanctioned, and may have acted in ways that Ogbu (1991) may view as "choosing academic success" (p. 456), he was not a high-achieving student. In fact, academic achievement as such was not a crucial issue in his life. He was mostly in the low-track classes, and he did not achieve high grades at either school. And, until the time he moved to the private school, he was very disenchanted with school and disengaged from classroom work. Jeff may have been able to name and embrace certain cultural practices associated with whiteness, but at the same time he was penalized through institutional and cultural practices because of the location of African Americans in a race hierarchy in the United States.

Emerging Masculinities in Relationships With Peers

The images of friends presented here are only a few of the images of African Americans that Jeff and Marcus talked about with me, and only some of the images that shaped their racialized and gendered sense of self and the racial sense of others. Their narratives about friends and friendship reveal how the context of school became one of the many sites in which these young men interacted that influenced the meanings they developed of themselves and of others. Through my analysis of their friends, I have tried to show that masculine identities are not universal, that their friendships were tenuous, and that there was an iterative process between the meanings given to racial identity and the peers Jeff and Marcus connected with. As we discussed these various racialized images, for example, "acting white," it became apparent that much of what they represented as African American cultural practice was shaped in part by their opposition to or embrace of conceptions of hegemonic white cultural practices. For example, Marcus described students at his school who "acted white": "To me it's people going against their own race. Like turning over their whole life to please the white man." Marcus situated his notion of racialized ways of being through power relations between white and black people. But the image is not a simple dichotomous one; it is relational. Marcus constructed the image of being African American in relation to white people and in relation to African American people who, in his mind, "acted white." These images, as I explain later, are not only racialized, they are simultaneously gendered.

Marcus's rejection and Jeff's embrace of "whiteness" may not be surprising, as they had white cultural practices thrust upon them, with little or limited opportunity in school to learn and affirm their own histories and cultural practices that would strengthen their self-image. Instead, they were struggling to define themselves in schooling contexts that were overwhelmingly shaped by institutional and social practices that seemed to perpetuate racial division through privileging some images, representations, and social practices, and subordinating others. These two young men's versions of masculinity may reflect their sense of powerlessness in larger society yet also create a sense of power through the connections and patterns of behavior that their various peer groups sanctioned. The emergence of their racial masculinities, as Connell (1993) noted, "is a collective process, something that happens at the level of the institution and the organization of peer group relationships" (p. 96).

They both felt the need to trust others and to stand by others; however, it was only Marcus who felt as though he was able to achieve this. At the same time, not all Marcus's relationships represented close connections with others. There were many friends with whom he chose not to share his innermost thoughts or feelings. Jeff, on the other hand, did not trust anyone besides Sharon, his white girlfriend. Clearly, peer groups and friendships were complex and multilayered and were a context for the shaping of the young men's racial masculine identities. It wasn't just the relationships they experienced that defined their masculinities, it was also the relationships that they felt they could not experience that perhaps revealed the possibilities and limits of who they were prepared to be as young African American men.

Gender-Race Meanings in Peer Relationships

The nature of Jeff's and Marcus's relationships shaped their sense of self; so did the gendered and racialized meanings and images that were interwoven through these relationships. These images are important in understanding how school contexts and the very relationships they encountered with peers in and out of school influenced the versions of racialized masculinities they enacted.

White Women, Black Masculinity, and Schooling

Jeff's relationships with others at Central and the friends he grew up with were not terminated solely because he transgressed an apparent racial boundary through the way he acted. The relationships also were tenuous because of his relationship with Sharon, who was white. Jeff said that a lot of his African American peers did not associate with him because of the way he acted or talked. At the same time, however, because of the way he talked and acted, Jeff believed, "It was just like a lot of more white girls was more attracted to me, dancing and start dating with them." But Jeff not only went out with white young women, he fathered a child with a white young woman. It was his relationship with Sharon that additionally provoked a tenuous relationship with his boyhood friends and many of his African American peers at school, male and female. He said,

> Yeah, a lot of people don't like me at Central also because of Sharon. They don't like to see somebody happy. You know you've got something good going on. [They say,] "If I can't have nothing, you can't." You get rumors goin' around.

After probing Jeff further to uncover the nature of the rumors, he told me,

> I think another thing is that Sharon used to be a virgin, a lot of guys get jealous, because "how come I couldn't get it?" and all this other stuff.

Thus, being "proper" was not just about talking and acting, it was also about his sexuality. As Lorber (1994) noted, "The social construction of sexuality is tied to the social construction of gender by marking off categories of who it is proper to mate and have children with" (p. 64).

The fact that Jeff mentioned Sharon losing her virginity, and Jeff being her sexual partner, suggests ways in which sexual conquests are viewed as status symbols among *young men* and are integral to proving a certain kind of masculinity, a heterosexual masculinity. This talk about Sharon potentially confirmed not only Jeff's masculinity but also a kind of masculinity where his heterosexuality was part of the fabric of his masculine identity as an African American. Another way in which he was able to live out his quest of "acting white" was not only to date a white girl but to father her child. The image of Jeff becoming a father enthralled him: "I was happy, I was overjoyed," he told me. The relationship with Sharon may have contributed to the affirmation of the gendered identity he embraced. At the same time, his relationship with Sharon took on an important gendered significance in his relationships with other men, particularly African American men.

Although the talk about Jeff and his relationship with Sharon may or may not have affected his relationships with others, he seemed to place emphasis on the need to assert his masculinity in the arena of school. It was through making public at Central his sexual relationship with Sharon that he was able to accomplish this. Through this relationship, "sex is prized not as a testament of love but as testimony to control of another human being" (Anderson, 1990, p. 114). The relationship became a vehicle to prove his self-esteem and pride and his heterosexual masculinity. As Massey (1991) argued, "Black boys engage in sexual activity earlier as a result of other blockages in the opportunity structure in our society" (p. 119). Sexual activity possibly becomes a way to exert his sense of masculinity, given a context imbued with distorted and hegemonic images of African American men and his harrowing experiences with school and the criminal justice system. He fathered the child before his encounter with the criminal justice system, but it was after the experience that he became almost entranced with the idea that he was a father. It seemed as though the criminal justice system had stripped him of his sense of manhood, and fatherhood thus became a mechanism whereby he was able to regain his sense of masculinity.

Interestingly, while Jeff made public his sexual relationship with Sharon at Central, he chose to be silent about his fatherhood at ACS. He decided that revealing such information to peers at ACS was inappropriate. His decision not to share these details of his life with white peers at ACS further revealed how Jeff used the social context of schooling to live out certain images of race and masculinity. At Central, it seemed important to his sense of manhood to reveal aspects of his relationship, while at ACS he made a different decision. He seemed to use fatherhood to define his identity in relation to African American men at his old school, but not in relation to the white men at his newer school, ACS. An interesting question that I did not explore with Jeff was whether he chose not to talk about his fatherhood because he thought sexual activity as a teenager would tarnish his image at ACS, or whether he chose not to talk about his fatherhood because he had a relationship with a white young woman. Clearly, Jeff did not make these decisions arbitrarily. He seemed strongly influenced by different institutional and cultural contexts of the two schools and his sense of connection with other peers in these contexts. These two different responses reveal how masculinities are actively and relationally made in context, and the influence of the institutional and cultural forces in schools and in peer relationships in the making of masculine identities.

Jeff's relationships with peers in school, then, were not only about his racialized identity, they were also about his gendered identity. While gender seemed to enter Jeff's conversations only in his talk about the sexual relationship between himself and Sharon, gender was present in *all* his conversations about his identity. When he "acted" in particular ways, he was not wanting to embrace femininity but a version of masculinity. In this way, it seemed that his embrace of "acting white" was not only about his racialized identity, it was also about his gendered identity. When students accused him of "acting white," they meant that he "acted" as a white man as opposed to their images of a white woman or black man. There were implicit gendered meanings embedded and intertwined in his racialized ways of being and talking. This relationship with Sharon was important to his sense of racial identity, just as it was important to his sense of masculinity. It can be seen as giving him an avenue to assert his power and control as a black man.

Although Jeff and Marcus shared some similar experiences, such as in the passing of their heterosexuality, their social identities were quite different. What was strikingly different were the ways in which they talked about images and ideas of others, and yet each used these images to develop a sense of who he was and wanted to be.

"What do you want with a white girl?"

For Marcus, as with Jeff, gendered images intermingled our conversations through talk about women and sexuality. For example, at one point,

Marcus told me that he was "not really into relationship black and white thing. I hate to see my black sisters with white males. I think we need to stay with our own color." However, I suggested I occasionally saw black men with white women, but rarely see black women with white men. Curious about this, I asked Marcus if he agreed with my observations.

Marcus: Let me tell you about that. The reason is because, white girls are easier to get than black women. Black males don't want that challenge, black females will give you a challenge. They ain't gonna let you get them real easy. You have to prove yourself to them.

JP: Like what?

Marcus: The way you treat them. Basically you can get in their [white women's] pants easily. That's what it is. And I don't really like it, that's stupid. I don't really like it, I always say, "Come back to us."

While Marcus related the issue of sexuality through his images of women, intertwined with his ideas about women, sex, and men as "challengers" were also ideas about race. His images were also imbued with the objectification of African American and white women. He argued that having sex with African American women was a "challenge" as opposed to the "easy" white women. He used the idea that black women are more difficult to "conquer" as a way to strengthen his image of black women, but this image of African American women was not only shaped by racial meanings, it was also shaped by his version of masculinity. Having a relationship with a black woman implicitly suggested Marcus's heterosexuality, and his sense of being a *black man*. Strands of sexuality, race, and gender identity came to the fore as he talked about women. Lorber (1994) correctly noted that sexuality is not just about behavior; it also involves "desire and actual sexual attraction and fantasies" (p. 60).

Marcus, therefore, enhanced his version of masculinity as a black man through his commitment to, and the image he carried of, black women:

Farrakhan says whites are an imitation woman. Anything black, you've got all the different shades of color in the black female, you've got big, you've got small, dark skinned, light-skinned. What do you want with a white girl? Hey, I'm not trying to cut. But ain't got no booty. And you know, black females, they've just got, everything is there, the perfect woman.

Marcus, like Jeff, used images and connections with women to develop his sense of self. However, it was a sexualized image that was interwoven with Marcus's talk about African American women. In his mind, the black woman is "the perfect woman." He sexualized the body of African American women and white women to argue his position about the beauty of black women. He denigrated white women, suggesting they are easy to "conquer," and conquest was part of the image of masculinity he constructed for himself. But his embrace of the beauty of black women was not arbitrary. It was connected to his sense of identity—his African American masculinity and heterosexuality.

Race-Gender Images and Emerging Masculinities

These images of women and relationships with women and men were connected to the young men's construction of their sexualities. The identities were simultaneously gendered and raced. Most important is that their talk about images of women was significant in their relationships with men. Talk with other men about women became a site for their affirmation of their version of masculinity, where men wielding power and control was a significant strand. For example, Jeff's relationship with Sharon saw him rejected by his African American peers but apparently the target of jealousy because he engaged in a sexual relationship with Sharon. Jeff's relationship with Sharon was not just about him having a relationship with a white woman; as a way to affirm his version of masculinity, the relationship could possibly be seen as a way of both challenging and trying to access white men's power (Collins, 1990). The relationship with Sharon, however, could also be seen as a story about competing masculinities among African American and young white men at school: Jeff fathered a child with Sharon and thereby was able to prove his manhood to his peers who seemed to place value on sexual conquests of women, yet the relationship could also challenge the power of young white men. This challenge is complex, however, because such challenging of power could have been an issue in relation to the young white men at his old school, Central, but at his new mainly white school, ACS, he chose to withhold the personal details.

The young men developed meanings and images of social identities in contexts that were historically shaped through relations of power and privilege. For example, Marcus's seemingly oppositional identity was constructed in relation to the hegemonic images of African American masculinity—images of black men as violent, aggressive, and socially irresponsible. But they were also constructed in opposition to hegemonic versions of white masculinity. For instance, Marcus criticized white identities and tried to live out an identity that was somewhat in *opposition* to the hegemonic images of black men; and at the same time, in *opposition* to images of white people.

Through exploring the ways in which these young men's sense of racial and masculine identities were constructed in relation to images, representations, and relations with others, we are able to catch a glimpse of the complexity of examining the ways in which race and gender interweave through their relationships. The discussion reveals that these two young men asserted their racialized masculine identities in different ways, but they both suggest images of men overpowering women through sexualized images and relationships as significant in their versions of masculinity.

Peer Relationships and Emerging African American Masculinities

Thus far, the discussion has uncovered these young men's different relationships with peers in and out of school and the gendered and racialized meanings that are intertwined within the relationships. Yet these stories are also about their emerging identities. Important to note is the fact that the relationships in their lives were uneven, and that the relationships they sought in school were complemented with relationships they developed through organizations outside of school. In this section I will focus on some of the themes that have dominated this chapter: peer relationships as sites of connection and alienation and peer relationships as contexts that are dynamically shaped by race, class, and gender relations of power.

Connection and Alienation

Most centrally, Jeff's and Marcus's talk about their friendships raises some interesting questions about the dynamics and conflicts among friends within peer groups. Many writers characterize the peer group as an all-encompassing place of reference, and rarely articulate the multiple layers of conflict and connection that interweave peer relationships. This is particularly true for literature on young African American men. For example, Taylor (1991) argued,

> The peer group becomes the principal means through which they seek both a sense of belongingness and feelings of self-esteem. In fact, for males whose fathers are absent from the home, affiliation with street-based peer groups is a crucial step towards learning many of the socially defined and normative aspects of the male role in the black community and the larger society. (p. 150)

Taylor raises some significant points about the centrality of the peer group. In my larger study, the peer group was important for all the young men, *including* Marcus and Jeff who had fathers at home. They all sought peer relationships in and out of school. There were various contexts in which Jeff and Marcus lived out their versions of masculinity, through their talk about their lives and the lives of others and through the beliefs and values emerging from and dominating the very group(s) to which they belonged. But these relationships with peer groups were not solely places to develop a sense of "belongingness," they could also be seen as places to spur alienation. For Jeff, in particular, being on the fringes of many groups meant that he learned about hurt and alienation. And even within most peer groups, Marcus admits he didn't share all aspects of his emotional and personal self. Peer relationships were complex and, while they may have influenced the young men's sense of self-esteem, were simultaneously inhibiting and sources of disconnection.

Perhaps amiss in many of the discussions about African American peer groups is the sense of conflict, frustration, affiliation, and alienation that were also defining aspects of the groups, particularly from Jeff's perspective. Taylor (1991) and Mincy (1994) both tend to underplay these dimensions of the peer groups. Mincy wrote,

> Adolescent black males have a propensity to exhibit real, honest, and authentic behavior in all interactions—that is, for "being for real" or "telling it like it is." They tend not to stifle their true thoughts, feelings, or behaviors in most social situations. While such authenticity may not always be appreciated or understood by others, black male youths tend to cut to the heart of a matter with their genuineness. (pp. 37-38)

Mincy argues an important point about the authentic nature of interactions among black men, but I wonder if he manages to capture the variation—social class, race, sexuality, masculinity, geographical location—and the multiple contexts and complex ways in which African American men interact with each other and with others, and the various kinds of peer groups that they may simultaneously belong to. Certainly, authenticity seems an important dimension of peer relationship. The dynamic, contradictory, and contextual aspects of authenticity in friendships, however, may be underplayed through his characterization of authenticity in friendships.

I have argued that peer groups and friendships were complex and multilayered as a context for the shaping of the two young men's racial masculine identities. At the same time, however, there were differences in their relationships and the forms of connections they developed that reflected individual choices they made. But these choices were not made arbitrarily. These choices were influenced by structures of power that were reflected in school curriculum, the different classes these young men took, and the formation of racial peer groups in relation to other groups in their particular schools.

Racialized and Gendered Images at Play

Racialized and gendered images and meanings, however, came into being not only through Jeff's or Marcus's individual practices; collective actions, through connection to or rejection from seemingly cohesive peer groups at school, also seemed to be a further force in their affirmation of identities—their racialized masculinities. They seemed to hang out with students in certain groups to validate their sense of their racial identity and concomitant behaviors and beliefs. Marcus at once sought solidarity with other young African American men and rejected aspects of white culture that he defined as not African American culture. In his exclusively African American peer group at school, the talk and behaviors apparently were influential in their bonding. His sense of connection with other African American students was important to him and his friends, not only because of how he came to see himself in relation to teachers, pedagogy, and curriculum within school, but because of the limited and negative images about African American men that dominate society. Thus the sense of "belongingness" was also about an affirmation of his version of masculinity. This connection was not apparent for Jeff, who had few friends but still tried to embrace particular racialized images as he constructed his identity.

These images, while seemingly racialized, were also infused with gendered meanings. They defined their masculinities as African American men in relation to versions of African American and white femininities and masculinities. Through his peer relationships, Marcus tried to build an identity as a man that represented a distinctly African American, not white, version of masculinity, and that did not reflect some of the dominant ideas, values, and beliefs about African American men that permeate U.S. society. Such meanings about African American men are given dominance in our society, despite these images representing only a few of the lived experiences of many African American men. Many of these negative and limited images are constructed in ways that distort the experiences of African American men.

These two working-class African American young men in differing contexts experienced different kinds of relationships with peers. They were in the process of becoming young African American men, and though they may be "seen" as African American men, this identity reveals different meanings to them that reflect the multidimensional nature of their experience in the social world. Jeff's and Marcus's stories can *only* be understood if seen in the context of power, privilege, and inequality. This helps us understand how the complex interplay of race, class, and gender interwove their lives differently and how each experienced and gave meaning to the relationships he formed in and out of school. Both these young men lost some or all of their boyhood friends and sought various avenues to develop connections and relationships with peers. School, the source and center of their current ambitions, became a place of connection and also disconnection because not only were Jeff and Marcus unable to be themselves, they also had to limit who they could be.

This discussion leads me to ask important questions about how we come to understand the complex nature of peer groups, how different students have different kind of experiences with and in relation to peer groups, and, most important, how schools might support and sustain peer relationships in ways that expand possibilities for young men. These questions are intimately tied to larger questions about becoming men, about images and representations of masculinities in relation to the lives of marginalized youth, and questions about living out various versions of masculinities in schools. As Mac an Ghaill (1994) notes in his work about the process of construction, contestation, and reconstruction of gender and sexual relations, there are no quick-fix solutions. Building relationships and exploring social identities with young men, however, seems to demand more than extracurricular activities and support groups, a response that might lead to a continued marginalization of such issues. More attention needs to be given to classrooms, particularly in relation to official curriculum and pedagogy. This seems to demand meaningfully centering the lives of students in curriculum and pedagogy through promoting discussions with students about the multiple representations of masculinities and femininities in various cultures; about issues of power in relation to class, race, gender, and sexuality; and about the process of constructing social identities.

References

Andersen, M. L. (1993). Studying across difference: Race, class, and gender in qualitative research. In J. Stanfield & D. Rutledge (Eds.), *Research in race and ethnic relations* (pp. 39-52). Newbury Park, CA: Sage.

Anderson, E. (1990). *Streetwise: Race, class and change in an urban community.* Chicago: University of Chicago Press.

Baca Zinn, M., & Dill, B. T. (1994). *Women of color in U.S. society.* Philadelphia: Temple University Press.

Baron, A. (1994). The making of a gendered working-class history. In A. Shapiro (Ed.), *Feminist revision history* (pp. 146-171). New Brunswick, NJ: Rutgers University Press.

Carrigan, T., Connell, R. W., & Lee, J. (1985). Towards a new sociology of masculinity. In H. Brod (Ed.), *The making of masculinities* (pp. 63-100). Boston: Allen & Unwin.

Coleman, J. S. (1961). *The adolescent society.* New York: Free Press of Glencoe.

Collins, P. H. (1990). *Black feminist thought—Knowledge, consciousness, and the politics of empowerment.* Boston: Unwin Hyman.

Connell, R. W. (1987). *Gender and power.* Oxford, UK: Polity.

Connell, R. W. (1993). Disruptions: Improper masculinities. In L. Weis & M. Fine (Eds.), *Beyond silenced voices: Class, race, and gender in United States schools* (pp. 191-208). Albany: State University of New York Press.

Connell, R. W. (1995). *Masculinities.* Oxford, UK: Polity.

Cusick, P. (1973). *Inside the high school.* New York: Holt, Rinehart & Winston.

Dill, B. T., & Baca Zinn, M. (1990). *Race and gender: Re-visioning social relations.* Memphis, TN: Center for Research on Women.

Franklin, C. W. (1984). *The changing definition of masculinity.* New York: Plenum.

Franklin, C. W. (1991). The men's movement and the survival of African-American men in the '90s. *Changing Men, 21,* 20-21.

Franklin, C. W. (1992). "Hey, Home—Yo, Bro": Friendship among black men. In P. M. Nardi (Ed.), *Men's friendships* (pp. 201-214). Newbury Park, CA: Sage.

Gibbs, J. T. (1988). *Young, black, and male in America.* New York: Auburn House.

Gilligan, C., Lyons, N. P., & Hanmer, T. J. (1990). *Making connections—The real worlds of adolescent girls at Emma Willard School.* Cambridge, MA: Harvard University Press.

Glasgow, D. G. (1980). *The black underclass.* San Francisco: Jossey-Bass.

Hammersley, W., & Woods, P. (Eds.). (1984). *Life in school.* Milton Keynes, UK: Open University Press.

Harding, S. (1987). *Feminism and methodology*. Bloomington: Indiana University Press.

Hearn, J. (1987). *The gender of oppression*. New York: St. Martin's.

hooks, b. (1992). *Black looks: Race and representation*. Boston: South End.

Hunter, A. G., & Davis, J. E. (1994). The hidden voices of black men: The meaning, structure, and complexity of manhood. *Journal of Black Studies, 25*, 20-40.

Kimmel, M. S. (1987). *Changing men: New directions in research on men and masculinity*. Newbury Park, CA: Sage.

Kimmel, M. S., & Messner, M. A. (1992). *Men's lives*. New York: Macmillan.

Lesko, N. (1996). Denaturalizing adolescence: The politics of contemporary representations. *Youth and Society, 28*(2), 139-161.

Lorber, J. (1994). *Paradoxes of gender*. New Haven, CT: Yale University Press.

Mac an Ghaill, M. (1988). *Young, gifted and black: Student teacher relations in the schooling of black youth*. Milton Keynes, UK: Open University Press.

Mac an Ghaill, M. (1994). *The making of men: Masculinities, sexualities and schooling*. Bristol, PA: Open University Press.

MacLeod, J. (1987). *Ain't no makin' it*. Boulder, CO: Westview.

Madhubuti, H. (1990). *Black men: Obsolete, single, dangerous?* Chicago: Third World Press.

Majors, R., & Billson, J. M. (1992). *Cool pose: The dilemmas of black manhood*. New York: Lexington Books.

Marriott, D. (1996). Reading black masculinities. In M. Mac an Ghaill (Ed.), *Understanding masculinities* (pp. 185-201). Buckingham, UK: Open University Press.

Massey, G. (1991). The flip side of teen mothers: A look at teen fathers. In B. P. Bowser (Ed.), *Black male adolescents: Parenting and education in community context* (pp. 117-128). Lanham, MD: University Press of America.

McCall, N. (1994). *Makes me wanna holler—A young Black man in America*. New York: Random House.

Mincy, R. B. (1994). *Nurturing young black males*. Washington, DC: Urban Institute Press.

Ogbu, J. U. (1991). Minority coping responses and school experiences. *The Journal of Psychohistory, 18*, 433-456.

Oliver, W. (1988). Black males and social problems: Prevention through Afrocentric socialization. *Journal of Black Studies, 20*, 15-39.

Price, J. N. (1995). *Against the odds: The meaning of school and relationships in the lives of six young African American men*. Unpublished doctoral dissertation, Michigan State University, East Lansing.

Roberts, G. W. (1994). Brother to brother—African-American modes of relating among men. *Journal of Black Studies, 24*, 379-390.

Smith, D. E. (1987). *The everyday world as problematic*. Boston: Northeastern University Press.

Solomon, P. (1992). *Black resistance in high school*. Albany: State University of New York Press.

Staples, R. (1982). *Black masculinity: The black male's role in American society*. San Francisco: Black Scholar Press.

Staples, R. (1986). Black male sexuality. *Changing Men, 17,* 3-5.

Staples, R. (1987). Black male genocide: A final solution to the race problem in America. *The Black Scholar, 18,* 2-11.

Stern, L. (1990). Conceptions of separation and connection in female adolescents. In C. Gilligan, N. P. Lyons, & T. J. Hanmer (Eds.), *Making connections—The real worlds of adolescent girls at Emma Willard School* (pp. 73-87). Cambridge, MA: Harvard University Press.

Taylor, R. T. (1991). Poverty and adolescent black males: The subculture of disengagement. In P. B. Edleman & J. A. Ladner (Eds.), *Adolescence and poverty: Challenge for the 1990s* (pp. 139-162). Lanham, MD: Center for National Policy Press.

Ward, J. V. (1990). Racial identity formation and transformation. In C. Gilligan, N. P. Lyons, & T. J. Hanmer (Eds.), *Making connections—The real worlds of adolescent girls at Emma Willard School* (pp. 215-232). Cambridge, MA: Harvard University Press.

Weis, L. (1988). *Class, race, and gender in American education.* Albany: State University of New York Press.

West, C. (1993a). *Keeping faith.* New York: Routledge.

West, C. (1993b). *Race matters.* Boston: Beacon.

Willis, P. (1977). *Learning to labor.* New York: Columbia University Press.

Wilson, W. J. (1987). *The truly disadvantaged: The inner city, the underclass and social policy.* Chicago: University of Chicago Press.

PART THREE

POSTSECONDARY SCHOOLS

7

"New Times" in an Old Country

Emerging Black Gay Identities and (Hetero) Sexual Discontents

MÁIRTÍN MAC AN GHAILL

Introduction

I always remember that day you asked, what are schools for. Typical sociologist you really upset the teachers and the students. To them it seemed obvious. I began to think, well what has school been for me. Whatever schools are for, they are obsessed in trying to make sure every one is keeping to the heterosexual rules. Its funny, given that they think that heterosexuality is natural that they have this obsession like religious fundamentalists that you have to keep the faith, keep to the straight and narrow. Given that it is supposed to be normal to be heterosexual, you would think that they would not have to work so hard at it. I suppose gays are a dreaded reminder of what they might become or what they might want to become.

Denton, student

. . . the society makes its will toward you very, very clear . . . the macho men—truck drivers, cops, football players—these people are far more complex than they want to realize. That's why I call them infantile. They have needs that for them are literally inexplicable. They don't dare look

163

the mirror. And that is why they need faggots. They've created faggots in order to act out a sexual fantasy on the body of another man and not take any responsibility for it. Do you see what I mean? I think it's very important for the male homosexual to recognize that he is a sexual target for other men, and that is why he is despised, and why he is called a faggot. He is called a faggot because other men need him.

James Baldwin quoted in Troupe, 1989, pp. 178-179

We are living at a time of rapid global socioeconomic and cultural changes in a period of late capitalism (Harvey, 1989; Jameson, 1991). These changes, such as deindustrialization, feminization of local labor markets, and the diversification of family forms, are contesting and fragmenting traditional lifestyles. Alongside this, education in advanced capitalist societies as a postwar representation of the modernist project, involving comprehensive reorganization, child-centered pedagogy, and antisexism and antiracism underpinned by a belief in universalism, collectivism, humanism, rational progression, and social justice is being destablized by this emerging socioeconomic uncertainty. For example, fundamental changes in the relationship between the reward structures of the school and the labor market seem to be leading to great confusion among large sectors of male and female students concerning the purpose of school in preparing them for occupational and social destinies. However, education continues to be a social and cultural refuge for the projection and temporary resolution of English social anxieties, as media representations of school standards are portrayed as national exemplars of the social, moral, and economic standards. At the same time, schools are actively involved in the production of these anxieties. Current controversies around boys' underachievement and middle-class students' disaffection are shifting concern away from social minorities to a reexamination of social majorities, with the implication that we are no longer sure about the purpose of education. This may be read as part of a broader social and cultural interregnum that we are presently experiencing in England. As Rutherford (1990) proposes,

> we are caught between the decline of the old political identifications and the new identities that are in the process of becoming or yet to be born. Like Laurie

Anderson's "urbanscape" in her song "Big Science" the imagery traces of the future are present, but as yet have no representation or substance. (p. 23)

It is within this process of political and media displacement that educational researchers are developing frameworks to make sense of the formation of young people's identities. Against this background the young men in this chapter provide an interesting insight into the making of "new times" in their discussion of emerging black gay identities in a postcolonial society (Mac an Ghaill, 1998).

During the 1980s in England we witnessed the ascendancy of the New Right agenda occupying the moral high ground with its projected images of a consumer-based acquisitive individualism, the patriarchal family, the strong state, and a patriarchic British nation. As Gordon and Klug (1986) cogently pointed out, the emergence of the social authoritarians' discourses converged around issues of "race" and sexuality. They argued, "For there is clearly an overlap in ideology which opposes black immigration on the grounds that white Britain could be swamped and one that advocates measures to strengthen the British family, both physically and ideologically, on the grounds of the moral integrity of the nation is at risk" (p. 11). In response, the paucity of the mainstream political Left involved a defensive reaction in terms of vague conceptions of a social-democratic, welfarist, and multiethnic citizenship. The main political and theoretical challenge to this Conservative "high moral" discourse, which was underreported, came from new social movements, including radical women's, black, lesbian, and gay social collectivities. For example, Kelly (1992, p. 22) offered a radical critique of the legacy of the 1980s' nationalist enterprise culture that involved, she argued, a recomposition of the English social landscape with the resulting repositioning of minority social groups.

By the 1990s, alongside the New Right critique of equal opportunities, we see the implosion of new social movements and their accompanying organizing categories, including notions of patriarchy and color racism. A major strategic flaw of new social movement theory has been its failure to conceptualize adequately, albeit in a hostile environment, a comprehensive and inclusive rationale for antioppressive education. The failure to offer an alternative social vision has contributed to the continuing ascendancy of the New Right popular authoritarianism with its invidious media-orchestrated attacks on progressive local educational authorities. The new Labor government has not signaled its intent to restore political losses that new social movements experienced under the Conservative government. The Left's additive model with its hierarchy-of-oppressions approach that conceives of working-class black gays as triply oppressed has limited explanatory power. Unintendedly, it serves to reinforce the pedagogical "common sense" view that recent policies, developed in response to the demands of the new identity politics of "race," gender, sexuality, and disability have displaced policies on class and are primarily concerned with minority interests and needs (Mama, 1992, p. 80). English schools find themselves with disparate policy documents that fail to address the complex and contradictory articulation between different forms of oppression. Equally important, they have failed to acknowledge the complex multifaceted nature and the contextual contingency of the mediation of these oppressions in state institutions located within a deindustrializing economy and accompanying disintegrating civil society.

The Study

The gay Asian[1] and African Caribbean working-class young men involved in this qualitative study were aged between 16 and 19 years. They were all attending local post-16 education institutions situated in the Midlands. I taught a number of them who were following academic courses. Within their schools and colleges they were not "out" as gay. My own students informed me that they were open to me about their sexuality because of my antihomophobic stance. In the Staff room, classroom, and more informal school arenas I presented a progay perspective. They introduced me to their friends, who in turn introduced me to their friends. We operated as an informal support group. Mercer and Julien (1988) contextualize for themselves, as black gay men, the positive political significance of the inner-city civil disobediences in opposition to the 1980s Conservative government hegemony:

> For us, 1981 was a profoundly empowering moment, mobilizing energies and abilities to challenge our conditions of existence. The feeling of empowerment came from the collective identity we constructed for ourselves as black gay men, enabling us to overcome the marginality we experienced as black people and the individual isolation we felt as gay people. Politics is about making connections practically, with the forming of alliances between different social groups, and at a cognitive level with the recognition of diverse categories of race, class, gender, ethnicity and sexuality in articulation of power relations.

The gay black group enabled us to start a conversation amongst ourselves, making connections between patterns of our common experiences to recognise the structures responsible for the specificity of the oppression in the first place. (p. 97)

There is a certain resonance here for the young gay black men and I who took part in this study. Reading through this chapter, we are surprised that at a time of the continuing influence of the New Right Moralism that we continue to be optimistic (Weeks, 1989). Our being together provided the conditions for us to start a conversation about the politics of oppression with particular reference to modern schooling and the telling of sexual stories (Plummer, 1995). This produced an unexpected and unintended effect. By the early 1990s in schools and colleges there tends to be less evidence among minorities of the "black unity" of the mid-1980s, with its emphasis on the shared experience of antiblack racism. The black gay students here, in exploring the politics of the interrelationship among homophobia, heterosexism, and racism, are a sector of the younger generation among whom "syncretic black identities are being formed" (Mama, 1992, p. 80), focusing on racial, gender, and sexual commonalties as well as on the specificities of personal histories, memories, and desires.

Space does not allow for a detailed discussion of the study's methodology, particularly with reference to questions concerning the politics and ethics of researching oppressed groups (see Mac an Ghaill, 1989, and Mac an Ghaill & Haywood, 1998). Much of the material reported here was collected from observation, informal discussions, and recorded semistructured interviews with the students and their teachers at their schools and colleges. It is taken from life and school histories that involved discussion of family/kinship networks, peer groupings, work experience, political views/activities, and school/college experiences. This methodological approach helped to locate schooling within the larger sociopolitical processes (Connell, 1989; Morgan, 1992). Sharing our life histories helped to challenge the power asymmetries between the students and myself. My main influences include feminist methodology and praxis-based pedagogy. I have attempted to operationalize an emancipatory research methodology as advocated by such critical theorists as Lather (1986), with an emphasis on the principles of collaboration, reciprocity, and reflexivity. At the same time, in adopting a student-centered methodological approach that prioritizes their epistemological accounts of schooling and popular culture, I have attempted to operate within a framework that seeks active student involvement in the construction of the research stance.

A main argument of this chapter is that, in order to grasp what is going on in schools with reference to sexual identity formation, it is necessary to bring together young gay people's accounts of schooling and recent theoretical developments in sexual politics. From both these sources, sexual/gender categories can be seen as being shaped by and shaping the processes of colonization, of racism, of class hegemony, of male domination, of heterosexism, and other forms of oppression. In short, sexual/gender relations can be seen as a crucial point of intersection of different forms of power, stratification, desire, and subjective identity formation (Fanon, 1970; Hemphill, 1991). The main focus in this theory-led empirical work is a rethinking of sexual/gender categories in relation to the complex interconnections of multiple forms of oppression. Of key significance here is the deconstruction of dominant forms of heterosexuality.

> Rajinder: One of the pluses of being a black gay person is that you see that you have to try and understand how different oppressions come together. White gays might only be interested in homophobia and blacks only interested in racism but what is important is looking at the complex ways homophobia and racism work in schools. And then again how these might affect gays or lesbians or working-class kids in different ways.

Rethinking Schooling as a Sexualizing Agency

We are only beginning to understand the complex interrelationship among schooling, masculine formations, and sexual and racial identities. Feminist theory has enabled us to move beyond the ahistorical gender essentialism and determinism of sex-role theory, acknowledging that young people are not such "tablae rasae, to be injected or even constructed with the ideology of the day" (Rowbotham, 1989, p. 18). Carrigan, Connell, and Lee (1985) claim that,

> The history of homosexuality obliges us to think of masculinity not as a single object with its own history but as being constantly constructed within the history of an evolving social structure, a structure of power relations. It obliges us to see the construction as a social struggle going on in a complex ideological and political field in which there is a continuing process of mobilization, marginalization, contestation, resistance and subordination. (pp. 588-589)

Connell, Ashenden, Kessler, and Dowsett (1982) and Davies (1993) have persuasively presented the case against biologically based and sex-role theories, suggesting that they are inadequate to explain the complex social and psychological processes involved in the development of gendered subjectivities that are underpinned by institutional and wider material powers. Such work acts as a critique of the dominant theoretical and commonsense explanations of sexual/gender differences that inform current pedagogical practice in English schools. These approaches often take for granted a definition of femininity and masculinity that are implicitly assumed to be unitary, universal, and unchanging categories. For Davies (1993), one of the major weaknesses of theoretical work on schooling and subjectivity has been inadequate conceptions of sexual/gender identity formation. More recently, theorists drawing on post-structuralism, psychoanalysis, and semiology have provided new ways of thinking about subjective identities (Henriques, 1984). For example, Hall (1990), in his discussion of the new politics of black culture, has argued that identities are not historically fixed entities but rather that they are subjected to the continuous interplay of history, culture, and power.

Rajinder: The old ethnicity studies saw different ethnic groups in very fixed terms. I think it's easier to see with the younger generation that you have to re-make who you are as a people. We have to make our own history that is not just about what white people are doing to us or have done to us. And this is probably most obvious with black gay people. It's nearly obvious that we have to invent ourselves. It is not clear how as a group we will develop as part of the wider community.

Earlier feminist research has been very successful in identifying the ways in which gender relations operate in favor of male teachers and students and the resulting inequalities experienced by girls and women (Delamont, 1982). Later feminist work has illustrated how dominant forms of sexuality circumscribe female students' and teachers' lives (Skeggs, 1991). However, for the students in this study the "visibility" of gender relations could be contrasted with the "invisibility" of sexuality. At a time when it is common practice for policy and professional documents to subsume issues of sexuality within a more general discourse on gender, there is a need to emphasize that sexual and gender relations are not totally separate, as is usually assumed. Staff room, classroom, and playground everyday behavior all serve to carry important messages about sexual identities and practices. Schools treat student sexuality as a latent by-product of an emerging adult status. When sexuality does "break into" the public arena, it is conceptualized as natural and normal. At the same time, it remains located within the private sphere, reflecting a popular conception of sexuality as being "special" or "exceptional." In contrast to schools' attempts to erase sex and sexuality from the formal curriculum, the young men in this study recognize that sex and sexuality are pervasive within the official and hidden curriculum while at the same time being made invisible (Mac an Ghaill, 1991). Sex and sexuality reappear in an extensive repertoire of student-student interactions, including name-calling, flirting, classroom disruption, harassment of girls, homophobic abuse, playground conversations, desk-top graffiti, and students' dress codes, as well as teacher typifications and student-teacher interactions.

> Assim: At our school they had a good antisexist policy that I think helped the girls. But there was nothing on sexuality. It seems strange when you think of it that they don't see gender and sexuality going together.

> Stephen: The teachers try to deny or suppress it but sex is everywhere in school and that includes the way that teachers use it all the time to control kids and at the same time the way that kids use their sexuality that often mixes the teachers up.

These wide-ranging schooling activities are central in making available dominant and subordinate sexual subject positions. In other words, schooling processes can be seen to form gendered identities, marking out "correct" or "appropriate" styles of being (Butler, 1993). It is suggested here that it is within these historically specific school sexual/gender regimes that we may locate the development of black working-class male gay sexualities (Mac an Ghaill, 1988, 1994). Equally important, the identification of sexuality as part of a wider schooling process reconceptualizes sexuality as a key element of a public agenda that structures school experiences. Presenting sexuality as enmeshed in a set of power relations serves to highlight that rather than individualizing sexuality, the deployment of sexuality works within social relations of domination and subordination.

> Denton: Teachers try to make out sexuality is something that is just private, something not to be talked about in public. But if you come out as gay, suddenly sexuality is the biggest story in the school. Of course they cannot see that het-

erosexuality is also not simply a private affair but a very public one that controls us all, all of the time.

Deconstructing Heterosexuality

In England, during the 1980s particularly, as a result of feminist, gay, and lesbian writing, and AIDS activism (and more recently the influence of "new queer theory"), the changing nature of men's lives and their experiences were much debated within a range of literatures, drawing upon sex-role, psychoanalysis, and gender and power theories (Dollimore, 1991; Plummer, 1992; Sedgwick, 1991; Sinfield, 1994; Weeks, 1986). By the early 1990s, we have been provided with theoretical frameworks that enable us to analyze systematically and document coherently the material, social, and discursive production of masculinities (Brod & Kaufman, 1994; Connell, 1995; Segal, 1990). Queer theorists and AIDS activists have argued that sexuality is a key element in the construction of contemporary identities, both internally as a significant dimension of the self, and externally as a social category imbued with cultural expectations by others and as a primary marker of difference (Dollimore, 1991; Mac an Ghaill, 1994; Sedgwick, 1991). More specifically, such work has suggested that heterosexuality is both the assumed reference point of sexual/gender identity formation, while at the same time remaining unspoken. Furthermore, heterosexual relationships and, more emphatically, homosexual relationships are assumed to refer primarily to intimate sexual relations with the gender of the objects of our desire. What is missing from such common-sense perceptions is the fact that heterosexuality and homosexuality are key social, cultural, and political arenas in which we are positioned and position ourselves (Butler, 1990, 1993; Dollimore, 1991).

Gilroy: The teachers think that being gay is all about having sex. I think they can't see it's a whole way of living your life, just the same as them. But they just can't see that their being heterosexuals affects the way they see the world, the way they act and everything they do.

Assim: I think what gays have done in this society is to show how important sexuality really is in the way in which we all live our lives.

Brah (1992, p. 134) has written very persuasively of the need to problematize the racialization of white subjectivity. It is relevant to apply her argument to the category of sexuality. In English schools there is a tendency to see questions of sexuality as something primarily to do with gays and lesbians. However, it is politically and pedagogically important to stress that both gay and straight people experience their class, gender, and ethnicity through sexuality. The sexualization of straight subjectivity is frequently not acknowledged by straights because "heterosexuality" signifies "normality" and dominance. Furthermore, there has been little understanding of sexuality as a relational concept in which different nonessentialist sexual identities are defined in relation to each other, with homosexuality always present in heterosexuality. A major task for educators is to deconstruct the complex social and discursive practices that serve to position teachers and students as "black and white, male and female straights," "black and white gays and lesbians."

In contrast to the conventional approach within sex-role theory that erases issues of sexuality by subsuming it within a broader discourse of gender, Butler (1993, p. 238) suggests that gender is often spoken through a "heterosexual matrix" in which heterosexuality is presupposed in the expression of "real forms of masculinity and femininity." This provides a useful framework within which to explore the interconnectedness between gender and sexuality as it is lived out in schools. In structuring the attributes of being a "real boy"/"real girl," the various forms of masculinity/femininity that are hegemonic in schools are crucially involved in policing the boundaries of heterosexuality alongside the boundaries of "proper" masculinity/femininity. For example, to be a "real boy" is publicly to be in opposition to and distance oneself from the feminine and the "feminized" versions of masculinity. At an institutional level, student identities are formed in relation to the formal curriculum and the categories it makes available, including the academic/vocational, the arts/science, and the academic/sporting polarities. These categories are highly gendered, with the "soft feminine" academic and arts subjects juxtaposed to the "hard masculine" vocational, scientific, and sporting options. Similarly, involvement in sport can be read as a cultural index of what it means to be a "real boy," while not to be involved in sport and its associated "lad" subculture is to be a "bit of a poof" (homophobic term).

> Raj: A lot of people at school, teachers and students, would want to deny that the subjects we did had anything to do with gender and sexuality. But really they can't deny it. At our school some of the boys who took arts subjects and particularly if they did not play football were persecuted. It's hard to know what was going on here. Just because they took certain subjects and did not act in a certain

macho way they were bullied every day. They were called "poofs" and all that but I don't think they were thought of as gay. It was like they were not proper straight boys but of course it can or does slide into homophobia. It's amazing really the way that these things are put together and lived out.

It must be added that it is important not to see heterosexuality as a unitary and cohesive subjectivity. In this study we explored the question of what constitutes male students' heterosexual identity. More specifically, we examined the constitutive cultural elements of dominant modes of heterosexual subjectivity that informed male students' performing their sexual apprenticeships within a school arena. These elements consisted of contradictory forms of compulsory heterosexuality, misogyny, and homophobia, and were marked by contextual contingency and ambivalence that served to challenge the hetero/homo divide. Male heterosexual identity can be seen as a highly fragile socially constructed phenomenon. Hence, the question that emerges is: How does this fragile construction become represented as an apparently stable, unitary category with fixed meanings? Schools, alongside other institutions, attempt to administer, regulate, and reify unstable sexual/gender categories (Foucault, 1979; Skeggs, 1991). Most particularly, this administration, regulation, and reification of sexual/gender boundaries is institutionalized through the interrelated material, social, and discursive practices of Staff room, classroom, and playground microcultures.

> Rajinder: I sometimes have the feeling that schools must be so tired with all the energy they put into making sure that people stay straight. They don't ask the kind of questions you ask. Like, what's going on here?

Psychosexual Dynamics and Masculine Identity Formation

Recent cultural theory reveals a tension between materialist, deconstructionist, and psychoanalytic critiques of sexual/gender identity formation. In materialist accounts, gender and sexuality are viewed as a matrix of power relations. In contrast, deconstructionist theorists have emphasized that the living of sexual/gender categories and divisions is more contradictory, fragmented, shifting, and ambivalent than the dominant public definitions of these categories suggest. As Davies and Hunt (1994) assert: "Deconstruction is a strategy for displacing the hierarchy, for revealing the dependence of the privileged or ascendant term on its other for its own meaning: deconstruction moves to disrupt binary logic and its hierarchical, oppositional constitutive force" (p. 389). Psychoanalysis has developed highly productive accounts of the complex psychic investments that individuals have in dominant sexual and gendered discourses (Butler, 1990). At the same time, psychodynamic explanations illustrate the limits of overrationalist accounts of sexual politics that fail to acknowledge that what we *feel* is as important as what we *know* in relation to the maintenance of dominant gendered and heterosexual discourses and social practices.

Currently, cultural theorists have placed on the educational agenda the urgent need for policy responses to acknowledge that key elements of the complexity of the construction of the sexual/gendered identities are the realities of differential power relations and sexual diversity. As the students point out below, their schooling cannot be reductively conceptualized in terms of a simple binary social system, composed of a juxtaposed white middle-class straight superiority and a black working-class gay inferiority. The relations between them also involve a psychic structure, including such elements as: desire, attraction, repression, transference, and projection in relation to a racialized "sexual other" (Pajckowska & Young, 1992). This echoes one of the main themes of Isaac Julien's film, *Young Soul Rebels*. In its exploration of the construction of black masculinity, he focuses upon such issues as white men's ambivalences, transgressions, and envy toward black men. There is much work to be done in this area in order to understand the ambivalent structure of feeling and desire embedded within social institutions (Fanon, 1970). In the following accounts, the young men discuss the range of split responses from white males to themselves that were manifested in terms of the interplay between racial and sexual fear and desire and the accompanying contradictory elements of repulsion, fascination, and misrecognition (Klein, 1960).

Andrew: It's like with the straights, all the bits they don't like about themselves or they're afraid of, they push onto us.

Rajinder: Thinking about it, it's very complex. Straight men don't really have a problem with gays, they have a problem with themselves. Straight men seem to fear and love women but fear and hate gay men. Then whites, especially white men, have that fear and hatred for Asians and African Caribbeans. So, black gay men are a real threat to white straight men. Like James Baldwin says, they act out their fears on us, on our bodies. . . . But then there's other complications. Like at our school, you could see some of the white teachers, the men, they really admired the Caribbeans and not just in sport and music, where it was really homoerotic, though of course they could never admit it to themselves. I think for a lot of teachers there, who felt trapped in their jobs, the macho black kids represented freedom from the system. There were antischool macho whites and Asians but the teachers with their stereotypes fantasized about the Caribbean kids, who they saw as antiauthority, more physical and athletic, everything they couldn't be but greatly admired.

Stephen: Like you say, black kids know that most white teachers would never live in our areas even though they make their living here. English middle-class people have always lived off immigrants—the blacks and the Irish around here. The teachers' kids go to their white grammar and private schools on the backs of the miseducation that their parents impose on us every day. . . . But at night the teachers creep out of their white ghettos to live it up among the "black folk." Emotionally they're really screwed up. And somehow although they don't want us as neighbors, they are obsessed with our food, music, dance, with our sex. You see they fantasize that these poor black folk they're not repressed like the whiteys and in a different way their kids are doing the same . . . another generation of patronization from the white boys and girls!

In schooling arenas, the black gay students identified different masculine heterosexualities as constitutive of different relationships with African Caribbean and Asian males and females. For the students, "race" created a number of complexities for white English males in their articulation of particular masculine heterosexualities. Those males, who were part of a heterosexual culture that was premised on sexual athleticism, experienced a range of psychic and microcultural contradictions because of their racist and homophobic disidentifications with Asian and African Caribbean men and women. These disidentifications limited, restricted, and thus contested their claims to a sexual desire that was "uncontrollable." In contrast, those males in sexual cultures that emphasized remaining virgins till they met the "right" person reflected few contradictions in forming relationships with African Caribbean or Asian females. If African Caribbean and Asian gay male sexualities are worked out against heterosexuality, it is necessary to see that what we understand as being "heterosexuality" is made up of individual, microcultural, and institutional complexities. The continuities of relations of domination and subordination embodied in heterosexual practices across different arenas have received vital and necessary critical attention. If schools are constituted by a range of heterosexualities, discontinuities arising between different heterosexualities in different and multiple social relationships need to be taken into account. As Andrew suggests, mapping out the diverse and incohesive forms of heterosexualities offers an alternative way of identifying the complexities present in the cultural landscape of gay experiences that moves beyond a construction of them as "mere victims."

Andrew: Its not a question of all straights being against gays. Like it depends where you meet the straights and whether it's a public or private place. Nor is it a question of all gays being mixed up about their sexuality and straights being sorted out. We need to know more about straights and the different ways they act out their sexual lifestyles. There's a lot of pressure on them to act in certain ways, probably especially when they're not sure about their sexuality. You get the feeling that straights have to perform all the time.

Vijay: Adults—gays and straights—tend to generalize their own experiences onto us. But there are things that are happening that are different for the younger generation. We have grown up in the decade of AIDS. We know about different sexual lifestyles, from the soaps, etc. I think sexual preference is different for our generation. And no one has begun to ask, how this is affecting young heteros. And especially, as Andrew says, there a lot of young people that are sexually experimenting. This is still the biggest surprise for me as a gay person, how many straight people are sexually attracted to you. This desire thing is really strange isn't it?

Gay Students as Active Agents: The Complexities of Contestation and Resistance

The students in this chapter have grown up in a society in which there are no positive images of gay or lesbian people. There is no acknowledgment of gay and lesbian history, sensibility, lifestyle, and community. There is no recognition of gay or lesbian achievement. For example, the research showed that when texts written by gays or lesbians were read in school, no reference was made to the authors' sexual orientation. In fact, in formal situations homosexuality was rarely discussed and on the few occasions when it was introduced, it was presented in a negative way; most recently in relation to AIDS. For the students this silence, reflecting that in the wider society, pervaded the whole of the formal curriculum, serving to reproduce and legitimate dominant heterosexual hierarchies. From this perspective, heterosexuality was presented as natural, normal, and universal, simply because there are no alternative ways of being (Egerton, 1986). The students emphasized the personal isolation, confusion, marginalization, and alienation that this engendered. Most significant, without a positive reference group they tended to internalize ambivalent negative messages about themselves as gay men.

Denton: Its terrible when you're younger, you think you're the only gay person in the world. And everyone is saying all these bad things about gays and lesbians. So, of course, you begin to think some of these things. And then you're really mixed up. Because you think, well this is the way I am and I don't fit into the stereotypes. I'm not surprised so many young gays feel suicidal.

Raj: If you think you are gay as you are growing up, it is easy to become homophobic and deny your feelings. You go on the defensive and try and distance yourself from *them*. The whole society is pushing you that way. All the talk about young people wanting to be different. It isn't true. Everyone wants to belong, everyone is looking to be the same.

However, there is a danger in examining black gay working-class students' schooling experiences of unintendedly adopting a passive concept of subject positioning, with the student portrayed as unproblematically accepting an overdetermined racial and gender/sexual role allocation (Walkerdine, 1990). In this study I set out to reconceptualize black students' experience of schooling by adopting an antireductive approach, in moving beyond monocausal explanations and examining the multifaceted dimensions of racially and sexually structured English schooling. The Asian and African Caribbean young men in this study, all of whom are academically successful, recall schooling biographies that have significant convergences and differences. What emerges is how racialized/sexualized social and discursive practices with their own local histories are grounded in specific material cultures at school, classroom, and playground levels. For the students, the white teachers' racial and gender/sexual typifications did not take a unitary form but rather were differentially structured and experienced, mediated by the specificity of different school cultures and individual student responses. In particular, the racial and gender composition of each school was a significant variable in the construction of teacher typifications. As the students make clear in this chapter, they were active curriculum and masculine makers. Furthermore, their accounts of schooling help to highlight the complexity of student resistance to cross-cutting multiple forms of oppression that queer theorists and postcolonial writers have suggested (Bhabha, 1990; Mercer & Julien, 1988).

As Cockburn (1987) has pointed out, "The social construction of gender is riddled with resistance and the resistance is complex. While some boys refuse the macho mode of masculinity and pay the price of being scorned as a 'wimp' or a 'poofter,' others resist the class domination by means of masculine codes" (p. 44). For African Caribbean and Asian male students this resistance is also developed in relation to racially administered schooling systems. Here, the students reflected on the specific dynamics and interplay between state schooling and the construction of African Caribbean and Asian ethnic masculinities. They were aware of how class-based differentiated curricula helped to shape differentiated masculinities, with sectors of black and white working-class students developing compensatory hypermasculine forms in response to their experience of academic failure. They were also aware of how black students defensively responded to racialized and gendered discourses that constructed juxtaposed images of "weak" Asian and "tough" African Caribbean males (Mac an Ghaill, 1994). They acknowledged the colonial legacy and present-day validity of Mercer and Julien's (1988) argument that,

whereas prevailing definitions of masculinity imply power, control and authority, these attributes have been historically denied to black men since slavery. The centrally dominant role of the white male slave-master in 18th and 19th century plantation society debarred black males from the patriarchal privileges ascribed to the male masculine role. . . . Shaped by this history, black masculinity is a highly contradictory formation as it is a subordinated masculinity. (p. 112)

What emerges are the specific dynamics for young black men in their psychosexual development within a school system and a wider culture that systematically devalues and marginalizes black masculinities while elevating and celebrating dominant forms of white straight masculinity. In the following extracts, the students make clear the contextual contingency in which racial and sexual typifications operate.

Amerjit: Teachers can't see the way that schools make kids act bad. For a lot of blacks, it's the low classes, the nonacademic subjects and being pushed into sport that makes them act macho. It's the way that black and white boys having being failed on the school's terms, try to get some status, some self-respect. At school you only hear of all the great whites. Most teachers don't respect black men, so the kids think they have no choice but to act it out.

Assim: At our school when we started the whites and the Caribbeans were seen as the toughest. But by the fifth year, the Asian gangs were the worst. They were like the Warrior gang in "Young, Gifted and Black." They formed gangs, smoked, wore the right gear, trainers and track suits, watched violent videos and hung around with older kids with fast cars and the music. Things that a lot of white working-class pupils do, acting hard all the time. But for the Asians, there is also racism. Outside of school, outside our own area, we are always under suspicion and likely to be attacked from the N.F. [National Front—racist political organization] and respectable whites. We know that we get attacked because whites see us as easy targets, as weak. They also knew that the teachers were afraid of the Caribbeans because they saw them as tough. Like at school the teachers would avoid walking through groups of African Caribbean kids but not Asians.

Stephen: In the last place [secondary school] the African Caribbeans were seen as the hardest and most anti the teachers. There were only a few of them involved in the main antischool gang but they were the leaders of the posse, as they called themselves. I think a lot of the teachers stereotyped all blacks as aggressive. And I think some of the kids came to believe this about themselves or thought the teachers believed it, so they may as well act it out as they were going to be picked on anyway.

As suggested above, the students' accounts find resonance in postcolonial writing that has provided ways of understanding power relations that move beyond additive approaches emphasizing the limitations of conceptualizing experience in terms of competing oppressions (Bhabha, 1994). These accounts of the experience of oppressions emphasize the simultaneous relevance of sexuality, gender, "race," and class. For Young and Dickerson (1994), "Hierarchies of domination are constructed and experienced simultaneously, their dynamics permeating one another" (p. 5). The exercise of power from a range of structures is refracted through individual experiences as a cohesive form of domination. In order to understand Asian and African Caribbean gay young men's experiences, we need to take into account the ways that their economic position, their ethnicity, and their age constitute *relational configurations* on the social and individual experience and understanding of being gay.

Feminist scholarship, in critiquing male ethnographic work on schooling and masculinity, has argued that antischool male student behavior cannot be reductively read as simply a product of resistance but also acts as a "legitimation and articulation of power and subordination" (Skeggs, 1991). The black gay students reported widespread forms of sexual harassment experienced by female and gay students. They examined the links between the institutional and male peer-group surveillance, regulation, and control of female and male gender and sexual reputations. They were surprised at the way in which straight male teachers and students conflated assumed gay behavior with femininity in order to disparage the former. The assimilation of masculine nonmacho behavior to feminine behavior was most evident in relation to the ubiquity of the term *poof* (homophobic term), which in "denoting lack of guts, suggests femininity—weakness, softness and inferiority" (Lees, 1987, p. 180). Furthermore, they linked this form of gay-bashing to that of the use of the term *paki* (racist term) as a form of "paki-bashing" (physical and verbal attacks on Asians). Both these labels, poof and paki, have several meanings: Sometimes they are used with a specific sexual or racial connotation, while at other times they are used as general terms of abuse. The notoriety and frequency of these labels acted as major mechanisms of policing gender and sexual boundaries with specific implications for straight and gay black youth.

> Rajinder: Nearly all the tough kids, the really hard lads were in the bottom two bands, especially the bottom one. They got their status by fighting the system that they saw abusing them. Some of the toughest ones were the white kids from the estate, always in trouble with the police and teachers. They were obsessed with proving they were real men, like those kids you talked about with their fighting, football and fucking—that was really them. They hated "poofs" and "Pakis" and used to argue with the teachers when they tried to stop fights, say things like, "sir, he's only a 'Paki' or a 'poof.'" They felt that the teachers agreed with them and in some ways they were right. A lot of the men teachers were really into violence but it was official, so that was okay to them. Anything seen as soft in their terms was despised. Like there was all this sexist talk by teachers. They thought that the best way to control a boy was to say to him, "stop acting like a girl." And they always said it loud so all the student's friends could hear. You see then outside the class the lads could carry on the sexual bullying that the teachers had set up.

There is much evidence from lesbian and gay literature of the physical, psychological, and verbal abuse that lesbian and gay people systematically experience in homophobic and heterosexist societies (Burbage & Walters, 1981; Mac an Ghaill, 1991). The young men in this chapter report similar personal and institutional experiences of such abuse. However, it is important for educationalists, in understanding the social positioning of these young people, not to adopt a reductionist pedagogical approach that sees gays and lesbians as mere problems or victims. Without reducing

Asian and African Caribbean gay masculinity to a unitary category, the students provide much evidence in this study to suggest that being gay is in many circumstances a positive and creative experience.

Rajinder: Teachers, especially male teachers assume your being gay is a problem but there are a lot of pluses. In fact I think one of the main reasons that male straights hate us is because they really know that emotionally we are more worked out than them. We can talk about and express our feelings, our emotions in a positive way. They can only express negative feelings like hatred, anger and dominance. Who would like to be like them?

Raj: It's like when you gave that talk at the university about having several identities. I don't think that the most people could understand because really everything about them is taken for granted. Their Englishness, their whiteness, their culture, their gender and sexuality—it's just the norm for them. And that's what's really good about being a black gay, you have no choice, you have to question these things. I think what I've learned most in us being together for the last two years is that the questions can be on our terms not theirs.

Denton: I agree. That's why people like James Baldwin and Langston Hughes are so important for us. Yes, the world is going to hate us but people like them got through and in a lots of ways it was worse, much worse for them. And you feel very proud that they are part of our history. They've made me more aware of other outsiders who are oppressed in this society. I used to feel really bad about being gay and I still get really down at times. But through being black and gay even if I don't stay gay, I know myself more than white men, than straights do.

Conclusion

As the young men in this chapter point out, the major problem in the schooling of black gay students is not their sexuality but the phenomena of homophobia, heterosexism, and racism that pervasively circumscribe their social world. Furthermore, these phenomena are mediated and reproduced both through existing formal and hidden curriculum, pedagogical, and evaluative systems that serve to regulate all subordinated young people, and through gender/sexual specific mechanisms, such as the processes of gender/sexual typifications, which in turn are "race," class, and age specific. For example, the students' teachers claimed that they found it difficult to discuss lesbian and gay issues within the school context. An idealist analysis of the curriculum, which reduces the heterosexist structuring of schooling to aberrant teacher prejudice, is insufficient here to explain the complex interaction of white teachers with black male gay students. In English schools, specific age relations operate that serve to marginalize and alienate many young people. White teachers' difficulty in communicating with gay black students is not simply an issue about sexuality and racism. Also, it is circumscribed by the low epistemological status ascribed to all students (Mac an Ghaill, 1994).

Vijay: I don't think teachers really know how deep feelings are about sexuality in schools and it's more complex when they are dealing with black gays. They think its just about bad stereotypes but in fact the whole place is organized to exclude gays and lesbians.

The Asian and African Caribbean working-class gay students here, in exploring the politics of complex difference involving the articulation of homophobia, heterosexism, racism, and class oppression, are a sector of the younger generation among whom syncretic black identities are being formed, focusing on social commonalties, as well as on the cultural specificities of personal histories, memories, desires, and expectations (Mama, 1992).

Andrew: Reading through this study it shows, yes we are pushed to the margins of society as black gays. But that doesn't mean we have to accept that position. We can educate ourselves to understand the different oppressions. And you can see here that our position can be positive in helping us to work out ways forward not just for gays and blacks but for others as well because we are questioning whiteness and heterosexuality that are usually very hidden.

For progressive social activists located within schools, the students suggest political and pedagogical spaces to identify and challenge dominant social practices. In so doing, we may build on their reconstruction of new forms of sexualities that they are living out, which in turn is helping to produce "new times" in an old country.

Note

1. *Asian* is used to refer to those students who identified themselves as Indian, Pakistani, or Bangladeshi.

References

Bhabha, H. (Ed.). (1990). *Nation and narration*. London: Routledge & Kegan Paul.

Bhabha, H. (1994). *The location of culture*. London: Routledge & Kegan Paul.

Brah, A. (1992). Difference, diversity and differentiation. In J. Donald & A. Rattansi (Eds.), *"Race," culture and difference* (pp. 126-145). Milton Keynes, UK: Open University Press/Sage.

Brod, H., & Kaufman, M. (1994). *Theorising masculinities*. London: Sage.

Burbage, M., & Walters, J. (1981). (Eds.). *Breaking the silence: Gay teenagers speak for themselves*. London: Joint Council for Gay Teenagers.

Butler, J. (1990). *Gender trouble, feminism and the subversion of identity*. London: Routledge & Kegan Paul.

Butler, J. (1993). *Bodies that matter, on the discursive limits of "sex."* London: Routledge & Kegan Paul.

Carrigan, T., Connell, R. W., & Lee, J. (1985). Hard and heavy phenomena: The sociology of masculinity. *Theory and Society, 14,* 551-604.

Cockburn, C. (1987). *Two-track training: Sex inequality and the YTS*. London: Macmillan.

Connell, R. W. (1989). Cool guys, swots and wimps: The inter-play of masculinity and education. *Oxford Review of Education, 15*(3), 291-303.

Connell, R. W. (1995). *Masculinities*. London: Polity.

Connell, R. W., Ashenden, D. J., Kessler, S., & Dowsett, G. W. (1982). *Making the difference: School, families and social division*. Sydney: Allen & Unwin.

Davies, B. (1993). *Shards of glass: Children, reading and writing beyond gendered identities*. Sydney: Allen & Unwin.

Davies, B., & Hunt, R. (1994). Classroom competencies and marginal positioning. *British Journal of Sociology of Education, 15,* 389-408.

Delamont, S. (1982). *Sex roles and the school*. London: Methuen.

Dollimore, J. (1991). *Sexual dissidence: Augustine to Wilde, Freud to Foucault*. Oxford, UK: Clarendon.

Egerton, J. (1986). *Danger: Heterosexism at work*. London: Greater London Council.

Fanon, F. (1970). *Black skin, white masks*. London: Paladin.

Foucault, M. (1979). *The history of sexuality, Vol. 1*. Harmondsworth, UK: Penguin.

Gordon, P., & Klug, F. (1986). *New Right, new racism*. London: Searchlight Publications.

Hall, S. (1990). Cultural identity and diaspora. In J. Rutherford (Ed.), *Identity: Community, culture and difference*. London: Lawrence & Wishart.

Harvey, D. (1989). *The condition of postmodernity*. Oxford, UK: Basil Blackwell.

Hemphill, E. (Ed.). (1991). *Brother to brother: New writings by black gay men*. Boston: Alyson.

Henriques, J. (1984). Social psychology and the politics of racism. In J. Henriques, W. Hollway, C. Urwin, C. Venn, & V. Walkerdine (Eds.), *Changing the subject: Psychology, social regulation and subjectivity*. London: Methuen.

Jameson, F. (1991). *Postmodernism, or the cultural logic of late capitalism*. Durham, NC: Duke University Press.

Kelly, L. (1992). Not in front of the children: Responding to right-wing agendas on sexuality and education. In M. Arnot & L. Barton (Eds.), *Voicing concerns: Sociological perspectives on contemporary education reforms*. London: Triangle Books.

Klein, M. (1960). *Our adult world and its roots in infancy*. London: Tavistock.

Lather, P. (1986). Research as praxis. *Harvard Educational Review, 56*(3), 257-277.

Lees, S. (1987). The structure of sexual relations in school. In M. Arnot & G. Weiner (Eds.), *Gender and politics of schooling*. Milton Keynes, UK: Open University Press.

Mac an Ghaill, M. (1988). *Young, gifted and black: Student-teacher relations in the schooling of black youth*. Milton Keynes, UK: Open University Press.

Mac an Ghaill, M. (1989). Beyond the white norm: The use of qualitative research in the study of black students' schooling in England. *Qualitative Studies in Education, 2*(3), 175-189.

Mac an Ghaill, M. (1991). Schooling, sexuality and male power: Towards an emancipatory curriculum. *Gender and Education, 3*(3), 291-309.

Mac an Ghaill, M. (1994). *The making of men: Masculinities, sexualities and schooling*. Buckingham, UK: Open University Press.

Mac an Ghaill, M. (1998). *Sociology of "race," ethnicity and racism: Social and cultural transformations*. Buckingham, UK: Open University Press.

Mac an Ghaill, M., & Haywood, C. (1998). The making of men: Theorizing methodology in "uncertain times." In G. Walford (Ed.), *Doing research about education*. London: Routledge & Kegan Paul.

Mama, A. (1992). Black women and the British state: Race, class and gender analysis for the 1990s. In P. Braham, A. Rattansi, & R. Skellington (Eds.), *Racism and antisexism: Inequalities, opportunities and policies*. London: Sage/Open University Press.

Mercer, K., & Julien, I. (1988). Race, sexual politics and black masculinity: A dossier. In R. Chapman & J. Ruthford (Eds.), *Male order: Unwrapping masculinities*. London: Lawrence & Wishart.

Morgan, D. H. J. (1992). *Discovering men: Critical studies on men and masculinities*. London: Routledge & Kegan Paul.

Pajckowska, C., & Young, L. (1992). Racism, representation and psychoanalysis. In J. Donald & A. Rattansi (Eds.), *"Race," culture and difference* (pp. 198-219). Milton Keynes, UK: Sage/Open University Press.

Plummer, K. (Ed.). (1992). *Modern homosexualities*. London: Routledge & Kegan Paul.

Plummer, K. (1995). *Telling sexual stories: Power, change and social worlds*. London: Routledge & Kegan Paul.

Rowbotham, S. (1989). *The past is before us: Feminism in action since the 1960s*. Harmondsworth, UK: Penguin.

Rutherford, J. (1990). A place called home: Identity and the cultural politics of difference. In J. Rutherford (Ed.), *Identity: Community, culture and difference*. London: Lawrence & Wishart.

Sedgwick, E. K. (1991). *Epistemology of the closet*. London: Harvester Wheatsheaf.

Segal, L. (1990). *Slow motion: Changing masculinities, changing men*. London: Virago.

Sinfield, A. (1994). *Cultural politics: Queer reader*. London: Routledge & Kegan Paul.

Skeggs, B. (1991). Challenging masculinity and using sexuality. *British Journal of Sociology of Education, 12*(1), 127-140.

Troupe, Q. (1989). *James Baldwin: The legacy*. New York: Simon & Schuster/Touchstone.

Walkerdine, V. (1990). *Schoolgirl fictions*. London: Verso.

Weeks, J. (1986). *Sexuality*. London: Tavistock.

Weeks, J. (1989). *Sexuality and its discontents: Meanings, myths and modern sexualities*. London: Routledge & Kegan Paul.

Young, G., & Dickerson, B. J. (1994). Introduction. In G. Young & B. J. Dickerson (Eds.), *Color, class and country* (pp. 1-9). London: Zed Books.

8

Preparing to ~~Teach~~ Coach

Tracking the Gendered Relations of Dominance, On and Off the Football Field

NANCY LESKO

The faces of the [football] players were young, but the perfection of their equipment, the gleaming shoes and helmets and the immaculate pants and jersies, the solemn ritual that was attached to almost everything, made them seem like boys going off to fight a war for the benefit of someone else, unwitting sacrifices to a strange and powerful god.

Bissinger, 1990, p. 11

Competitive athletics is a high-status dimension of U.S. schooling, a domain dominated by men's sports. More than half of all student participation in extracurriculars is in the athletic/sports category (Berk, 1992). Despite male athletic programs' preeminence in school budgets and politics, little scholarly attention has been given to the significance and effects of competitive athletics, coaching, and their brand of masculinity within contemporary discussions of teaching, schooling, and school reform. That is, the masculinity of sports in schools, especially in high schools, has been generally treated as a separate sphere with limited impact. The examination of male-dominated athletics as a delimited phenomenon—extracurricular, court- or field-based, rather than as a systemic "logic of

AUTHOR'S NOTE: I am grateful for support from the Maris Proffitt Foundation, Indiana University, and for Sharon Sperry's assistance.

practice"—has truncated our analyses of how a competitive, athletic masculinity influences school culture, teaching, and curricula.

Several recent studies of high school athletes and sports do begin to map the connections across gridiron and classroom, coaching and teaching. For example, Bissinger's (1990) study of one Texas high school football season shows how the players were treated as demigods and exempted from routine attendance and classwork. Lefkowitz's (1997) research on the Glen Ridge, New Jersey, rape of a "mentally impaired" girl by a group of football players portrays the ways classroom teachers and administrators supported the privilege of male athletes by systematically ignoring their bullying and assaults of other students. Both studies describe schools in which policies, discipline, and educational aims are strongly dominated by male athletes and competitive athletics.

This chapter seeks to expand our understanding of the sports culture in schooling by tracing linkages between the football field and the classroom, beginning with the popular representation of exemplary teachers as "coaches." I examine the social relations of playing football, the spectacular linkages between nationalism, militarism, and community-school spirit, and the implications of these masculinized, stratified gridiron social relations for high school curriculum and teaching. I utilize the life history narratives of one preservice teacher, a football star in high school, to help map the circulation of hypermasculine perspectives and their social relations from the gridiron to the classroom. Thus, I am in pursuit of how affect becomes harnessed to political life (Stoler, 1995, p. 136), or how nation and school team become fused with desire. This analysis, although speculative, offers cautions for the eager employment of coaching-as-teaching in educational reform movements.

The Teacher as Coach in Contemporary Educational Discourse

Ted Sizer, a towering presence in the secondary school restructuring movement, proposes that good teaching is analogous to *coaching*. In *Horace's Compromise* Sizer (1984) writes about students learning skills,[1] including reading, writing, speaking, listening, measuring, estimating, calculating, and seeing, and suggests that coaching is the best way for these abilities to be imparted:

How are skills learned? By experience. How, then, are they best taught? By *coaching*. . . . Ironically, it is the athletic coach, often arrogantly dismissed by some academic instructors as a kind of dumb ox, unworthy of being called a real teacher, who may be a school's most effective teacher of skills. (p. 106)

Sizer argues that the process of teaching/learning is abstract and incomplete until a student actually writes (for example) and a teacher criticizes it, or a novice throws a javelin, the instructor criticizes it, the student throws again, and the coach gives further criticism. Sizer's equation of coaching = good teaching has been widely circulated as part of the influential work of the Coalition of Essential Schools.

Competitive athletics are clearly masculinizing dimensions of schools (Connell, 1996). Recent British scholarship suggests that there is a *remasculinizing* of schools and school management occurring. Lynn Davies (1992) finds that a particular version of masculinity—"competitive, point-scoring, over-confident, sporting, career and status conscious" (p. 135)—has come to dominate school management. Mac an Ghaill's (1994) description of the masculinities of teachers in one secondary school supports Davies's thesis: Mac an Ghaill found a resurgence of English nationalism, which was linked to boys learning their place through coercive discipline and to a professionalism yearning for the old days of all-male schooling and enacting some of that past by emphasizing traditional "masculine" subject areas, such as natural sciences, mathematics, and competitive team sports. I suggest that the reimagining of *teaching as coaching* is part of a remasculinizing of U.S. schools, which has gone hand-in-hand with broader social remasculinization via film and literature on the Vietnam War (Gibson, 1994; Jeffords, 1989) and through nationalistic aggression.[2]

Positioning Football, Masculinity, and the Gulf War

My interviews with Woody Rockne,[3] the subject of this chapter, were part of a larger study of a secondary teacher education program.[4] My interviews with Woody began in August 1993, slightly more than a year after the Persian Gulf War ended. The emotional tenor of his narratives, coupled with the alleged efficiency and rationality of his life, sounded familiar. For me, Woody's stories echoed the mix of irrationality and reason around the U.S. invasion of Iraq during the Gulf War. I *felt* a similarity between the plot and emotional pitch of this preservice teacher's life stories and the popular response to the attack on Saddam Hussein by George Bush. My mental, emotional, and visceral responses to Woody's stories focused on the mix of rationality and boosterism in his tales of his school years, his sports involvements, his coaching practices, and his beliefs about teaching and coaching. Ann Laura Stoler (1995) has termed this intersection the link between nationalism and desire, or the "harnessing of affect to political life" (p. 136). It was the peculiar *fervent rationality,* sometimes amusing but often arrogant and frightening, that this analysis seeks to describe and understand. Connell (1990) suggests that life history narratives afford an invaluable and unique perspective on schools as masculinizing institutions that is elided in other approaches.

This re-presentation of Woody's stories of playing football, coaching, and preparing to teach within the context of the Gulf War's nationalistic aggression begins with the need to view the following topics as linked: (a) sports and war, (b) sports and nationalism, (c) football as nationalist spectacle, and (d) the militarization of civilian life through "permanent war." The latter part of the chapter examines the individual and classroom dimensions of these sports-war-masculinity connections.

Sports, War, and Nationalism

There are strong historical, political, and ideological connections between *sports and war.* Organized team sports and imperial wars developed simultaneously in the United States. Sports often became a preparation for war (Wakefield, 1996), and the way the military kept noncombat soldiers busy, fit, and with a steady morale. Teddy Roosevelt and others of his generation linked the development of masculinity with both sports and wars.

In addition, the language of football draws heavily on military argot: attack, blitz, bombs, ground and air assaults, offense, defense, penetrations, flanks, conflicts, and battles for territory are standard terms in sportscasters' vocabularies. Both coaches and generals speak of victories, defeats, and casualties. In addition, sport/war metaphors have had currency in U.S. politics since the Civil War (Jansen & Sabo, 1994). The government often uses sports language as code words; for example, Richard Nixon's pseudonym for himself was *Quarterback.* George Bush dubbed the Gulf War his "Super Bowl" (Nadelhaft, 1993, p. 27). Jansen and Sabo (1994) conclude that football imagery has become the "root metaphor of American political discourse" (p. 3).

Connections between sports and the Gulf War were everywhere. "[F]rom the beginning sports and the actual [Persian Gulf] conflict were linked in the media" (Nadelhaft, 1993, p. 25). Nadelhaft points to sports-inflected language in the Gulf War coverage, references to the war appearing on the sports pages, and the *Chicago Tribune*'s full-page, brightly-colored "Young Reader's Guide to the Gulf War" at the back of the sports section. Columnist Mike Royko made these connections:

> In football, the coaches say careful preparation, planning, discipline and execution are everything. That's what the generals say too. In football, the coaches say it's essential to establish the air game and the ground game. That's exactly what the generals said we did in the desert. And most coaches loathe the press. So do the generals. They have so many qualities in common. (cited in Nadelhaft, 1993, p. 27)

Scholars suggest that sports imagery both rallied support for the war (Jansen & Sabo, 1994) and justified it:

> Sports, used as a metaphor for the Persian Gulf war, provided a sense of parity between the combatants and a sense that the war was governed by a neutral structure. . . . Sports metaphors, wrestling included, helped to legitimate the war and show merit and Justice to lie with the United States. . . . They imparted a structure to the war and made it into a contest, not a slaughter. (Nadelhaft, 1993, p. 29)

To emphasize the intimacy of sports and war is simultaneously to demonstrate strong connections between *sports and nationalism*. Historian George Mosse (1985, 1996) finds masculinity and nationalism linked through sports; the sports realm provides the ideal of physical fitness and its related moral health. The physical body—portrayed as a strong, white, muscular male body—represents the nation and its moral health.

With the fading of the 1992 Gulf War from view, skeptical readers might question the close association between football and war. However, scholars of the Cold War argue that the United States is in a state of "permanent war," a militarization of nationalism and civilian life that occurs on the terrain of ignorance and knowledge, and the psychologies of good citizens and threatening others (Lutz, 1997). Persistent ideas of dangerous others who might brainwash upright citizens and images of subversion of the American way of life are aspects of Lutz's "epistemology of the bunker." The "permanent war" mentality can be mobilized through complex, evil portraits of "others" (Aksoy & Robins, 1991; Levidow, 1995) who threaten invasion or the takeover of American institutions or interests. The mobilization of emotions, discussed in the next section, is a crucial component of wartime dichotomies of us/them. The mobilization of emotions is essential to the appearance of a noncoercive political order.

Sports as Nationalist Spectacles

Conceiving of sports as nationalistic spectacles broadens our analysis to include visual, collective, emotional, and symbolic dimensions of football. Guy DuBord's (1977) work on the spectacle is useful here:

> The spectacle is not a collection of images, but *a social relation among people, mediated by images.* . . . The spectacle is the present model of socially dominant life. (emphasis added; pp. 2-3)

DuBord continues with his description of the spectacle:

> [The spectacle] says nothing more than "that which appears is good, that which is good appears." The attitude which it demands in principle is passive acceptance, which in fact it already obtained by its manner of appearing without reply, by its monopoly of appearance. (p. 12)

The monopolizing visual spectacle asserts the dominant social relations as an accepted fact, and charges these images with emotion. Sporting events are highly emotional occasions, although thoroughly structured and scripted.

> Apathy and boredom are considered bad form; if the game is that bad, you're expected to get mad and boo. Fans are expected to be *enthusiastic* in the literal sense of the word: possessed by gods they identify with. (Friedenberg, 1980, p. 180)

Friedenberg views sporting events as channeling feeling and awareness:

> Spectator sports arouse intense emotion and surround its expression with so much anxiety and such stereotypical constraints that *it can be directed only into approved and conventional channels:* like competition or school or national spirit. . . . Sport has become institutionalized as . . . hostile to all spontaneous feeling. (emphasis added; p. 184)

Spectacles and Invented Communities

Historian Anne McClintock (1995) sees spectacles as central to the formation and performance of nations.[5] Spectacles, and especially commodity spectacles such as World's Fairs and athletic contests, invent nations and, by extension at the local level, imagine communities: "The singular power of nationalism has been its capacity to organize a sense of popular, collective unity through the management of mass national commodity spectacle" (p. 71). Nationalism takes shape through the visible, ritual organization of fetish objects: flags, uniforms, anthems, and through collective fetish spectacle—in team sports, military displays, mass rallies, and the like.[6]

Bissinger's (1990) portrait of high school football in Odessa, Texas, overflows with evidence of ritual organization, from the watermelon feed in August to the motorcades of cars and vans trekking to away games; football was the site of Odessa community-making, of "compulsive self-gorging" (Berlant & Freeman, 1993, p. 195) on ritualized community.[7]

> Nationalism presents itself both as a modern project that transforms traditional attachments in favor of new identities and as a reflection of authentic cultural values culled from the depths of a presumed communal past. (McClintock, 1993, p. 73)

This "imaginative" role of nationalist spectacle, as transformer of past social relations and as a reflection of authentic cultural values from a common past, is also present in high school football. McClintock suggests that nationalistic spectacle invents images of the past to identify what is "new" about current efforts. Bissinger's (1990) account of Odessa's Permian Panthers positions the tradition of the enormously successful football team against the grim realities of a town consistently named among the 10 worst places to live in the United States: "The legends of Odessa football had a deep and abiding sense of place and history, so unlike the town, where not even the origin of the name itself could be vouched for with any confidence" (p. 34).

The townspeople were "desperately devoted" to the football team and considered all the players like their own children. As Bissinger notes, however, injured African American players quickly reverted from beloved sons to no-good blacks. The start of each football season gave townspeople something to live for, which the gritty, grimy, economically depressed realities of their lives did not. Football in Odessa, and likely elsewhere, provided an imagined community out of economic boom-and-bust cycles and dust storms, an imagined community with a glorious past (in football victories) and a record-breaking future.

Summary. In this section, I have argued that sports are intimately linked with war and nationalistic political discourse. The concept of "permanent war" establishes sports/war/nationalism in imagery and language as a continual process of the militarizing of civil society. But it is necessary to supplement language analyses of sport/war/nation associations with considerations of material spectacles, the preeminent form of contemporary mediated nation building. Spectacles invent group ties by creating both pasts and futures; as illustrated in Bissinger's study of one Texas high school team, football calls forth community; scripted emotions; and enacts, legitimates, revivifies a dominant form of social relations. Thus, I am postulating a permanent discourse of sports/war/ nationalism as the context in which school athletics operates and within which it must be viewed.

The football spectacle as "the present model of socially dominant life" will be explored at the individual level with Woody's stories of his football career, his disciplined body, and the social relations of playing and coaching football. I will investigate Woody's narratives on football as parables for the correct life and attitudes, policy statements, really, for how individuals should act and how society should be organized—as on a playing field. If we are encouraged to imagine schools as "level playing fields" and teachers as "coaches," we need to look more closely at the social relations carried in those images. Woody's life history will help us specify the social relations of football and coaching before examining their implications for teaching.

Woody's Disciplined Body

> Strength of will was one of the distinguishing marks of the proper male ideal as opposed to so-called weak and womanly men. . . . Willpower was usually equated with courage, knowing how to face danger and pain. Steeling the body through sport was universally advocated as one of the best ways to accomplish this end. (Mosse, 1996, p. 100)

Woody was a 20-year-old junior in college, white and middle class, dividing his coursework among physical education, history, and secondary education, when he narrated his own adolescence. Unlike the adolescents he characterized as "trying to become as adult as possible as quickly as possible," or those he described as reactors to stimuli, without self-determination, Woody presented himself as fully rational and purposeful.

> I knew, probably from day three in the womb, I was going to play football. . . . My parents swear on my babybook that the first two words I ever put together were my high school, Holy Cross. They swear that ever since day one, it was just football and that was it. That's all I wanted. (Interview 2: 29-30)

In contrast to his descriptions of confused teenagers bending to whims, Woody portrayed himself as masterful, reasoning, and autonomous.

> I never did anything because I had to do it. . . . I did what I thought was right . . . 99% of the time. It wasn't like, Well, I'm in high school now and if I want to be a big, big star, I'm going to play football and get A's and B's. Na, I just lived my life how I was going to do it. . . . Did I succumb to peer pressure? No, I never did . . . other than like styles or clothes . . . I was just, you know, I think I should do this. It would be right if I did this. (Interview 3: 44)

Woody's story portrayed a boy-man[8] who knew exactly what he wanted; he wanted, like other adolescent males, to be an athlete, for boys are judged according to their ability in competitive sports (Messner, 1992, p. 24). He pursued his goal single-mindedly, except for his 8-month "James Dean" period.

> I guess my teen years did not start until I was 16, when I got a car. . . . [A]ctually like 14 I bought an old Mustang, '68 Mustang. Me and dad restored it. . . . When I turned 16, everyone thought I became this big James Dean kid, . . . and I kind of started trying to live up to that attitude. I was driving fast and getting into all kinds of trouble. . . . I was running around with some guys that were a little older than me and they were a lot crazier than I was. . . .[9] After they graduated [and entered the Marines], I went back and re-found myself. . . . The only thing that mattered to me, after the rebel period, was playing football and getting grades, because I had been recruited to play ball by Notre Dame, so I was just kind of straight and narrow. . . . I just kind of wanted to be a football player, go to work, come home, and coach my little brother is all I really wanted. (Interview 2: 45)[10]

Except for the lapse of 8 months, strategically positioned between the end of one football season and the beginning of the next, Woody never was an adolescent, if an adolescent is rebellious, confused, and prone to be influenced by others. He was purposive, focused, and his life was an orderly progression toward football stardom and academic achievement. He did not *learn* rationality; his orderly development was naturally occurring. Woody's life exemplified the manly leadership advocated by the sports and war booster, Theodore Roosevelt: "Courage, hard work, self mastery, and intelligent effort are essential to a successful life" (Haraway, 1989, p. 28).

In describing his younger brother (about to turn 13 at the time of the interviews) and his brother's best friend, Woody elaborated on the themes of self-directedness, purposive living, decisiveness, and competition.

> Those two kids are more mature than any other kid I've every coached. . . . They're not totally independent, but *they're in control of what's going on. They tell their parents what they want to do instead of just sitting back. . . . [T]hey pick out what they want and they take it. They are more determining kids.* (emphasis added; Interview 3: 55)

Being mature is being "in control" and "determining."

When Woody talked about his coaching experiences, he admitted that he found it difficult to work with kids who were not like himself. The "lackadaisical athlete" reminded him of his middle brother, an irritant, who barely made it to practice on time.

> The kids that are lackadaisical that I coach . . . I've been known to run them to death. . . . It doesn't work, but it rids me of the problems of having to deal with them. (Interview 2: 17-18)

In these excerpts, Woody portrayed several aspects of ideal masculinity: rational, purposive, disciplined, and focused. Woody and his younger brother remained self-determining, except for Woody's short "rebel" period. As we track these rational, disciplined, self-determining men into competitive sports, additional aspects of the social world governed by football are clarified.

Producing Woody's Privileged Position

In this section, I trace some connections between sports and the establishment of a sense of privilege, the belief that one is superior and deserves special treatment. The limitations of regular people drop away for superior athletes as they receive adulation from fans, families, and the media; the "pain principle" mandates that they give until it hurts (and beyond), conferring a sense of superior will and courage. The ability to take pain is part of the embodiment of masculine privilege that distinguishes them from weak others.

Privilege

Both in Woody's narratives and in other sociological studies, success in sports creates a sense of privilege that involves specific material rewards, status, and an exemption from ordinary routines. In Odessa, Texas, the football coach began the new season with, "You guys are a very special breed" (Bissinger, 1990, p. 24). Don Sabo (1994) recalled the pull toward football in very specific terms: "Winning at sports meant winning friends and carving a place for myself within the male pecking order" (p. 83). Girls were part of the bounty won by athletes, as Woody explicitly described:

> Our football coach used to always say, "If you guys win this sectional or if you win this big game, there's going to be girls waiting for you when you get back." (Interview 2: 32-33)

Having been deemed special, athletes come to believe that they are "supposed to win—every game" (Messner, 1992, p. 50) and they count on other entitlements. Both Bissinger's report on West Texas and Lefkowitz's account of athletes in New Jersey demonstrate how successful athletes assumed they were above the law.

Woody's sense of superiority was also produced through a private school education:

> I competed in Catholic leagues, but then I played football and baseball in the city leagues and . . . the kids I played with, I always thought they had no manners, I was more adult acting than they were. . . . *I just always had an idea in my head that they were lolly-gagging around all the time while I had to sit and study and learn. Our grade scale was higher, so we definitely thought we were smarter when we graduated.* (emphasis added; Interview 2: 15-16)

Woody's sense of superiority is a phenomenon widely chronicled in scholarship on masculinity and sports.

Don Sabo (1994) connects the privileges of competitive athletics with domination of women and other men. It is a hierarchical system in which men dominate women and also a

> system of intermale dominance, in which a minority of men dominates the masses of men. The intermale dominance hierarchy exploits the majority of those it beckons to climb its heights. Patriarchy's mythos of heroism and its morality of power-worship implant visions of masculine excellence and ecstasy in the minds of the boys who ultimately will defend its inequities and ridicule its victims. (p. 86)

The social relations of sports create a small group of privileged males who dominate women and lower-status men.

The Pain Principle

Michael Messner (1992) writes evocatively about pain and aggression toward others:

> The athlete is often encouraged to see his body as an instrument. An "instrumental male" is an alienated creature: he is usually very goal-oriented (in his work and in his personal relations), and he frequently views other people as objects to be manipulated and defeated in his quest to achieve his goals. The ultimate extension of instrumental rationality is the alienation from one's own body—the tendency to treat one's body as a tool, a machine to be utilized (and "used up") in the pursuit of particular ends. . . . Physical or emotional pain are experienced as a nuisance to be ignored or done away with [often through the use of alcohol or other drugs]. A common result of this focus on the body as an instrument is violence expressed toward others, and ultimately toward oneself. (p. 62)

Football, of course, is especially brutal. In a recent survey of retired football players, 78% reported that they suffer physical disabilities related directly to football, and 66% believe that having played football will negatively affect their life spans (Messner, 1992, p. 62). "Boys are taught that to endure pain is courageous, to survive pain is manly" (Sabo, 1994, p. 86). Reflecting on his own football career, Sabo writes,

> I learned to be an animal. Coaches took notice of animals. Animals made first team. Being an animal meant being fanatically aggressive and ruthlessly competitive. If I saw an arm in front of me, I trampled it. Whenever blood was spilled, I nodded approval. The coaches taught me to "punish the other man,"

and to secretly see my opponents' broken bones as little victories within the bigger struggle. (p. 84)

The path to privilege and domination was via becoming an animal. Masculinity draws vigor from animality.[11]
Athletes who rejected the pain principle became pariahs among their teammates, coaches, and fans. Messner (1992) tell the story of Bill S., who injured his knee before the state championship game:

> I was hurt. I couldn't play, and I got a lot of flack from everybody. The coach said, Are you faking it? And I was in the whirlpool and a teammate said "You fucking pussy." That hurt more than the injury. Later, people told me it was my fault that we lost . . . not just other players and coaches, but people in the whole town. It hurt, it just really hurt. (p. 72)

Players with suspicious injuries receive the silent treatment, which often makes them frantic to play. "They will plead with the team physician to shoot them up so they can play. The player will totally disregard the risk of permanent injury" (Messner, 1992, p. 74).

Painkillers are an illegal, but necessary, part of the brutal culture of professional football. As National Football League (N.F.L.) medical staffs try to contain the use of prescribed painkillers, players trade tickets or locker room passes to pharmaceutical sales representatives for drugs. Playing in pain is typical in the N.F.L., since the sport consists of 300-pound guys smashing into one another. The New York Giants quarterback Dave Brown stated that painkillers are a necessity, since "No one cares about how hurt you are. The coach doesn't care, the fans don't care and the media doesn't care. They just want you to play" (cited in Freeman, 1997, p. 22).[12] Donald Sabo (1994) summarizes the effects of the pain principle:

> It stifles men's awareness of their bodies and limits our emotional expression. We learn to ignore personal hurts and injuries because they interfere with "efficiency" and "goals" of the "team." We become adept at taking the feelings that boil up inside us . . . and channeling them in a bundle of rage which is directed at opponents and enemies. (p. 86)

As the following stories indicate, Woody exemplified Sabo's connections: the stifling of personal pains; the prioritizing of the team, efficiency, and doing one's best; the trivializing of others' hurts and pains; and the channeling of feelings toward opponents and those who did not subscribe to the same principles that he did.

Woody listed his injuries: a separated shoulder, a fracture in his left hand, a torn-up ankle, and, of course, his major knee injury.

> When I was a freshman, I got hit by a kid who is the middle linebacker for the University of Illinois now. I actually went unconscious, the only time I've ever been blacked out, and my kneecap was laying on the inside of my leg when they woke me up. (Interview 2: 20-23)

Woody elaborated on playing through the pain, a story that resembled innumerable ones reported by sports sociologists and journalists.[13]

> I played sometimes in so much pain I didn't know if I could make it through the game. I mean my knee would act up in the middle of the game, and I'd come off the sidelines and tell the coach, "I don't know if I can go anymore." He'd say, "You've got to go. You have to do it." It's just that . . . I mean, I never really had, I always had like not bad knees but kind of weak knees, even when I was younger, you know, I would twist it or something. I wore a knee brace from when I was 11 on and . . . I anticipated it because I always watched ball players get hurt all the time. I mean, I remember when I was little, my dad always wanted me to play regardless. . . . [N]one of us are quitters. They [his parents] never wanted to see anybody quit if you started something. . . . I've always lived by that and always tried to do that as much as I could, play as hard as I could for however long. (Interview 2: 20-23)

Woody restated his perspective on the pain principle:

> I just learned I'm not going to live forever and that's how I've always lived, is that I'm going to try as much as I can do. . . . I'll probably get real crippled at some point with arthritis, but I don't care as of now. (Interview 2: 20-23)

The pain principle has an additional implication for social relations off the field. Violent sports support male dominance, not only through exclusion of women, but through the association of males and maleness with sanctioned use of aggression, force, and violence. Thus, modern sport helps to naturalize the equation of maleness with physical power (Messner, 1992, p. 15).

In this section, we saw how sports is a means for producing and reinforcing social hierarchy of a small group of men over women and other men, and channeling emotions against structurally ordained enemies. But in "permanent war," the enemy can take many forms (Jeffords, 1989; Lutz, 1997). As the next section demonstrates, sporting spectacles likewise signify deficiencies/superiorities of class and race.

Weak Others

Lack of control of passion characterized all outsiders. (emphasis added)

Mosse, 1985, p. 134

My interviews with Woody occasionally moved to educational and public policy, and he invariably emphasized hard work within an assumed meritocracy.

I always had to work for whatever I got, so I think everyone should have to do that. . . . No one's going to get anything for free. I don't believe in the free stuff, and I don't care how much you have to work for everything, I won't give grades. I won't give playing time. . . . I've had parents come up to me and holler that my kid's not playing enough. Well, he's not good enough, you know. I'm sorry, he's not, and maybe if he practiced or whatever. I mean, I'm not going to just give anybody anything. (Interview 3: 32)

Woody's backing for "the level playing field" image of schooling and social policy became emotionally charged when I asked about youth rights. Woody advocated prohibition of rights, such as voting, marriage, and so on, for persons under 21 years of age: "These kids are so immature, they have no clue of what's going on. . . . you just end up with too many problems" (Focus Group 3: 11). I asked him if parents are abusive or neglectful, should youth be able to instigate a termination of their parents' rights? Without knowing much about the case, Woody wondered whether "Gregory K."[14] wasn't just a whiner:

How was his father abusive? What did his dad do? Holler at him? Well, you're a little girl, kid—not little girl, but you know what I mean—little baby. I'm sorry you're a little baby, but things happen. You're going to get yelled at in your life. (Focus Group 3: 14)

Woody proceeded to portray teenagers as apt to make up stories about things that happened to them. On a rhetorical roll, he asserted that "35 to 40 percent of date rape is a farce" (Focus Group 3: 14). He was convinced that it was a combination of teenagers lying about what had happened or whining over trivial occurrences. In this way he trivialized both child abuse and date rape, saying that many of these kids were either wimps or liars.

Summary. In this section, I have highlighted the intertwined construction of privilege through success in high-status sports and the value placed on the attendant discipline and pain. In the deadening of athletes' attention to their own bodies and emotions, and in the conscious fostering of an animality to beat the opponent, a complex and volatile emotionality/rationality brew occurs.

Woody portrayed himself and other good athletes as self-directed, autonomous, and moving rationally toward a goal. He spoke almost lovingly of his disciplined body and mind. Weak or emotional people, notably girls, people of color, and other whiners are chastised for not being able to take a little of what life offers.[15] Woody's ideas are in line with a broader recasting of national patriotism as "proper public expression, loyal self-censorship, and personal self-discipline" (Berlant & Freeman, 1993, p. 195).

What becomes of this emotionality/rationality construct when Woody moves from coach to classroom teacher?

The Social Relations of Teaching-as-Coaching

Woody: Let's put it this way. I'm not going into education because I want to teach children.

Interview 3: 55

In this final section, I examine implications for the social relations of teaching drawn from my critical analysis of competitive athletics as a hypermasculine domain. I situate Woody's specific views on teaching, described below, within an understanding of schools as engaged in a process of remasculinizing, a renewed emphasis on competition, confidence, and status. Mac an Ghaill (1994) portrays the remasculinizing of one British secondary school via the concerns of one group of teachers, whom he dubs the Professionals:

> The Professionals saw their primary task to be that of making real men of the male students. They tended to be more interested in the male than female students' schooling. They believed in coercive discipline, and there was much talk among them of order, discipline and academic and moral standards. The Professionals . . . missed the "common culture of maleness" that is found in all-male secondary schools and attempted to recreate a fantasized past within specific school spaces, including traditional "masculine" subject areas, such as the natural sciences, mathematics and competitive team sports. (p. 26)

The regendering of schools—coded as patriotism, academic rigor, the importance of math and science, and competition and moral standards—should be kept in mind as I turn to Woody's ideas about teaching: the classroom as level playing field; the Terminator meets traditional teacher-centered pedagogy; and anti-multiculturalism.

Classroom as "Level Playing Field"

Woody articulated his position for a level playing field in and out of the classroom:

> [J]ust because your big brother, Steve, was an athlete, I don't think that automatically you are. . . . I just don't believe in that . . . everybody's equal. No one's better than anyone else. (Interview 3: 33)

As noted above, the level-playing-field rhetoric projects an image of fairness and justice on situations where that is far from the case (Nadelhaft, 1993).

Traditional, Teacher-Centered Pedagogy Meets the Terminator

In a discussion about expectations for and fears of teaching, Woody portrayed himself *against* images of student-centered teachers who might try to make mathematics relevant and try to understand students' lives outside school.[16]

> I want to teach at the biggest school I can possibly go to. . . . I don't want to be a teacher. I just want to coach football, and you've got to go to a big place to get a good square where you can move on. (Interview 3: 50)

With relish and zest, Woody fleshed out his image of the highly carica-
tured, well-worn, and strategically upwardly mobile approach to teaching:

> I guess I'll be the kind of teacher that every social studies teacher is: puts a
> movie in two days a week and the other three days gives notes for 35 of the 50
> minutes and then says, "Read your books and I'm going to be up here." (Focus
> Group 3: 18)

This disengaged perfunctory teacher knows what really counts—coaching. The fantasy image of Woody-as-Terminator-teacher utilized athletic
power:

> I guess I want to be the ... one that everybody wants to take as a teacher, but the
> players are just scared to death of him, you know. They respect him, but they're
> just scared to death that at any moment he could just blow up and just smash
> them, you know. (Focus Group 3: 18)

I quote at length here to provide a stronger feel for Woody's teacher-
centered, authoritative-yet-playful, boy-man pedagogy, a pedagogy sure
to connect with athletic boys:

> I base my teaching, or how I want to teach, on three teachers I had in high school.
> One was the social studies, one was the science, and one was the econom-
> ics/psychology/sociology type area. The history teacher ... was the most popu-
> lar teacher. He was my football coach. He was the wrestling coach, but he was
> just laid-back. The tests were hard, but as long as you came to class, you knew
> the material. As long as you took notes and read your notes, you knew the mate-
> rial, nothing more than that. You watched movies a lot, and you watched stuff
> that interested you and you talked about stuff that interested you. I didn't care if
> Betsy Ross made the flag. I mean, I could care less if she made it or not, so you
> didn't talk about that. You talked about Vietnam, something that mattered to
> you.
>   And then like my chemistry teacher, he was always in control of the class,
> but it was always just like right on the verge of just going out of control. You
> made comments to him and he'd holler back at you ... but when he wanted con-
> trol, you totally were in control. He was in control. The same with the psychol-
> ogy teacher. You know, discussion is mostly what should occur in psychology
> and sociology classes, I think, and he'd allow discussions, but when he wanted
> control, he'd say be quiet and everyone was quiet. I mean those guys were
> popular because they allowed you to learn basically what you wanted to learn

or what they needed you to learn, but they also allowed you to enjoy your classroom. (Focus Group 3: 19)

When I asked, "What kinds of teaching situations or students will be hard for you?" Woody replied in his hyperbolic mode: "I can't handle idiots." He explained:

I can't handle below level. I mean if I'm teaching seniors, I have an opinion on how seniors should act, and I think it should be across there, you know. I can't handle the little kid over in the corner, I don't know, blowing up balloons, you know, because that's just not the level he should be performing at. That's what, I guess, I'm most worried about is not being able to handle the below level kid. (Focus Group 3: 20-21)

In humorous and powerful images, Woody presented his aspirations to be a worshipped teacher who could hammer any male student into obedience in or out of the classroom. He pulled from classroom experiences with three male teachers who promoted discussion of topics that interested him (e.g., Vietnam), allowed banter (at which Woody excelled), and could draw the disciplinary line in the sand when necessary. The social relations he described were based on male-to-male relationships, with laughter, competitive talking, and put-downs, but always in the context of total control. Woody acknowledged that patience, necessary for teaching of diverse students and historically linked with women and nurturing, was not in his repertoire.

Against Multiculturalism

The rage of a white male deprived of his privilege (Weis, 1993) surfaced when Woody discussed his experience with the required multicultural education course. Woody filed a formal complaint for reverse discrimination against the African American woman instructor.

I seriously think that she is the worst teacher that I ever had because everything that she did was to degrade white males, regardless. White males were the downfall of everything. White males cause abortion. White males cause black kids not to get educations. White males cause Chinese kids to be, you know, come over here on boats from Bangkok and be sick. You know, the last time I checked, I never chartered a group of aliens over here and I never caused a black kid to not get an education. (Interview 3: 49-50)

The focus of the course on racism in schools and society was intolerable for Woody, who reached his limit one day and gave an "I'm mad as hell" speech:

> I said, "Look, I'm sorry if I have offended anyone for being a White male, but you know this is ridiculous. I'm really pissed so I'm just going to leave now" and [I] walked out of class. This was in fact during one of our panel discussions. . . . I just got up and left for lieu of later, you know, causing myself to be an ass. . . . In all honesty I was really disappointed with this university at that time. (Interview 3: 50-51)

In these statements, Woody took the position of the beleaguered white male who was held responsible for all the nation's shortcomings. He deflected the criticism by saying that he personally never did any of those things. Woody concluded by saying that he had never been prejudiced, and could not agree with a class that emphasized past patterns of race relations:

> I think everything that occurred in that class was prejudged on past racial tendencies, and . . . I don't want that [racial or economic or ethnic discrimination] to occur in anything I've ever done or will do. (Interview 3: 50)

I can only describe Woody's response to the multicultural education class as *rage;* and his rage led to contesting his grade and the instructor's approach to the course. That is, he challenged her authority to grade him and her legitimacy in teaching about racism. Given Woody's descriptions of good teachers and his expertise in exerting control over classroom dynamics, pacing, and topics, it is small wonder that he reacted so strongly to the multicultural course. The social relations, topics, and perspectives were not only beyond his control, but his usual privileged position (as clown, as articulate student, as smart, as domineering) was diminished.

Although Woody occasionally critiqued high school history courses for presenting a sanitized version of the past, we can expect that his curriculum will remain Eurocentric and dominated by the study of the accomplishments of white men, and that his classroom will similarly be dominated by young men who are skilled at athletics and verbal repartee and demand a disproportionate amount of the teacher's time and attention.

Conclusion

The problems of hypermasculinity in athletics and in gendered violence have begun to receive some national attention as a social problem, no longer completely dismissed as "boys being boys." Nevertheless, given the scholarship on gendered violence and athletics (Katz, 1995; Miedzian, 1991; Stein, 1995), schools have a long way to go in seeing, understanding, and changing the hypermasculinity that is now identified as problematic among students. This chapter extended concerns about aggressive masculinity in athletics to coaching and teaching and, thus, to the broader school environment and discourse.

The starting point for this analysis was a critical look at the popular image of teacher-as-coach in the secondary school reform literature. Utilizing critiques of competitive athletics and explorations of the hegemonic masculinity of sports, I emphasized the social relations produced in football spectacles, with their scripted emotions and strong linkages with war and nationalism. The hierarchy through unity of competitive athletics, its violence, nationalism, and emphasis on winning are principles that would seem quite distant from classroom life. However, using one preservice teacher's life history narratives, I began to track the circulation of dominance across the playing field and the classroom. Woody's ideas about teaching were rooted in its unimportance, whereas coaching counted. Through flashbacks and imaginary forwards, Woody figured himself as a domineering teacher, a boy-man who moved between jokes and serious history, between being the most popular and the most feared teacher. These teaching fantasies gave preeminence in the classroom to those with Woody's characteristics: athletic, joking, articulate, dominant, and competitive. Woody eschewed all student-centered teaching and acknowledged an impatience with all but the best and the brightest.

The social relations of coaching repudiated multicultural education, at least any version that contains a serious examination of structural racism and sexism in schools. Woody's view of the classroom as a level playing field glossed the educational process as an athletic event, with the imputation of fairness and justice; everyone was equal. This perspective, combined with his violent rejection of the existence of racism or sexism ("these people just need to stop whining") and the failure to see his own privilege, kept Woody-as-teacher/coach within practices that will connect with the male athletes. The social relations of the gridiron are smoothly embraced within a teacher-centered, level-playing-field approach that is staunchly against affirmative action and antiracist policies and practices.

In these social relations, persons who do not hold the same values and physical prowess will be labeled weak or whining and will be dismissed. The hierarchy within the alleged unity of the "team" perspective will prevail in classrooms and curriculum.

Competitiveness, aggressive masculinity, dominance, and privilege are key players on and off the football field. If educators embrace the idea that exemplary teachers = coaches and accept the inevitability of high status athletics in secondary schools, it is questionable whether these problems of hegemonic masculinity, school management, and hierarchical social relations in the classroom can be raised, much less changed. This chapter raises serious questions about "athletic discourse" and its logic of practice in schools.

Furthermore, Woody's ideas are in line with a broader recasting of national patriotism as "proper public expression, loyal self-censorship, and personal self-discipline" (Berlant & Freeman, 1993, p. 195). Community-spirit and mass spectacles can be seen as training grounds for these new "civic values." In Woody we see the harnessing of affect to a political order via football. The political order he espoused was a peculiar blend of the New Right, team spirit, and can-do masculine football fervor, companioned with a sense of privilege masquerading as merit. The Persian Gulf War was one occasion in which this football-and-nationalistic discourse was clear and wildly popular. That event stands as a reminder of the power of desire linked to nation and mobilized against Others. The Persian Gulf War is also a marker of the connections between nation, war, and football, and a glaring instance of the necessity to critique spirit-building events and the related body images, affect, and discipline. Educators must pay heed to the masculinized and racialized spirit embodied and advocated by Woody, for it offered no hope for progressive school change. Woody's version of coaching was not a model for future teachers who will teach an ever more diverse student body. Although the pleasures of playing well and winning football games must be acknowledged, it is imperative to evaluate Woody's perspectives in relation to what we believe the future of public schooling ought to be. Woody's version of coach-as-teacher does not carry the public school toward a more responsible position in society. Nevertheless, the seeming "naturalness" of football and the logic of competitive athletics in schools makes the interrogation of aggressive masculinity imperative and immensely difficult.

Notes

1. Sizer categorizes reading, writing, and so on, as "skills." It is noteworthy that Sizer defines educational learning as the accumulation of "skills," thereby accepting an approach to educational reform that reduces knowledge and understanding to the stockpiling of isolatable abilities, what many term a technocratic approach to education. However, the analysis of that aspect of Sizer's work is beyond the scope of this chapter.

2. Stuart Hall (1993) argues that the 1990s witnessed a return of recharged nationalism in England and elsewhere. There was great impetus for restoring national culture as the primordial source of national identity.

3. Participants in this study chose their own pseudonyms, and the football influence on Woody's choice is evident.

4. The research project occurred over the academic year 1993-1994 in a midwestern university. A research assistant and I interviewed four undergraduate preservice teachers across two semesters while they were enrolled in teacher education courses, specifically educational psychology and multicultural education. We conducted both group and individual interviews to understand the participants' experiences in secondary schools, in their families, and in college, as well as their expectations for teaching.

5. Drawing on Anderson's (1983) work on the imagining of nations, nationalism can take various forms and need not only take the form identified here. See also Parker, Russo, Sommer, and Yaeger (1992).

6. Working in a similar vein, John Hargreaves connects sports with British national identity: "Since the 1950s especially, with the expansion of TV coverage of international events, media sport has increasingly provided opportunities for people to identify with the nation through sport. The notion of the 'national interest,' frequently invoked in media discourse when 'our' competitors and representatives are made the focus of the media's attention on international occasions: how are 'we' going to fare? and how have 'we' done? . . . The ceremonial and ritual surrounding these occasions, prominently displaying the national symbols—the flags, the parades, the uniforms, the patriotic hymns and anthems, the participation of elite figures symbolic of national unity—. . . signal preferred conceptions of national unity which powerfully invoke feelings of identity" (Hargreaves, 1986, p. 154).

7. For other accounts of high school football, see also Foley (1990), Gruneau and Whitson (1993), Robins and Cohen (1978), and Walker (1988).

8. In using the descriptor boy-man, I draw on Jeal's (1990) biography of Baden-Powell, the founder of the worldwide Boy Scout Movement.

9. When asked to describe in more detail what occurred, Woody recounted getting a flat-top haircut (like a Marine), getting an earring, driving fast, partying (but not drinking much), "just popping off to anybody I could" (i.e., "mouthing off" or "talking back" to people), and losing all his manners. Friends of his parents, for example, avoided him because he was obnoxious.

10. From R. W. Connell's (1990) work on the Iron Man, we can see the car-based, masculine rebellion as a collective social practice, involving his dad, close friends, acquaintances, and various other performers. Also like Connell's Australian Iron Man, Woody leads a life narrowly focused on sports training, studying, and coaching his younger brother.

11. The direct exploitation of animality (savagery) for Western male domination has a long history in the United States. Gail Bederman (1995) directly links psychologist

G. Stanley Hall and Theodore Roosevelt with this turn-of-the-century association between developing masculinity and promoting civilization by using animal or primitive energy. These primitive energies were gathered by being in nature, by hunting, by competitive games and righteous wars.

12. Freeman (1997) adds that many players face drug withdrawal rigors at the end of each season.

13. The pain principle and its collective making and remaking is an example of what Connell (1995) calls body-reflexive practices, which are an important dimension of masculinity.

14. "Gregory K." was the plaintiff in a high-profile lawsuit to replace his biological parents with different, more responsible parents of his choosing. The case was heard in Florida in 1992.

15. Woody exhibited a rhetorical "privilege" to make amazingly contradictory statements about youth. One minute he would say teenagers just needed to be left alone and be given responsibility and they would be fine. Then he would state that as a teacher, he was not going to pamper kids, but just give them lecture notes and test them on those. He suggested that his own children would be strictly limited in what they did; for example, no dating before they were 16 years old. What emerged as the most important issue was that Woody remained the ultimate authority in all situations. The substance of his decisions or policies did not matter; what mattered was his authority to make absolute calls, which he labeled as rational, in each of these different domains.

16. Following Cuban (1993), I utilize the language of student-centered and teacher-centered teaching to denote sets of different practices. In general, Woody's comments place him in the teacher-centered perspective on teaching.

References

Aksoy, A., & Robins, K. (1991). Exterminating angels: Morality, violence and technology in the Gulf War. *Science as Culture 12*, 322-337.

Anderson, B. (1983). *Imagined communities: Reflections on the origin and spread of nationalism*. New York: Verso.

Bederman, G. (1995). *Manliness and civilization: A cultural history of gender and race in the United States, 1880-1917*. Chicago: University of Chicago Press.

Berk, L. (1992). The extracurriculum. In P. Jackson (Ed.), *Handbook of research on curriculum* (pp. 1002-1044). New York: Macmillan.

Berlant, L., & Freeman, E. (1993). Queer nationality. In M. Warner (Ed.), *Fear of a queer planet: Queer politics and social theory* (pp. 193-229). Minneapolis: University of Minnesota Press.

Bissinger, H. G. (1990). *Friday night lights: A town, a team, a dream*. New York: HarperCollins.

Connell, R. W. (1990). An iron man: The body and some contradictions of hegemonic masculinity. In M. A. Messner & D. F. Sabo (Eds.), *Sport, men, and the gender order* (pp. 72-90). Champaign, IL: Human Kinetics Books.

Connell, R. W. (1995). *Masculinities*. Berkeley: University of California Press.

Connell, R. W. (1996). Teaching the boys: New research on masculinity, and gender strategies for schools. *Teachers College Record, 98*(2), 206-235.

Cuban, L. (1993). *How teachers taught: Constancy and change in American classrooms, 1880-1990* (2nd ed.). New York: Teachers College Press.

Davies, L. (1992). School power cultures under economic constraint. *Educational Review, 43*(2), 127-136.

DuBord, G. (1977). *The society of the spectacle.* Detroit, MI: Red and Black Press.

Foley, D. E. (1990). *Learning capitalist culture: Deep in the heart of Tejas.* Philadelphia: University of Pennsylvania Press.

Freeman, M. (1997, April 13). Painkillers, and addiction, are prevalent in N.F.L. *New York Times,* pp. 19, 22.

Friedenberg, E. Z. (1980). The changing role of homoerotic fantasy in spectator sports. In D. F. Sabo, Jr., & R. Runfola (Eds.), *Jock: Sports and male identity* (pp. 177-192). Englewood Cliffs, NJ: Prentice Hall.

Gibson, J. W. (1994). *Warrior dreams: Violence and manhood in post-Vietnam America.* New York: Hill & Wang.

Gruneau, R., & Whitson, D. (1993). *Hockey night in Canada: Sport, identities and cultural politics.* Toronto: Garamond.

Hall, S. (1993). Culture, community, nation. *Cultural Studies, 7*(3), 352-360.

Haraway, D. (1989). *Primate visions: Gender, race, and nature in the world of modern science.* New York & London: Routledge & Kegan Paul.

Hargreaves, J. (1986). *Sport, power and culture: A social and historical analysis of popular sports in Britain* New York: St. Martin's.

Jansen, S. C., & Sabo, D. (1994). The sport/war metaphor: Hegemonic masculinity, the Persian Gulf War, and the new world order. *Sociology of Sport Journal, 11,* 1-17.

Jeal, T. (1990). *The boy-man: The life of Lord Baden-Powell.* New York: William Morrow.

Jeffords, S. (1989). *The remasculinization of America: Gender and the Vietnam War.* Bloomington: Indiana University Press.

Katz, J. (1995). Reconstructing masculinity in the locker room: The Mentors in Violence Prevention Project. *Harvard Educational Review, 65*(2), 163-170.

Lefkowitz, B. (1997). *Our guys: The Glen Ridge rape and the secret life of the perfect suburb.* Berkeley: University of California Press.

Levidow, L. (1995). Castrating the other: The paranoid rationality of the Gulf War. *Psychoculture: Review of Psychology & Cultural Studies, 1*(1), 9-16.

Lutz, C. (1997). Epistemology of the bunker: The brainwashed and other new subjects of permanent war. In J. Pfister & N. Schnog (Eds.), *Inventing the psychological: Toward a cultural history of emotional life in America* (pp. 245-267). New Haven, CT: Yale University Press.

Mac an Ghaill, M. (1994). *The making of men: Masculinities, sexualities, and schooling.* Buckingham, UK and Philadelphia: Open University Press.

McClintock, A. (1993). Family feuds: Gender, nationalism and the family. *Feminist Review, 44,* 61-80.

McClintock, A. (1995). *Imperial leather: Race, gender and sexuality in the colonial context.* New York: Routledge.

Messner, M. A. (1992). *Power at play: Sports and the problem of masculinity.* Boston: Beacon.

Miedzian, M. (1991). *Boys will be boys: Breaking the link between masculinity and violence.* Garden City, NY: Anchor Books.

Mosse, G. L. (1985). *Nationalism and sexuality: Middle class morality and sexual norms in modern Europe.* Madison: University of Wisconsin Press.

Mosse, G. L. (1996). *The image of man: The creation of modern masculinity.* New York and Oxford, UK: Oxford University Press.

Nadelhaft, M. (1993). Metawar: Sports and the Persian Gulf War. *Journal of American Culture, 16*(4), 25-33.

Parker, A., Russo, M., Sommer, D., & Yaeger, P. (1992). *Nationalisms and sexualities.* New York: Routledge.

Robins, D., & Cohen, P. (1978). *Knuckle sandwich: Growing up in the working-class city.* Harmondsworth, UK: Penguin.

Sabo, D. (1994). Pigskin, patriarchy and pain. In M. A. Messner & D. Sabo (Eds.), *Sex, violence and power in sports: Rethinking masculinity* (pp. 82-88). Freedom, CA: Crossing Press.

Sizer, T. R. (1984). *Horace's compromise: The dilemma of the American high school.* Boston: Houghton Mifflin.

Stein, N. (1995). Sexual harassment in school: The public performance of gendered violence. *Harvard Educational Review, 65*(2), 145-162.

Stoler, A. L. (1995). *Race and the education of desire: Foucault's* History of Sexuality *and the colonial order of things.* Durham, NC & London: Duke University Press.

Wakefield, W. (1996). *Playing to win.* Albany: State University of New York Press.

Walker, J. C. (1988). *Louts and legends: Male youth culture in an inner-city school.* Sydney: Allen & Unwin.

Weis, L. (1993). White male working-class youth: An exploration of relative privilege and loss. In L. Weis & M. Fine (Eds.), *Beyond silenced voices: Class, race, and gender in United States schools* (pp. 237-258). Albany: State University of New York Press.

9

Striving for Educational Rigor

Acceptance of Masculine Privilege

MELODY J. SHANK

A Nation in Search of Educational Rigor

Rigor seems to be what we all want in the education of our youth. Although the word is not often used and people have difficulty explaining what it is, rigor is an educational value easily accepted by both the public and educators. Nowhere is this more true than at the high school level, where there is the most contention over the proper preparation of young people for adult and societal roles and responsibilities. A principal, being interviewed on National Public Radio, talks about the implementation of a rigorous curriculum as part of his urban high school's reform efforts. Ted Sizer (1996) advocates for a "rigorous general education" for all high school students. Parochial high schools are often viewed as having more rigorous curricula than public high schools. A school with many honors and Advanced Placement courses is seen as rigorous. College preparation courses are viewed as more rigorous than their regular or basic cousins. Academic courses are valued over vocational and technical courses for their rigor. Rigor is a part of the "grammar of schooling" (Tyack & Cuban, 1995); one of the assumptions of "real" school.

It is not immediately clear, however, what we are assuming when we accept rigor as a criterion for the quality of learning, curriculum, or education in general. The most recent wave of school reform, with its tensions, struggles, and conflicting strands of thought, provides an apt terrain in which to explore the underlying assumptions and beliefs that bolster a quest for educational rigor. Regardless of the philosophy and aims of education espoused by prominent high school reformers, rigor is a quality desired.

The most recent wave of high school reform was initiated by the release of *A Nation at Risk* in 1983 by The National Commission on Excellence in Education. The crafters of the report seemed to have one understanding of educational rigor and how to attain it. In their portrayal of the educational crisis in America's high schools, the lack of rigor was found in "homogenized, diluted, and diffused" secondary school curricula of the "smorgasbord" variety; decreased amounts of homework; little time spent on academic subjects in comparison to other nations; high levels of elective course work; testing of only minimum competencies; and unchallenging course and textbook content. To remedy the dire situation, the report called for excellence for all students. For individual learners, excellence meant "performing on the boundary of individual ability in ways that test and push back personal limits, in school and in the workplace" (National Commission on Excellence in Education [National Commission], 1983, p. 16). For schools, it meant establishing high expectations for all students and creating programs to help students reach those expectations; thus, "stretching minds to fullest capacity" (p. 17).

Although these goals, focused on the equitable fostering of the intellectual capacity of individual students and schools, seem laudable, the commission's recommendations to remedy the dire educational situation did not challenge traditional school structures or address the educational disparities among students based on gender, socioeconomic status, access, and resources. The commission, rather, recommended more of the same: increased graduation requirements in the expanded *Five New Basics:* English, mathematics, science, social studies, and computer science, with courses designed separately for college-bound and non-college-bound students; and the adoption of "more rigorous and measurable standards" (National Commission, 1983, p. 73), which were to be achieved through stricter standards for grades given, raised college admission requirements, implementation of standardized achievement tests, and upgraded instructional materials to "ensure rigorous content" (p. 74). For the National Commission on Excellence in Education, educational rigor was represented in an externally designed system of quantitative accountability measures: the type and number of courses students completed, the content of textbooks and other instructional materials, the content expertise of teachers as indicated by completed course content and grade point average, student achievement as measured through grades and standardized tests, and the amount of assigned homework.

Policymakers—state legislators and department of education officials—readily embraced these indicators of rigor. During the 1980s they mandated increases in graduation requirements, statewide standardized achievement testing, high-stakes school accountability plans, inclusion of Advanced Placement courses, and special diplomas for high academic achievement. By 1990, 39 states had increased the number of Carnegie units required for high school graduation (Rossman & Wilson, 1996), and by 1994, 18 states had implemented a graduation examination (Bond & King, 1995).

The attainment of rigor has been differently conceived in other studies of American high schools of the same period. Educational researchers—John Goodlad and Theodore Sizer, among others—were crisscrossing the country in the early 1980s, looking beyond the external indicators of excellence, investigating what was actually happening within America's high schools. What they found were disinterested, disengaged students; exhausted, compromising teachers; overloaded, shallow curricula; and school structures and practices barely changed in 80 years of high school education. Although confirming the findings of the *Nation at Risk* report, in contrast to it, the recommendations of these educational researchers indicated that more of the same for more students was not going to produce increased engagement, achievement, or competence. What the *Nation at Risk* report called for was more rigorous academic curriculum and testing for more students. What the inside view of high schools called for was intensified student engagement in more rigorous work; rigorous work of a different kind than had been conventionally known, however. As Goodlad (1984) noted,

Many students successfully go through the motions of rote learning, pass requisite tests, and move on to more of the same in college. What they have had little of, however, are encounters that connect them with the major ideas and ways of knowing that the fields of knowledge represent. (p. 317)

It is better to learn a few concepts well and to know how to apply them than to cover long lists of topics for purposes of recall. The search is for understanding and for the processes basic to acquiring this understanding. (p. 339)

Sizer (1984) was of a similar mind in his call for centering the purpose of high school on the development of the mind and character. He advocated that high school curriculum be based on "the intellectual and imaginative powers and competencies that students need, rather than on 'subjects' as conventionally defined . . . [or on] 'content coverage' " (pp. 225-256). He promoted a "less is more" approach to curriculum and a focus on personalized learning. He claimed that adolescents develop and learn in unique ways; hence, the learning process should be molded to each student's exceptionalities and be flexible, and public means of demonstrating their competence should be designed. In addition, he advocated creating schools where students' intellectual capacities are nurtured through teacher coaching and cultures of decency, trust, and fairness.

For Goodlad and for Sizer, the focus on intellectual development and deepened understanding required not more of the same, but changes in curricular frameworks, pedagogy, assessment, school structures and practices, and educational beliefs initiated by those closest to the educational process: teachers and administrators, students, parents, and communities. Rigor, still accepted as a criterion for quality learning, would be grounded not in external standards of excellence, but in locally determined standards of engagement in the development of the intellect.

Almost 15 years have passed since this most recent cry for educational reform was sent out, and overall student achievement has improved only minimally. Nationally, SAT scores have improved only slightly. Colleges continue to chide high schools for not preparing graduates better and to deplore the fact they must provide remedial programs. International comparisons still find the United States behind other countries in some areas of academic achievement. There is a cacophony of debate about best solutions, including the institution of national standards and a national curriculum. Policymakers still clamor for rigor and continue to raise the stakes. But, if one walked into the majority of high schools in the country, one would likely see classroom and school practices that have barely changed.

Meanwhile, Sizer and colleagues at the Coalition of Essential Schools have sustained a dynamic national school reform movement based on his ideas of 1984. Implementing innovative school structures and pedagogical practices based on Sizer's nine common principles[1] has been difficult for educators in the Essential Schools across the country, especially for those in conventionally structured schools. As Essential School educators attempt to narrow their schools' curriculum, focus on students' public exhibition of competence, create personalized school environments, and center the work of the schools on students' work, not teachers' expertise, the conventionally understood signs or measures of rigor—or tough learning—are replaced with unknowns. Nonetheless, rigor is what is strived for (Cushman, 1995).

Understanding the conceptual underpinnings of rigor is not as simple as it may seem at first look. The concept is tied not only to aims of education, but also to theories of learning, conceptions of curriculum, and epistemological orientations. The term is used in a perfunctory manner, but conceptually it is laden with cultural assumptions about how we come to know, conceptions of the mind, and values of schooling. It is in the exploration of the heritage of the concept of rigor that its hidden meanings and implications are revealed. These two approaches to high school reform epitomize the epistemological inheritances that intertwine and diverge to undergird prominent educational thought regarding rigor.

In this chapter, I will first outline how the term *rigor* and its opposites are commonly used and what these common understandings imply about our values in education. I will explore how the notions of rigor are tied to our epistemological inheritances and how these inheritances have shaped our thinking about schooling and curriculum to perpetuate exclusionary education. I will conclude by examining how these inheritances are still embedded in Sizer's otherwise provocative reform agenda and challenging those of us who espouse his philosophy to interrogate the pernicious underlying assumptions.

What Is Rigor?

Rigor, as defined in the dictionary (*Random House,* 1995), means strictness, inflexibility, meticulousness, accuracy, and precision. The definition connotes hard work, difficulty, persistence, and focus. It implies discipline in and adherence to either a prespecified procedure or set of laws followed with great exactness. In its conventional denotation, rigor is fittingly applied to technical pursuits: being a mechanic, doing science experiments, building something to specification, engineering a bridge; to rational pursuits of the mind: doing mathematics, reasoning logically and developing a sound argument; and to physical activities of mastery: climbing a mountain, running a marathon, or training for a sports competition.

Its opposites include laxness, lenience, sloppiness, inaccuracy, carelessness, incoherence, slovenliness, and easiness. These opposites connote a lack of direction, an aimlessness, and a lack of discipline. Rigor is also contrasted to creativity, flexibility, innovation, imagination, and play. It is therefore not easily applied to a stroll or frolic in the woods, dancing expressively, exploring the artifacts in a museum, listening to music, creating a design, adjusting procedures to a particular situation, or envisioning possibilities. It is also unfitting to socially oriented activities, activities requiring nurturance and caring: being a good neighbor, parenting, being a friend, attending the sick, or listening patiently. Lastly, rigor is not applicable to the realm of emotions or aesthetic experience: one doesn't laugh or cry rigorously, nor is one rigorously moved by a painting, words, or music.

From this brief examination of the definitional connotations of the word *rigor* we discover that rigor is a criterion of particular domains of activity: technical, rational, and physical. It is a criterion used either in judging the precision in the use of a particular technical method, the acquisition or development of the skills of logical reasoning, or the disciplined training of the body. It does not pertain to pursuits of creativity or imagination, the heart, or human interaction. If rigor is a criterion for judging the soundness of aspects of the educational enterprise, then we can assume that education is a technical, rational, or physical pursuit, and not social, creative, or emotional in nature. From this, we can either deduce that the valued realms of activity or knowing are of a technical, rational, or physical nature, and therefore the basis for educational and curricular decisions; or that the realms of knowing that are valued in the education arena must be evaluated as technical, rational, or physical processes regardless of their nature.

Either of these assumptions reveals the worldview and privileging that is inherent in using rigor as a primary criterion for the soundness of an education. And, they also ultimately reveal who this privileging accommodates. The split in realms of experience or ways of coming to know also reveals the privileging of areas that have traditionally been constructed as masculine realms over those that have been realms of the feminine. Thus, the use of rigor as a criterion for judging the soundness of education, learning, and curriculum both reflects and maintains the privileging of the masculine over the feminine. Although both strands of school reform under consideration in this chapter recommend reforms/changes that will benefit all students through a more rigorous education, both suffer from these inherent inequities embedded in an adherence to rigor.

The Legacy of Rigor in Western Philosophy

The privileging of certain realms of knowing—thus certain approaches to education—has a long heritage in Western philosophy, beginning at least with Plato. Within this heritage, a rigorous education takes on different meanings for different people. In his Just Society, Plato envisioned that people would be educated according to their natural abilities as either ruler, artisan, or warrior, thus taking their proper place in society. The most educated man, who would be steward/ruler of the Just Society, thus entering public life, needed to be trained in theoretical knowledge, finely tuned powers of reasoning, emotional restraint and distance, and objectivity (Martin, 1994c). "For Plato, truth [was] accessible only in the realm of pure and absolute being, a realm reached . . . by learning to see through and beyond the realm of the purely physical" (Keller, 1985, p. 22). He was required to transcend the private realm—the realm of intimacy, compassion, and care, the ordinary and everyday—to a higher plane (Martin, 1994c). His education was one of the mind, not the hand or the heart. To be worthy of the position of steward, an educated man needed to learn self-discipline and self-governance.

Of course, only a few worthy men could be the stewards of Plato's Just Society, for example, those few men who had the social and economic position, capacity, and will to undergo the rigors of attaining theoretical knowledge, the powers of reason, and control of passion and subjectivity. Men of lesser ability and status remained the hands and backs (artisans and warriors) for the Just Society. Although Plato claimed that women too could be guardians of the Just Society, his philosophical descendants maintained the place of women in the realm of obedience, irrationality, and emotion (Martin, 1994b; Warmington & Rouse, 1956).

Even though Plato's education for a Just Society required rigor—a rigorous contemplation of ideas and control of emotions—it is Descartes's legacy that gives rigor its form. Seventeenth-century reason, championed by Descartes, was "encapsulated in a systematic method for attaining certainty" (Lloyd, 1996, p. 152). This systematic method entailed breaking complex rational operations down into parts and sharpening the mind's ability to perform the mental operations of intuition and deduction.

> For Descartes, then, all knowledge consists of self-evident intuition and necessary deduction. We are to break down the complex and obscure into what is simple and self-evident, then combine the resultant units in an orderly manner. In order to know we must isolate the "simple natures," the objects of intuition, and "scrutinize them separately with steadfast mental gaze." We then combine them in chains of deductions. (Lloyd, 1996, p. 153)

These operations could only be employed if they were free of the influences of the senses and the imagination. Therefore, the mind had to be separated from the corporeal senses, desires, and emotions.

Descartes also viewed the mind's ability to order things as a mirror of the order of reality. Hence, if man could order things through rigorous method, he would arrive at the truth of reality (Lloyd, 1996). This theory of mind created "an epistemological chasm separat[ing] a highly self-conscious self from a universe that now lies decisively outside the self" (Bordo, 1986, p. 444). With this separation of mind/self from the external world, the aim of cognition was to represent that world accurately.

There could not be assurance of stability of either the self or the world, so accurate representation—truth—was doubtful. Therefore, Descartes had to rely on a veracious God. According to Lloyd (1996), "Introspection of the nature of thought in an individual mind ultimately yields access to universal reason, God given and God guaranteed" (p. 153). The development of reason, then, had a divine endowment that placed man next to God.

To become a Cartesian rational man required training. It required learning to separate the nonintellectual from the rational mind. It required controlling emotions and desires and shedding impulses and imagination. It required introspection, rigor, and discipline. The Cartesian method meant "subjecting the erratic, unreliable vagaries of individual consciousness to the demands of rigor and discipline" (Lloyd, 1996, p. 160).

By the time Descartes introduced his method of truth-finding, women were already viewed as incapable of reason—thus impulsive, emotional, and imaginative. With the introduction of the Cartesian method, women could, then, be excluded from the acquisition of the method of reason as well. Women were left with the "erratic, unreliable vagaries of individual consciousness." "If they are excluded from training in rationality, women are perforce *left* emotional, impulsive fancy ridden" (Lloyd, 1996, p. 154). Because they were incapable of Cartesian rationality, they were also not capable of the divine standing—being in God's image—through introspection. Hence, not only were women left in the realm of impulsivity, emotion, subjectivity, and imagination, they also were incapable of morality.

Their banishment to the realms of nonrationality or irrationality meant that women became the preservers for this realm. "It can now be seen as woman's role to preserve [for the rational man] the areas of warmth and sensuousness that training in reason demands that he himself transcend" (Lloyd, 1996, p. 154). Women became the preservers of that part of life that men could no longer indulge in, a part of life that was necessary for the rational man and yet despised/desired by him. Thus, the education of women was preparation for service to the rational man—to rationality itself, and to embody the realm that the man escaped and repudiated, but desired.

The "Man of Reason" Becomes Scientific

The ideal of the autonomous, rational man, separated from the particularities and corporeality of the physical world, has survived challenges to its exclusiveness and denial of feeling and imagination (Lloyd, 1996), but has been perpetuated in the scientific mind and ways of knowing. With the rise of science and then empiricist philosophy, the "Man of Reason" turned his gaze from his own internal mental processes to the Earth/nature and his senses for the source of truth. The emerging scientific rational man, however, maintains the split between mind and body, reason and emotion, and himself as knower and the knowable/nature. In his detachment and distance, he assumed a new universalized persona, with heightened superiority and a more aggressive epistemic project.

Method in truth-finding, no longer strictly reliant on the fine-tuning of rational mental powers, became the primary focus in science. The credibility of the method was secured through impartiality, objectivity, and rigor. The method and the inquirer were stripped of any interests or particularities. "The methodology and epistemology of modern science assume[d] that people are interchangeable as knowers" (Harding, 1991, p. 51). In this process the scientific mind became neutral and universal, sanitized and faceless.

This scientific mind inherited the legacy of the Cartesian mind and of course was not neutral, featureless, or universal. Code (1991) claims that this Cartesian notion of the autonomous, rational thinker as free of any biases of social interaction, as separate from the objects of his knowing, and as producer of knowledge that is objective, neutral, and true for "everyman" is in itself a biased conception. She maintains that all knowers have a history, a cultural and social embeddedness, that instills in them certain ways of seeing the world. Knowledge claims traditionally made by privileged rational thinkers (primarily white men) have been from their viewpoint and based on their interests and questions. Therefore, neither knower or knowledge are fitting for "everyman," or unbiased. Rather, it should be understood from the subjective perspective from which it is derived. The scientific mind is very much a masculine mind with his subjectivities deeply planted in superiority and privilege.

According to Harding (1986, 1991), masculine bias has permeated science "in both the definition of what counts as a scientific problem and in the concepts, theories, methods, and interpretations of research" (Harding, 1986, p. 82). With science as its paradigm, the epistemological ideal, too, is based in this masculine bias, through the attempt to describe and explain the natural and social worlds from a detached, objective view in the explication of universal laws. The standards and criteria for carrying out scientific inquiry and justifying knowledge claims have been the exclusive right of those trained—male or female—in the processes dominated by the masculine bias.

This is particularly apparent in the conception of the knowable/nature created by the masculine bias of the scientific mind. Code (1991) notes that the separation between the knower and the object to be known creates a hierarchical relationship in which "a primary purpose of cognitive activity [is] to produce the ability to control, manipulate, and predict the behavior of its objects. Such a relation is taken for granted in hegemonic conceptions of science practice" (p. 139). In the 17th century, nature, which was imbued with all that was not masculine and rational—uncontrollability, corporeality, passivity, and the feminine—was viewed as something to be mastered and controlled. The words of Francis Bacon, the noted father of science, provide a powerful image of science's project of domination: "It is Nature herself who is be the bride . . . in a chaste and lawful marriage between Mind and Nature, [and] . . . who requires taming, shaping, and subduing by the scientific mind" (Keller, 1985, p. 36). The superiority of the rational, scientific mind became more firmly planted not only in our cultural practices, but in the whole epistemological enterprise. Women and now nature settled into their positions as inferior, passive, controllable entities. They lost their existence as living subjects; as entities with agency. They became objectified and scrutinized under the masculine gaze. They were viewed increasingly in mechanical ways (Keller, 1985).

These Legacies in Modern Times

These classical philosophical legacies intertwine to perpetuate a hierarchy of rationality (Lloyd, 1996) and educational prerogatives/opportunities in our modern times. Armed with mastery of the disciplines of the mind and the methods of science, the rational man is qualified to determine his destiny and to govern and control others. Those to be governed—the less or nonrational women and laboring men, not capable of rigorous training of the mind—are viewed as needing a different kind of education, a different kind of discipline. Women and laboring men, as nonrational or irrational, cannot transcend their corporeality, so their education requires bodily discipline and hard work even to learn rudimentary skills and knowledge for survival. The transcended, rational man must discipline them into "docile bodies" (Foucault, in Rabinow, 1984). It is disciplined, rigorous training of the body and hand that women and laboring men assumedly need to ensure the elimination of bad habits and societal problems. School becomes "the arena for the development of one set of techniques for 'disciplining' the population" (Walkerdine, 1990, p. 20), thus alleviating these problems (especially crime and poverty) and bad habits of the masses, while at the same time maintaining the exclusive arena for the education of reason.

This notion was especially evident in our country at the beginning of this century in the turn to scientific management techniques for the establishment of school structures, procedures, and curriculum development. The archetype of mechanistic organization of the scientific management movement, Frederick the Great of Prussia (reign: 1740-1786), was fascinated by mechanical toy men and used them to fashion his military training program. He developed his inherited slovenly Prussian army into an efficient automatized machine through the standardization of language, rules, and equipment; specialization of tasks; and regimented training. This meant, without a doubt, strict discipline, as the master of military training hoped to take "raw material" and shape it into a disciplined soldiery (Morgan, 1986).

This mechanistic notion of human nature and need for discipline heavily influenced the scientific management movement in education. As masses of immigrants entered the United States at the turn of the 20th century, a very structured, standardized system of education—standardized language, rules, structures, learning tasks, and teaching techniques—seemed like the only recourse to some educators, especially Charters, Bobbitt, Snedden, and Judd (Kliebard, 1986), for educating those students who were viewed a threat to the norms of American society. The goal of these educators was to specify all aspects of educational practice through techno-scientific methods to produce the best rudimentary outcomes for students. This would not only ensure assimilation into the American way of life, but also placement of children in their proper social strata and careers.

Any attempt to provide immigrant or lower-class children with an education that might "liberate" them or forge a connection between their everyday lives and the world of the rational—like Dewey's school or Kilpatrick's activity curriculum[2]—was contested with a cry for rigor and discipline. Note William Bagley's response to activity curriculum. In 1926, William Bagley claimed that the activity curriculum advocated in some elementary schools "lacked rigor, and as a result, the children of America were simply not learning what they needed to know" (quoted in

Kliebard, 1986, p. 230). He further claimed that the "American [educational] enterprise needed a theory that was 'strong, virile, and positive not feeble, effeminate, and vague' " (p. 231).

Education as a Technical-Rational Pursuit: A Nation at Risk

The drafters of *A Nation at Risk* too wanted to create an educational enterprise that was strong, virile, and rigorous. They claimed that America's prosperity rested on developing a strong workforce. Their recommendations were all too familiar and represent centuries of inheritances—the combination of rationalism and science—that place development of the Cartesian rational mind through techno-scientific means at the forefront. They have accepted the superiority of the scientific mind and methods to create the best means for improving education and view the process of learning as a rational-technical pursuit.

In the framework of *curriculum as technology* (Eisner, 1985), knowledge is viewed as structured disciplines that are complete and coherent; have been validated through verifiable, value-neutral means; and are passively described as factual and explanatory, not evaluative (Cherryholmes, 1988). These neatly ordered boxes of verified structures of knowledge, with their specified conceptual frameworks and intellectual habits, then can be broken into component parts for easy acquisition by learners new to the discipline. These knowledge components can be easily measured in efficient, reliable, controllable ways.

Valued realms of knowledge, regardless of their nature, are "technicized"—quantified—so the inputs and outputs can be easily measured and controlled. At the high school level this means that the majority of student work is characterized by sameness: routine acquisition of units of knowledge. Students cover the curriculum and move on to the next unit. In this conception of education, the rational mind has become mechanized, with the metaphor of machine—or, more recently, computer—prevailing. Students take in knowledge through reading or lecture and give it back in the form of responses to worksheets, quizzes, and tests. Students progress mechanically through the process in predictable and measured ways. Social interaction, expressions of emotion, and sparks of creativity where not appropriate only obscure this progress.

This all-too-familiar conception of learning and curriculum is highlighted in the recommendations for high schools of the *Nation at Risk* report. The assumption of the report is that if educators initiate a controlled increase in the amount of content covered through required course credits and homework in a more focused curriculum, more learning will occur. Curriculum is deemed rigorous through the transfer of a certain amount of predetermined content to students in a certain amount of cost-effective time (Shor & Freire, 1987). Rigorous learning is the lockstep progression through outlined chunks of content.

The conception of curriculum and learning are easy for educators to reject. Even though it may be a more manageable way to educate students, it perpetuates inequities through the norming of standardized testing, renders knowledge as inert and disconnected from students' lives, "deskills" teachers (Apple, 1982; Ginsberg, 1988), and disempowers communities. More important, it emasculates the rational man, now an ingrained cultural ideal.

A Return to a Rigorous Education of Reason: Sizer's Project

The epistemological legacies inherent in the concept of rigor are more subtle and classical in Ted Sizer's reform project. He challenged the technical rationality (Schön, 1983) of the 20th-century scientification of education and the factory model of submission that differentiated education for the rationally capable and those (women and less-capable men) banished to the realms of heart and hand. He saw that the educational rigor touted by technical rationalists was backfiring for students, with most becoming "docile bodies" *and* minds, and many choosing exclusion from *any* formal education. He advocated an education for all students that focused on the development of mind and character. He wanted all students to be afforded an education that had previously been for only a few.

His call was appealing to many educators. Since 1983, the Coalition of Essential Schools network has expanded from 12 schools to more than 1,000 in 37 states. Sizer's call for an intellectual focus and locally designed reform excited many educators' desire for a more meaningful educational purpose and enlivened action. The promise of an education for all, grounded in the development of the mind, is an inviting one to many educators—including me—who want to wish beyond the instrumentalist notion of education with its focus on learning as handmaiden to the workforce and market. We know schooling that promotes sorting and selecting is attuned neither to the ideals of our nation nor to authentic learning for students. The scientification of curriculum and learning has made all of education a technical pursuit and is not conducive to engagement or thoughtfulness. Yet in our rejection of the technical rationalist notion of education and the acceptance of education of the mind for all through

Sizer's guiding principles and premises, are we truly proposing a framework for education that embraces our increasingly diverse population of students and engages them in the multiplicity of a pluralistic democracy, or are we merely advocating an expansion of the highly exclusionary, "rigorous" education promulgated by the legacy of Western philosophy?

Although Sizer proposes his educational ideal to eradicate the inequities in learning opportunities and is deeply committed to creating schools where all students develop their mental capacities, his call for high-quality intellectual work evokes an image of a classic liberal education that traditionally has been the entitlement of only a few. He calls for high-quality intellectual work.

> Scholarship—and it is scholarship that we must expect of secondary school students—is both precise and personal, a product of both the accumulated imagination of thinkers and doers from the past and of the individual learner herself. . . . [W]ork of a high standard . . . must be presented to all students, and there must be an end to the lamentable intellectual sloppiness one sees in too many American high schools. (1996, p. 46)

The use of the word *scholarship* invokes an image of the university academic who pursues an autonomous attempt to understand the world from afar. It maintains the separation between the knower and the knowable. And, it invokes the image of privilege. Only the most capable have traditionally had the privilege of stepping into the world of scholarship. It does not invoke the image of a midwestern farmer's daughter, whose interest is in the riding and breeding of horses, or of the factory worker's son, whose dream is to own and operate his own auto mechanic shop.

As Martin (1994a) notes, the goal for the educated man—one worthy of scholarship—is reasoned understanding that is fostered through objective analysis, rational thinking, and an interest in ideas and things. Employing R. S. Peter's conception of an educated person, Martin maintains that such a person

> has a body of knowledge and some kind of conceptual scheme to raise this knowledge above the level of a collection of disjointed facts which in turn implies some understanding of principles for organizing facts and of the "reason why" of things. (p. 211)

Learners must be intentionally initiated into these esteemed bodies of knowledge, conceptual schemes, and the respective "standards of proof and adequate evidence." To be initiated into these disciplines of knowledge—the traditional academic subjects: mathematics, science, literature, fine arts, philosophy, and history, as Martin claims, students must separate themselves from the particulars of the everyday and realms of emotion and body to acquire the habits of quiet reflection, reasoned deliberation, dispassionate inquiry, and abstract analytical theorizing. The well-educated person then has knowledge about the world, but is not directed to be of the world, compassionately solving problems. Martin implies that rigor within the traditional notion of an educated person is mastery of theoretical knowledge, being able to think abstractly within abstract disciplines, to develop habits of mind.

Such is the ideal Sizer (1992) holds for all students. His "rigorous general education" includes only those subjects that have been deemed "basic fields in the arts and sciences [that] best exemplify and exercise the human's rational abilities" (Eisner, 1985, p. 67). He adheres tightly to traditional academic disciplines—mathematics-science, history-philosophy, the arts—and development of habits of mind in his proposed educational program, without analyzing how their structures and their traditions have privileged and excluded many ways of knowing.

Rigor, in Sizer's project, is a disciplined initiation into the accepted structures of knowledge and the sharpening of rational powers. As we have seen, this project has been an exclusive masculine endowment at the expense of the interpersonal, emotive, and creative realms of knowing and of a majority of peoples. It has also disconnected learners from the realness of their lived experience and the realities of our world. It has allowed us to disavow the contributions of those whose lives have been built on the accomplishments of the hand and heart, those whose work has valued the land, the craft of their hands, or the giving of their heart to children and the community. It has blinded us to the contributions of those people who have been on the margin of privilege, who, as Harding (1991) claims, are in the best position to make claims to knowledge.

As a person who traversed the world of privilege, of the academy, and ultimately found her home again, bell hooks (1996) claims she now can make her home on the margin, in the center, and in between. These fragmented home locations have enabled her to have multiple and changing perspectives:

> To be in the margin is to be part of the whole but outside the main body. As black Americans living in a small Kentucky town, the railroad tracks were a daily reminder of our marginality. Across those tracks were paved streets, stores we

could not enter, restaurants we could not eat in, and people we could not look directly in the face. . . . We could enter the world but we could not live there. . . . Living as we did—on the edge—we developed a particular way of seeing reality. We looked both from the outside in and from the inside out. We focused our attention on the center as well as on the margin. We understood both. (p. 51)

It is from this position of being on the periphery of the whole that hooks gains her strength. If she had co-opted her voice to the man-of-reason's rationality, masking the worlds that she transverses, forgetting the home world she left behind, she could not possess her critical perspectives. Her voice would be silenced, her resistance disciplined, her critical position subdued.

If we uphold the desire to shape all students into Cartesian rational beings, then we are accepting that reason comes only from the disconnection of self from our cultural, social, and personal situatedness. We in essence are disconnecting the students (knowers) from their particular identities and crafting them into a specific mold of rationality. We are succumbing to our "Cartesian anxiety," our fear of uncertainty and instability, that compels us to trust technical methods and standards more than people (Bernstein, 1985). This project is subtle and is sustained through the subject matter we chose and the ways in which we engage students in the act of knowing. And, it is perpetuated by an adherence to rigor as a primary criterion for a quality education.

In the call for a rigorous education for all, we must critique the legacy of the rational, autonomous man who has been privileged in our heritage. We must ensure that we do not perpetuate the Western "man of reason," thus denigrating the experience, expertise, and realms of knowing that have been the legacy of women and laboring men; that is, those who hold the land or their craft as dear; and those who nurture our children and nature. We must beware, for "in creating our own centers and our own locals, we tend to forget that our centers displace others into the peripheries of our making" (Probyn, 1990, p. 176). By advancing the education of the man of reason for all, we may be enlarging the circle at the center, silencing and fading the voices and lives of those at the periphery. We may conceal the lives of others, disconnecting them from their existence, creating at best fragmented selves in the hope of them becoming the ideal rational thinker. It hides their lives, their identity. In our hope for an educational system that expects all students to believe in the promise of the man of reason, we may mask the differences of experience and existence of the many "others" in our country, put a silencer on their voices, and leave them powerless to critique its very premises.

In our naive, hasty acceptance of rigor as a criterion for a sound education, even for an education of the mind, we are blinding ourselves to the privileging inherent in that conception. If we want a rigorous education, we must unearth this privileging and seek new ground upon which to make our claims. Or, perhaps we need to find more appropriate criteria for judging the quality of education.

Notes

1. Sizer's principles call for an intellectual focus for all students; an essential curriculum, thus following the recommendation of "less is more"; a school tone of decency, trust, and fairness; personalization through a teacher-student ratio of 1:80—now modified to a maximum of 1:50 (Sizer, 1996); graduation by exhibition of mastery; engaging the students as the workers, teachers as coaches; teachers as generalists first; and only a small operational budget increase. In 1997 the Congress of the Coalition added a tenth principle, which calls for democratic and equitable practices in schools (Coalition of Essential Schools, 1999).

2. The activity curriculum engaged children in project-oriented learning.

References

Apple, M. (1982). *Education and power.* Boston: Routledge.

Bernstein, R. (1985). *Beyond objectivism and relativism: Science, hermeneutics and praxis.* Philadelphia: University of Pennsylvania Press.

Bond, L., & King, D. (1995). *State high school graduation testing: Status and recommendations.* Oak Brook, IL: North Central Regional Educational Laboratory.

Bordo, S. (1986). The Cartesian masculinization of thought. *Signs: Journal of Women in Culture and Society, 11*(3), 439-456.

Cherryholmes, C. (1988). *Power and criticism.* New York: Teachers College Press.

Coalition of Essential Schools. (1999). [Information brochure.] (Available from: Coalition of Essential Schools, National Office, 1814 Franklin St., Suite 700, Oakland, CA 94612)

Code, L. (1991). *What can she know? Feminist theory and the construction of knowledge.* Ithaca, NY: Cornell University Press.

Cushman, K. (Ed.). (1995). Making the good school better: The essential question of rigor. *Horace, 11*(4).

Eisner, E. (1985). *The educational imagination: On the design and evaluation of school programs* (2nd ed.). New York: Macmillian.

Ginsberg, M. (1988). *Contradictions in teacher education and society: A critical analysis.* London: Falmer.

Goodlad, J. (1984). *A place called school.* New York: McGraw-Hill.

Harding, S. (1986). *The science question in feminism.* Ithaca, NY: Cornell University Press.

Harding, S. (1991). *Whose science? Whose knowledge? Thinking from the lives of women.* Ithaca, NY: Cornell University Press.

hooks, b. (1996). Choosing the margin as a space for radical openness. In A. Garry & M. Pearsall (Eds.), *Women, knowledge, and reality* (2nd ed., pp. 48-55). New York: Routledge.

Keller, E. F. (1985). *Reflections on gender and science.* New Haven, CT: Yale University Press.

Kliebard, H. (1986). *The struggle for the American curriculum, 1893-1958.* New York: Routledge.

Lloyd, G. (1996). The man of reason. In A. Garry & M. Pearsall (Eds.), *Women, knowledge, and reality* (2nd ed., pp. 147-165). New York: Routledge.

Martin, J. R. (1994a). Becoming educated: A journey of alienation or integration? In J. R. Martin, *Changing the educational landscape: Philosophy, women, and curriculum* (pp. 200-211). New York: Routledge.

Martin, J. R. (1994b). The ideal of the educated person. In J. R. Martin, *Changing the educational landscape: Philosophy, women, and curriculum* (pp. 70-87). New York: Routledge.

Martin, J. R. (1994c). Sophie and Emile: A case study of sex bias in the history of educational thought. In J. R. Martin, *Changing the educational landscape: Philosophy, women, and curriculum* (pp. 53-69). New York: Routledge.

Morgan, G. (1986). *Images of organizations.* Newbury Park, CA: Sage.

National Commission on Excellence in Education. (1983). *A nation at risk: The full account of the National Commission on Excellence in Education.* Cambridge, MA: USA Research.

Probyn, E. (1990). Travels in the postmodern: Making sense of the local. In L. Nicholson (Ed.), *Feminism and postmodernism* (pp. 176-189). New York: Routledge.

Rabinow, P. (Ed.). (1984). *The Foucault reader.* New York: Pantheon.

Random House Webster's college dictionary. (1995). New York: Random House.

Rossman, G., & Wilson, B. (1996). Context, courses and the curriculum: Local responses to state policy reform. *Educational Policy, 10*(3), 399-422.

Schön, D. (1983). *The reflective practitioner.* New York: Basic Books.

Shor, I., & Freire, P. (1987). *A pedagogy for liberation: Dialogues on transforming education.* New York: Bergin & Garvey.

Sizer, T. (1984). *Horace's compromise.* Boston: Houghton Mifflin.

Sizer, T. (1992). *Horace's school.* Boston: Houghton Mifflin.

Sizer, T. (1996). *Horace's hope.* Boston: Houghton Mifflin.

Tyack, D., & Cuban, L. (1995). *Tinkering toward utopia.* Cambridge, MA: Harvard University Press.

Walkerdine, V. (1990). Progressive pedagogy and political struggle. In V. Walkerdine, *Schoolgirl fictions* (pp. 18-27). London: Verso.

Warmington, E., & Rouse, P. (1956). *Great dialogues of Plato.* New York: Mentor Books.

10

"What's This About a Few Good Men?"

Negotiating Gender in Military Education

DIANE DIAMOND
MICHAEL S. KIMMEL
KIRBY SCHROEDER

Daily, the headlines shout at us. Tailhook. Aberdeen Proving Ground. Several of the highest ranking career military officers have resigned over allegations of sexual harassment and adultery. The nation's highest ranking noncommissioned officer stood accused by five women of rape and sexual misconduct. A West Point cadet was expelled for rape. In one survey, two of three women in the military report having been sexually harassed (Schmitt, 1990, p. A22). Suddenly the U.S. military has become the chief theater of operations in the war between the sexes.

At the same time, the last two remaining publicly supported military-style all-male institutions of higher learning have submitted to a court order to admit women. By a 7-1 vote, the United States Supreme Court decided that the Virginia Military Institute had to end its 158-year-old tradition and admit women to its Corps of Cadets. A week after that decision, The Citadel, South Carolina's all-male military college, voted to admit women to its Corps of Cadets.

How would VMI and The Citadel face the daunting problems of integrating women? Preliminary anecdotal evidence indicated that the answer was "not very well." Shannon Faulkner, the first woman to enter The Citadel's Corps of Cadets, left the school after 1 week, much to the gleeful celebration of many of the male cadets—a vulgar display of anger toward women that was at least tolerated, if not encouraged, by The Citadel administration. In the fall of 1996, four more women entered The Citadel's gates; two of them were gone by Thanksgiving, citing violent hazing and sexual harassment by their training officers that included having deodorant sprayed into their mouths, and having their uniforms doused with lighter fluid and set on fire and then commanded not to break their "brace" position.

Having participated in both the VMI and Citadel cases as an expert witness of gender relations and masculinity for the Civil Rights Division of the Justice Department, the senior researcher of this team was familiar with those schools and their sense of making a last stand against federal regulation of states' educational institutions and preserving the nation's last arena of untrammeled, undiluted masculinity. But VMI and The Citadel were not the first military institutions to face the crisis of gender integration. All the federal military academies admitted women under Congressional mandate in 1976; Norwich University, a private military school in Northfield, Vermont, had admitted them voluntarily—willingly—2 years earlier. How had they accomplished their task of gender integration? What were the remaining obstacles they faced in the full integration of women into their Corps of Cadets? These were the questions that guided this research. Under a grant from the Small Grants Program of the Spencer Foundation, we interviewed a sample of women from the first classes to graduate from Norwich and West Point, as well as a sample of women currently enrolled at those two schools.

We take our title from a current recruiting poster for Norwich University in which two female cadets stand proudly and prettily in uniform (see Figure 10.1). Their eyes are clear and blue, their hair neat and feminine, their lipstick perfect, their mouths in near-smiles. They stand at attention, posing the rhetorical question, "What's this about a few good men?"—at once mocking and appropriating a traditional Marine Corps recruiting slogan that became the title of a popular film. They thus visually resolve the paradox of women's participation in the military—here are women who have sacrificed not one drop of their femininity in order to become decorated and disciplined military leaders. The effort to resolve the paradox between femininity and military competence has plagued efforts to integrate women into the military, just as it has also haunted efforts to exclude them (see, for example, Greene & Wilson, 1981; Johnson et al., 1978; Segal & Woelfel, 1976; Segal, 1978; Stein, 1981; Vitters & Kizner, 1977).

What's this
about a few good men?

NORWICH ⊛ UNIVERSITY
Northfield, Vermont   1-800-468-NORWICH

Figure 10.1. "What's This About a Few Good Men?"

This research is a preliminary investigation into the ways that the first cohorts of women negotiated gender at two military institutions, and the legacy they have left the current cohort of students.

Arguments Against Coeducation

Perhaps the most convenient place to begin is to see how the experience
of gender integration at West Point and Norwich addresses the arguments
advanced by VMI and The Citadel against women's entry. VMI and The
Citadel made three linked sets of arguments to support their claim that
women neither belonged nor would benefit from their educational methodologies: (a) *demand*—that women did not want the kind of adversative
educational experience that military education offered; (b) *abilities*—that
the natural, biologically based differences between women and men
would make it impossible for women to succeed; and (c) *dilution/pollu-
tion*—that women's entry would destroy the fragile male-bonding experiences of the men, experiences that were essential for successful military

training. Each of these contentions was disproved by the experiences of women at West Point and Norwich, although the persistence of these ideas created, and still creates, particular dilemmas for women who seek a military education.

Demand

Virtually all available research suggests that women enter military institutions for the same reasons men do. A longitudinal study of 3,700 male and 300 female cadets (Adams, 1984) found that the women and men were similar on personality variables and in their work and family orientation. Our interviews confirmed what current survey data revealed—that women and men, in both the first and current cohort, have similar reasons for selecting West Point: (a) quality of education; (b) desire for discipline; (c) opportunities; and (d) challenge (see Ace Survey, 1995-6; see Tables 10.1 and 10.2). Slightly more than half the women came from families with military histories.

As can be seen from Table 10.1, male and female cadets differ only slightly in their motivations for attending West Point. Similarly, they differ very little indeed when compared with male and female students at other public or private 4-year colleges (see Table 10.2). (Of course, it is equally interesting how little men and women differ at these colleges as well—this from people who are said to be applying for admission from different planets!)

In the first cohort at West Point, women said they "wanted to go to a very very good school to get a good education" (also applied to MIT and Wellesley) (WP I-1)[1]; they wanted to place themselves "under stressful conditions, overcome obstacles and succeed" (WP I-2). Current female and male cadets at West Point and at Norwich give similar reasons for wanting to attend the school, with the only significant difference being that far fewer females said they were preparing for careers as army officers. (*Candidates, Cadets and Graduates*, 1997). Several mentioned academic programs available at a select few colleges, including physics with an engineering emphasis in nuclear science (WP, II-6); criminal justice (N III-6).

Two current female cadets summarized their cohort's motivations: "I wanted to be in a place where I could live to the extreme," said one West Pointer (WP II-6); "I like running around in the mud and doing that sort of stuff," added a Norwich sophomore (N III-8). "I wanted discipline and I wanted a military lifestyle," commented one 22-year-old engineering major at West Point (in Schmitt, 1997, p. 26).

TABLE 10.1 First Priority Reasons for Selecting the U.S. Military
Academy at West Point (Classes of 1996-2000)

	% Women	% Men
USMA's overall reputation	23	24
Desire to be an army officer	11	21
Self-development	22	18
Academic program	20	16
Leadership training	12	10
Other:	12	11
Athletics		
Economics		
Family Influences		

SOURCE: Prepared by: USMA, OPA (IRAB), Aug. 1996. Class Characteristics, Classes of 1996-2000.

Demand for military education actually increased as opportunities became available, illustrating the sociological axiom that opportunity creates demand. Numbers of applications have remained at the same level for nearly three decades, with minor fluctuations. Interestingly, predicted drops in applications among men also did not occur; in fact, when women were admitted to Norwich, for example, applications from men went up as well—to the fourth highest level in the school's history. Alumni giving also reached an all-time high, which led the president to state that the introduction of women had been "a major consequence in increasing revenues and the quality of our academic performance" (*Report of the President,* 1975). This year, VMI admitted the largest class in its history, including 32 women (Janofsky, 1997).

Stereotyped Differences: Negotiating Sameness

In its VMI decision, the U.S. Supreme Court found that VMI relied on anachronistic stereotypes about women's abilities in their decision to exclude them. This position is aptly summarized by then Speaker of the House of Representatives, Newt Gingrich; as he put it, "If combat means living in a ditch, females have a biological problem staying in a ditch for 30 days because they get infections. Males are biologically driven to go out and hunt giraffes."

TABLE 10.2 Reasons for Selecting "This College"

% Cadets/Students Rating Each Reason for Selecting This College as Very Important

	% USMA		% Four-Year Public Colleges		% Private Universities	
	Women	Men	Women	Men	Women	Men
Good academic reputation	87.7	86.2	61.2	51.6	80.3	76.8
Good career opportunity	89.0	88.9	53.8	48.5	70.5	67.3
Grads go to top grad schools	62.2	70.6	33.6	26.9	55.8	49.6
Offered financial assistance	42.3	48.8	41.6	35.6	42.3	37.7
Offers special programs	40.5	34.8	27.0	18.9	29.3	20.5
Low tuition	38.0	37.0	28.0	21.9	6.8	4.3
Recruited by athletic dept.	20.4	17.1	5.0	13.1	3.9	7.1
Good social reputation	17.8	21.5	25.7	24.2	31.4	32.1
Relatives wanted me to come	18.4	16.1	9.4	8.9	8.3	8.0
Recruited by college rep.	7.4	6.0	4.7	7.7	3.2	4.6

SOURCE: Prepared by: USMA OPA/IRA (MAOR-R), 23 Jan 97. *Ace Survey,* AY 1995-1996

Reliance on such ideas of the natural, biologically based differences between women and men confronted women entering military education with the same dilemma as the women who have successfully entered every field of endeavor traditionally the homosocial preserve of men, from the business world to medicine, law, and even the university—the assumptions that women who seek military education cannot be "real women." Military service is seen as gender-conforming for men, gender nonconforming for women. Thus, women were trapped in a paradox: To the extent that they are successful cadets, women cannot be successful women; to the extent that they are successful women, they cannot be successful cadets. Women are either successful cadets or successful women; they cannot be both, and thus either way they lose. "When women deviated from their feminine role, despite the appropriateness of this behavior to the cadet role, they were regarded unfavorably by their classmates," wrote a team of researchers (Yoder, Adams, & Prince, 1983, p. 330); and females often "do not believe they are as accepted as the males" in their training squadrons (DeFleur & Gilman, 1978, p. 176).

Adherence to stereotypes was most evident in the attitudes of male cadets and staff at West Point during the first years. "The greatest obstacle the academies encountered in integrating women was, and continues to be, the attitudes of men—faculty members and students," was how one writer put it (Holm, 1982, p. 311). Female cadets found the males "closed-minded," believing in 'women should be barefoot, pregnant and in the kitchen' outlooks" (WP I-2). These hostile attitudes began at the top of the chain of command and filtered down to the lowest first-year students. At West Point, for example, the chain of command was not at all supportive of women's entry, vowing that "over my dead body will women come here" (WP I-1). Prior to the women's arrival, the Superintendent had the entire corps of cadets come to an assembly, "have them close their eyes and raise their hand if they thought it was a good idea for women to be there [laughter]" (interview, WP I-4; see also Barkalow, 1990, p. 62). It was hardly a surprise that the last all-male class (1979) made a big deal of being "the last class with balls" (WP I-3).

By contrast, Norwich administrators were supportive of women from the beginning. The college decided to become coeducational voluntarily, in 1974, 2 years before the service academies. General Hart, the college president, even raised the issue before women were introduced, saying, "I would very much like to see women enrolled in the Corps of Cadets" (*Guidon,* November 2, 1973, p. 1). An editorial in the student paper (Fall 1974) commended the administration for their "careful and deliberate handling" of this controversial issue and concluded with the message to the women to feel "at ease," because "the majority of the Norwich community welcomes you" ("One Man's Opinion," in *Guidon,* Fall 1974). Most male students were supportive. "At present," reported the student newspaper as the first cohort of women entered,

> it appears that the only serious hassle evolves from the few members of the Norwich community who are not mature enough to adapt to the new environment. These poor people feel that it is necessary to direct rude remarks or cat-calls in order to express their opinions. It is these few people who make it rough and embarrassing for these girls who are trying to accomplish something worthwhile. ("The New Resident Norwich Students," 1974, p. 1)

It is therefore not surprising that at West Point, stereotypic assumptions about women's capabilities and ambitions were more prevalent than at Norwich. Stereotypic assumptions about putatively natural differences between women and men led to the problems typically associated with tokens in any large organization (cf. Kanter, 1977; Laws, 1975). Because the women believed the chain of command was not especially supportive, they felt isolated from the institution. As one female put it, "we could not let the authorities know what was happening because if we did we would be harassed further" (cited in Rogan, 1981, p. 196).

And because, like all tokens, they felt invisible as individuals yet hypervisible as members of their group, they felt isolated from the other female cadets. "Obviously you stood out like _ sore thumb," commented one female cadet from the first class at West Point. "You got longer hair and you got boobs. You're gonna stick out" (WP, I-1). Another commented that "one minute we were supposed to do bayonet training, and the spirit of the bayonet is to kill. And screaming and yelling and you're in camouflage. And then the next half hour you're cleaned up. . . . But what's the real woman, what's the real girl?" (WP I-4).

Diluting the Purity of Homosociality: Negotiating Difference

At the same time as these military institutions stressed traditional assumptions about natural gender differences, they also relied on traditional military assumptions that equal treatment means treating everyone the same—and the delicate line between equality and sameness is especially complicated in a "fundamentally masculinized" military that no woman has a chance of transforming into a place of genuine gender equality (Enloe, 1988, p. xvii). To the extent to which women were perceived as different, these institutions believed that women's admission would lead to the dilution and pollution of the experience for the men. Women, the argument went, would distract the male cadets, introducing sexual tension that would undermine the fragile imperatives of male bonding upon which the schools were founded. Gen. Josiah Bunting III, now the Superintendent at VMI, argued that women would represent "a toxic kind of virus" that would destroy The Citadel. "Adolescent males benefit from being able to focus exclusively on the task at hand, without the intrusion of any sexual tension," he added (quoted in Vojdik, 1997, p. 76).

This was originally a fear at service academies as well. Air Force Academy Superintendent Lt. Gen. Albert P. Clark argued that

[t]he environment of the Air Force Academy is designed around these stark realities [of combat]. The cadet's day is filled with constant pressure. His life is filled with competition, combative and contact sports, rugged field training, use of weapons, flying and parachuting, strict discipline and demands to perform to the limit of endurance mentally, physically, and emotionally. It is this type of training that brings victory in battle. It is my considered judgment that the intro-

duction of female cadets will inevitably erode this vital atmosphere. (cited in Holm, 1982, pp. 307-308)

Army secretary Howard Callaway agreed: "Admitting women to West Point will irrevocably change the Academy. The Spartan atmosphere—which is so important to producing the final product [combat leaders]—would surely be diluted" (cited in Holm, 1982, p. 308)

As a result of these assumptions about women's abilities and the experience of their presence, the first cohorts of women, and subsequent ones as well, have had to negotiate gender carefully and constantly. They were constantly negotiating sameness and difference with each other, with male cadets, with faculty and staff, and with themselves. When they stressed sameness, they were seen as different; when they stressed difference, they were treated the same. Since so much was at stake, and both so fragile and fluid and so constantly scrutinized, the women were constantly "doing gender," negotiating publicly the meanings of femininity. What is typically left for backstage preparations had taken a very visible center stage.

Strategies of Negotiation

How, then, did the first classes of women negotiate sameness and difference? The first classes of female cadets at Norwich and West Point faced difficult and often contradictory demands. In a sense, the phrase "woman cadet" was an oxymoron—one could not be both a woman and a cadet at the same time. How did they negotiate equality with the men in a context of gender differences and the military's emphasis on same treatment?

One strategy, what we call "emphatic sameness," was to downplay gender identity as women in favor of being seen as cadets. To the extent that they were not seen as women, they could be seen as successful cadets. "Needless to say it's been no picnic here," wrote Air Force 2nd Lt. Marianne Owens:

Yet many of us have made it through under the same conditions as the men. Therefore we say: Don't point us out; don't applaud us or you'll be ruining what we've been trying to establish. We've come so far in fighting the hard feelings. . . . It is the goal . . . for us, to simply leave this institution, not as the first women graduates, but as deserving, hard-working graduates to enter the Air Force. in (Little, 1980, p. 12)

As one West Point graduate told us, "Once I was accepted as 'not one of those women' then I was O.K." (WP I-4).

Asserting any elements of traditional femininity was frowned upon. One cadet described this situation:

> A sexual double standard was operating. In the beginning, it was the ones who were the prettiest or the most feminine, who wore perfume and makeup in formation. The guys didn't like that at all; they felt that if the women had time to do that, they should have been polishing shoes. They turned on the pretty women because they felt they didn't belong at West Point. They wanted to drive them out. (quoted in Rogan 1981, p. 196)

Women from the first cohort at West Point described low levels of solidarity and support networks among the women. They rarely appeared in public in groups of more than two, a strategy that seems to have developed in response to comments made by faculty, students, and administrators. "Literally, my class, we stayed away from other women," one graduate said. "You didn't want to have more than two women together at one time, then somebody would make a comment" (WP I-1). "A group of women together was always seen as a cabal," wrote one of West Point's first female cadets (Barkalow, 1990, p. 138). Another said: "When we were there as cadets, we tended to not go around as groups of women because that caused attention to be focused on women and usually it was negative attention" (WP I-2).

Of course this increased the women's sense of isolation. "I wish there were another female out here I could talk to—someone who was going through the same things I am, having the same feelings," wrote one first-year West Point cadet in her diary at the time (Barkalow, 1990, p. 125). But their decision seemed to have been based on an accurate reading of the situation. When some of the female cadets tried to initiate group lunches, the men would make derisive comments, as did one male instructor who said, "So what's going on? You plotting the revolution?" as he walked by.

A second gender strategy—*strategic overcompensation*, developed by the first classes of women—was to work twice as hard as the men to succeed. As tokens fighting against both minority status and stereotypic assumptions about their capabilities, many believed that they had to work twice as hard to remain "equal" to the men. In our interviews, well over 75% of the women at Norwich and West Point felt that they have to work "twice as hard" as the men to be treated the same—to be taken seriously as cadets (this is true both of the first cohorts and of the current cadets).

"You're put in a fishbowl here cause there's so few women in comparison to guys," commented one woman. "I think that maybe you do have to be a little bit tougher just because you are in the minority" (WP II-4). Sometimes, one woman told us, "you have to work twice as hard to be considered half as good" (WP I-5).

Third, since formal networking was suspect and the first cohorts did not have upper-class women as mentors and role models, the first cohorts developed *informal networks of support*. As one early graduate put it, "Those women badly needed a support network, which, institutionally, wasn't there for them. They had to create it for themselves" (Barkalow, 1990, p. 138). "We really needed contact with women officers. We needed their experience, their advice and their example," said another. "We needed to be able to talk to them without suspicion or fear. We needed their empathy and their concern. We needed to be brought up the way men at the Academy had been brought up by their own for almost 200 years" (Barkalow, 1990, p. 96). One woman made friends with one of the officer's wives. Officers' wives "were, to us, I think, outside the system enough that we could use them," she said (WP I-4) (unlike West Point, the Air Force Academy provided women as upper-class surrogates for the first female cadets enrolled, creating institutional support structures).

Finally, the first cohort of women cadets negotiated their contradictory experiences of femininity through *strategic deployment of gendered display*. Often, they asserted traditional femininity in social situations while they downplayed it in professional situations. Such minimizing and maximizing of gender difference, depending on the situation, is probably only an exaggerated version of what women do in virtually all public domains in which their participation is gender nonconforming, from the legal and medical professions to institutions of higher learning and Wall Street investment houses.

Concerned that military training would "masculinize" its women cadets, the institution responded initially by exacerbating the problem. The USMA offered its first women a class in how to apply and wear makeup (WP I-4). They put out a press release in 1979 to reassure the public that their cadets had not become masculinized. Its first two sentences read: "Female cadets here adopt traditional masculine personality traits to be accepted as leaders. They also want both marriage and a full time military career" (cited in Rogan, 1981, p. 201).

Yet research undertaken by the school found little cause for worry. Priest, Prince, and Vitters (1978) found that the women became slightly less masculine and more feminine, though the data were not statistically significant. Thus, they concluded, "the environment was not psychologically defeminizing to the women" (ironically, data indicated that their male counterparts became *both* more masculine and more feminine). Both male and female cadets were more masculine and less feminine than a sample of their counterparts at University of Texas (Priest et al., 1978, p. 215).

Much of the women's strategic maneuvering to reconcile being women and cadets was rhetorical. In the tortured, twisted, and often incoherent narratives offered by both first-cohort graduates and contemporary students, one hears most clearly and poignantly these efforts. One woman said, for example,

> I mean there's always going to be differences because there's differences between men and women. I hope I'm different from the guys. You know, I still like to be a woman, as well as a cadet. Especially outside. At the same time, you know, when I'm at school I don't want to get treated any different because I'm still a professional. I do the same things, so I don't want to get treated any different in that way. (WP II-3)

Current Cohorts of Students

Research from studies in the early 1980s indicated that some of the problems of tokens were alleviated by subsequent classes by (a) the increased number of women enrolled; (b) the development of institutional supports; (c) changes in the dominant group's attitudes; and (d) increased cohesiveness among tokens (Yoder et al., 1983).

Today, both Norwich and West Point have supportive chains of command. General Goodpaster, who took over at West Point in 1977, supported women cadets:

> Women are participating in the Army in large numbers and making a fine contribution. With women in the Army, you must have women officers. If you're going to have women officers, they're entitled to be trained at as good an institution as there is. The notion that you could have a mini-West Point for women is nonsense. And so you come to say that they should be here. (cited in Rogan, 1981, p. 210)

The current Commandant of cadets at Norwich adds that "our women will really make them understand that women are very capable in all those positions as long as you treat them all alike and realize that there are some biological differences" (interview).

Both West Point and Norwich have developed and utilize extensive sexual harassment training. Norwich President Richard Schneider has also instituted effective sexual harassment training. Calling it a "front burner" issue, Schneider commented that "It's illegal, it's immoral . . . and I feel very strongly about it" (Walsh, 1993, p. 2D).

The presence of upper-class women and increased women faculty and staff have also enhanced formal and informal structures of support. One current West Point cadet said, "you can always talk to female upperclassmen" (WP II-1). Another said, "There's all these senior girls that have had four years here that you know you can always go talk to. Or there's a lot of female officers here that I feel really comfortable with. There's a lot of graduates also" (WP II-4). Another offered this account:

> the first couple of weeks, they took us aside and said "if you ever, you know, issues like female issues that you can't talk with your male platoon sergeant, whether it be about going to the hospital or about having your period and what to do . . . or if you run into a sexual harassment situation or something," that their door was always open. They didn't treat us any different but they came in and they told us that that support net's there. That we could come. (WP II-3)

In addition, women's sports teams build solidarity among the team members; sports have become a larger and larger portion of women's experiences at military academies. Women's sports participation, in the words of Sheila Tobias,

> has challenged age-old views of what is normal for males and normal for females. The qualities it takes to make a woman an athlete—go for the jugular, learn to be a team player, learn to be a leader—conflict with old ideas. The bottom line is that once women are as strong and confident physically as they can be, they won't be pushovers. (cited in Goodman, 1997, p. A 17)

Increased formal and informal structures of support, increased cohort solidarity, and increased numbers of women have gone far in making Norwich and West Point more inviting to women. Yet the problems of earlier classes have not entirely disappeared. Women cadets today still face the same contradictory demands of succeeding as cadets and as women. Being seen as successful cadets—the same—leads them to desire to be seen differently, while being successful at being women—different—leads them to want to be seen as the same. One female cadet notices the way the male cadets look at the women from other colleges:

You get kind of jealous because here we are in these uniforms, hair pulled back, trying to do 50 push-ups and stuff like that. And the guys see us like, as other cadets, pretty much, to be honest, and not as girls. There's that desire to be feminine at the same time the desire to be a really good cadet. So it can sometimes tear you apart. (WP II-6)

And they are still adapting tortured and contradictory narrative strategies to negotiate this dilemma:

I think people are pretty much treated the same, but as a female you have to prove yourself a lot more. You have to put forth 110% instead of just 100% because they look at you and they're like "Well, is she going to be good?" but in the long run after you prove yourself to everyone that you can do it and that you're not expected to be treated . . . You have to come in with an attitude that we're all the same not "Well, I'm a girl, I can't do this, and I can't do that." I think they treat you pretty much the same. (N III-2)

The chief obstacle to women's successful integration remains their perceptions of the attitudes of the male cadets. On the one hand, some cadets see significant changes among the men: One woman says she believes that "most of the guys feel that they want the girls in your company to do well" (WP II-1); while another says she feels "very much" supported by the male cadets (WP II-2). "When people are used to working together, the social relations calm down," one female cadet commented. "It's cooling here now; there were real passions, but now we're more like brothers and sisters. You can feel good about somebody and have it be friends" (cited in Rogan, 1981, p. 219).

But for other men, there is, at best, a grudging tolerance of the inevitability of women's presence. "It's inevitable," one current VMI cadet said, resignedly. "I'm not out to get anyone, but at the same time I'm not out to help them either" (quoted in Schmitt, 1997, p. 31).

What Do the Women Want?

Why do they put up with it? What do they get out of it? The answer is simple—the same reasons that the men put up with the incessant barrage of humiliations and harassment. An institutional self-study at West Point reported that the women, just like the men, "earn their way into USMA; perform to the same standards as other cadets; make significant contributions as officers" (*Candidates, Cadets and Graduates,* 1997).

For the most part, the women who graduate from West Point and Norwich get the same benefits as the men—a feeling of accomplishment, of leadership experience, of successful navigation of a very difficult and demanding regimen of physical and mental training. "This place made me realize I could do a lot more than I thought I could do," said one (WP II-3). Competitive, ambitious, assertive, these women thrive on their successes, including those in which they compete directly with men: "I'm out there with the guys doing the same thing with the guys, doing better than some of the other guys," one current cadet said (WP II-1). "If you're running and there's some guy there and you're almost at a line and you outsprint him, that the best feeling in the world. . . . It's like 'I'm here. I did better than you.' "

Both male and female graduates have had the experience of success in a coeducational setting, a more adequate preparation for a heterosocial military as well as for civilian life.

As Col. Craig Lind, at Norwich, said, "I tell these young men, 'You're going to work for, and work with, women. The sooner you understand that the better' " (quoted in Rimer, 1996, p. 16)—a sentiment echoed by current students, both female, like Capt. Tonya Thorne, who hopes "these guys aren't so blind or stupid they think they'll never have to take orders from a woman," or Lt. Col. Dianna Zito, who suggests that men "have to know how to deal with women, to feel comfortable giving them orders and taking orders from them—that's the real world" (both in Ford, 1994, p. 37). In fact, VMI and Citadel graduates are at a decided disadvantage, according to one current male Norwich cadet: "It's an all-boys club, they go off in the military and they've never played with girls, never dealt with the female aspect of things, whether they're a soldier, a sailor, a marine, whatever, and they're hindered by that" (N III-2). By contrast, West Point and Norwich have been transformed by the experience of coeducation, and for the better. A woman from the first West Point cohort recounted what one male West Point graduate told her: "I think one of the best things that ever happened to West Point was women coming because it used to be a boys' school and now it's a school of leadership. It's a professional school" (WP I-4).

Conclusion

Classical liberal theory was preoccupied with the relationship among equality and inequality, difference and sameness. It was a Lockean axiom that different talents, different motivations, and different abilities would lead to different, that is, unequal, economic and social outcomes. This is, of course, a bedrock principle of capitalist economic systems that emphasize meritocratic principles. By contrast, equality has always meant the fear of sameness. Thus anti-Communists play on fears that economic equality would mean that we would all look, act, and think the same things. Antifeminists play upon a fear of androgyny, a blending of masculinity and femininity into an amorphous mush, to maintain traditional gender inequalities. Difference leads to inequality; equality means sameness.

So too is sex discrimination law replete with the articulation and elaboration of this sameness-difference equation. To the extent that we treat unalikes as alike, or alikes as unalike, are we not practicing sex discrimination? The development of the "reasonable woman" standard in sex discrimination, critical legal theory's efforts to establish guidelines about sexual harassment and date rape that stress the experience of the woman over the intentions of the man, point to the dilemmas of this negotiation.

And so, too, the nation's military is currently grappling with questions of sameness and difference at every turn. Does equal treatment require that all cadets be treated exactly the same—for example, to have their heads shaved, to be subject to sexualized humiliations? Of course not. But how to dislodge the casual equation of equality = sameness? Today the military joins its educational institutions, as well as virtually every other institutional arena in American life, in exploring what it would mean to develop theories of equality that embrace and appreciate difference. As one young current cadet put it, "They don't seem to understand that equality does not mean we all have to be the same" (quoted in Rogan, 1981, p. 185).

But perhaps they have—or at least have *begun* to do so. It may also be that the male and female cadets have stumbled, inadvertently, on a cooperative strategy to accommodate gender difference within a context of the most rigidly hierarchical lines of authority and the absolute equality of all within the same rank. They're becoming family. Recall the words of the cadet quoted earlier: "It's cooling here now," she said. "There were real passions, but now we're like brothers and sisters. You can feel good about somebody and have it be friends."

Consistently, surprisingly, female cadets used family as a metaphor to describe what was good about their relations with male cadets. "The guys seem to look at the women as their little sisters," comments one current Norwich female cadet. And it appears that some of the men, at least, agree. "It's almost like being brothers and sisters," says 2nd Lt. Scott Owings, at Norwich. "If you come here with the idea of entering the military, you'd better get used to [the] idea of working with, for, and in command of women" (quoted in Mace, 1995, p. D1).

And the family is becoming more than a metaphor for the way differences can be accommodated within a hierarchy that also stresses equality. Mike Mentalvos, one of The Citadel's most decorated cadets, resigned from the school when his younger sister, Jenny, resigned after being sexually harassed in November 1997. And the school's new superintendent, appointed to steady an institution listing from so much adverse publicity, is Maj. Gen. J. Emery Mace, the father of Nancy Mace, one of the two remaining second-year female cadets at the school.

The family as political metaphor, of course, has a long history. For centuries, it provided the analogy for patriarchal political rule, theocratic domination, and misogynist familial life. But *that* family was always defined as the relations between father and "others," either wives or children (at best, the more democratic family proposed relatively equal parents and their children). As the father ruled the family, so too did the king rule the country. But the family also contains an alternative reading: Even within the structure of authority and hierarchy that is the relationship between parents and children, there is also the relationship among siblings, between brothers and sisters, each valued for his or her individuality, distinctiveness, difference, and yet each an irreplaceable part of the family, equally valued and equally loved (imperfect incest taboos to the side, brothers do not torture, rape, and harass their sisters; parents do not abuse their authority by permitting one child to lord over the others). Of course, the validity of this familial model depends less upon the attitudes of the parents (the administration and faculty) and more on the changing attitudes of the male cadets. For those answers, we must return to our sources.

Note

1. References to interviews are coded as follows: WP or N indicates whether the cadet was from West Point or Norwich, respectively. The roman numeral indicates the cohort: I (1976); II (1985-1986); III (current cohort, 1997).

References

Ace survey. (1997). [Prepared by USMA OPA/IRA (MAOR-R), January 23, 1997.]
Adams, J. (1984). Women at West Point: A three-year perspective. *Sex Roles, 11*(5/6), 525-541.

Barkalow, C. (1990). *In the men's house: An inside account of life in the army by one of West Point's first female graduates.* New York: Poseidon.

Candidates, cadets and graduates. (1997). Report for the Conference on Women Cadets, Office of Policy, Planning and Analysis, United States Military Academy, West Point, 1997.

DeFleur, L. B., & Gilman, D. (1978). Cadet beliefs, attitudes, and interactions during the early phases of sex integration. *Youth & Society, 10*(2), 165-190.

Enloe, C. (1988). *Does khaki become you? The militarization of women's lives.* London: Unwin Hyman.

Ford, R. (1994, May 1). The uniforms of diversity. *The Boston Globe,* pp. 37, 39.

Goodman, E. (1997, June 20). A winning idea in sports: A level playing field. *Boston Globe,* p. A17.

Greene, B., III, & Wilson, K. L. (1981). Exploring the new integration of women into the military. *Journal of Political and Military Sociology, 9*(3), 241-254.

Holm, J. (1982). *Women in the military.* Novato, CA: Presidio Press.

Janofsky, M. (1997, July 20). Military college awaits its first female cadets. *New York Times,* p. 12.

Johnson, C. D., et al. (1978). *Women content in the Army—REFORGER 77 (REF WAC 77).* Alexandria, VA: Army Research Institute for the Behavioral and Social Sciences.

Kanter, R. M. (1977). *Men and women of the corporation.* New York: Basic Books.

Laws, J. L. (1975). The psychology of tokenism. *Sex Roles, 1,* 51-67.

Little, C. (1980, Spring). *A look at women cadets after four years* [photocopy]. Colorado Springs, CO: U.S. Air Force Academy.

Mace, D. (1995, August). Being coed is not at issue at Norwich. *Rutland Herald and Times Argus,* pp. D1, D2.

The new resident Norwich students. (1974, September 21). *Guidon, 58*(1), 1.

One man's opinion. (1974, September 21). *Guidon* (Norwich University).

Priest, R. F., Prince, H. T., & Vitters, A. G. (1978). The first coed class at West Point: Performance and attitudes. *Youth & Society, 10*(2), 205-224.

Report of the President of Norwich University. (1975, July 15). Loring Hart papers, Krietzberg Library, Norwich University.

Rimer, S. (1996, September 6). Women are "no big deal" at an old military college. *New York Times,* p. 16.

Rogan, H. (1981). *Mixed company.* New York: G. P. Putnam.

Schmitt, E. (1990, September 12). Two out of three women in military study report sexual harassment. *New York Times,* p. A22.

Schmitt, E. (1997, April 6). A mean season at military colleges. *New York Times,* Higher Education Supplement, pp. 26, 31.

Segal, D. R., & Woelfel, J. C. (1976). *Interacting with women: Interpersonal contact and acceptance of women in the U.S. Army.* Alexandria, VA: Army Research Institute for the Behavioral and Social Sciences.

Segal, M. W. (1978). Women in the military: Research and policy issues. *Youth & Society, 10*(2), 101-126.

Stein, J. H. (1981). *Bring me men and women.* Berkeley: University of California Press.

Vitters, A. G., & Kizner, N. S. (1977). *Report on the admission of women to the U.S. Military Academy* (Project Athena). New York: United States Military Academy.

Vojdik, V. K. (1997). Girls' schools after VMI: Do they make the grade? *Duke Journal of Gender Law and Policy, 4*(1), 76.

Walsh, M. (1993, May 25). "One of the few" women to give military school a try. *Burlington Free Press.*

Yoder, J. D., Adams, J., & Prince, H. T. (1983). The price of a token. *Journal of Political and Military Sociology, 11*(Fall), 325-337.

PART FOUR

PEDAGOGIES, POLICIES, AND LEADERSHIP

11

Tempering the Masculinities
of Technology

JOHN WILLINSKY

Men and their machines (boys and their toys) forms an underlying theme for the history of the West and many of our childhoods. Those constant images of young boys earnestly playing with their trucks, microscopes, and guns tells its own history of a technology engaged in building, exploring, and otherwise wreaking havoc on the world. Whether the machines are used to discover or conquer, with the two often inextricably mixed, technology was to become for the West the very measure of man (Adas, 1991). During its Age of Empire, spanning from the Renaissance to our own day, the West mounted what was, in effect, a *political science* that cast reason and its machinations as a masculine dynamo against a feminine nature that was seen to be embodied in women, children, and natives. And so today it is tempting to imagine that the *phallotechnologies,* as Jane Caputo (1988) identifies them, of instrumental reason are now approaching some sort of culminating moment with the thinking machines that aptly manage our words, work, and worth. It is all vastly more complicated than that, of course, but gross characterizations have a way, sometimes, of capturing rough truths.

The development of technology is often cast in the form of a creation myth in which a given race of men have come to produce the world through a technology that others are meant to consume and *man.* Certainly, women are more often the bar-code readers, the word- and data processors, the human extensions of the machines that constitute and regulate their work.

And to show for it, they bear more than their share of repetitive strain injuries or RSI (the black-lung disease of the info-age), as well as a greater part in the polarization of the economy brought about by automation and downsizing, and the off-shore globalization of manufacturing (Hayes, 1995).[1] Women suffer this technology because it is part of a fiercely competitive economic system and, in the argument this chapter pursues through the high schools, because technology has come to define a masculine space.

Technology, in the sense that I am using it here, is something more than the application of device and technique. Technology represents a mobilization of resources and reason; it creates a place in the world of privilege and exploitation. That space, at this point, has been made thoroughly masculine, beginning in childhood, in ways that are being challenged. This chapter describes an exploration and challenging of that masculine space in a high school computer studies program.

Shaping Technology

The approach I am taking to technology emphasizes what people have made of machines, rather than asking what the machines have made of us. I say this because there is no shortage of prophets pointing to the profound changes the technology has wrought. Educator Neil Postman (1992) warns that "it is not always clear, at least in the early stages of a technology's intrusion into a culture, who will gain most by it and who will lose most" (p. 12). I think it is clear. Physicist Ursula Franklin (1990) finds herself "overawed by the way in which technology has acted to reorder and restructure social relations" (p. 13). I think that changes to the order and structure of social relations are not the result of an overawing technology, but of the uses to which the machinery has been put. This technological determinism recalls Marshall McLuhan's *the medium is the message,* and while I wouldn't deny technology's impact on the feel and tone of our lives, I fear that we are losing sight of the ends to which the medium is messaged.[2]

So I am left to wonder when Sherry Turkle (1995) wants us to believe that Multiple-User Domains (MUDs), which are network games based on the role-playing model of Dungeons and Dragons, offers a new form of identity. She holds that in these *computer-mediated worlds,* the thinking of the postmodernist giants, Lacan, Foucault, Deleuze, and Guattari, comes to life, or, as she captures it: "The self is multiple, fluid, and constituted in interaction with machine connections; it is made and transformed by language; sexual congress is an exchange of signifiers; and understanding follows from navigation and tinkering rather than analysis" (p. 15). The MUDs may well feature men constructing female characters posing as men and so on, but this really does little to alter the masculine tenor of the "navigation and tinkering" of the human-machine-human interface, despite the free flow of virtual fluids. Real life, or RL as MUD-sters name it, goes on. Technologies do not so much create new spaces, I think it can be argued, as render them quicker, brighter, bigger, and noisier. It takes a far more deliberate and focused effort to turn the machines away from reproducing the world of those who direct them.

But if changes in the technologies are not the answer, what about changes in the men? As Mary Bryson and Suzanne de Castell (1993) perceptively warn, "re-tooling" an old-style masculinity in favor of a men's movement version of a New Age technology only risks a further entrenching of a masculine monopoly over these resources in the West. What we need, rather, are ways of speaking to how the devices that govern our lives have been constructed as the reasonable domain of men and how that could be otherwise. This is to distinguish between the *masculinity* ascriptions of technology and what men and, for that matter, women really do with machines. It has been Eve Kosofsky Sedgwick's (1995) seemingly obvious point that not everything that men do counts as masculine and vice versa. It is better to think of masculinity as a particular performance of gender, which is what Judith Butler (1991) does in making sense of sexual identity. In the case of technology, the machine is read as a natural and powerful extension of the male body, whatever the order of the body that happens to be driving the car or laptop. Mastery of the machines has been made to define masculine space. This chapter considers how schools give students lessons in occupying that space, even as one might hope that the schools hold, in the name of education, the possibility of reclaiming that space for other sorts of performances.

Technology and Gender

Not so long ago, the controversy over the gendered divisions of technology in the schools was about who hammered together a step stool in industrial arts or who sewed an apron in home economics. That great gender frontier has since been bridged with coed classes in both areas, while the educational focus on technology has grown to encompass the far more academically respectable areas of computer studies and information technology. While technology has yet to achieve the academic status of physics or mathematics, it does seem clear that where, during the 1950s and 1960s, the sciences were seen as key to the West's Cold War triumph, technology has now become the great white hope of the New World Order. As I write, President Clinton is helping volunteers lay an Internet link to a California high school. "We are putting the future at the fingertips of your children," he solemnly declared to the gathered crowd, "and we are doing it in the best American tradition" (Purdum, 1996). Where once President Kennedy pledged to place a man on the moon in the ideological space race against the Soviet Union, this president has committed himself to connecting every school in the nation to the Internet by the turn of the century through a partnership of volunteers and corporate sponsors that is intended to place America at the forefront of the age of information.

The post-Sputnik Cold War funding of science education three decades ago drew attention to the gendered nature of this society's most valued form of knowledge. Women were largely staying away from math and science, and this meant, given the urgency of this national agenda, an alarming loss of human resources for the Free World. The federal government responded by holding conferences on women in science and taking other measures.[3] Gains in female participation were made through the mentoring of women scientists, the implementation of all-girl science classes, and the active recruiting of young women. In what is again becoming a familiar refrain, as we shall see, these programs often ended up blaming the girls who were not otherwise inclined to pursue these difficult but beneficial subjects (McLaren & Gaskell, 1995).

Now that Information Technology (IT) is paving the highway to the future, a similar concern has arisen over how few young women are drawn to this field of study and work, a concern shared by education and business, by those committed to equity issues and those bent on tapping human resources and retail markets. The news today on this year's Take Our Daughter to Work Day (April 25) was that 50 homeless girls in New York City were given the opportunity to surf the World Wide Web. One can't help feeling that something more has still to be done, and whether one puts it down to expediency or opportunism, one way of effecting change in education is to play on existing energies. It seems only fair to expose this great educational interest in technology to alternatives concerned with making a difference in the ordering and structuring of gender relations in the schools.

/St

The first step would seem to be to identify the qualities of technology readily associated with masculinity, and to do so within the scope of this chapter, I work from close analogy, exact instances, interpreted data, and risky practices. The close analogies come from the masculine tendencies of athletics, the military, and the sciences. The exact instances are to be found in the computer and gender research, along with gendered innovations in electronic games and the Net. The interpreted data are based on interviews with high school boys and girls who are participating in the risky practices. They are risky practices, at least from my perspective, because the interviewed students are taking part in an Information Technology Management (ITM) program that Vivian Forssman and I are in the midst of developing for the schools in a business-academic partnership. Vivian Forssman is a glass-ceiling refugee from the IT industry who now heads Knowledge Architecture, a start-up educational company that is not waiting for new technologies to change the classroom but seeks to change the classroom as a new way of working the technologies. This review of where gender sits with technology, then, has as its final measure the promise and shortcomings of our program in trying to reorder and restructure social relations.

The ITM program, designed for Grades 10 through 12, has grown out of work with teachers over the past 2 years and is currently being piloted in 17 high schools. With ITM, the class runs on the model of a high-tech consulting company that provides technical design, planning, implementation, support, and ongoing services that help people realize the value (and reduce the frustrations) of increasingly sophisticated technologies. Students in the ITM program work in teams, developing their skills with people, projects, and technology, in offering a similar array of services to the teachers and students in their school and community. This often involves shifting power structures around learning and teaching in the school, often reversing the institutional roles of student and teacher. It draws the school's hackers away from a life on the screen to some greater contribution to the school community, while offering some reason and pleasure to take computers for some of those students who otherwise tend to say no to the machines. Yet it is equally cautious about the masculine temperament that haunts the information technology sector from which we have taken our model.[4] This partnership is about technology in both business and education, and what we have learned after this first round of development is that restructuring the school program is insufficient in and of itself for altering the governing ethos. The nature of this masculinity, as reviewed below, has to become an object of study in the program. The critique has still to become the curriculum.

Masculine Domains: Athletic and Military

In trying to understand the masculinity of technology in the high school, especially in its more heroic aspects, extracurricular sports provides a valuable point of comparison. While the football players are out on the field during the fading light of afternoon, the computer nerds are gathering round their monitors, each dedicating himself to going farther than anyone has gone before, to mastering the exhilarating moves that define their place on the field or screen. Both athlete and hacker operate within a specialized work ethic, devoting long hours to improving specific skills, focusing on self-improvement, on staying competitive (without letting other school subjects totally collapse). The key is focus, being able to enter the *zone,* as this space of total concentration is known in athletics. In his novel on the lives of Microsoft employees, *Microserfs,* Doug Coupland (1995) has his narrator reflect on how "nerds overfocus. . . . But I guess it's precisely this ability to narrow-focus that makes them so good at [computer] code writing: One line at a time, one line in a strand of millions" (p. 2). The body becomes a tool, in a merging of flesh and apparatus, in what is now being identified as a *cyborg.*[5] There is that masculine form of bonding that comes of sharing these concentrated moments of lone achievement and daring, of personal bests and private failures, marked by the taboo language of bravado. Athletics and technology are decidedly different routes to masculinity that envision the male body in different ways, and yet athlete and hacker share a way of being in the school that distinguishes these students. Of course, girls take to the fields and the screens, too. In my experience, however, the young women are still fighting for equity in the schools, a fight often focused on the school gym, and there is little sense that these are no longer masculine spaces, if under siege. On the other hand, this is clearly not about how well women or men can do any of these activities.

At this level, the masculine bent of athletics and technology is largely extracurricular—leaving behind physical education and computer literacy classes—which is where the real life of the school exists. It is a space in which athletes and hackers are learning a masculine hold on power that both enforces, and plays against, established forms of order. They have found a sanctuary in the school, whether in the gym or computer lab, where they reign, however much they may flounder in calculus or French class.

Yet who am I kidding? Hackers and crackers are also known as nerds and geeks. The best of these keyboard artists cannot hold a candle to the head-turning that follows the school's top athletes. To go deep with computers is to join a subculture, running underground and behind the scenes, at best in close conjunction with the teacher in charge of the school's systems. Pulling cable into wiring closets and establishing password access does not generate the glamour or sense of presence afforded the public athlete; it does not solicit the often personal commitment of the school coach, who believes that he can make men out of boys (and out of girls, too) (Sherlock, 1987). At best, the revenge-of-the-nerds will lie in the world beyond schooling, where athletic and computer stars hold a similar hope for greatness. Michael Jordan has his match in the towering figure of Bill Gates, the boy-inventor and a household-name of legendary, self-made financial worth. In looking to heroics of athletics and technology, I also wouldn't want to discount the race-and-aspiration issue that falls between Jordan and Gates. They represent a particular masculine take on the world (with the computer far more the great white hope for America at this point of global struggle for economic domination). Although the posters of dynamic Michael leaping heavenward abound, the image of rumpled Bill lording it over his cyber-empire recalls the Boy's Own Adventure series of the 19th century, in which imperial adventurers explored the world of their own true manhood and race.

A further link between athletics and technology is their shared military genealogy that defines warrior forms of masculinity. Student athletes tend to speak in metaphors of war (Lesko, 1996). Working from sports' military sensibility, Michael Messner (1990) has described how, "in many of our most popular sports, the achievement of goals (scoring and winning) is predicated on the successful utilization of violence—that is, the human body is routinely turned into a weapon to be used against other bodies" (p. 203). By the same token, the most popular of the computer games—Doom, Marathon, Heretic—are largely track'em/blast'em games in which the machine is a virtual body/weapon. In these games, the computer monitor becomes one's eyes; the joy stick one's deadly handle on the world (Coyle, 1996).

Apart from all of the shared metaphors and images, however, it is well to remember that the military has been a primary sponsor of the computer revolution. One of the earliest full-scale computers, the ENIAC, was developed at the Army's Ballistic Research Laboratory in the final years of

World War II (after being initially programmed by women), while the Internet was first established to link research universities and the military-industrial complex. Donna Haraway (1995) goes a step farther in capturing the connections by using the Terminator, the movie hero who stands as the athletic and technological tool ("the beast on the face of post-modern culture") of the New World Order:

> The Terminator can be the transfused blood fraternity of information machine and human warrior in the cyber-enhanced airforce cockpit, those pilot projects for the equally—maybe more—profitable commercial cyborg theme parks and virtual reality arcades to follow in the great technology transfer game from military practices to the civilian economy that has characterized cyborg worlds. (p. xv)

The sci-fi transfer between military and civilian economies appears, however, to go both ways. So Eliot Cohen (1996), in a recent article in *Foreign Affairs,* waxes enthusiastic over the coming military-technical revolution in which " 'information warriors,' for example, might supplant tankers and fighter pilots as groups from which the military establishment draws its bulk of its leaders" (p. 39).

In the context of the high school, both athlete and hacker line up as more or less celebrated warriors on the side of the school's power structure that formalizes the competition and violence necessary to sort and cool out the young. While women participate in this play of significance at the school, the space is still largely defined by the relationship between the male body and machine (as opposed to the female body and nature). This defines the particular site of power shared by athlete and hacker in the high school, while contributing to a larger lesson about the masculine claim on the technologies of the West.

A Manly Science and Technology

A second approach to this dynamics of a masculine technology, and one more closely related academically to computer studies, is through the example of science education. Theories have abounded about the masculine bent of science, not least of which has been Brian Easlea's (1983) idea of womb envy which postulates that men have compensated for their inability to give birth by making bigger and ever-more powerful things that took life and death back into their manly hands. If Cold War psychoanalysis seems a little passé, Nancy Chodorow's (1978) object relations theory also has much to say about this masculine association with scientific order, as the young boy looks for a detached ordering of his difference from his mother, which the young girl does not need to find in her identification.

Science has been presented to generations of students as a man's world of mental gymnastics (Bryne, 1992; Whyte, 1986). The post-Sputnik research on why girls have said no to a science that said no to them indicates that something more fundamental than a greater display of women in science is needed. In an effort to establish what set science and "feminine roles" apart, Herbert Walberg (1969) established at the time that "girls value people and religious unity more than boys while boys value practicality, power, and theoretical ideas more" (p. 52). He adds that "the girls are less dogmatic and have higher needs for affiliation and to be outgoing, and they regard the universe as more friendly" (p. 52). While Walberg was ready to accept "the apparent trait discontinuities in feminine and scientific roles," there was something pedagogically interesting in women's rejection of science in favor of something more engaged with the world and people. In surveying young women through the 1970s, Ormerod (1971, 1979) found that those who could perceive science's social relevance were more likely to take the subject. Young women were more likely to be interested in the therapeutic use of lasers, for example, rather than in their military functions. Young women had, it seems apparent, something to add to the tone and substance of the science program.

In the mid-1960s, the Project Physics Course, out of Harvard University, was aimed at turning around the declining number of students taking the discipline in high school. It used this very point of relevance, with science portrayed as "a cultural force," to increase the subject's reach to a more "diverse" audience. It involved teamwork and performance contracts, and the "instructor was available as 'consultant' to each of these groups" (Holton, 1978, pp. 293-294). A similar concern with the social place of science was present in the science-technology-society (STS) approach that arose in the early 1970s in various English-speaking countries. As a result, it, too, has appealed to young women through its pursuit of issues that "relate to people and their predicaments," as well as its collaborative approach in examining the moral implications of scientific activity, although these topics interested the young men equally well once they were introduced (Solomon, 1994, p. 144).

Despite the success of these curricular developments, the trend through the 1980s, at least, was that fewer women entered the sciences and engineering than a decade earlier (Haraway, 1991b, pp. 14-15). A gender balance in textbook illustrations has been achieved, while more demanding modifications to the teaching of science have not been as extensive. A good instance of what might be required is found in Jane Butler Kahle and Léonie Rennie's (1993) research on how, as Australian and American girls get older, they increasingly think science less relevant or useful than boys do.[6] Their research in the United States shows that the teachers who attended gender equity workshops were able to overcome this gap and provide 9-year-olds with "classes where girls generally enjoyed the activity as much as boys" (p. 333). They also worked with changing the style of teaching to a more activity-based approach, pointing to the importance of addressing the style of the subject as well as its masculine definition, at least among the teachers.

It is not hard to see the parallels between the sciences and technology, with young women finding themselves put off, for example, by the abstract and unforgivable logic of writing tiny perfect computer programs. The interest that young women expressed in the social relevance of science might well find equal application, we are hoping with the ITM program, in keeping the school's networks running, or bringing a senior generation of teachers on-line and on-board with new learning technologies that assist them in their work, or developing Internet access policies for students and staff, to take three instances that have occurred within the ITM program.

Computers, Gender, and Education

While the literature on gender and computers makes it plain that males predominate in the use and study of computers on a global scale, one is still left feeling cautious about the significance of this *fact*.[7] A key measure in this literature is student attitude toward computers, and Leslie Francis (1994) reports how the studies she has reviewed are divided between those showing boys possessing a more positive attitude and those that found no difference, whether she looked at the elementary, high school, teacher trainee, undergraduate, or teacher levels (p. 283). Her own study found little difference at the undergraduate level in either student attitudes toward computers or their gender stereotyping in association with the machines. To take another point of caution, Janice Woodrow (1993) has found that boys' greater experience and more positive attitude toward computers did not translate into superior performance in computer courses. In Woodrow's judgment, "students will master various uses of computers *for a purpose*—one that is immediate and obvious, and one which much more closely resembles the acquisition of computer skills in the workplace" (p. 334, original emphasis).[8]

The greater confidence of the boys on the machines is certainly related, as Lily Shashaani (1994) has found, to the greater amount of time and the number of courses taken. But given that, young women may well tend to benefit more from specific learning experiences with computers, as Harriet Taylor and Luegina Mounfield (1994) found at the college level. There is nothing so profoundly at odds between gender and technology, this research suggests, other than how one chooses to spend one's time. This is a small but important point, as women attempt to overcome a long history of ascribed aptitudes and assigned spheres of activity. Bente Elkjær's (1992) work among eighth-grade Danish schoolchildren has led her to focus on how girls become " 'guests' in a sphere of content that is dominated by symbolic masculinity," while "boys are regarded as 'hosts' in the sense that they feel compelled to try to maintain their dominating position in a sphere defined by masculinity" (p. 38). Elkjær suggests that gender is best understood as it is produced by the relationship struck between male and female (the *opposite* sex) and what she calls "the subject content of the concrete sphere" (p. 38). Unsettling those domestic relationships, of guest and host, of gender-specific spheres, seems a fair aim of any equity program that goes beyond seeking a balance in enrollment numbers between the sexes.

One measure of the public concern in the United States on this issue has been the Carl D. Perkins Vocational and Applied Technology Education Act of 1990, which has led to a series of Women in Technology projects that have included mentoring, summer camps, speaker bureaus, and job shadowing (Cunanan & Maddy-Bernstein, 1993). This was to follow the earlier example of science and, without denigrating these efforts, it seems clear that getting more women to spend more time in front of a computer will not necessarily temper the masculinity of technology. At least one study reveals that women who show a positive attitude toward computers score higher on the masculinity scales used in the psychological literature, which I take to confirm the assumption that an interest in machines is a masculine trait (Colley, Gale, & Harris, 1994). Are we to increase participation with computers on that basis? I see the far more promising direction to be, as it was with the sciences, changing the way the subject is taught. Thus, I am encouraged by Geoffrey Underwood and Nishschint Jindal's (1994) finding that organizing boys into cooperative relationships can lead to gains in their problem-solving abilities. Still, when computer teams consist of boys and girls, the research shows that girls tend to be heard from less often than the boys (Lee, 1993). It would seem that the old patterns tend to repeat themselves in new settings.

While there are signs of hope in this literature, it tends, as Bryson and de Castell (1995) point out, to locate the failure to enroll in the young women who are assumed to be oblivious to technology's benefits (p. 26). While much is made of changing girls' attitudes toward technology, Bryson and de Castell convincingly argue, in what has become a theme for this chapter, that the "beliefs reported by female students appear, in fact, to be a close to accurate characterization of the culture of computers and their users in and out of schools" (p. 27). To take one example, the undergraduate female students whom Ann Beer (1994) interviewed about computers "often [saw] computers as isolating, even psychologically dangerous; they [spoke] critically of teenage boys who are 'hackers' or, obsessed with computer games, seem in a world of their own," which she contrasts with one young man's reference to the computers as "the perfect slave," a metaphor that she had not heard in 5 years of working in this area (pp. 22, 26). Girls have been to computer classes and know what they offer. They are just saying no, thank you. Real-world relevance is very much at question, as it was with science (one inspiration for Vivian Forssman's involvement in the ITM project was her exasperation at the sight of computer labs filled with boys and a few girls spending hours learning programming languages that in her decade in the Information Technology business she had seen very few employees use).

The young women's rejection of computer courses, Bryson and de Castell (1995) hold, cannot be reduced to the vocational shortsightedness or to "cognitive/dispositional differences" commonly thought to distinguish women's ways of knowing (p. 31). The gender differences, as they see them, are "constructed in the context of institutional schooling by the differential treatment of students according to their group membership" (p. 31). They call for more attention to be paid to "the ways in which differences are produced through social relations and institutional practices" (p. 31). Women's ways of knowing have taken shape within these patriarchal practices, and simply catering to these assumed dispositions among the female students only strengthens the institutionalized differences while doing little to change the balance of power or the ends to which technology is directed. The boys'-club atmosphere that surrounds technology in the school has to become the object of scrutiny, a piece of the curriculum. Placing the keyboards in the hands of those from whom it has been kept needs to be accompanied by a deliberate attempt to challenge and change what is aptly cast by Bryson and de Castell as a "thinking man's tool" and its institutionalization.

Emasculating Computer Games and Feminizing the Net

Among those actively seeking to break the masculine hold on the computer among the young are the producers of computer games. Young women are turning away from the machine as a toy. As already noted, they will go on in great numbers to work with the technology, but the masculine take is still to find in the machines an absorbing daydream of power and adventure. (Microsoft has shown a video at computer conferences in which an 8-year-old boy says that girls should get more violent so that they can really play computer games.) The masculinity of the machines has been largely defined by the games that have been developed and fervently taken up by boys, games that tend to leave young women cold. The solution, as it is commonly cast, is to develop games that attract young women.

From the corporate game-maker perspective, girls represent an untapped market that can be fostered under the banner of gender equity. To take one example, Her Interactive, a division of Laser Games Inc., has developed a game for young women aimed at capturing some part of the 43 billion dollars that "teen girls" have been identified as spending each year (Flannigan, 1996). Laser Games claims to be responding to "teachers [who] want software to keep girls enthusiastic about computers." The company reports that young women want "emotional involvement with characters; advancing storyline through decision-making, creative outlet, and adventure without violence" as opposed to "victory through killing." It also reports that the content preferences among young women are also for "fashion/shopping" and "make-up experimentations."

To meet this market, Laser Games has produced Mackenzie & Co., an adventure game that promises that "The Ultimate Prom Experience is yours with the hottest CD-ROM game ever." The player reports are enthusiastic: "I found myself feeling like a computer nerd because I wanted to play so often." The letters attest to how grateful young women and their parents are that, finally, there is a game for them, "the first and only girl type computer game we have found." Where once a young woman might have said that "the whole technology thing just didn't appeal to me," she can now say, as one did in writing to Her Interactive, that "now I can actually get into this 20th century computer stuff . . . and like it." Laser Games goes a step farther with its commitment to gender equity by letting the young women know why it donates part of its proceeds to breast cancer research. The larger question that remains, however, is how do we make computers something more than a game for the young, and are there content opportunities that provide real engagement without reinforcing the narrow range of gender performances that Mackenzie & Co. and Doom feed?

Another corporation in this business is Brøderbund, which reports that until the age of 10, girls are as likely to equal or surpass boys in their devotion to playing computer games, with a falling away of interest at the onset of puberty when girls tend to invest their time in personal rather than prosthetic relationships (Strand, 1996). Brøderbund's Laurie Strand reports that they come back to the use of the computer when they are pushed to do so in high school, favoring "productivity and reference products." Again, we have the idea of the computer as a tool to get a job done, but not quite as the power tool that boys have learned to leverage by this age. This focus on productivity might seem an encouraging point, if you are not in the business of computer games.[9] Still, games are where computers continue to hook into young lives. In looking at "traditional adventure games," Strand reports that 82% of the players are males, with Brøderbund taking credit for raising the percentage of girls playing their adventure game, Myst, from the typical 18% to 30%. She cites Myst's fantasy qualities and non-violent style as being gender balanced. Apparently young women especially enjoy Myst when they play with a partner. Brøderbund, along with several other companies such as Electronic Arts, involves women in the game's design, software development, its "playtesting," and through what it describes as "licenses that leverage other female recognition factors."

One research group devoted to bringing greater educational content to games is the Electronic Games for Education in Math and Science (E-GEMS) project at the University of British Columbia. It has conducted research on games and girls that confirms girls' preference for games that feature narratives with distinctive characters and social relationships, as well as collaboration among the players (Inkpen et al., 1994). E-GEMS has worked with Electronic Arts in creating games such as Counting on Frank that are intended to create a space for girls that has educational value, while increasing what might be thought of as their bonding time on the machines.

A second way forward is to look, as almost everyone is, to the Web. While Laser Games has brought out a companion net-site, Her OnLine, for its girls' game, Mackenzie & Co., a more radical guide to crashing the boy's club comes in Carla Sinclair's (1996) web-manifesto/whole-grrrl guidebook to the Internet, *Net Chick:* "So wait not, fair grrrlie," insists Sinclair in the foreword, "Hie thee to a modem connection and get thine ass online! This ain't a passing fad; this techno stuff is real, and, in case you haven't heard from Madge, you're soaking in it" (p. x). While pointing to the 40% female membership in Prodigy and Online Internet access services, Sinclair allows that the web is still home to the patriarchal order, comparing it to the Wild West and quoting Rosie Cross on its domination by "boring conservative righteous sexist bloody men who really need to get a life" (p. xi). But against such bores, she stakes her claim to this wired world, declaring it nothing less than the natural domain of women: "The root forces driving this medium—communication, community, and creativity—are inherently feminine. They are things women innately excel at. Plainly put, this means we were built to do this" (p. xi). This *feminine* essentialism—biology is (computing) destiny—is bound to alarm postmodernists, yet to reject stand-alone computing in favor of networking and community challenges the masculine individualism of technology. The point is that we do not need to find women's (true) ways of computing to move it out of the boys' club, we just need *other* ways of working with machines and that, too, is what Net Chicks is about.[10]

Electronic games and web sites that speak to and for women do create alternative spaces within these new technological realms. They claim a place for women within the playing field of this technology, sometimes under the same ethos, sometimes with what are taken as female variations. In commercial hands, this may seem nothing more than a grab at the missing 51% of the potential edutainment market, or they can be seen as a female refusal of the isolated and violent struggles of rugged individualism, in favor of building sites where relationships and collaboration matter. This is still about making incursions into masculine space, creating a gender safe-zone for the other sex. These other-gendered games and web sites have their educational applications, some directly, others as sources of information not otherwise available to young women. Yet they only begin to speak to other ways of working with the technology, as variations on masculine themes.[11] I am obviously inclined, given this work on the ITM program, to argue for something more than creating a safe house for girls to work comfortably with computers or of drawing girls into the computing marketplace. Vivian Forssman and I are seeking to build a program that goes farther in students' use of technology to contribute to the learning environment of school and community.

ITM program

The ITM Students Speak

The Information Technology Management (ITM) program is being piloted in 17 high schools in the province of British Columbia, whether as a full-year Grade 12 course or an extracurricular club. Two of the schools are in the second year of the program, while the rest are in their first year of implementation. Thus far ITM has not attracted anything close to an equal number of girls to the program. There are a number of schools with no girls in the ITM class, with most having 2 or 3 girls, and one with 10 girls in a Grade 10/11 class of 26. The interviews with the ITM students, conducted by Diane Hodges and Blane Després, included three girls and four boys at a school situated on the outskirts of a large urban center, in its second year of the program. The school offers a wide array of courses in computers, from graphics to advanced programming. The boys were in a Grade 10/11 ITM class, taught by a woman with a master's degree in computer science. There were 3 girls and 20 boys in the class. The girls interviewed had been in the class the previous year. Sarah and Natasha were interviewed together, as were David and Aaron, and Frank and Paul, while Candice was interviewed by herself. The interviews were loosely structured around the involvement of girls and boys in the school's technology courses, and gave the students a chance to demonstrate an awareness that reflected in larger measure the same understanding achieved by the research literature in computers and gender.

The interviewed boys spoke readily of the masculine bond with machines. David drew an analogy with auto mechanics—"you know how there is never any girls in mechanics classes"—and Frank based it on the use of the machines to play such manly games as Doom:

> I think that just in general nature guys get on computers more because they like to play Doom more and you see a lot more guys playing video games, and I think computers is just, you know, just another way of playing video games and they just get hooked.

This element of addiction, which forms an apt characterization of gaming culture, at least allows that there could well be other, more salutary, ways of working with machines. Other sorts of games and activities, David might permit, could create different patterns of use. Paul also referred to boys and games, while his suggestion that computers had other uses introduced a rather vocationally limited vision of women's computing:

Like, at work, if girls need to use it, they will use it for word processing and everything. But I don't think they go out of their way to use it, to, like, go and play games because . . . most games, for one, were made with a male attitude behind [them]. But quite a few of the secretaries use computers to do word processing and . . . all sorts of programs for businesses, accounting and stuff like that.

The boys were not fazed by the questions on gender. They understand that it is an issue. Frank did note an element of change in the school that year, which he put into daunting perspective:

> One of the things I found interesting, this year for the first time, I heard a girl say that she wanted to go into computers, and I've never, I mean it's just not something that girls generally want to do. I don't know why that is, but they just generally don't really want that you know.

Among the girls interviewed, Sarah also pointed to the mechanical aptitude of boys in explaining their greater interest in computers:

> They like to break them down, see what like how they function and everything like they go way more in-depth with computers than girls do.

Natasha, on the other hand, felt that there was an element of self-fulfilling prophecy to it all:

> They are stereotyped knowing more and more, so they . . . try and fulfill it, I think, something like that.

Both Sarah and Natasha identified how girls tend to take an instrumental approach to computers: "Girls will like just do like a project or something on a computer and that's it," was how Sarah put it. "They don't really like care." For Natasha, the issue was also one of girls seeking relevant applications for computing:

> I think girls would be more interested in it if there was . . . computer programs and stuff that dealt with . . . everyday things, not just programming. Like, if it has to do with our lives . . . to help run them or something, I think we'd probably use them.

There is not the same investment in the machines as an end and pleasure in themselves, or as a means of taking control over part of the world.

Yet Natasha and Sarah recognized that, despite this difference in interest, there persists a pressure to get with the technology: "I think it's important that more kids should [take computers] because the whole future is based on technology," Sarah put it, "and if they don't know it, then they are not going to get anywhere." Natasha, however, countered,

> I don't think they need to be encouraged that much because they know what's out there, and if they need it or not. So, it's up to them.

Sarah certainly felt pressured to become more involved with technology:

> I think it would be in my best interest to [take further technology courses], but I don't know if I will or not.

There is just that sense of not getting excited about the machines: "I don't really like computers," Sarah told the interviewer. "I have a computer at home and I just do homework on it and stuff. That's it. That's my computer (laughs)."

When Candice was asked why she decided to take ITM rather than one of the other computer courses, she made reference to "that independent thing . . . where you learn on your own." This was key to the program for her: "Learning about how to develop your own type of program . . . instead of just learning about one thing one day and then changing to another one, so that was the most positive thing for me." Candice also commented on the increased number of girls in the class, again pointing to the self-directed nature of learning in ITM as a contributing factor:

> As I got into Information Technology Management, it seemed to be more girls, actually, and I think it is, I don't know why, but it seems to be that the boys seemed to be more attracted to it for some reason, and that's why I was surprised that it seemed to be more girls, maybe because of the independence thing. But I think that over the next few years it's going to get more equal between them, that's for sure.

Sarah also addressed the importance of self-paced learning to her interest in the class: "We learned at our own pace sort of thing, so it was a change." Yet in terms of why she signed up, Natasha spoke of how she had been actively recruited into the program: "Miss Jones came and talked to me she wanted me to take it cause she wanted girls in the class to take it. So that's why I took it." To which Sarah responded in the interview: "I actually took it to be with Natasha in a class."

When asked about girls' participation in the ITM program, Frank allowed that the program had advantages that expanded the possibilities for participation for girls in the program:

> The fact that ITM doesn't have to be in one specific area of computing could be something to encourage them, I think that . . . are some, the two girls that are in our class, they are, they don't have to be programmers or whatever, which I find is most often guys, or something like that, but they can pursue their own areas like, one of the people really likes graphics and she can draw well on the computer so she has been able to pursue that as opposed to having to fit the norm of computing class.

In accounting for why he thought that ITM might appeal to young women, Paul pointed to how ITM "doesn't even have to be a computer class; it's a management class more than anything else; you don't even have to know computers to be in it." It follows that the girls in the program will need to rattle the typecasting by taking on different roles within the ITM teams, from project manager to systems architect. Paul's own interest in having young women study Information Technology was based on the contribution he felt women could make to the industry:

> I think that there should be [more girls taking technology courses] because if you look at our computer industry right now . . . almost everyone is male, and women give a different outlook. And I feel that the more people, the more that come into the field, then the more it diversifies.

David agreed that women had much to contribute—"There is a need for women in the computer world too, just because the different sexes, different opinions"—but he also made it clear that the girls' problem was still that "the interest isn't there" for computers. For these two boys, women's participation appears to be a human resource issue. Candice also identified a lack of interest among the young women, but she was clearly less concerned with the state of the computer world: "Even though they might not want to go into the computer field, I think it's good if they still keep up with what's going on with computers."

David was unsure of how to make the classes more interesting for girls, but he "definitely" supported the idea, when it was posed to him, of running an all-girl computer class. He pointed, in defense of the idea, to the lack of respect that young women receive in such manly subjects as computer studies. This is an important point that counters the focus on girls' lack of interest. Aaron expanded on the negative reception: "Right now it's a pretty hostile environment. It's not like the best place for girls to be. Some of the people in there are just crude when it comes to girls." While that is troubling enough, the hostile boys he is referring to are, presumably, in the girls' other classes, leaving us to imagine that they feel a particular license for crudity in the presence of machines as demarcating a man's world and as no place for a lady. A note of regret entered Aaron's comments about this harassment, and he spoke of taking "one graphics course [that] was like half girls; it was the best year of my life."

The increased range of activities in the ITM program did have an impact on the boys. David explained how he had been thrown into teaching a graphics software package to adults, which then proved to be the highlight of the program for him:

David: It was about November. Miss Jones just handed me this Corel Draw booklet and said learn the program. I'd never used it before, never touched it. So, "learn it because in 2 months you've got to teach a seminar on it to teachers," and I was just like, "I can't do this," you know. And then when I came out of it, I taught the whole thing, and . . . no negative comments came back.

Interviewer: Really, so you did teach the seminar.

David: I taught the whole thing and taught, there was about 17 adults that I taught. Everybody was really happy when I left.

Interviewer: That must have felt good too?

David: Oh, it was a total, a total great achievement.

This sense of achievement in teaching others provides an excellent instance of how the ITM program at least begins to temper the masculinities of technology, not because teaching is emasculating, but because of how working in this way with teachers and students runs against the man-machine identification of programming, hacking, and gaming. In a similar vein, Aaron adds, in a mixed review, the element of learning can come through teaching:

I took, you know, the computer program they have upstairs, 3-D Studio. I ended up teaching other people in the room. . . . It gets kind of boring because you are showing them everything you know. In a way, you start learning more. While you are teaching you find more stuff.

Aaron also spoke of how this approach to teaching could shift the power relation between student and teacher:

> I think my most positive experience . . . through ITM . . . was helping out . . . one of the teachers in the school, he was so sure of himself, felt that no student could ever be better than him. And I felt that when I went in there and showed him that actually we knew not more than him but different things, that could really help him, and how it more or less humbled him into thinking that students can do this. That would be the most positive thing. I like just seeing him like, in the end, like, just going, "Yes, you can help me. Maybe I'll come to you next time."

This theme of helping others carried through David's and Aaron's discussion of the emphasis on deadlines in the program: "It makes it like a job. You have to meet the deadline," Aaron said, putting it in terms of his grades: "Last year, you just had to show up, and this year you have to make the deadline, like I said." David added, "If you don't meet the deadlines, basically, you let everybody down in the class." He went on to explain, "What it is is like a bunch of different groups and everybody knows what everybody is doing and all the different groups are doing different things. There is usually about five or six people in each group." The considerable coordination of the teams is handled through a special project management software used in industry: "It's all done through MS-Project," David pointed out. "You know exactly what your plan is, how long it's going to go on for, when you plan on having it done."

ITM's focus on teamwork and management also figured in Frank's discussion of his role in the class:

> I find that the ITM course is good because I get to pursue what I want and I am, right now I'm more in a managerial role than in learning the technical stuff or doing anything like that. I feel that it's beneficial.

Frank went on to draw its relation to the world of work:

> It teaches you how to take initiative or lets you learn how to take initiative and how to take things into your own hands and it's more realistic for the world as opposed to just sitting down and listening.

There is that subtle shift in his position, between "it teaches you" to "lets you learn how," that captures the element of independent learning in the program. What the ITM program provided and called for was a coordinated effort among the people providing services to the school and community: "Organization has been one that has been emphasized quite a bit," Frank explained, "I guess more of, for me, due to my style." For his part in this team process, Paul has been learning to step back, as a way of giving help:

> Helping others is the big one for me. Most of my classes, I'm one of the top students in computers, and [it's] emphasized to help others . . . in ITM. . . . When I was project leader of a group earlier this year, I . . . looked at the other people and said, "I'm better than them and I should be able to take this on myself and they could just rattle my coat-tails," but I found out, no, I can't do that. I've got to help others by giving them responsibility, and they'll come through if you give it to them.

For Paul to learn how to delegate responsibility to others, or for Frank to improve his managerial skills, hardly presents a serious blow to the male order. Yet this focus on teams, organization, and service represents a change in how students work with technology, a change that wears as well for the young women as the men.

In explaining the sort of work that she did in ITM, Candice referred to a conference presentation that her group made at the university, in which "we had to present what our year-long project was and how it helped the school." She also served as a "computer helper," where she "used to teach some of the kids up in the Mac lab how to use different programs." The highlight of the program for her, however, combined service and technical expertise as she designed and built a career database for the school's Counseling Centre:

> I think learning more about how to develop your own type of program which you're interested in . . . like, I did for the Counseling Centre that was the most positive thing, because I had to do the whole thing all together, instead of just learning about one thing one day and then changing to another one. So that was the most positive thing for me.

Candice worked alone on this project, and I am struck by how teamwork did not figure in the girls' comments, while two of them mentioned the importance of independent learning. This, in conjunction with the boys' comments about the sometimes hostile atmosphere for girls, suggests that much still has to be done to create a more cooperative atmosphere.

Given the students' experiences in the ITM program, we can see that much more needs to be done if the program is to have a significant impact on the gendered ethos that surrounds technology in the schools. The program has begun to alter the ways, I think it fair to say, in which the students see learning and the ways in which they relate to computers, their classmates, and the school at large. These students' comments do speak to the pedagogical possibilities of putting the question of gender on the table, beginning with their own observations, which are not far removed from the findings of the research that, for example, relate extent of use, largely tied to gaming, with positive attitude or interest. Yet placing the focus on providing services to the school and community is not going to be enough, this preliminary inquiry suggests, to present a serious challenge to the gender stereotyping long associated with technology, We shouldn't be surprised. We will need to work with ITM teachers and students to make sure that gender ascriptions form part of what gets openly discussed and explored in ITM classes in this process of changing the way students work in the school and workplace.

Conclusion

The research literature on gender in science and technology education makes it clear that creating the conditions for greater collaboration and service challenges the patterns commonly identified with technology's masculine bent. The ITM program offers students a chance to experience the social relevance of working with Information Technology; it calls for teamwork and collaboration in the noncompetitive provision of support for others. Whether one envisions women's interest in relational and narrative forms of knowing, in collaboration and support, as inherent or learned, these approaches to technology do appear to challenge its otherwise masculine tendencies in schools and across history.

ITM may alter the way students work with people and technology, but that is proving to be only half of the story. The structural changes to computer studies introduced by the ITM program are not sufficient in themselves to change the ideas that students in the program have about gender and technology, let alone the thinking of their "clients" and other members of the school community who are also intended to benefit by the program (which is proposed as a further step in this research process). Based on this school's second year with the program, ITM has yet to build a fully inclusive setting for students' working together in supporting the learning environment of the school. It has yet to deal explicitly with the gender question in the classroom and through the history of technology. It has yet to eliminate the misogyny that besets technology classes.[12] These changes to the structures by which students work and learn in the school will lead to other changes in the school, and those human-technological consequences will need their own forms of attention as part of the ITM program. When John Dewey (1916) addressed the value of introducing forms of work (and play) into the curriculum in *Democracy and Education,* he was careful to warn "that while manual skill and technical efficiency are gained and immediate satisfaction found in their work, together with preparation for later usefulness, these things shall be subordinated to *education*—that is, to intellectual results and the forming of a socialized disposition" (pp. 196-197). We need to increase that intellectual and educational focus on the implications of those socialized dispositions.

Further to this critical reflection on the nature of this work, the ITM program clearly has a responsibility to make the impact of information technology, as the principal work process of the future, a component of the curriculum. Students need to see how information technology has led to the deskilling of certain jobs, affecting the large numbers of women working at the low end of the pay scale, while adding in some cases to the greater regulation and intensification of work processes. Attention also needs to be paid to related areas of work, such as the struggle for professional standing among women in the helping professions. Otherwise, ITM may seem to build false expectations around what lies ahead, even as it offers students something more during their class time than the routines of data-entry work, which appears to be the direction some schools are taking, according to the valuable critique of technology in the schools mounted by Monty Neill (1995).[13]

This inquiry into technology's impact could well form an aspect of what students bring to the school community, creating a space for the cultural critiques of technology offered by Haraway, Bryson and de Castell, and others. It needs to begin with the teachers' becoming aware of this work (through this chapter, perhaps, in the first instance) in the professional development workshops in which they are introduced to ITM, and it needs to find its way into the service ethos of the students' programs. Think of it: Students who not only can fix the machines but can offer students and teachers a critique of their use, considering not only the negative implications but the utopian visions and science fictions of technology's application that dare to imagine and thus, perhaps, guide change. The students will need to see examples of how undermining the masculine hold on technology will require explicitly feminist perspectives such as those of Sharlene Hesse-Biber and Melissa Kesler-Gilbert (1994), who have designed a classroom in which computers are used cooperatively in nonhierarchical ways for studying topics that are grounded in personal experience and deal with inequities, such as the gender gap in earnings or the impact of sexual harassment.

It is all too obvious that we need new kinds of programs for the schools, when the world can still seem young to the young, that begin remaking how they should expect to live with technology, how they should expect to share in the power of teaching and learning. This is an experiment in *seeing through* theories of gender (with the pun intended). It is based on understanding how gender is about the way that machines and space are defined. It is based on the belief that machines and space can be redefined in ways that challenge what has been made historically of gender and difference. We have a responsibility to press against this history by finding new ways of working together in schools, by drawing on new models that seem to break with the past.

The ITM program is itself no technological panacea; its value lies in how we are learning to make something different out of an amalgam of practices in the IT industry and research on computers in education. As we explore how to reorder and restructure social relations and socialized dispositions and partial identities, we are holding to education's utopian and ameliorative aspect. This program attends selectively to corporate models and tools, in an effort to prepare students for the world after school, while giving them a taste of what it means to support and contribute to their community. Rather than waiting for an analysis of the impact of new technologies, we are working with teachers and students to reflect on and change how they are already being used in educational settings. It is a matter of trying to make something (else) of a difference that has for too long been taken to define the nature of technology.

Notes

1. Kyle Pope (1994) reports that women make up two thirds of computer users on the job.

2. See David Noble (1984) for a history of industrial technology that has been developed to ensure the dominance of capital over worker skills and crafts.

3. See Alice Rossi (1965) for an example of a conference presentation of that period. Donna Haraway (1991a) writes, "A PhD in biology for an Irish Catholic girl was made possible by Sputnik's impact on U.S. national science-education policy. I have a body and mind as much constructed by the post-Second World War arms race and cold war as by the women's movement" (p. 173).

4. Doreen Massey (1995) has described how high-tech industries contribute not only to a deskilling of the workplace through automation, but to a superskilling among high-level workers, consisting of a "competitive workaholism" of perpetual boyhood: "We have toys which they can't afford," one company representative explained. "You know engineers, big kids really; buy them a computer, you know you've got them" (pp. 490, 496). See also Hacker, 1990; Ullman, 1995.

5. See Haraway (1995) for the origins of *cyborg* (cybernetic organism) in laboratory forms of machine-regulated life-forms.

6. In McLaren and Gaskell's (1995) research on science education, a female physics student, when asked how the class could better reflect her interests, conveys the sense of the subject as fixed: "I guess there is no way. It's the same subject; you can't change it. Movies or something, I don't know, there is nothing you can really change about it" (p. 152).

7. On gender and computers in education, see Ingeborg Janssen Reinen and Tjeed Plomp, 1993; Kay, 1992; Collis, 1987; Makrakis, 1993.

8. Schubert (1986) also found that young women are more likely "to value the computer as a means toward an end" (p. 271).

9. The research review of Carole Nelson and Allen Watson (1990-1991) contradicts this assumption of early equality of use, as they found that preschool boys spend significantly more time with computers than girls.

10. *Net Chicks* is complemented by its own "Net Chick Clubhouse" web site (http://www.cyborganic.com/People/carla/). The Association for the Promotion and Advancement of Science Education runs a number of web sites that offer access to female role models drawn from science and gender equity activities in science (http://www.etc.bc.ca/apase/apasehome.html).

11. See Susan Clerc (1995) for women's on-line participation in media fandom forums that center on television programs, while Constance Penley (1991) treats the female resistance to male domination of technology and sex in the underground circulation of erotic Star Trek fan-zines written by women.

12. Bryson and de Castell (1993) point out that special policies, curricular modifications, and pedagogical approaches for women often avoid dealing with the more immediate problem of misogyny (p. 352).

13. See Neill (1995, pp. 183, 187) on the savage inequalities in school access to technology.

References

Adas, M. (1991). *Machines as the measure of men: Science, technology, and ideologies of Western dominance*. Ithaca, NY: Cornell University Press.

Beer, A. (1994). Writing, computers, and gender. *English Journal, 26*(2), 21-29.

Bryne, E. (1992). *Women in science and technology: The image of science.* Unpublished paper, University of Queensland.

Bryson, M., & de Castell, S. (1993). En/gendering equity: On some paradoxical consequences of institutionalized programs of emancipation. *Educational Theory, 43*(3), 341-355.

Bryson, M., & de Castell, S. (1995). So we've got a chip on our shoulder! Sexing the texts of "educational technology." In J. Gaskell & J. Willinsky (Eds.), *Gender in/forms curriculum: From enrichment to transformation* (pp. 21-42). New York: Teachers College Press.

Butler, J. (1991). *Gender trouble: Feminism and the subversion of identity.* New York: Routledge.

Caputo, J. (1988). Seeing elephants: The myths of phallocentrism. *Feminist Studies, 14*(3), 439-456.

Chodorow, N. (1978). *The reproduction of mothering: Psychoanalysis and the sociology of gender.* Berkeley: University of California Press.

Clerc, S. (1996). Estrogen brigades and "big tits" threads: Media fandom online and off. In L. Cherny & E. R. Weise (Eds.), *Wired women: Gender and the new realities of cyberspace* (pp. 73-97). Seattle, WA: Seal.

Cohen, E. A. (1996). A revolution in warfare. *Foreign Affairs, 75*(2), 37-54.

Colley, A. M., Gale, M. T., & Harris, T. A. (1994). Effects of gender role identity and experience on computer attitude components. *Journal of Educational Computing Research, 10*(2), 129-137.

Collis, B. (1987). Adolescent females and computers: Real and perceived barriers. In J. Gaskell & A. McLaren (Eds.), *Women and education: A Canadian perspective* (pp. 21-29). Calgary, AB: Detselig.

Coupland, D. (1995). *Microserfs.* New York: HarperCollins.

Coyle, K. (1996). How hard can it be? In L. Cherny & E. R. Weise (Eds.), *Wired women: Gender and the new realities of cyberspace* (pp. 42-55). Seattle, WA: Seal.

Cunanan, E. S., & Maddy-Bernstein, C. (1993). *Working together for sex equity: Nontraditional programs that make a difference.* National Center for Research in Vocational Education, Berkeley, CA. (ERIC Document Reproduction Service No. ED 358 363)

Dewey, J. (1916). *Democracy and education.* New York: Free Press.

Easlea, B. (1983). *Fathering the unthinkable: Masculinity, scientists, and the nuclear arms race.* London: Pluto.

Elkjær, B. (1992). Girls and information technology in Denmark—An account of a socially constructed problem. *Gender & Education 4*(1/2), 25-40.

Flannigan, P. (1996, May). *Her Interactive: A case study.* Paper presented at Software Publishers Association Annual Conference, San Francisco.

Francis, L. J. (1994). The relationship between computer related attitudes and gender stereotyping of computer use. *Computers & Education, 22*(4), 283-289.

Franklin, U. (1990). *The real world of technology.* Montreal: Canadian Broadcasting Corporation.

Hacker, S. (1990). *Doing it the hard way: Sally L. Hacker* (D. E. Smith & S. M. Turner, Eds.). London: Unwin Hyman.

Haraway, D. (1991a). A cyborg manifesto: Science, technology, and socialist-feminism in the late twentieth century. In *Simians, cyborgs, and women: The reinvention of nature* (pp. 149-182). New York: Routledge.

Haraway, D. (1991b). Cyborgs at large: Interview with Donna Haraway. In C. Penley & A. Ross (Eds.), *Technoculture* (pp. 1-20). Minneapolis: University of Minnesota Press.

Haraway, D. (1995). Cyborgs and symbionts: Living together in the New World Order. In C. H. Gray (Ed.), *The cyborg handbook* (pp. xi-xx). New York: Routledge.

Hayes, R. D. (1995). Digital palsy: RSI and restructuring capital. In J. Brook & I. A. Boal (Eds.), *Resisting the virtual life: The culture and politics of information* (pp. 173-180). San Francisco: City Lights.

Hesse-Biber, S., & Kesler-Gilbert, M. (1994). Closing the technological gender gap. *Teaching Sociology, 22*(1), 19-31.

Holton, G. (1978). On the educational philosophy of the Project Physics Course. *The scientific imagination: Case studies* (pp. 284-298). Cambridge, UK: Cambridge University Press.

Inkpen, K., Klawe, M., Lawry, J., Sedighian, K., Leroux, S., Upitis, R., Anderson, A., & Ndunda, M. (1994). "We have never-forgetful flowers in our garden": Girls' responses to electronic games. *Journal of Computers in Mathematics and Science Teaching, 13*(4), 383-403.

Kahle, J. B., & Rennie, L. J. (1993). Ameliorating gender differences in attitudes about science: A cross-national study. *Journal of Science Education and Technology, 2,* 321-334.

Kay, R. (1992). An analysis of methods used to examine gender differences in computer-related behavior. *Journal of Educational Computing Research, 8*(3), 277-290.

Lee, M. (1993). Gender, group composition, and peer interaction in computer-based cooperative learning. *Journal of Educational Computing Research, 9*(4), 549-577.

Lesko, N. (1996). *Team and nation: At play with hegemonic masculinity.* Paper presented at meeting of the American Education Research Association [AERA], New York.

Makrakis, V. (1993). Gender and computers in schools in Japan: The "we can, I can't" paradox. *Computers & Education, 20,* 191-198.

Massey, D. (1995). Masculinity, dualisms and high technology. *Transactions of the Institute of British Geographers, 20*(4), 487-500.

McLaren, A., & Gaskell, J. (1995). Gender as an issue in school science. In J. Gaskell & J. Willinsky (Eds.), *Gender in/forms curriculum: From enrichment to transformation* (pp. 136-156). New York: Teachers College Press.

Messner, M. M. (1990). When bodies are weapons: Masculinity and violence in sports. *International Review of Sports, 25,* 203-219.

Neill, M. (1995). Computers, thinking, and schools in the "New World Economic Order." In J. Brook & I. A. Boal (Eds.), *Resisting the virtual life: The culture and politics of information* (pp. 181-194). San Francisco: City Lights.

Nelson, C., & Watson, J. A. (1990-1991). The computer gender gap: Children's attitudes, performance and socialization. *Journal of Educational Technology Systems, 19*(4), 345-354.

Noble, D. (1984). *Forces of production: A social history of industry automation.* New York: Knopf.

Ormerod, M. (1971). The social implications factor in attitudes toward science. *British Journal of Educational Psychology, 41*(3), 335-338.

Ormerod, M. (1979). Pupils' attitudes to the social implications of science. *European Journal of Science Education, 1*(2), 177-190.

Penley, C. (1991). Brownian motion: Women, tactics, and technology. In C. Penley & A. Ross (Eds.), *Technoculture* (pp. 135-161). Minneapolis: University of Minnesota Press.

Pope, K. (1994, March 18). High-tech marketers try to attract women without causing offense. *Wall Street Journal,* p. B1.

Postman, N. (1992). *Technopoly: The surrender of culture to technology.* New York: Vintage.

Purdum, T. S. (1996, March 10). President helps schools go on-line. *New York Times,* p. Y13.

Reinen, I. J., & Plomp, T. (1993). Some gender issues in educational computer use: Results of an international comparative survey. *Computers and Education, 20*(4), 353-365.

Rossi, A. S. (1965). Women in science: Why so few? *Science, 148*(3674), 1196-1202.

Schubert, J. G. (1986). Gender equity in computer learning. *Theory Into Practice, 25*(4), 267-275.

Sedgwick, E. K. (1995). "Gosh, Boy George, you must be awfully secure in your masculinity." In M. Berger, B. Wallis, & S. Watson (Eds.), *Constructing masculinities* (pp. 11-20). New York: Routledge.

Shashaani, L. (1994). Gender-differences in computer experience and its influence on computer attitudes. *Journal of Educational Computing Research, 11*(4), 347-367.

Sherlock, J. (1987). Issues of masculinity and femininity in British physical education. *Women's Studies International Forum, 10*(4), 443-451.

Sinclair, C. (1996). *Netchick: A smart-girl guide to the wired world.* New York: Henry Holt.

Solomon, J. (1994). Learning STST and judgments in the classroom: Do boys and girls differ? In J. Solomon & G. Aikenhead (Eds.), *STS education: International perspectives on reform* (pp. 141-154). New York: Teachers College Press.

Strand, L. (1996, May). *Bridging the gender gap in computer games.* Paper presented at the Software Publishers Association Annual Conference, San Francisco.

Taylor, H., & Mounfield, L. C. (1994). Exploration of the relationship between prior computing experience and gender on success in college computer science. *Journal of Educational Computing Research, 11*(4), 291-306.

Turkle, S. (1995). *Life on the screen: Identity in the age of the Internet.* New York: Simon & Schuster.

Ullman, E. (1995). Out of time: Reflections on the programming life. In J. Brook &
I. A. Boal (Eds.), *Resisting the virtual life: The culture and politics of information*
(pp. 131-144). San Francisco: City Lights.

Underwood G., & Jindal, N. (1994). Gender differences and effects of co-operation in
a computer-based language task. *Educational Research, 36*(1), 63-74.

Walberg, J. A. (1969). Physics, femininity, and creativity. *Developmental Psychology
1*(1), 47-54.

Whyte, J. (1986). *Girls into science and technology.* London: Routledge & Kegan
Paul.

Woodrow, J. (1993). The development of computer-related attitudes of secondary students. *Journal of Educational Computing Research, 11*(4), 307-338.

12

The Sounds of Silence

Notes on the Personal Politics of Men's Leadership in Gender-Based Violence Prevention Education

JACKSON KATZ

Introduction

Why is it that after 30 years of the modern women's movement, gender-based violence prevention education, where it exists at all, is usually still seen as "women's work"?[1] The American pandemic of men's violence against women is one of the great tragedies of our time. Political leaders, public health advocates, educators, and the general public have had more than three decades to respond to what feminist activists and scholars famously termed a "war against women" in our society, a war that has, shockingly, claimed more victims in the years since Vietnam than the number of Americans who died there. Even according to conservative estimates, the incidence of rape, sexual abuse of children, battering, and wife-murder in the United States has for a long time far exceeded rates in similar industrialized countries. How could we, as a society, not have faced up to men's responsibilities in all of this? How could we, as educators, not have made addressing these issues with young women *and* men an absolute priority?

Considering the fact that some studies show that as many as a third of high school and college-age youth experience violence in an intimate or dating relationship during their dating years (Levy, 1992, p. 4), why isn't teen dating violence talked about in every high school in America? Why, when more than half of all rape victims are assaulted by the age of 18, and

29% are assaulted *by the age of 11* (National Victim Center, 1992), is there such a meager amount of antirape programming in high schools and middle schools—if not elementary schools?

Part of the answer, not surprisingly, lies in the sexual politics of educational leadership. Most gender-based violence prevention education has historically, and understandably, been initiated and implemented by women. Women have been foremost among the pioneers, the reformers, and the guiding forces in this work. Their achievements are especially impressive considering that, while struggling against predominantly male institutional leadership, they have also had the responsibility to educate not only girls, but boys, too. At the same time, they've had the unenviable task of educating their male colleagues and friends.[2]

The purpose of this chapter is to examine some of the reasons why, to date, relatively few *men* in K-12 educational institutions have been actively involved in leading gender-based violence prevention efforts with girls and boys. This subject can be approached from any number of theoretical and practical perspectives. For example: Is it naive to think that men, as the dominant sex-class, would work to diminish their own power? How has the societal definition of "gender" issues as synonymous with "women's" issues contributed to men's lack of engagement with them? How much of an effect does homophobia have on men's silence? Is continuous political pressure exerted by antifeminist (male and female) administrators, school board members, and community groups successfully impeding progress? How about the failure of graduate schools of education to prioritize this subject in the training of professional educators (female and male)? What effect do fiscal constraints have on the ability of impoverished school districts to pay for effective programming or training for staff? How much of the problem is due to the scarce and contested space for new subject areas in already-crowded curricula?

I have chosen to outline some ideas about what I'm calling the personal politics of male educators. By "personal politics" I mean such factors as an individual's gender and sex ideology, his level of self-awareness, his relationships with men as well as women, his peer culture status, his body image, and his overall concept of his masculinity. How do these factors influence the exercise of a man's educational role, especially his potential for activism around gender-based violence prevention? How do men's personal politics contribute either to problems or to potential solutions?

Schools function as institutional systems that construct gender/sexual hierarchies; structure knowledge dissemination and acquisition; and police dissent against dominant sexual, racial, and class ideologies. But they are also, by definition, institutions that are attended, operated, and led by men and women who bring to their roles and responsibilities their own gendered identities; life histories; and sexual, race, and class biases. In the case of male educators involved in (or avoiding) gender-based violence prevention education, it seems relevant to examine how their identity as *men* affects their work and their roles.

While grounded in some of the basic ideas of critical pedagogy and feminist theory, the ideas in this chapter are derived mainly from my work as an activist educator. For more than 10 years I have run racially diverse gender violence (primary) prevention programs with men in colleges, high schools, and the military; spoken about men's violence against women at hundreds of high schools, middle schools, and colleges; and conducted gender violence prevention training with male and female educators in schools and colleges across the United States. I have worked with, and trained, dozens of male colleagues. I have observed firsthand the ways that many male educators—including myself—approach these issues. I have also participated in numerous professional conferences, devoted to such issues as gender equity and teen dating violence, where only a handful of men were present. And I have talked to countless committed women educators, and some men, about the widespread absence of male input and participation.

This absence represents, to a large extent, an absence of vision and a failure of leadership. Leadership can come from anyone in a position to effect change, including teachers, guidance counselors, health coordinators, coaches, other staff, students, parents, and others. In many schools, those prevention initiatives that do occur are initiated by one impassioned person, usually a woman, who devotes personal time above and beyond her professional obligations. Some of the most effective efforts I have seen, and been a part of, were initiated by women (and, rarely, men) who held no formal positions of institutional power.

Administrators, including principals, superintendents, and athletic directors, by virtue of their authority, bear a disproportionate share of responsibility for what goes on (or doesn't go on) in their schools. Decisions about what a school might do to prevent violence and trauma in students' lives should not be determined by something as idiosyncratic as how much extra time the health educator has. This is a leadership issue, and we know that most formal positions of leadership in education, including a significant majority of principals and an overwhelming percentage of superintendents and athletic directors, are occupied by men (U.S. Department of Education, 1996). So to say that educational administrators, with important exceptions, have failed to provide strong antisexist education to the young people in their schools is to say that in education, as in numerous other institutions, antisexist men's leadership has been sorely lacking.

It is true that educational leaders face numerous, and sometimes overwhelming, pressures. This is particularly true in school systems in resource-poor areas, where educators daily confront numerous and seemingly intractable social problems, including racism and many forms of interpersonal violence. The challenges—and the opportunities—for educators in those systems have been powerfully addressed by numerous academic as well as popular writers. Gender-based violence, which is disproportionately perpetrated by young males and is a fact of life in every socioeconomic and racial category, has widely come to be recognized as one of our most urgent and far-reaching social problems. This violence hurts tens of millions of girls and women, boys and men, directly or indirectly. It affects impoverished city schools as well as wealthy suburban school districts. The family issues and social problems that educators contend with obviously vary according to socioeconomic and racial differences. But the pervasiveness of men's violence against women—and the need to develop strategies to prevent it—transcends these categories. Activists and theorists are also increasingly seeing its links to other serious social problems, including child abuse, homelessness, depression, eating disorders, and substance abuse. It hardly seems a radical proposition, at the end of this violent century, to argue that our educational institutions should be forthrightly and systematically addressing it.

Violence Against Women Is a Men's Issue

Educational administrators have an enormously influential platform. Their leadership, or lack thereof, sets the tone for how an institution will address any number of issues. For example, when male administrators choose to take an active antisexist stance themselves, overseeing prevention programming efforts; influencing personnel practices to facilitate the hiring of feminist women and antisexist male faculty; meting out strong punishment for violent, abusive, or harassing students; arranging for staff development and training (within the limits of collective bargaining agreements); and playing an active public leadership role both in the school and in the community, they send a strong message to other male administrators, as well as faculty, students, and parents, that violence against women is a *men's issue* that responsible men have no choice but to face.

This message is critical, because the first step in motivating boys and men for antisexist efforts anywhere is getting them to reconceptualize issues like sexual assault, dating violence, and sexual harassment as *their* issues. Without this reconceptualization, and to the immense frustration of many feminist educators, many men will simply not give these issues serious time and attention. This is, of course, not true across the board. Some male principals, superintendents, athletic directors, college presidents, and deans have devoted significant resources, including personal time, to gender-based violence prevention work. Unfortunately, however, many male administrators, even those who support gender equity efforts and are generally responsive to feminist concerns, do not often recognize the extent of their potential for antisexist leadership. Instead, they see it as their responsibility to delegate administrative authority in this area to a woman. Their explicit or implied rationale is that it is more appropriate for women to be handling "gender-related" issues.

The leadership of women, of course, has made possible the very discussion of how men should be involved. Women have long been at the forefront of numerous societal efforts to achieve sex equity and fairness at every level of the educational system, as well as to reform laws to hold abusive males accountable, and to create institutions, such as battered women's shelters and rape crisis centers, to serve victims and survivors. But pandemic rates of men's and boys' violence have persisted despite these feminist efforts. And while it would be reductionist to ascribe this persistence to any single factor, one factor is surely the absence, society-wide, of effective antisexist male leadership, including active male involvement in primary prevention education efforts aimed at boys and men.

Administrators have to cater to the concerns of various constituencies, including at the K-12 level school boards, faculty, students, parents, and community groups (and at the college level numerous competing academic and nonacademic departments). It would be unfair to minimize the political sensitivity of their position. But antisexist male leadership, in professional as well as personal spheres of life, requires making decisions and taking actions that might be personally uncomfortable, unpopular, or controversial. Exercising this leadership can sometimes feel very lonely. A certain degree of isolation is one of the consequences of breaking the historical conspiracy of men's silence around sexism. You risk being seen as having "broken ranks" with your fellow men, few of whom appreciate having to be accountable to other men about the way they treat women—either in the school setting or in their private lives.

As a result, too often, men in positions of influence, instead of speaking out about the sexist attitudes and behaviors of boys and men, leave it to women—mothers, teachers, female colleagues or co-workers—to raise concerns or try to hold abusive males accountable. For many male leaders this is an unconscious process; they have never been forced to think through their responsibilities as antisexist *men* in these situations. But counting on women is also a way of avoiding some of the difficult burdens of leadership. Conscious or not, characterizing men's violence against women as a "women's issue" allows these men both to camouflage their own fears and anxieties and to avoid having to learn the difficult interpersonal skills required of effective antisexist male leadership.

Why has this leadership been so lacking in the classrooms, on the playing fields, in the main offices, and on school boards? It is important to note that this phenomenon is not specific to education. Relatively few men in the corporate world, the professions, or in blue-collar occupations have distinguished themselves as powerful antisexist advocates. Most men and boys are not abusive; they just haven't spoken out about the sexism and abusive behavior of their peers and other males in their circles of influence.

One possible explanation for why relatively few educational administrators have made gender-based violence prevention a major priority is concern for the "good name" of a school and its public image. This is particularly true in communities that pride themselves on their relatively low rates of street or school-related violence. If the school is seriously addressing gender-based violence, the reasoning goes, it might call attention to the existence of problems in the school. The subsequent (journalistic?) spotlight might reveal problems with male—and female—students that were previously ignored, minimized, or covered up. This could then potentially cause a defensive reaction, particularly from parents of boys, and greater scrutiny and criticism of the administration, particularly from the parents of girls.

Another reason for male administrators' relative inaction is that it rarely even occurs to them that they—as men—have an extra responsibility to be doing something about men's violence. They might see themselves as administrators with a set of professional responsibilities, and not *male* administrators with special obligations. Robert Hanke (1992), in an article about hegemonic masculinity in transition, explains this mind-set by arguing that masculinity, like whiteness, "does not appear to be a cultural category at all" (p. 186), but is rather the unexamined norm against which nondominant groups are defined as other.

A classic example of this "othering" in the service of leaving the dominant group uninterrogated is the stereotypical question asked of battered women: Why do they stay? Our fixation is on the behavior of the women. Why are we so quick to ask why she stays? Why aren't we more concerned with *why so many men beat women?* Doesn't battering, which, according to the Surgeon General, is the leading cause of injury to women in the United States (and a growing problem in high school and college populations), say as much or more about the boys and men who do the assaulting as it does about the women and girls they victimize?

Another reason to reconceptualize gender-based violence as a men's issue is that effective prevention, by definition, means addressing root causes. According to many researchers, a key cause of rape, battering, and sexual harassment is cultural ideas about manhood that at best tolerate and at worst promote sexist and abusive behavior. Addressing and counteracting this cultural approval needs to be an important part of violence prevention efforts. But calling a crime like rape a "women's issue" has the opposite effect. It subtly, though powerfully, steers attention away from the fact that whether the victim is female or male, *men* commit 99% of all rapes. This shift of focus from perpetrator to victim also has the effect of absolving nonabusive men of their responsibility to speak out. If they're "women's issues," what can men really add to the conversation?

Challenging men to think "out of the box" on the subject of so-called women's issues is one of the goals of a series of exercises I use in gender-based violence prevention work with male educators or other men, either in single-sex or mixed gender groups. I call them "remedial empathy" exercises. After establishing the seriousness of our society's problem of men's violence against women, I ask just the men to raise their hand if they have a wife, daughter, sister, girlfriend, mother, grandmother, or female friend. This usually prompts laughter, and some grumbling, but eventually they all put up their hand. The message is clear: It is simplistic and divisive to reduce gender-based violence to a "battle between the sexes" where one side wins at the expense of the other. Men's and women's lives are too interconnected. I remind them that during the course of this presentation, every woman we talk about who has been raped or abused by her boyfriend, or assaulted by a man in some other way, is somebody's sister, mother, daughter. This violence doesn't happen to some abstract category of "women." It happens to women we know, and love.

By personalizing the issues, this exercise challenges men to examine how their self-image as responsible fathers, brothers, husbands, sons, and friends of women and girls is or can be consistent with continued inaction in the face of the widespread reality, or threat, of men's violence against them. For male educators, it helps them to think about how they can use the influence, mentoring role, visibility, and resources of their professional positions to serve better the needs of their students, families, friends, and community.

How can these men be most helpful? Broadly stated, male educators attempting to help reduce gender-based violence can perhaps be most effective by breaking the customary silence and engaging boys and other men in critical dialogue—in assemblies, in classes, on the playing fields, and in private conversations—about what it means to be a man, especially as this relates to attitudes and behaviors toward women. In facilitating this dialogue, we need to provide ample opportunities for young men, in safe and respectful educational spaces, to talk about their life experiences as *males*, not simply as "kids," or "teens," or "youth." This is not an easy thing to do, because both the educators and the students live in a culture that often reads male introspection and vulnerability as weakness. Thus part of our challenge is to model strong-but-gentle antisexist masculinity as a stark contrast to the omnipresent cultural images on television, in movies, comedy, sports, and music that equate strength in men with power over other men and dominance and abuse of women. One way of doing this is to co-teach classes and cofacilitate workshops with women. By working together we can model the very sort of intergender partnership and respect that stands in diametric opposition to sexism and abuse.[3]

Overcoming Men's Defensiveness

Feminists have long known that many men react defensively to the slightest attempts to hold them accountable for sexist beliefs or actions. Many feminists in the antirape and antibattering movements, for example, have been called "male-bashers" for arguing passionately against male violence. This Orwellian inversion, using a violent term (*bashers*) to refer to antiviolence activists, nonetheless has the effect of silencing a lot of women, and men, who might otherwise vocalize their condemnation of sexist abuse.

The notion that holding men accountable for gender-based violence—as perpetrators or bystanders—is tantamount to attacking men is a critical hurdle in attempts to convince educational leaders to address this subject in schools. Sometimes youth outreach educators from battered women's shelters or rape crisis centers have to demonstrate explicitly that their curriculum will not offend or unfairly attack the boys. For pragmatic reasons, it is usually a good idea for these educators, female and male, to preempt this criticism by emphasizing the need to inspire more male *leadership* in this area. Calls for preventive antisexist male leadership, combined with calls for perpetrator accountability, are more likely to provoke a positive response than are calls addressed exclusively to perpetrator accountability. It is also a good strategy to tout, explicitly, the benefits to both girls *and* boys of healthy, nonviolent relationships.

Until mainstream educational practice more fully incorporates a feminist sensibility about gender and power, men's defensiveness, as well as some women's knee-jerk and self-defeating attempts to defend men, will continue to block progress. I have encountered this type of resistance many times, from male and female educators as well as parents. On several occasions, plans to have me or a colleague come speak about gender-based violence and men's responsibility at a high school or middle school have been scuttled as a result of administrators' or activist parents' fears that we would be too critical of the boys. In one instance, a woman who was active in her New England small town's parent-teacher organization contacted me about coming to give a speech and some workshops at the middle school. She had two teenage daughters in the school and was worried about a dangerous climate of sexism and abuse that (she felt) wasn't being dealt with by anyone in the school system. We had several conversations, and I provided her with written literature about my work with high school and middle school boys and girls, along with several references. We had gotten as far as choosing dates when she reluctantly, and somewhat apologetically, informed me that the whole idea had been rejected because a woman on the school board, who had three sons in the middle school, had blocked the effort out of concerns about potential male-bashing. This was ironic, because the woman who had initially contacted me had done so after hearing about my work with high school and college male student-athletes and college fraternity members—hardly groups who would embrace, and recommend, an "antimale" approach.

The idea that gender-based violence prevention education targeted at boys is inherently "anti-male" has undoubtedly hampered the implementation of effective approaches. The antimale charge has, of course, been part of the backlash against gender equity efforts in general, and antirape, antibattering, and anti-sexual harassment strategies in particular. In recent years, books, articles, and high-profile media appearances by Camille

Paglia, Christina Hoff Sommers, and Katie Roiphe have bolstered the position of antifeminists who have long opposed the very idea of gender-based violence prevention work with men.

Hoff Sommers, for one, has been prominently featured in the conservative corporate media deriding feminist attempts to address what she considers the dramatically overblown problem of gender violence. She refers repeatedly to supposed feminist efforts to attack and blame boys, and she is even writing a book on the "war against boys." She and the others, by virtue of their sex, have also provided a useful patina of intellectual female cover for the radical right-wing opponents of progressive educational reform, who continue to organize against the public schools' addressing what they regard as private, "family" issues. Thus armed with putatively reputable critiques of antimale bias, traditionalist educators and parents—men and women—can hide their personal fears and anxieties about exposing the dark underside of family life behind vague accusations that typically conflate male-bashing with perfectly reasonable efforts to educate males *and* hold them accountable.

In the face of this sort of predictable conservative resistance, the strategy that I developed originally at the Mentors in Violence Prevention (MVP) Program at Northeastern University's Center for the Study of Sport in Society is positive and nonblaming. Rather than provoke men's (and in some cases, women's) defensiveness, the MVP approach frames the need for men to respond to the societal crisis of men's violence against women as a leadership issue. It differentiates between male guilt for sexism and men's responsibility to work against it. The MVP pedagogy also highlights the ways that nonabusive men can create a peer culture climate whereby the abuse of women by some men and boys is seen as completely socially unacceptable, uncool, and "unmanly." Focusing on men as "bystanders," and not as potential perpetrators, allows the men to take in the ideas without feeling defensive. Instead, they feel challenged to make a difference on an issue that up until now has seen precious little male initiative.[4]

"Walking the Talk": The Personal Perils of Coming Out as an Antisexist Male

One legitimate concern of male educators contemplating whether to become involved in school-based antisexist efforts is the likelihood that their personal behavior will, as a result, be more thoroughly scrutinized. A male principal, teacher, or coach who takes a public antisexist stance, which inevitably means talking about male responsibility and accountability, invites attention to his own "walking the talk." Before teaching classes, initiating programming for students or faculty, or otherwise providing antisexist leadership, he must assess whether or not his private life, personal history, or daily conduct in interactions with women in any way contradicts his public role. If it does, he invites the charge of hypocrisy, both from others and, if he's honest, from himself. Men in any visible line of work or profession who take a public antisexist stance must be aware of this dynamic.

In part because we are still a small minority of men, the personal motives of avowedly antisexist or profeminist men are constantly under suspicion. Of course, because of this suspicion, it is even more critical for those seeking to increase the number of antisexist men, inside and outside of schools, to be very cautious about embracing men who might have personal transgressions to hide. This does not mean that all men who want to be effective antisexist educators have to have a perfect record. Young people can learn a lot from a man who openly takes responsibility for abusive behavior in his past, especially if he's done the personal and intellectual work required to understand how and why he chose to act violently against women (or gays, people of color, etc.). On the other hand, if he's not fully disclosive, he risks providing motivation for women or girls—from his past or present—to reveal his duplicity. This sort of unmasking not only causes pain and embarrassment to the parties involved, it also impacts the level of trust afforded all men who speak out against sexism, and it deepens the skepticism of those who wonder why a man would really care about these issues in the first place. Admittedly, this degree of mistrust is not unfounded. There have been numerous cases across the country in the past few years where seemingly supportive male educators, clergymen, coaches, politicians, and business leaders have sexually assaulted and/or harassed either young girls and boys or their own female peers.

Fortunately, most potentially active antisexist male educators are not paralyzed by fears of being found out. Most men have never assaulted a woman. Rather, their reticence to get involved has more to do with a self-critical appraisal. Some men have confessed to me that they feel reluctant to "tell other men how to behave" on account of their having had "politically incorrect" experiences like being sexually aroused by pornographic images. There is clearly a need for much more honest dialogue among men, and between women and men, about issues such as the sometimes hard-to-define distinctions between sexual attraction, objectification, and abuse. It is also important that men are honest with ourselves and confront our own sexist attitudes and behaviors. In the meantime, however, scandalous rates of rape, battering, and sexual harassment continue unabated, and few men speak out. In this context it seems necessary to mention that for men to be effective antisexist leaders, we must dispense with self-righteousness—and the self-defeating notion that we have to be free of any ideological inconsistencies or inevitable human contradictions.

In addition to being able to "walk the talk," to be effective male educators we need to have an adequate personal comfort level in talking to other males about these issues. Considering the intensely competitive male hierarchies in which most of us were socialized, this is easier said than done. There are many personal reasons why men might be uncomfortable talking about issues that literally hit close to home. What if a man grew up in a home where his father abused his mother, and he has never talked about it outside of his family? What if he has an abusive relative or friend, and he has never confronted him? What if a woman close to him is a rape survivor? What if a male educator is himself a survivor of childhood sexual abuse or some other sort of violent mistreatment? How do these life experiences affect a man's willingness to talk to young people about these and other issues?

Some men are silenced by their continuing shame at having been bullied, as kids or even as adults. One embarrassing secret of many male high school teachers is that many of them are intimidated by outwardly tough male students. The popular discourse around teachers-being-intimidated-by-students typically conjures up the setting of a decaying urban high school with a teacher scared of his or her young black or Latino students who might have (or have access to) knives or guns. But this phenomenon is present in upper-middle-class white towns as well.

As Bernard Lefkowitz (1997) reports in *Our Guys,* his book about the 1989 rape of a mentally retarded girl by a group of popular high school male athletes in Glen Ridge, New Jersey, the inside clique of abusive "real jocks" in the school intimidated everyone around them:

> The peacock image they projected was not something they had picked up overnight in high school. They had spent years perfecting it. For these young men, the essence of jockdom was a practiced show of contempt for kids and teachers alike. They tried to humiliate any wimpy guy who got in their way, but they reserved their best shots for girls who ignored them or dared to stand up to them. (p. 111)

Lefkowitz reports one incident where a girl tells of being grabbed by the arms and legs by two of the boys, who began dragging her through the hallway of the school:

> They are carrying me off the ground, and they're trying to pull off my pants. I'm screaming my head off, and this teacher sticks her head out the door and she doesn't say anything because none of the teachers wanted to deal with them. So nobody did anything until they finally let me go. (p. 148)

In this case the intimidated and irresponsible teacher was a woman, but Lefkowitz makes it clear that these aggressive young men silenced male teachers, administrators, and coaches as well. This type of abuse by young males is hardly unique to suburban New Jersey; it occurs in hallways and classrooms across the country. In the face of this sort of brazen bullying, is it surprising that many male educators hesitate before jumping into overt antisexist advocacy?

Pedagogical effectiveness, argues bell hooks (1994), requires paying attention to the fact that teachers are not abstract dispensers of knowledge but, rather, sexual human beings:

> Trained in the philosophical context of Western metaphysical dualism, many of us have accepted the notion that there is a split between the body and the mind. Believing this, individuals enter the classroom to teach as though only the mind is present, and not the body. To call attention to the body is to betray the legacy of repression and denial that has been handed down to us by our professorial white male . . . and black male . . . elders. . . . The public world of institutional learning was a site where the body had to be erased, go unnoticed. (p. 191)

Calling attention to the male body and its various constructions raises important questions about the challenge of finding men to teach other men and boys about sexism. For example, how does the antisexist pedagogical strategy of a man who is short and slight of build differ from one who is tall and muscular? How does a male physical education teacher and coach, wearing a warm-up suit, differ in the way he talks about issues, and is responded to by students, from a math teacher who is less athletic but, say, more bookish and cerebral? Each can be effective, but perhaps for different reasons. If men in every ethnic and racial group are, in the words of the anthropologist Alan Klein (1993), "in a dialogue with muscles" (p. 4), how does that dialogue influence pedagogical choices in gender-based violence prevention education efforts?

Consider the following scenario. A male English teacher is leading a discussion of a book or short story with an explicit gender theme. In the course of conversation, a charismatic and aggressive male student says something sexist or victim-blaming (e.g., that a woman who was raped was asking for it). The teacher does not respond directly, challenging the sexism of the statement, but instead moves on to another point. Some of the female students quietly fume; the teacher gradually develops a reputation for being insensitive to girls.

This scenario seems all too common. I have heard variations of this very situation from female educators, as well as from college students about their high school teachers or college professors. The women often assume that male teachers are silent in these circumstances not because they are insecure or unprepared to respond, but because they likely agree with the sexist statements.

This might be true; it would be silly to deny that such blatant sexism still exists among men (and women). But in the aforementioned scenario, there is another, perhaps more subtle, explanation for the teacher's silence. He might appear to be a mature, confident adult man, but in truth he's frightened by the sexist student and his male peers, and he also worries about what other male faculty will think of him. The intimidation, from students or colleagues, rarely takes the form of a physical threat. Rather, it has to do with the teacher's confidence and security *as a man* and whether or not he can withstand potentially overt or covert ridicule. For male teachers in their twenties and thirties, memories of sexist and homophobic male high school and college peer cultures might still be fresh. They might have experienced these peer cultures as oppressive, but never had the strength or standing to speak out. If in college or graduate school—or psychotherapy—they have never addressed the issue of their silence and insecurity in the male group dynamic, they will be much less likely to respond to other men's sexism, inside or outside of a classroom.

Male teachers who themselves are not hegemonically masculine in body type, clothing style, or personal affect might also be compromised in their ability to confront belligerently sexist male students. They might even, in some circumstances, feel physically threatened or bullied. Closeted gay teachers might not want to risk being outed by the inevitable gossip that follows antisexist men ("He must be gay; a 'real man' wouldn't be talking about 'masculinity' "). Many homophobic heterosexual men also chafe at this sort of gossip. Many men are so policed by their own internalized homophobia that just the possibility that others will think they're gay is enough to keep them silent, even if they're uneasy in the face of other men's sexism.

There might also be relevant racial and cultural factors. Antisexist African American men who teach in majority white suburban schools, for example, have to be prepared to deal not only with the sexism of their students, but potentially with their racist beliefs about black male sexuality. Asian American male teachers who dare to challenge young men's machismo posturing have to be self-confident enough to overcome their stereotypical image, in the words of the Japanese American actor Mark Hayashi, as "the eunuchs of America" (Mura, 1996, p. 17).

On the other hand, conscious white male teachers who have a large percentage of students of color might be hesitant to confront sexism out of fear of being accused of ignorance or insensitivity. It is very difficult for any educator, male or female, to maintain a strong antisexist position in a discussion when being forcefully told that "you don't know what it's like in my culture." Then again, some white male educators might themselves believe the myth of the hypermasculine, hypersexual black or Latino male, and as a result feel inferior to them as men, on a bodily level, and hence not feel comfortable mentoring them or commenting on their manhood.

In any cultural setting, teachers who are privately antisexist might not want to risk losing whatever credibility or popularity they've acquired in the school's dominant male culture, whether it be jock-centric or not, by calling some boys out on their sexism, or calling girls out on their complaisance. In some cases, the motivation might be related to concerns about career advancement. There is little reason to suspect that men who challenge the male power structure are likely to be speedily promoted as a reward for principled dissent or ideological independence.

Lite Beer and Men's Leadership

The sports culture is often accurately viewed as one of the key sources of sexist and heterosexist male attitudes and behaviors. Don Sabo (Sabo & Messner, 1994) says that "sports, especially contact sports, train boys and men to assume macho characteristics like cut-throat competitiveness, domination of others, tendency toward violence, emotional stoicism, and arrogance toward women" (p. 191).

Men and boys in the male-dominated school sports culture often have a disproportionate impact on what sorts of masculine styles and sexualities in that school are accepted or marginalized, celebrated or bullied. But while many critiques of the relationship between sports culture and gender-based violence understandably stress the complicity of this culture in covering up if not actively promoting men's violence against women, the male sports culture is also, paradoxically, a source of creative antisexist strategies.

As noted earlier, the dearth of male participation in gender-based violence prevention efforts over the past generation is partly a failure of male leadership. Due to the popularity, power, and privileged status of boys' sports (particularly team sports) within many suburban, rural, and urban school "jockocracies," the school-based athletic subculture—in the persons of athletic directors, coaches, and student-athletes—is in a position to provide some of that missing leadership.

The story of a famous beer advertising campaign illustrates this principle by analogy. In 1972, Miller Brewing Company bought the rights to Meister Brau Light, a beer that Meister Brau, a small Chicago brewery, had been attempting to market to women as a diet beer ("Beer Advertising," 1983). Not surprisingly, the effort had failed. Still, Miller's market research had shown that beer drinkers would welcome a beer that wasn't filling, but men didn't want to drink a beer that could be seen as "feminine."

So Miller had a problem, because in 1972, much more so than in the late 1990s, concern with calories was seen as a decidedly "feminine" preoccupation—and in the early seventies men made up more than three quarters of the U.S. beer market. Their solution was to initiate a television ad campaign that featured a series of macho football players and other sports icons, with Dick Butkus, who is white, and Bubba Smith, who is African American, among the first cohort. They placed these football stars in a crowded bar, surrounded them with their buddies, and put a Lite beer in their hands. (They also featured hegemonically attractive women as visual subplot, a near-obligatory presence in contemporary beer commercials.)

The message: Dick Butkus and Bubba Smith can drink light beer, and no one is going to accuse them of being wimps. You can, too. The result was that the Miller Lite television commercials became among the most celebrated ads in TV history, winning numerous Clio awards for advertising excellence in the 1970s. Today, Miller Lite is the official beer of the National Football League.[5]

This stunning shift came about because some savvy marketers nearly three decades ago figured that men would change their gendered behavior if given "permission" to do so by men with more status in the masculine hierarchy. In other words, if men in positions of cultural leadership would take risks and model new ways of being male, large numbers of men were likely to respond in turn by changing their attitudes and attendant behaviors (albeit, in this case, consumer behaviors).

The same leadership principle can be applied in efforts to increase the involvement of male educators and students in gender-based violence prevention education in the schools. If one reason so few male educators have participated in this work is that it has been stigmatized as "unmasculine" to do so, what better strategy than to enlist some of the most traditionally "masculine" men in the work? Of course, this approach is not without its contradictions. One could argue that affirming the centrality of the male school sports culture, by utilizing its potential for leadership, merely reinforces its legitimacy, when what is called for is a diminution of the power of this and other patriarchal institutions.

But if high-status male student-athletes (e.g., varsity members, team captains, seniors, all-stars) could be offered special antisexist training that focuses on their role as leaders and does not target them, with predictably negative results, as potential perpetrators, then their leadership could help make this work more acceptable for other males with less social standing. This is just as true for athletic administrators and coaches, who belong to their own peer culture in the school and community. Their willingness to attend gender-based violence prevention trainings, cosponsor events with school-based health educators or community-based women's programs, and otherwise endorse antisexist efforts makes it more likely that their nonathletic peers, on the faculty or in the administration, will get involved. Politically, the interdepartmental and community contacts fostered by these sorts of coalitions could also help indirectly to reduce the resistance of influential male athletic directors, coaches, teachers, and others to school-based gender equity and antihomophobia efforts.

My colleagues and I have given speeches and presented workshops in numerous schools where the athletic department has been a cosponsoring partner. In most cases, a woman administrator or teacher initiated the effort and solicited support from the athletic department in part by emphasizing our sports backgrounds and credentials. The success of these partnerships, however, is hardly assured. Many male athletic administrators, coaches, and student-athletes resist efforts to involve them in such educational interventions, due either to antifeminist ideologies or to circle-the-wagons defensiveness. Some are angry about the widespread public perception that male athletes, at the high school, college, and professional level, are out of control generally, and specifically are disproportionately involved in crimes against women. Advocates for African American male athletes are concerned that in the national media, black males are the stated or unstated focus of much of this discussion, allowing white male athletes and nonathletes to avoid the same level of critical scrutiny. As a result of these and other concerns, in some cases it is necessary to defer talk about positive leadership and instead spell out how athletic departments have a self-interest in getting involved (e.g., preventing student-athletes from getting themselves, their coaches, and the school, into trouble).

There are many other strategies that school systems, through athletic departments, can implement to help mandate and institutionalize male participation in gender-based violence prevention efforts. One is to provide regular training for coaches and student-athletes. Another is for school boards, superintendents, and principals to write job descriptions for prospective athletic directors that explicitly mention gender-based violence prevention programming as part of the job. Hiring preference would go to candidates, male and female, who had previous experience in this area or who had done related college or graduate school work.

Likewise, if athletic directors communicated, in their job postings for coaches' positions, that undergraduate and graduate course work and other demonstrated knowledge of and interest in gender issues would help (male and female) candidates distinguish themselves, this would prompt many otherwise indifferent undergraduate or graduate students (who have an interest in the coaching profession) to take these kinds of courses. While there is no national uniformity in this sort of coursework, and no guarantee that education will always result in an increase in commitment to activist progressive principles, one effect on many men of taking gender studies courses is an increased awareness of the pervasiveness of sexism and all forms of men's violence against women. Studying gender is also likely to lead to a better understanding, by men who are training to be leaders in athletic departments, of the potential abuses of masculine power and privilege. This insight, and the self-knowledge it often catalyzes, is one of the reasons why this education is still politically controversial.

Conclusion

It would be one thing for educational policymakers to agree, in principle, that more male participation is needed in school-based gender violence prevention education. But who would decide which men? What if the majority of current male faculty, for many of the reasons outlined in this chapter, resist taking on these issues? Can a small minority of concerned men in a school system make a sufficient impact to affect the school climate? If so, who trains them? Out of whose budget?[6]

The most common model of gender-based violence prevention programming in schools consists of a mix of various components, including classroom presentations, forums for teens, theater troupes, peer leadership programs, and support groups for at-risk students (Hanson, 1995, p. 18). While there are no comprehensive data documenting the sex of faculty involved in this work, there are, to be sure, male educators who have been teaching and mentoring students, attending trainings and conferences on gender equity and violence issues, and providing other sorts of antisexist male leadership. But we're a long way from this sort of participation being the norm.

In the meantime, or until gender-based violence prevention education is incorporated directly into the training of all teachers and administrators in colleges, graduate schools of education, and in K-12 curricula, most schools that want a knowledgeable, confident antisexist male presence realistically will have to bring in educators from the community. Currently, only a few communities in the United States have antisexist men's groups that could provide this service. Battered women's and rape crisis programs often have youth outreach programs, but many more men are needed to co-facilitate classes with the women who typically present the material. Unfortunately, chronically underfunded women's programs rarely can provide compensation for these positions.

There are significant limitations to the model of (male) community educators coming into the schools to teach antisexist masculinity. For one thing, time limitations are always a factor. Even if they can gain the respect and attention of the students, community educators are only briefly in the school. And if they can manage to be effective despite the constraints, sometimes the very teachers and coaches who brought them in can easily undermine their influence. At one urban high school where two of my colleagues were conducting a series of all-male workshops, a student told them that his football coach had called him a "fucking pussy" for not diving to block a punt. At another session in the same school, a physical education teacher, in his late twenties, handing out passes to students about to participate in a workshop, said to one boy, "you're not only a member, you're the president of the fag club" (J. O'Brien, personal communication, 1997). This was in front of my colleagues, who were there to talk and facilitate dialogue about men's sexist and heterosexist attitudes and abusive behaviors. Another swaggering male teacher told my colleagues later that day that he was "so on top of these issues," he "could have done this training myself" (J. O'Brien, personal communication, 1997).

While this is highly debatable, what is not in question is whether enough male educators have accepted the responsibility of full participation in gender-based violence prevention efforts. Clearly they have not. Until now, women have led the way and have accomplished a great deal, often in spite of male apathy or even outright hostility. It is time, as we approach the 21st century, for more men to move beyond passivity and resistance, and instead join women in creating a safer, nonviolent, and more egalitarian world for the young women and men who are counting on us.

Notes

1. For the purpose of this chapter I am using the definition of "gender-based violence" adopted in 1997 by the U.S. Department of Education's Subpanel on the Prevention of Sexual and Racial Harassment and Violence Against Students in Higher Education: "A continuum of violent and controlling behaviors perpetrated by an individual's partner, former partner or acquaintance, including physical violence, sexual relations without affirmative consent, and acts of verbal, nonverbal, or physical aggression, intimidation, or hostility based on sex." This definition also includes hate crimes committed against people for reasons of gender, race/ethnicity, or sexual orientation.

Also for the purpose of this chapter, I have narrowed the scope of my focus to men's violence against women, and not other aspects of gender-based violence, such as gay-bashing or the small percentage of serious violence perpetrated by females against males. These areas, particularly male leadership in education against (men's) violence against lesbians and gays, require a much more thorough treatment than I could provide here.

2. Some recent pedagogical theory examines the complex dynamics of women teaching boys and men about sexism, dynamics that can be even more challenging when factoring in issues of race, class, and sexual orientation. See Roof and Wiegman (1995) and hooks (1994).

3. For a discussion of some of the dynamics of male and female cofacilitators leading a discussion of sexual abuse and dating violence with girls and boys, see reference to the work of Fernando Mederos in Caterina (1992, p. 4).

4. For more information about the development and practical application of a bystander-focused pedagogy applied to gender-based violence prevention education and practice, see Katz (1995).

5. A more recent example of this phenomenon is the Procter & Gamble marketing campaign for Zest Body Wash, an "all-family soap." After the company enlisted St. Louis Rams running back Craig "Ironman" Heyward to pitch the product in a TV ad campaign, sales doubled in less than 6 months. Mark Schar, head of skin care products for the consumer products giant, was quoted by Gary Straus (1998) in *USA Today* as saying that the impetus

for the campaign was that "we realized men didn't have permission to buy the product" (p. 1).
6. A promising new interdisciplinary teaching curriculum by N. Stein and D. Cappello (1998) builds gender violence prevention education into existing courses. This integrative approach holds great promise for increasing the number of men who will address the issue of gender violence in the classroom.

References

Beer advertising: Coming through for you? (1983). *Consumer Reports, 48*(7), 349.

Caterina, M. (1992). Conference on sexual violence and adolescents highlights need for treatment and intervention. Newton, MA: Center for Equity and Cultural Diversity.

Hanke, R. (1992). Redesigning men: Hegemonic masculinity in transition. In S. Craig (Ed.), *Men, masculinity, and the media* (pp. 185-198). Newbury Park, CA: Sage.

Hanson, K. (1995). *Gendered violence: Examining education's role.* Working Paper Series #4, Education Development Center, Center for Equity and Cultural Diversity, Newton, MA.

hooks, b. (1994). *Teaching to transgress: Education as the practice of freedom.* New York: Routledge.

Katz, J. (1995). Reconstructing masculinity in the locker room: The Mentors in Violence Prevention Project. *Harvard Educational Review, 65*(2), 163-174.

Klein, A. (1993). *Little big men: Bodybuilding subculture and gender construction.* Albany: State University of New York Press.

Lefkowitz, B. (1997). *Our guys: The Glen Ridge rape and the secret life of the perfect suburb.* Berkeley: University of California Press.

Levy, B. (Ed.). (1992). *Teen dating violence: Young women in danger.* Seattle, WA: Seal.

Mura, D. (1996). *Where the body meets memory: An odyssey of race, sexuality, and identity.* Garden City, NY: Anchor Books.

National Victim Center. (1992). *Rape in America: A report to the nation.* Washington, DC: Author.

Roof, J., & Wiegman, R. (1995). *Who can speak? Authority and critical identity.* Urbana: University of Illinois Press.

Sabo, D., & Messner, M. (Eds.). (1994). *Sex, violence, and power in sports: Rethinking masculinity.* Freedom, CA: Crossing Press.

Stein, N., & Cappello, D., with Tubach, L., & Katz, J. (1998). Gender violence/gender justice: An interdisciplinary teaching guide for teachers of English, literature, social studies, health education, peer counseling and family and consumer sciences (Grades 7-12). (Available from Wellesley College, Center for Research on Women, Wellesley, MA)

Straus, G. (1998, February 5). Being incorrect, politically and otherwise, sells. *USA Today,* p. 1.

U.S. Department of Education. (1996, December). National Center for Education Statistics, Schools and Staffing Survey: 1993-94. *Education Vital Signs,* pp. A19-A21.

U.S. Department of Education Sub-panel on the Prevention of Sexual and Racial Harassment and Violence Against Students in Higher Education. (1997). [Sub-panel guidelines]. (Unpublished document, available from Higher Education Center at Education Development Center, Newton, MA.)

13

The "Facts of the Case"

Gender Equity for Boys as a Public Policy Issue

LYN YATES

In many countries, the final decades of the 20th century have seen "gender equity" enter the discussions of education policy, school systems, schools, and education researchers. Today, a very widely held story about what has been happening would go something like this:

About 20 years ago, governments became aware that girls were being disadvantaged in schooling. They developed policies and funding to improve girls' career aspirations, to make curriculum and pedagogy more "girl-friendly," and to ensure equal spending on girls and boys. At the same time, a huge amount of research and writing was carried out on girls, their development, and their needs. New textbook guidelines were introduced; ways of teaching were reassessed; forms of assessment were rethought; ideas about girls' psychology began to influence curriculum materials, classroom organization, and teachers; concerns about the need in modern society for girls to be successful, to be mathematically literate, and to take on a broader range of post-school careers were promoted with significant effect among teachers, parents, and girls themselves.

AUTHOR'S NOTE: Earlier discussions of some material in this chapter were given as a paper presented at the 1996 AERA (American Educational Research Association) Conference in New York, and in an article "Gender equity and the boys debate—what sort of challenge is it?" published in 1997 in the *British Journal of Sociology of Education, 18*(3), 337-347.

The story goes on with the moral of the tale:

Over this period we have seen a large increase in the proportion of girls completing school as compared with boys, and their increasing success in "nontraditional" subjects such as mathematics. Now it is time for more attention to the boys. Boys' retention rates, learning difficulties, delinquency, suicide rates, and general self-esteem are all cause for concern. We don't want to take away from the girls' programs, and more needs to be done in relation to issues such as sexual harassment in schools, but there is a real dearth of good research and professional support for boys, and this is what should now occupy our urgent attention.[1]

This widely repeated story gives rise to a number of interesting questions, both conceptual and "factual." What *are* the "facts of the case" regarding sex-based inequalities and schooling—and to what extent *have* these changed in the past two decades of reform activity? Just what sort of project is gender-focused reform in schools? And, in policy contexts and in school reform agendas, what leads to certain claims (the needs of girls, say; or the needs of boys) being prominent or being no longer prominent?

In what follows, I want to look at some aspects of why as well as how boys and masculinity have become the interesting topic for policymakers, media, and, indeed, for researchers such as myself. I will begin by revisiting the matter of inequalities, and will show that some elements of the story I have just outlined are quite misleading. However, I will argue, the particular form in which the concern about the boys is now being heard does point to some interesting issues about school reform and gender issues. These relate to the treatment of inequalities within the shaping of public policy; to curriculum and pedagogy matters of just how "gender" is to be "reconstructed"; and to research methodologies, and what frames our interests and interpretations as researchers.

What follows, then, is not an attempt to give a comprehensive overview of the developments in relation to boys. It is an attempt to illuminate some aspects of these developments. And it is specifically grounded in an Australian context, where gender equity has been a very prominent reform program and where current discussions about boys are more strongly concerned with "equal opportunity" and men's movement concerns than with fears about gendered and racial patterns of poverty and violence in society, which seem to have been more prominent in public discussions about boys in the United States and the United Kingdom. The present discussion is not intended to suggest that the issues I raise are the only matters of relevance in current debates and in the changing agendas (some good discussions of other aspects of the issue can be found in Arnot, David, & Weiner, 1999; Lingard & Douglas, 1999; and MacKinnon, Elgqvist-Saltzman,

& Prentice, 1998), but to discuss one specific set of developments and to add some areas of discussion to the interpretation of the new developments.

Policy and Politics: Debates About Inequality and Equal Opportunity

Just how much was the policy attention to girls a response to facts about inequality and disadvantage, facts that have now changed and justify a new attention to boys on the same grounds? The answer is complex.

In the mid-1970s, in one of the government inquiries in Australia that investigated and justified the need to give more attention and support to girls in school, one member insisted on producing a Minority Report in which she argued that to see girls rather than boys as the disadvantaged group was a distortion of reality:

> Those who have experienced racism know how false are the analogies drawn between sexism and racism, and the equation of female "liberation" with models of liberation from colonial rule. When assessing the status of any disadvantaged or under privileged group, e.g. the blacks in the U.S. or Aboriginals in Australia, a number of criteria are used: infant mortality, life expectancy, incidence of disease, alcoholism, violence, involvement with drugs, crime, imprisonment, level of literacy, retention rates at school, success rates in examinations, employment and income levels. Applying these criteria to males and females in Victoria, on *every* count except the last, it is males who emerge as the disadvantaged group. (Victorian Committee on Equal Opportunity in Schools, 1977, p. iii)

Now we might complain about the way the list of "indicators" here is loaded (literacy but not mathematics; alcoholism but not those on welfare payments; imprisonment rates, but not rates of those in political office, etc.), but I want to draw attention to something else. In the 1970s, the statement just quoted was very much a minority voice. It was circulated, but otherwise, for school reform purposes, effectively ignored.[2] Yet, in terms of its "factual" underpinnings, and for the categories that are included, the case made in this statement is, broadly, correct—*both two decades ago, and also today.*

Then, as now, males rather than females predominated among those falling behind in school and being sent to "special education" classes. Then, as now, teenage boys were much more likely to commit suicide than teenage girls. Then, as now, girls' overall broad retention and success rates in school were not of the pattern that was previously associated with "disad-vantaged" groups. But then, as now, women went on in later life to have much poorer incomes and employment achievements than do men (Aus-tralian Bureau of Statistics, 1993; Kenway & Willis, 1995; Yates, 1986, 1993a; Yates & Leder, 1996). Equally, none of these indicators has an un-problematic meaning, but that is an issue for other discussions.[3]

To take one example: School retention rates were, and are, a traditional indicator of (class-based and race-based) inequality, but, in the statistics quoted in the 1975 Australian report that represented the initiating case launching a reform policy agenda for girls, the gap between the overall re-tention rates of girls and those of boys was extremely small (boys, 34.1%; girls, 31.7%—and girls' retention rates passed those of boys in *1976*), whereas class differences at the same period were extremely large (as one crude indicator, the retention rates of private schools were 90.3% and those of government schools, 27.3%). There were significant differences in patterns of subject-choice and success in mathematics and science, but to some extent the dramatizing of these rather than overall retention as in-dicators was a consequence rather than source of the concerns about what happened to girls. And there were very significant sex-based differences in entry to higher and further education. There were certainly grounds for being concerned about what happened to girls through schooling, but what I am trying to show is that the pattern of what is picked up as a significant feature of schooling shifts. Some broadly similar interpretations can be made using data in the U.S. report, *How Schools Short-Change Girls* (American Association of University Women [AAUW], 1992), which is *not* simply a story that girls do badly at school.

So the present debates somewhat misrepresent the nature of the in-equalities from which the gender reforms began. Women and girls did ex-perience social inequalities, and this fed a new attention to which aspects of educational processes were contributing to this (particularly subject-choice, career advice, share of teachers' attention). But on many other measures, in relative terms, even in the 1970s, girls were doing well *at school*. Similarly, boys' problems at school had already long been a sub-ject of fascination for sociologists (dropping out, school resistance, delin-quency), educational psychologists (remedial teaching), and policymak-ers. It was not the discovery that girls and not boys had problems that prompted the new reform, but a social movement, the Women's Move-ment, and the broader work, social and cultural changes of the late 20th century. These spawned a new concern about girls' outcomes from their education and a new commitment to investigate how girls' problems had been made invisible in the previous research and policy agendas, and to attempt to redress this (Yates, 1993a, 1998b).

In emphasizing some ways in which the "facts" about education patterns such as retention were not markedly different from those now being "discovered" and used as justification in the call for new attention to boys, I am not suggesting that no specific problems regarding girls were identified, nor that the education pathways and outcomes for girls and boys have remained unchanged. In Australia as well as in England and Scotland (Arnot, David, & Weiner, 1996, 1999; Powney, 1996) there has been both absolute and relative improvement in the educational achievements of girls. In the world economy, too, there has been a significant reshaping and relocating of work, involving the loss of many areas of traditional male employment. But a number of the grounds on which the case for attention to the boys is now being justified existed and were known at the beginning of the wave of reforming policy directed to girls. Yet at that time it was widely accepted that, insofar as policy reforms needed to deal with "gender" and "sex equity," then they were an issue about girls and women, not boys and men, whereas today boys are taken as a legitimate, indeed compulsory, concern for gender equity programs (Browne & Fletcher, 1995; Gilbert & Gilbert, 1998; Lingard & Douglas, 1999; Ministerial Committee on Employment, Education, Training and Youth Affairs (Australia) [MCEETYA], 1995; O'Doherty, 1994; West, 1996).

So it is not, after all, a simple story where the "disadvantage" of girls was discovered, attended to, at least partially fixed up, and then replaced by some of the same processes in relation to boys. The "facts of the case" are a useful reminder that the discourse, the broad context of action and research ("sex equity," "gender-based reform"), assumes a taken-for-grantedness that hides the politics of what is being taken up and whose definitions are being taken up.

Who Is Disadvantaged and What Does Inequality Look Like? What Is "Sex Equity" and "Gender-Based Reform" About?

Projects of gender equity in schooling, though by no means uniform in their politics or their framing assumptions, have been broadly concerned with inequalities and also with reassessing and changing school's part in the formation of gendered identity (student self-perceptions, values, ambitions, skills, social relationships).[4] The current concerns about boys pose a challenge to elaborate at a public level the broad agendas framing both enterprises.

The projects and discussions concerned with boys are not unitary (for good overviews see Connell, 1995; Gilbert & Gilbert, 1998; Lingard & Douglas, 1999). Some writers, such as Connell (1989, 1994, 1995), MacLean (1995), Gilbert and Gilbert (1998), and Lingard and Douglas (1999), have contributed complex analyses and research on the subject. But public and popular accounts of the need to reform schooling for boys most commonly draw on two simple themes: that it is boys who are now "losing out" at school, as evidenced by changing patterns of results in the final examinations; and that what is needed is to take over strategies that have been successful for girls, and apply these to boys.

In the next sections of this chapter I want to look at some assumptions and implications of those commonly heard themes. This popular form of the challenge to focus on boys, I will argue, sets aside the actual social/economic significance of the examination results that are the focus of so much attention; sets aside the historical construction of schooling as the site of gender reform; and, above all, fails to deal adequately with power and with masculinity and femininity as relational phenomena.

Inequalities and Examination Results as a Benchmark

Recent discussions about changes in the patterns of final examination results of girls as compared with boys have led to some detailed debate about which groups are and are not successful here, and which groups are and are not advantaged by current assessment and ranking procedures (see Arnot et al., 1996; Davy, 1995; Foster, 1994; Powney, 1996; Teese, Davies, Charlton, & Polesel, 1995). What is less remarked on is the assumption being made about the significance of school final year results as the benchmark for assessing inequalities (Yates & Leder, 1996). The specific event that sparked a major Australian inquiry into boys and education (O'Doherty, 1994) was the publication of some final year school statistics in which girls, for the first time, gained some of the highest mathematics results. The results that drew the debate concerned a minority of students, those students doing the very "hardest" subjects, and getting the very highest results. The newspapers, which have a long-standing preoccupation with the top results in the annual examinations, seized on some results where girls, for the first time, were top students in the highest level mathematics subjects, both as evidence of an enormous turnaround in gender patterns in school and as a signal that something now had to be done about the "underachievement" of boys (this debate is discussed more fully by Foster, 1994).

The results under discussion *were* a change in the patterns of school success in that, for a long time, although girls had been successful in many areas, success in the "highest" levels of the very "hardest" subjects had eluded them. But the emphasis given to this particular change very much narrowed and abstracted the focus on gender and inequality.

For almost 20 years, girls' overall retention and success rates in Australian schools had been higher than those of boys—but, in relation to girls, those examination statistics had never *sufficiently described or accounted for* the patterns of sex-related inequality in schools. Although girls' lesser participation and success in mathematics contributed to their more restricted educational and employment paths beyond school, the latter went far beyond what could be accounted for by the former (see Yates, 1993a). And the projects of gender reform for girls in schools had been concerned about inequalities in the curriculum and processes of schooling, about how schooling was contributing to different futures for girls and boys by what they learned there, how they developed there—and not just by what examination score they obtained (i.e., relative to a particular level of actual school success in mathematics, girls, on average, would make less of it in terms of future educational career and in terms of eventual career "payoff").

Reports on girls and inequality did look at patterns of school success, but they also drew attention to the different *outcomes* of schooling for girls, to the ways school *directed and limited* the paths taken by girls (stereotyping women; directing girls to a narrow range of post-school courses and jobs); and to ways curriculum and pedagogy *was biased* in taking men and not women as actors in the world, and in treating women and girls as "other."

Given this background, to argue that it is boys rather than girls who now need to be seen as the focus for sex equity work should require some attention to (a) whether the payoff of schooling for girls has now been turned around and (b) whether school curriculum and pedagogy are now focused on women's and girls' ways of knowing and their interests. Simply showing that girls' retention rates have continued to grow, or that some girls have increased their participation in mathematics and their success in this, is not enough.

Weiner, Arnot, and David (1997) make a similar point about the debate as it has been shaped in the United Kingdom: "Significantly, this pattern of *male advantage* in employment which is common in both the public and private sectors, is not alluded to within the current educational discourse of male disadvantage." David also makes the point that, "It is a comparative statement that boys are doing less well than girls. However, all boys and all girls are doing better than they did five years ago" (in Kemal, Leonard, Pringle, & Sadeque, 1996, p. 69).

In fact, in Australia, the picture regarding what has happened to males and females as a result of school reforms and labor market changes is mixed. While there has been change in some "outcomes" areas (more women now undertake degrees, and more enter medicine and law; and there has been some decline in women's unemployment rates), there is also evidence of lack of change in others: Overall, women in Australia still enter a relatively narrow range of jobs; are a minority in the senior ranks of most areas of employment and particularly in business; and their average weekly incomes relative to men's improved steadily from the early 1970s until the mid-1980s, but have remained static since the late 1980s at around 83% (Australian Bureau of Statistics, 1993; Kenway & Willis, 1995; Walpole, 1995).

So the continued focus on a small section of the year 12 results as if they are a straightforward indicator of what schooling does for girls and boys is misplaced.[5] This popular way of taking up examination results gives undue emphasis to what is happening to a small group at the top, in the process drawing attention away from how class differences operate within the groups of girls and boys. This approach not only constructs "girls" and "boys" as unitary categories rather than categories permeated by educationally important differences, it also deals inadequately with how *gender* is part of the process. By abstracting out the single indicator of year 12 results, the discussion fails to consider the specificity of the *form* of girls' inequality (as discussed above), and it also deals poorly with masculinity and with how gender can contribute to some patterns of failure for boys and to restriction in payoff for high-ability girls. The suggestion is that if there are some lesser results of boys, then it must be due to girls' having been given special assistance in recent years, or to school and assessment authorities now adopting "girl-friendly" strategies and failing to institute "boy-friendly" equivalents. Conceptually, the issue of girls and boys, pedagogy, and outcomes is treated as a rather mechanical process, in which discrete advantages are bestowed on groups through techniques of particular kinds.

Richard Teese's work, however, suggests that it is possible to look at the broader patterns of subject-choice, success, and failure with more subtle assumptions about gender as a phenomenon—assumptions that see gender as relational, and subject-choice and success as being embedded in broader discursive constructions of masculinity and femininity (and class and ethnicity; Teese et al., 1995). From a major survey of Australian year 12 subject-choice and assessment results, Teese argues that gender contributes to a much broader failure of boys than that picked out by the focus on a few top students—in that it persuades boys to "over-enroll" in mathematics and thus to produce a greater overall proportional failure for boys in this area—a pattern that has been evident for some time. Similarly, Teese argues, gender (in conjunction with the structure of the assessment system) contributes to a phenomenon of high-ability girls not getting the rewards and outcomes that accrue to high-ability boys (in that humanities choices bring penalties in relation to maximizing one's score and one's post-school career rewards).

Gender Reform Strategies

Just as the public discussion of year 12 results in Australia has tended to detach "sex equity" comparisons from the broader social location and effects of schooling, some of the reform strategies now being suggested for boys also take up the issue as if it were about abstracted technologies for success, rather than related to historical and social constructions (*sex equity* is also itself a problematic term that encourages detached mathematical comparisons rather than attention to social meanings of equality and inequality). The quote that follows, taken from the foreword to a recent book, *Boys in Schools,* intended for teachers, takes up the rhetoric earlier applied to reforms for girls:

> Boys will change when they are helped to understand themselves better, are affirmed and valued "as they are" and are given the tools to feel safe and equal around girls. . . . It's time we honoured and put a positive value on the unique qualities of boys. (Biddulph, in Browne & Fletcher, 1995, pp. ix, x)

This quote takes up the rhetoric of the earlier reforms directed to girls, but ignores both the institutional history of schooling and the concern about gendered power relations that formed their social foundations. For the past decade or two there has been, in Australia, some funding, research, and professional development specifically focused on girls, but this does not reproduce for boys a mirror image of the situation in which girls were earlier seen to be disadvantaged. Textbooks today are not full of women and silent about men; the "reproductive" aspects of society (cf. Foster, 1995; Martin, 1982) are still a minor and low-status element of the curriculum; and pedagogies that benefit girls have not made boys invisible to the teachers.

Even the concern about school practices limiting students by the ways they construct femininity and masculinity is not a mirror image argument for boys and girls (as Connell, 1989, 1994, and MacLean, n.d., 1995, have well argued). Individual boys (or categories of boys) may be distressed by their failure to measure up to desired masculine attributes such as sporting prowess, size, and technical and scientific achievement; but those characteristics of "hegemonic masculinity" (to quote Connell) were ones that bring social power, status, and financial reward. In the case of girls, however, a starting point agenda was that even what schools promoted for girls was socially disabling:

> An observer not raised with our cultural assumptions would be struck by the fact that one half of the population was assigned by birth to activities which, whatever their private gratifications and social importance, carried no economic reward, little public status, and very limited access to public power. (Schools Commission, 1975, p. 8)

The distinctions here are of considerable significance in terms of reform strategy and of policy in relation to public schooling. Both girls and boys may be made unhappy by their failure to measure up to what is ostensibly promoted and valued by schooling, or their peers, or the media. But a strategy whose aim is simply to extend the public power and status outcomes of the group in question is very differently located than one whose aim is to reduce or redirect that group's share of public power or is to challenge more broadly what is currently valued and rewarded in the broader society. The problem here is one that affects both the public policy formulation level of gender reform and also microlevel strategies of gender projects.

Reform Agendas and Their Limits Within Public Policy

Earlier I suggested that the recent taking up of boys' issues as a key concern in gender equity work was not simply a response to changes in patterns of school success or of social inequality. I now want to consider further why the boys' agenda may have arisen at this point, and the issues that this raises in relation to gender matters and school reform.

In Australia, the debate about boys' results took off not when it was discovered that boys, proportionally to those doing it, failed mathematics in higher numbers than did girls—that had been the case for some time.[6] It was a response to boys beginning to lose out to girls in the very top categories.[7] I would argue that the way in which this debate broke out, and the way it has been handled, points to some features of the sources and the discursive form of public policy. The case study of Australia that I will discuss I would suggest points to processes that can be seen in other countries, but with some contextual specificity. I am aware that the specific form of final school assessment and tertiary entrance, and the public discussions in Australia, more clearly take mathematics as the singular privileged indicator of prestigious intellectual achievement than do some other countries (consider the United Kingdom's A-levels, for example; or even more strikingly, Bourdieu's discussions of France).

In Australia, one notable feature of reforms concerned with girls has been that many of the beneficiaries have been middle-class girls. Private girls' schools have taken up feminist agendas even more strongly than public schools (Abbott-Chapman, Hughes, & Wyld, 1991; Connell, Ashenden, Kessler, & Dowsett, 1982; also, annual reports on *Girls in School* produced by the national Department of Employment, Education and Training since 1988). There has been an articulate and strong middle-class lobbying for women's interests in education. So, one might argue, for some time the gender agenda has represented an extension of middle-class interests without threatening middle-class interests.

The examination results that sparked the debate and inquiry, however, introduced something new onto the scene: the issue that there *is* some zero-sum aspect to schooling achievement patterns. Now it is becoming apparent that it is not only working-class boys and men who are being affected by the changes of recent years (many manual jobs were the first to disappear)—it is middle-class boys who may be being "deprived" of a place in medicine because a girl has done better; or who may be being "deprived" of optimum learning conditions because girls are going off to single-sex classes rather than being a supporting influence on their own learning environment (Foster, 1995). So two things are happening here: a threat to the group whose power has been greatest, and also the beginnings of an inkling that gender reform programs cannot just go on improving the competitive outcomes of schooling for some students without, in relative terms, affecting the outcomes of others.

What I have been suggesting in these sections is that the coming into force of the challenge to look at boys in gender work in schools raises more far-reaching problems than the problem of "what to do about the boys." It raises the problem of how gender equity in general can be maintained as a public policy issue. Schooling is a selecting mechanism in relation to post-school power, income, and privilege, but the policy discourse is one in which it is only possible to talk about improving outcomes for groups without acknowledging that it is not possible for all students to get the good jobs, and that it will not be politically acceptable to pursue a policy where those who already have power see the chances of their own children being overtly undermined. Debates of this kind have been seen already in relation to affirmative action programs in employment, but, until recently, in Australia, the idea that the increasing success of girls might have implications for boys, and for particular groups of boys, was not explicitly discussed or obvious.

The Complicity of Academic Researchers in Changing Policy Agendas

One of the aspects of the present debate that is most irritating to those who have been working in the gender area for the past two decades is the charge that there is a desperate need for research about boys because research to date in the gender area has been feminist research that is concerned only with girls.

A consideration of gender, by its nature, has involved the development of theories and frameworks for investigating how women *and men* and how femininity *and masculinity* work: their discursive construction, their patterns of achievement and life patterns, the meanings and implications of "gendered subjectivity," and so on.[8] The lines of research and strategy being discovered and "created" by those working on boys (Browne & Fletcher, 1995; West, 1996) often directly borrow earlier frameworks and findings of feminist gender research: concerns about role models, consciousness raising, concern for boys who are teased because they are not sufficiently masculine, and so on.

Yet it is also true that the great bulk of empirical qualitative work on gender, pedagogy, subjectivity, and schooling in the past two decades *has* studied girls rather than boys. Frameworks and theories might have been concerned with both, but the substantive "findings" and insights were not equally spread.

This issue and its implications have been brought to my own attention by the experience of embarking on a new empirical study after some years of focusing mainly on theory and documents. The study (McLeod & Yates, 1997; Yates & McLeod, 1996) is a qualitative, interview-based, longitudinal study of girls and boys at four different schools from the beginning to the end of high school.

In the project we are interested in some things that have been the focus of a great deal of research in the gender area—including the development of gendered subjectivity over the secondary schooling years, and the workings of gender in relation to schooling and out-of-school life over that time. What we found when we were looking at and attempting to interpret the tapes from our first round of interviews was that the boys in our study seemed interesting and our findings there "unexpected," whereas (for the purposes of research publication) we could find little to say about the girls. But, being good postmodern reflexive researchers, we were equally aware that this reaction was as much a comment on us and what we were bringing to the research as it was on what we were "finding."

To take one example, the boys' responses (at the end of primary school) to how they would describe their friends (being interviewed with them) spoke much more about caring and supportive relationships than we had expected (Yates & McLeod, 1996). The boys fantasized about sport, but also (in a number of cases) about their future married life. As well, we noticed considerable differences among the boys in our study. Now we could describe findings about the girls that parallel the points crudely summarized here: Many girls in the study were widely and intensely interested in sport and fantasized about future stardom in that arena; they, too, differed markedly in their values and hopes. As feminist researchers, however, we expected all this—a legion of books had now told us not to see girls in an essentialist way. We also expected boys not to be a uniform group—in principle. But in practice, we became aware that much of the feminist literature on schools with which we were familiar (particularly the literature directed to school-based action) did treat girls in sensitive detail, while leaving boys as a more shadowy "other"; and treated masculinity as a more crudely sketched out discourse against which femininities were examined.

My experiences in this project also touch on ways in which, as researchers, we find ourselves driven by some of the same forces (such as the search for a new issue) that can be seen in the press debate. An area of research and action (girls and gender) can begin to seem like "old news"; in Thomas Kuhn's terms, to be a paradigm that is providing fewer rewards; or in the harsh context of funding decisions, to be less attractive to funding bodies than the new public concerns about boys. Here I think there is some parallel with the way class issues have become a less prominent area of sociological research on education since the 1970s. Whatever the reason, it is clear from publishers' lists that at this time, very large numbers of researchers have begun to develop an interest in boys as an important issue and thereby to feed as well as benefit from the dominance of this issue within public policy "gender equity" debates—a trend in which I am clearly myself a noninnocent participant.

"Facts," Truths, Public Stories, Inequalities, Feminism . . .

This has been a discussion intended to disrupt some taken-for-granteds of the public form of the emerging boys' gender equity agenda, and to reflect on some different practices and the ways they converge—of class and gender interests; of researchers and the fields they ostensibly address. To go back to my starting story and my questions about this, what are the implications of what I have said?

First, on inequalities, there is more than one set of "facts" and more than one story to tell, even about the same set of figures. The issue of schooling and "gender equity" can look different if you abstract and focus on comparisons at one point (drop-out rate, or final achievement patterns, for example) than if you start with broad social patterns of gendered inequality and relate these to the education processes that produce them (which are not simply relative achievement); and of course all of these look different again if you work with class- and race-differentiated analyses rather than unitary ones.

Second, on policy agendas, we see through the changes of the past few decades the way in which social changes and movements can bring new issues onto the policy agenda (gender equity), but in which there is an ongoing "taming" and reclaiming of these in terms of dominant interests and in terms of how questions may be addressed. Mathematical, categorical comparisons are a common and acceptable tool; claims related to past injustices, or to adjusting the type of social "goods" that are being promoted are making much less progress.

The "what about the boys?" debate has marked an interesting shift in the discursive field of gender and schooling. *Why* it has arisen, *which* boys are getting attention, *what* is now being defined as the evidence of "inequity," and the agendas for further action are the questions that have been the subject of this chapter. These are all issues that warrant attention alongside the empirical investigations and the claims that are too easily taken for granted as "the facts" of the case.

Notes

1. This "story" that I have paraphrased in the opening is one I have seen represented in magazines, newspapers, television programs, and government-commissioned reports and that has been the theme of a number of academic conferences and writings. Three useful books that take up this story and provide interesting discussions of it in ways that are complementary to the present chapter are: MacKinnon, Elgqvist-Saltzman, and Prentice (1998), a collection of papers arising from an international feminist conference held in Umeå, Sweden, in 1995, at which reflection on past gender equity initiatives and a concern about the ubiquity of the "what about the boys?" question was a central focus of the discussions; Arnot, David, and Weiner (1999), a U.K. book arising from a government-initiated consultancy project to assess how the relative equity issues of females and males had been affected by various reform initiatives of past decades; and Lingard and Douglas (1999), a book about the current varied forms of men's relation to feminism and to gender equity issues in education, which includes a good discussion of some major popular publications and debates on these issues around the world.

2. I need to make a qualification here. Funding *was* being spent on areas such as remedial education, delinquency, and so on, that gave heavy attention to boys. But, in contrast to the present-day debate, such funding was not seen as connected with concerns about gender, masculinity, or sex-based equal opportunity in schools. Indeed, one of the problems spawning backlash responses to funding of girls' and women's programs over the past two decades is that these have always been very explicitly tagged as "girls" or "gender equity" spending, whereas the funding that in fact goes to boys and men often has more innocuous labels, such as "sports funding," "remedial programs," "special reading programs," and the like. A recent study in the United Kingdom has found this pattern in the allocation of special needs provision and makes some interesting points about how such provision is unequally distributed along both gender and race lines (see Daniels, Hey, Leonard, & Smith, 1996).

3. In another project (Yates & Leder, 1996), we investigated the meaning and problems of "indicators" used in various government databases in Australia: how they were defined; how the data were collected; what was left out; what perspectives and biases the measure produces about factors such as gender, ethnicity, disability, and more. The report from this study provides a major index, review, and critical discussion of the categories and indicators used in national databases in Australia (copies of the report are obtainable from the author: Dr. Lyn Yates, Graduate School of Education, La Trobe University, Bundoora, Vic 3083, Australia).

4. In other writings (especially Yates, 1993b, and Yates, 1998a) I have discussed differences and changes in the ways girls have been conceptualized as an object of educational research and reform and, implicitly, the fallacy of accounts (such as Moore, 1996) that reductively portray this as a simple and self-contradictory project concerned with "disadvantage."

5. On this issue there is a significant difference between Australia and England. In England (but not Scotland; cf. Powney, 1996), there has not been the same extent of achievement in relative success by girls at A-level; and the "turnaround" in achievement patterns that underlies much discussion is more strikingly seen at GCE (Arnot, David, & Weiner, 1996) and is more commonly discussed in relation to working-class boys (David, Arnot, & Weiner, 1996). But in each case, my point remains: that patterns of school achievement need to be read in the context of other social indicators.

6. Though boys had proportionally higher failure rates, many more boys were taking higher level mathematics, so despite the higher proportion failing, the actual numbers of those passing it were still considerably greater than the number of girls.

7. It was also influenced no doubt by the steady growth in the numbers of girls taking these subjects, though they are still distinctly outnumbered by boys (see Foster, 1994; Teese et al., 1995).

8. Feminist research has not been the only way into these issues. Paul Willis's important 1970s study of working-class masculinity developed from an interest in class-focused ethnography; and many studies (more commonly in the United States and the United Kingdom than in Australia) have developed research on gender as an outcome of a focus on race.

References

Abbott-Chapman, J., Hughes, P., & Wyld, C. (1991). *Participation and retention rates and social and educational factors which are related to them in Tasmania* (2 vols.). Hobart: University of Tasmania, Centre for Education.

American Association of University Women. (1992). *How schools short-change girls*. Washington, DC: Author.

Arnot, M., David, M., & Weiner, G. (1996). *Educational reforms and gender equity in schools*. Manchester, UK: Equal Opportunities Commission.

Arnot, M., David, M., & Weiner, G. (1999). *Closing the gender gap: Postwar education and social change*. Cambridge, UK: Polity.

Australian Bureau of Statistics. (1993). *Women in Australia*. Canberra: Author.

Browne, R., & Fletcher, R. (1995). *Boys in schools*. Syndey: Finch Publishing.

Connell, R. W. (1989). Cool guys, swots and wimps: The interplay of masculinity and education. *Oxford Review of Education, 15*(3), 291-303.

Connell, R. W. (1994). Knowing about masculinity, teaching boys and men. In J. Lemaire (Ed.), *Girls, boys and equity: A practical resource for use in schools*. Sydney: NSW Teachers Federation.

Connell, R. W. (1995). *Masculinities*. Sydney: Allen & Unwin.

Connell, R. W., Ashenden, D. J., Kessler, S., & Dowsett, G. W. (1982). *Making the difference: Schools, families and social division*. Sydney: Allen & Unwin.

Daniels, H., Hey, V., Leonard, D., & Smith, M. (1996). *Gender and special needs provision in mainstream schooling* (ESRC End of Award Report, July 1996). (Available from Dr. Diana Leonard, Institute of Education, University of London, London, England)

David, M., Weiner, G., & Arnot, M. (1996). *Feminist approaches to gender equality and schooling in the 1990s.* Paper presented to the American Education Research Association [AERA] Conference, New York.

Davy, V. (1995). Reaching for consensus on gender equity: The NSW experience. In *Proceedings of the Promoting Gender Equity Conference.* Canberra: ACT Department of Education.

Foster, V. (1994). *"What about the boys!" Presumptive equality, and the obfuscation of concerns about theory, research, policy, resources and curriculum in the education of girls and boys.* Paper presented to the Australian Association for Research in Education Annual Conference, Newcastle, NSW, Australia.

Foster, V. (1995). Citizenship education and *Whereas the people* . . . Another case of "add women and stir?" In L. Yates (Ed.), *Citizenship and education* (Melbourne Studies in Education 1995). Melbourne: La Trobe University Press.

Gilbert, R., & Gilbert, P. (1998). *Masculinity goes to school.* Sydney: Allen & Unwin.

Kemal, S., Leonard, D., Pringle, M., & Sadeque, S. (Eds.). (1996). *Targeting underachievement: Boys or girls?* London: Centre for Research and Education on Gender.

Kenway, J., & Willis, S., with Junor, A. (1995). *Dangerous opportunities: Gender and the restructuring of work and vocational education* (Melbourne, Victorian Education Industry Partnerships Forum Series). Canberra: Australian Government Printing Service.

Lingard, R., & Douglas, P. (1999). *Men engaging feminisms: Pro-feminisms, backlashes and schooling.* Buckingham, UK: Open University Press.

Mackinnon, A., Elgqvist-Saltzman, I., & Prentice, A. (Eds.). (1998). *Education into the 21st century: Dangerous terrain for women?* London: Falmer.

MacLean, C. (n.d.). Boys and education. In Dulwich Centre, *Men's ways of being.* Adelaide: Dulwich Centre Publications.

MacLean, C. (1995). The costs of masculinity: Placing men's pain in the context of male power. In *Proceedings of the Promoting Gender Equity Conference.* Canberra: ACT Department of Education.

Martin, J. R. (1982). Excluding women from the educational realm. *Harvard Education Review, 34*(4), 341-353.

McLeod, J., & Yates, L. (1997). Can we talk about girls and boys today, or must we settle for just talking about ourselves. Dilemmas of a feminist, qualitative, longitudinal research project. *Australian Education Researcher, 24*(3), 23-42.

Ministerial Committee on Employment, Education, Training and Youth Affairs (Australia). (1995). *Proceedings of the Promoting Gender Equity Conference.* Canberra: ACT Department of Education.

Moore, R. (1996). Back to the future: The problem of change and the possibilities of advance in the sociology of education. *British Journal of Sociology of Education,* 145-161.

O'Doherty, S. (Chair). (1994). *Challenges and opportunities: A discussion paper* (Report to the Minister for Education, Training and Youth Affairs on the Inquiry into Boys' Education 1994 by the NSW Government Advisory Committee on Education, Training and Tourism). Sydney: NSW Government.

Powney, J. (1996). *Gender and attainment: A review.* Edinburgh: Scottish Council for Educational Research.

Schools Commission (Australia). (1975). *Girls, school and society.* Canberra: Australian Government Printing Service.

Teese, R., Davies, M., Charlton, M., & Polesel, J. (1995). *Who wins at school? Girls and boys in Australian secondary education.* Melbourne: Melbourne University, Department of Education Policy and Management.

Victorian Committee on Equal Opportunity in Schools. (1977). *Minority report* (by Babette Francis). Melbourne: Government Printer.

Walpole, S. (1995). Gender equity in education: A view from outside the classroom. In *Proceedings of the Promoting Gender Equity Conference.* Canberra: ACT Department of Education.

Weiner, G., Arnot, M., & David, M. (1997). Is the future female? Female success, male disadvantage and changing gender patterns in education. In A. H. Halsey, P. Brown, & H. Lauder (Eds.), *Education, economy, culture and society.* Oxford, UK: Oxford University Press.

West, P. (1996). *Fathers, sons and lovers.* Sydney: Finch Publishing.

Willis, P. (1977). *Learning to labour.* Aldershot, UK: Saxon House.

Yates, L. (1986). Theorizing inequality today. *British Journal of Sociology of Education, 7*(2), 119-134.

Yates, L. (1993a). *The education of girls: Policy, research and the question of gender.* Melbourne: Australian Council for Educational Research.

Yates, L. (1993b). Feminism and Australian state policy: Some questions for the 1990s. In M. Arnot & K. Weiler (Eds.), *Feminism and social justice in education.* London: Falmer.

Yates, L. (1998a). Constructing and deconstructing "girls" as a category of concern. In A. Mackinnon, I. Elgqvist-Salzman, & A. Prentice (Eds.), *Education into the 21st century: Dangerous terrain for women?* London: Falmer.

Yates, L. (1998b). Education. In B. Caine, M. Gatens, E. Grahame, J. Labalestier, S. Watson, & E. Webby (Eds.), *Australian feminism: A companion.* Oxford, UK: Oxford University Press.

Yates, L., & Leder, G. (1996). *Student pathways: A review and overview of national data-bases on gender equity.* Canberra: ACT Department of Education and Training.

Yates, L., & McLeod, J. (1996). "And how would you describe yourself?" Researchers and researched in the first stages of a longitudinal qualitative research project. *Australian Journal of Education, 40*(1), 88-103.

14

Same as It Never Was

Masculinity and Identification in Feminism

BRIAN CARR

Although the political discourses that mobilize identity categories tend
to cultivate identifications in the service of a political goal, it may be
that the persistence of disidentification is equally crucial to the
rearticulation of democratic contestation. Indeed, it may be precisely
through practices which underscore disidentification with those
regulatory norms by which sexual difference is materialized that both
feminist and queer politics are mobilized.

Butler, 1993, p. 4

She is a girl who's trying not to become Woman, but remain responsible
to women of many colors and positions, and who hasn't really figured
out a politics that makes the necessary articulations with the boys who
are your allies. It's undone work.

Haraway, 1991a, p. 20

For Butler and Haraway, feminism is to be found in a peculiar place: It re-
sides not in an identification with "Woman," nor in any simple disidentification with "her." Rather, following Butler's "disidentification" and

323

Haraway's "girl who's trying not to become Woman," feminism makes possible and renders productive the vexed moment at which the subject both recognizes and rejects its place under the law of sexual difference. In this model, feminism arises out of a *conflict,* both identificatory and political, over the regulation of identification within a normative regime of sexual difference. As Haraway makes clear, feminism is never about simply avowing one's identification with Woman, for this would mean no more than the reinvestment of a patriarchal category. However, at the same time, feminism can never lose sight of what it means to "remain responsible to women of many colors and positions."

I begin the turn toward the masculine here, in the wake of feminist theories of identificatory disunity that Butler suggests feminism ought to exploit, precisely because this tension can offer us some important entries into the question of feminist pedagogy and identification in the context of masculinity. Thus, I inhabit the theoretical terrain where Haraway's "polychromatic girl" is left potentially caught—in the space between identification and disidentification—not to promise to rescue the "girl" or feminism from the complexities of identification, but instead to explore what this foundational paradox might offer a critical approach to this book's object of study: masculinity.

Perhaps it seems odd to turn to feminist formulations of the female feminist subject's constitution, since our project here is to understand the relations between masculinity and education conceived broadly. Though my gesture here may seem to move in the wrong direction—toward the "feminine" and away from the "masculine"—I begin here only to resist what I understand as a dominant methodological problem in theorizing the masculine: namely, a certain inability, indeed a refusal, to see a relation between feminism's long history of theorizing its (female) authorial subjects and the subject of masculinity, either as question of representation, practice, or as a potential feminist subject.

In the contemporary moment, debates both internal and external to feminism have produced a set of invigorating, though some have argued debilitating, critiques of the history of feminist methodological and political assumptions about experience, sexual difference, and the oppositional subject.[1] Where feminism has had its moments of characterizing the feminist subject as the possessor of a higher-level and thus more "radical" identification with "woman," contemporary feminism, particularly of the poststructuralist variety, has increasingly turned a critical eye toward this version of feminism where the feminist subject is thought to be an autonomous, transparent, self-knowing renegade beyond the intrusive knowledges of patriarchal practices. Feminists skeptical of this rather modernist rendering of the feminist subject suggest that feminism is not a politically pure or epistemologically unmediated thing one embodies whose privileged locus is the self-same Woman.[2]

But where feminist critics like Butler and Haraway argue against a simplistic notion of woman-identification as the ground of feminism, they have not elaborated on what it means to approach masculinity and men in a context in which a seamless identification with or "as" Woman is no longer revered as the horizon of feminist possibility. If feminism produces the possibility of disidentification as its enabling gesture, if it is the counter-avenue by which Haraway's "girl [is] trying not to become Woman," does it also involve some similar kind of subjective deterritorialization of "masculinity"? Where feminism is understood in the vein of disidentification, this chapter turns to theorize a pedagogy of feminist political identification, one that necessarily offers up a disorienting framework in which to consider the relationship among group and subjective identification, masculinity, men, and feminism. What happens to masculinity when it encounters feminism, and vice versa? Is masculinity under feminist scrutiny just any old masculinity after all? I want to suggest, in the context of thinking about masculinity and educational practices, that it may just be that feminism can seize the possible disjunction between primary (or gendered) identification and political identification characteristic of current feminist theorizing as a way of remaking the masculine subject. If feminism seeks to exploit the cleavage between one's (normative) gender and one's gender *politics*—not as a way of saying that one's politics have nothing to do with one's gender, but to say that one's gender might not overdetermine one's politics in some prescripted way—then this is a model worth pursuing with reference to the male subject whose gendered embodiment and political mobility is thought to be most fixed.

Men in/and Feminism

Though many feminisms, but by no means all, take as axiomatic the notion that any lone version of Woman is necessarily a political and social fiction, they are not always so sure that "Man," too, points toward a politically construed object, one that has its own set of protocols and exclusions. We see this categorical difference between feminist construals of "woman" and "man" most acutely in that by-now-famous early-1990s academic rhetorical marriage: men and feminism. It is no accident that feminism has increasingly turned to study men and masculinity at the same historical moment that it puts a great deal of critical energy into theorizing men's (possible) relationships to feminism. Given the history of the female authorial subject in feminism—that subject whose gendered experience secures for her a rightful, oftentimes politically transcendent place in feminist theory—it makes sense that the move to take men as an object of feminism would entail a consideration of men as feminist subjects. However, though the question is raised again and again of men's "place" in feminism, either as subjects or as disciplinary objects, it became quickly apparent, through much of the literature on "men and feminism," that a certain impossibility governed the idea of men as feminist subjects.

But how did we move so quickly from men and feminism, to the intimacy of the (im)possibility of men *in* feminism, the governing logic by which all questions of men and feminism are so commonly framed, as the infamous anthology in its name codifies (Jardine & Smith, 1987)? Figured primarily through a metaphorics of geographical location, the question of "men in feminism" works on a structural logic of property; one that relentlessly figures feminism as a "place" in which one does or does not categorically belong, through and over which one asserts rights, ownership, and authority. But if the opening critics see such essentialized logics of place as retrograde ways of understanding the psychic operations of feminist political subjects, how is it that men are figured as impossibly mired in a kind of primary identification with masculinity that precludes an identification with feminism, especially if, as critics like Butler argue, feminism is not to be understood as an identification with femininity or Woman?

We might begin to approach this question from the vantage of education (as a broad rubric), that modality that, in institutional venues such as Women's Studies, gives disciplinary legitimacy to identification in the first place and that first leads us to see an essential relationship between who we are (as gendered, among other things like raced and classed) and what we are for (politically). Supposedly, what we are is what we are for; but as feminism and all oppositional discourses know all too well, what we "are" is not always what we are "for," nor can we even separate these terms *are* and *for* from the radically asymmetrical normative and oppositional articulations to which they are bound. This is not meant to bind us to a trajectory of the never-ending game of language, but to ask us to consider the relationship between the psychic ambivalence of feminist political identifications and the materialist practices of institutions like Women's Studies and other modes of feminist practice in the academy.

I maintain that there is an unexplored relationship between these two registers—the psychic or subjective and the institutional or pedagogical—in much of feminist theorizing on the subject of masculinity. Since institutions provide the conditions of possibility for collective and individual identification, why have we not considered feminist pedagogical and institutional work to be an occasion to challenge the rehearsal of the normative identities of "man" and "woman" as fixed prior to one's engagement with feminism? Cannot feminism itself provide sites of productive disidentification, ones that cross the supposedly impossible divide of sexual difference? Might feminism be said to encode a specific set of political identifications that dislodge the categories of "men" and "women" as they are thought to be the only or eternal horizon through which a feminist politics can be waged?

For Avital Ronell, feminism is precisely about the production of counter-frameworks: "Feminism as a force or intensity has to disrupt all officially charted maps—it calls for the *remapping* of relationships" (cited in Juno & Vale, 1991, p. 134). Following Ronell's characterization of feminism as a rerouting of political and libidinal energies, what she calls a "force or intensity," I want to understand feminism not as a "place" or a "position," but as a force that, at its best, serves to render the categories of "men" and "women" always potentially out of their disciplinary place. It is here—in the potential for a feminist political identification to disorient our navigation of the "officially charted maps"—that the "ground" of men and women becomes decidedly inadequate as the only modality in which feminism's authorial speaking subjects can be understood.

To imagine feminism as a force that interrupts the seamless "reality" of sexual difference and its operation shifts feminism from its ontological mirings ("Are you a feminist or not?") toward a more dynamic understanding of feminism's reach. Though I use Ronell's language of feminism as a force here, she falls somewhat short of realizing its potential. Feminism is not just a *call* to remap relationships, though it is surely that. It is *itself* evidence of a remapping of relationships insofar as it offers us a counterreality, one that Elizabeth Grosz (1991) calls a form of "collective psychosis" (p. 39). In the space of this metaphorical psychosis, it may just be that feminism takes over, troubling anything we might easily call the "reality" of sexual difference. That is, if there is no one place to find any given masculinity—as surely this book would agree, the signs of gender are highly contextual—is feminism not itself the occasion in which the masculine is made different, contested, re-formed?

To theorize feminism's authorial subjects as the subjects of a political identification that refuses, in part, the categorical condensations of "men" and "women" requires engaging the set of feminist critiques of identity, experience, and politics that have governed so much of contemporary feminist critical thought. Such methodological inquiries can shift the terms of *men* and *women*—and the question of "men in feminism"—to a more productive engagement where, as Joseph Boone (1992) suggests, we can "formulate terms for presenting the issue of 'men and feminism' so as to not limit its possibilities, overdetermine its body, from the outset" (p. 11). For Boone, we must enact a pedagogy that refuses to foreclose the possibility of multiple feminist entries, ones that are not tied to normative logics of (hetero)sexual difference. This suggests that we must shift away from what can too often be the mere reinvention of men and women as the ground of feminism—from, that is, a practice that must continually redis-cover what it already thinks it knows: that men and women are differ-ent—and toward an interrogation of feminism's own categorical creations that have produced, however enabling, a set of regulatory avenues in which a feminist "becoming" can occur.

In attempting to account for feminism's rethinking of "men" and "women" as wholly adequate categories for a feminist politics, Sandra Harding (1987) claims that the untenability of a singular disciplinary ob-ject called "woman" comes chronologically after feminism's realization that "man" is itself a false uniformity. She says, "Once we realized that there is no universal 'man,' but only culturally different men and women, then 'man's' eternal companion—'woman'—also disappeared" (p. 7). However, Harding's gesture elides the ways in which feminism's critique of a universal "man" has historically inserted the additive category "woman" as the excluded term. It has not been, as Harding suggests, that when feminism saw the nonuniversality of "man" it therefore produced a nonuniversal woman; in fact, many have spent their efforts criticizing feminism's deployment of a supposedly universal Woman. Feminism has much more regularly worked on the assumption that if "man" is only a part of humanity, the rescue and addition of "woman" will make it whole. Thus, universality, though not complete with just "man," will be solved through the return of "woman" to the democratic social scene.

Positions, Territories, Locations

One of the problems of theorizing masculinity today, as my concerns hope to demonstrate, is that in fact feminism's proliferation of woman to women, from singular to plural, has worked precisely on a notion of a universal "man." Harding's observations work, in part, to elide the way in which feminism's recognition of categorical differences within the production of "women" has emerged decidedly before its recognition of "men" as fractured and fracturing category. Thus, the 1980s in the United States marked a particular methodological move where "man" still remained a totalized site of hegemony for feminist theory measured against "women" as the pluralist haven of "difference."[3]

To suggest that man is a differential category is not to say that it is as equally or analogously fissured as woman, nor that it does not carry with it a mark of privilege. Indeed, this would do no more than concede feminism to a kind of radical individualism in which a systemic critique of social relations has all but totally dropped out. What it is to say is that the sociosymbolic structure of sexual difference maps the supposedly given category "men" in differential terms, ones that refuse the monolithic elision of "masculinity" (as privileged) with all bodies historically regarded male.[4] To suggest that the logic of sexual difference *succeeds* in marking male and female bodies through a simplistic binary figuration of masculinity and femininity is to miss the constitutive failure in the social production of sexual difference. This failure, as Judith Butler (1990, 1993) has most famously suggested, constitutes one of feminism's most radically subversive, and forcefully enabling, claims.[5]

To trace the failures in the production of sexual difference—or the moments, nodes, and sites at which social power does not uniformly accrue along a pregiven male/female divide—is also not the same thing as marking the ways in which men are situated *as* women. Turning to men who supposedly occupy the structural positions of women in particular cultural formations has been one of the primary ways in which critics have attempted to think about the social privileges of gender in more complex terms. But the argument that sexual difference situates some men (usually framed as always already socially marginalized; read gay, "of color," etc.) in a structural relationship usually reserved as the "place" of women risks reessentializing this "position" of women as somehow a priori instead of interrogating the cultural work though which such a "place" is maintained.[6]

Moreover, any analysis of feminism's role in reproducing this faulty logic of "place" is rarely interrogated. In fact, it has been primarily through this essentialized logic of "place" that feminism has framed, either positively or negatively, the question of "men in feminism." For if men can be shown to stand in the structural place of women, it becomes possible, for much of feminist theory, to imagine them being "in" femi-

nism. For Cary Nelson (1987), "men in feminism" is only thinkable insofar as certain men are really, in the symbolics of patriarchal hierarchies,
women. He says:

> The West has numerous hierarchically disenfranchised others by way of which
> it asserts and maintains its confidence and prestige. Variations on categories of
> race, class, religion, and ethnicity regularly place men in some respects in the
> situation of women; indeed, these are the experiences that some men draw on in
> seeking ways of empathizing with and being "in" feminism. (p. 159)

Thus, for Nelson, one's "in-ness" vis-à-vis feminism necessarily requires
the "experience" of "being" in "the situation of women."

Nelson's reassertion of the rigidity of the place of women in a feminist
analytic begins to resolve into a theoretical lapse wherein, as Diana Elam
(1994) warns, there is "the danger . . . that women stop being a *question* for
feminism and that identity functions as a normative ideal" (p. 73). In the
wake of Elam's warning, it seems we might pose the question of men's
"experience" differently, asking to what extent Nelson's narrative of male
feminist "in-ness" rides on a rather facile (under)theorization of what it
means to talk about women's relationship to feminism. Nelson works precisely on a notion of "woman" as a "normative ideal" and thereby refuses
to take "women in feminism" as itself a question that has surely not, by any
means, been solved.

Since Nelson's way of thinking about feminism and experience is para-
digmatic of the "men in feminism" question as most critics have posed it, it
seems clear that the move to "men in feminism" itself entails a certain kind
of feminist disavowal of its own. It is too telling that feminism's move to
theorize this joinder "men and feminism" emerges at the same historical
moment in which feminist theory puts a great deal of critical energy into
displacing the epistemological security thought to govern that other rhe-
torical/political pair: women and feminism. That is, it becomes clear that
feminism's inability to grapple with the internal contradictions of
women's relationships to feminism (even their vehement refusals of it)
produces a reactionary turn to men as that site at which both these things
called "women" and "feminism" will be reconvened as stable and self-
evident. In this light, it may just be that the turn toward the masculine
within feminist theory has served a compensatory function: It has become
a sight for the resurrection of the humanist subject, the female version of
which was recently shot down by a certain strain of feminist theory.

We might thus rewrite Elam's warning about women "ceasing to be a question for feminism" somewhat differently through the detour of "men in feminism," suggesting that the very positing of men as a question can serve to alleviate the question of women altogether. The singularity with which the question of "men in feminism" is posed serves to elide the contractions at the very heart of a feminist identification (Is feminism about an identification with woman or a disidentification with "her"?). Here, the critical focus on "men in feminism" becomes that modality by which "women in feminism" is displaced as a nonquestion, and thus turned into precisely the kind of regulatory ideal with which Elam is most concerned. This is not to say that a critical engagement with the categories of men and masculinity (though not at all synonymous or uniformly linked) cannot be a productive turn for feminist theory. However, if such a shift in the object of study retains the methodological investments that its supposedly subversive shifting was meant to unmake or at least think differently, it risks reinscribing, in a newly disavowed fashion, the story of feminism's analytic of gender and sexual difference as unfettered once again. Indeed, a shift only in the object of study, from "woman" to "man," is really no shift at all.

To mark, as Nelson does, the sites at which the "feminine" is a structuring logic within the category "men" is finally never to take seriously the internal failures of sexual difference itself. Instead of grappling with the authorial narrative of "women's experience," which underwrites the assumption of what Rosi Braidotti (1990) calls the "female feminist subject," Nelson instead furthers the hegemony of "women's experience" in feminism by extending it across the board, to that locale in which it otherwise does not reside, as the newly discovered property of (some) men. Such an extension not only retains the fiction of a transparent, knowing, and experiential female subject for feminism, but does so in what can only be read as a strengthening of feminist models of the oppositional subject and her/his experience that were supposedly being critiqued precisely at this historical juncture.

As Diana Fuss (1989) argues, formulations of "place" such as Nelson's not only reveal the "place of essentialism" within the "men in feminism" question, but they betray a pernicious "essentialism of place" (p. 19). It is such a locational politics that motivates the newfound autobiographical maleness of the male feminist critic, one of the most regulatory rhetorical frameworks through which the male feminist finds access to a place in feminism.[7] Michael Awkward (1995), in his theorization of what he terms a "black male feminism," utilizes precisely this posturing: "At this early stage of male feminism's development, to speak self-consciously—auto-biographically—is to explore, implicitly or explicitly, why and how the individual male experience (the "me" in men) has diverged from, has created possibilities for a rejection of, the androcentric norm" (p. 44). Here, Awkward tropes a specific historical form of feminist knowledge—the personal autobiography—as a way of imagining men's "in-ness" with regard to feminism. But still, the particularization of the subject—its individualization as "me"—is about an ever-more normative discourse of proof: Men must prove that, really, their experiences differ from the supposed norm of patriarchal subject production and thus they can be "in" feminism.

Pedagogies of the Personal in Feminism

Women's Studies is no pedagogical stranger to the practices of autobiographical speech as a form of intellectual and political work. Indeed, as anyone who has ever taught or participated in a Women's Studies course knows, most of the students believe the Women's Studies classroom and its forms of knowledge to be highly personal and therefore ripe ground for a variety of autobiographical practices. And though there is nothing inherently wrong or conservative about autobiography, it usually appears only as the antidote to more theoretically based (read masculine) critical approaches within feminism. In such dominant formulations of autobiographical experience, the "personal" level of autobiography is understood as operative in the domain of "the real," against which some feminisms situate the symbolic "masculine" realm of theory and not-so-readily transparent forms of critical and political practice.

When the autobiographical provides the dominant frame of feminist identification and experiential mobilization, it risks, as all claims to the purity of the real do, eliding the institutional and social contexts that give rise to our understanding of our own experience and memorial history. Though, personally, I may narrate my relationship to feminism through a set of identifications and disidentifications with the regulatory production of sexual difference, my experiential story will nevertheless bear the trace of convention, no matter how oppositional it may be. That is, one's ability to make sense of one's place in feminism will always bespeak a set of ideological relations, not some "real" relationship between the subject and feminism.

For someone like Nelson, gay men and men of color have a more "real" connection to feminism because of their more "real" connection to women. However, there is no "real" proximity between, for instance, gay men and women. Indeed, such a linkage is really more the product of a phobic management of (homo)sexual difference that construes all forms of differences within the category of "men" into a binary logic of sexual difference. One may, however, use these phobic associations productively—as Nelson suggests, many disenfranchised men "draw on" their experiences of oppression as the source of a feminist identification. But we also must not forget that such routes into feminism are in part the effect of feminism's own normative ways of imagining what brings someone to feminism, what the condition of feminist authorial candidacy is. The autobiographical in feminism too often seeks an authentic relationship between the subject and feminism, instead of focusing attention on the set of explicitly social narratives, many of them feminism's own, through which the feminist subject is interpellated into feminism. These narratives are not to be confused with the real: They are entirely social, constructed, and, as the rest of this chapter will suggest, feminism's pedagogical responsibility.

The problem with autobiography as a pedagogical framework is that a feminist becoming is waged only in terms of the subject's knowledge about herself/himself—waged, that is, at the level of one's own always retroactive narrative of memorial experience. But might we shift the terms from experience to identification, asking what it might mean to stage a relationship to a feminist politics in terms of political identification? In doing so, we might question the identificatory ground of feminism that imagines the feminist subject only in terms of gendered identifications or "placement": The feminist subject is either a woman, a man supposedly situated in ways akin to women, or a (gay) man with the supposed psychic attributes of women. In shifting away from these notions of primary identification that always locate politically resistant identifications in personal (gendered) history, we can refuse the territorial metaphorization of feminism as a "place" to which one does or does not belong and also begin to think about feminism beyond a condition of "being." Perhaps it is not wholly adequate to ask whether one is or is not a feminist as such, but rather to talk about a political identification with feminism, one that—like all identifications—is surely not necessarily pregiven in one's gender, but instead subject to unprecedented forms of investment and detour that often serve to complicate the relations between one's identity and one's politics.

In order to understand what identification might have to do with the study of masculinity and the possibilities of that project within feminism, I want to turn to an interesting feminist pedagogical moment as outlined by

Barbara Epstein (1995) in her rather reactionary attack on poststructuralist feminist theory, "Why Poststructuralism Is a Dead End for Progressive Thought." Describing a methodological confrontation between herself and her students, who are "imbued with a poststructuralist mindset," Epstein says that the class

> was collectively appalled when I made the argument that there are innate biological differences between men and women and that these differences are socially important, though also socially constructed in an immense variety of ways. My students argued that such a view was antifeminist. . . . I was convinced that outside the classroom, every one of these students lived lives governed by the ordinary view that men and women are sexually different, and that these differences matter. I was struck by the "as if" quality of poststructuralist discourse: one asks not what one actually believes, or how one actually sees the world, but instead adopts a set of rules (everything is socially constructed, one should emphasize culture difference and celebrate it, one should deny innate difference, etc.) and then attempts to filter one's perceptions of the world accordingly. (p. 96)

Epstein's criticism of poststructuralist feminism's "as if" quality is surely a criticism one might make of this piece insofar as I am supposedly not talking about how "real men" and "real women" negotiate their relationship to feminism. However, her relentless anxiety about this kind of feminism's elliptical nature, its refusal to nail down its categories, indeed, its refusal to "get real," must be read in the context of her students' objections. When Epstein calls for us to talk about how we "actually see the world," she mistakes the citation of social norms—our simply admitting how we "actually" see something—with the possibility of actually changing it. To suggest that stating "how one actually sees the world" is adequately feminism's political project misses what poststructuralist feminism has been so insistent to explain: How we "see" the world is always the effect of ideology, and Epstein's claim that the students have "adopted" a set of poststructuralist "rules" misses the more pertinent ruse that what we "actually see" is itself a product of "rules" or norms that have adopted *us*. But the students seem to know, contrary to Epstein, that even though we may all "see" sexual difference a certain (normative) way, it will not be at the level of simply stating so that will bring "reality" into subversive or "unfiltered" focus.

What Epstein's students object to is on the register of *possibility,* of a future beyond modernity's rendering of bodies and selves, beyond Epstein's use of the "innate" to ground feminist political claims. Her students thus resist a certain pedagogical seduction, one entirely endemic to the answer-driven quality of most educational practices: They contest the demand to locate a point of essential difference and simultaneously question the necessity to do so. Indeed, Epstein lays bare that she simply wants them to "admit" to the answer that we all already know—that, after all, men and women are really different. However, for the students here, the answer will not suffice. It does not really matter (does it?) if we all "get real" and admit the "truth" to which poststructuralism has blinded us. They suggest, contrary to Epstein, that even without fictive recourse to the real, the class and feminism can still go on.

After all, we can all point to the supposed "obviousness" of sexual difference; and yes, Epstein is probably right that most of these students "liv[e] lives governed by the ordinary view that men and women are sexually different." But since when is feminist critical thought about pointing out the obvious? What constitutes feminism's difference when it obeys the hegemonic laws of gender's normative organization, denouncing as "lofty" those who refuse to obey the "truth" of sexual difference? And though these students lead lives where sexual difference is recognized, the question is still unanswered as to what the content of this "difference" is or what it means for feminism and the possibility of fostering a collective (classroom) identification. To be sure, the students did not say that they led lives that witness gender's disintegration. What they said, as far as Epstein suggests, is that sexual difference need not ground the classroom discussion in such a way that it goes unquestioned.

This tension between Epstein's invocation of the students' lives "outside" the classroom and their theoretical/political/methodological positions inside it reveals further the contextual nature of gender's signification. If we take seriously that gender is contextually produced, that its meaning is not essential or timeless, then we must confront the ways in which the categories of "men" and "women" do not translate uniformly from one disciplinary location to another. They are categories whose creation and maintenance must be ritualistically attended for their successful execution: They are, in the most saturated sense of the word, performative. What the students say in Epstein's example is that such categories need to be challenged by feminism, not safeguarded by it. They chime with Pat Califia (1997) when she says, "If we really want to be free, women must realize that at the end of [feminist] struggle, we will not be women any more. Or at least we will not be women the way we understand that term today" (p. 90). For Califia, feminism is not the occasion to (re)install gender's normative rule in the pressure to "tell the truth" about how one "really sees the world." Feminism must surely be more ambitious than that.

But there is always a territorial and political anxiety for many when claims to a "feminism without women" are advanced (Modleski, 1991). Once, in a graduate Women's Studies course I took, one of the women claimed, during a discussion of the study of masculinity in feminism, that, "Sometimes I just want to lock the clubhouse." This was a telling moment for several reasons: First, the conversation was not really about men in feminism, but rather it was focused on the study of masculinity and men from the vantage of feminism. Thus, the question of men as objects of feminist study was articulated as an anxiety about men as the subjects of feminist work. Second, it is worth considering how, despite the elaborate system of displacement and metaphor in her statement, everyone still knew what this woman was talking about. We knew, that is, that we had now moved from the original question of a feminism that (might) study men, to one of men who study feminism, and further that the "clubhouse" was feminism (or its institutional form in Women's Studies) and that the folks being locked out would be men. After all, we are all attuned to this logic of the "clubhouse": It is simply another one in a string of territorial metaphors for secret sociality and displaced property ownership.

But the clubhouse also necessarily marshals another set of terms—the clubhouse rules—that several of us in the course were not quite willing to follow. Instead of understanding the clubhouse to be the illegitimate social space where a discrete feminism (comprised of only women) can retreat and wage its war against an imagined monolithic patriarchal headquarters, we raised the question of how this student's use of the "clubhouse" and the exclusion of men from it worked to deny the operation of "competing" feminist clubhouses or of the possibility of a feminism that is not, thankfully, about a clubhouse at all. In fact, her comments were leveled in a course where it was very clear that all the self-identified feminist women where not fighting the same battle, much less doing so in the same way. The "clubhouse" metaphor of woman-identification and sameness as the ground of feminism could not have been more at odds with the way political identifications played out in the classroom, more often than not, across generational and sexual differences.

Primary and Political Identification

For many of us, it was a political identification with certain modalities of feminism (among other things), not one's primary gender identification, that informed the bonds of commonality we might have had with each other. Such a model of identification seeks politics as its common denominator, not essentialized notions of sexual difference that see gender sameness as the ground of feminism. To theorize feminism in terms of political identification requires considering how, as Fuss (1989) suggests, "it is coalitional politics which constructs the category of women (and men) in the first place" and thus it is not necessarily "affinity which grounds politics . . . but politics which grounds affinity" (p. 36).[8]

If politics (re)produces the categories through which it is enacted—if it delimits the field in the moment it appears to represent it—we can begin to imagine the ways in which the languages of feminist politics might themselves be a crucial site in which (political) subjects are framed, imagined, and produced. The question is thus not how does one come to feminism via a reified structure of sexual difference, but rather what kinds of displacements and reorganizations does such a "becoming" exact. More to the point, are not the categories of "men" and "women" deterritorialized through their subjective mobilization within feminism? If feminism has any personal transformative power, is it not precisely that it can produce new configurations of lived categories, that it can be the occasion for an unmaking of "women" and "men" as inevitable and timeless?

Part of what these questions betray is a concern that feminism take responsibility for the identificatory and pedagogical discourse it foregrounds. When a feminist pedagogy foregrounds essentialized understandings of "masculinity" and "femininity," normative gendered identifications are necessarily reinvested, tragically within a purportedly oppositional discourse. In the context of the Women's Studies course, such reinvestments in gendered norms take the form, for instance, of instructors asking men to speak to the "other side" of gender. Indeed, much of feminist work insists on the importance of men in Women's Studies for precisely this reason: Men can tell the women in the course what they supposedly cannot, but must, know about masculinity. But feminism should be refusing such simplistic forms of patriarchal authorization that, as we have surely all seen, allow men to claim that of course they think in sexist ways—after all, they *are* men. Feminist pedagogy should disallow both men and women such normative lines of flight from questions of social justice. It can begin to do so, I think, by foregrounding the trouble at the very heart of all identifications and identities, therefore refusing to provide convenient sites of gendered identification.

When a pedagogical practice begins from a position of sexual difference as the ground of feminism, it winds up overemphasizing the difference between men and women as *the* difference in political identification, instead of exploiting the potential gap between one's gender and one's politics. Importantly, this "gap" only appears as a contradiction or site of conflict within an essentialized notion of sexual difference, one that claims that sexual difference = political difference. Instead of providing a context in which sexual difference is merely recognized and cited, as in the model where men and women speak representatively to their "experiences," feminist pedagogy must foster an understanding of the workings of sexual difference—one of which is the belief that one's interests, politics, and identifications are can all be explained with reference to one's gender. To shatter the belief in the wholeness of one's gendered identity is to begin to move away from an investment in what Silverman (1996) calls the "principle of the self-same body" (p. 35), thus beginning the move out of "safety" in identity as the guarantor of one's politics.

Without the lie of the self-same body, the question of men in feminism is not theoretically impossible; it does not require the impossible ability of the man to project himself into the place of woman, for this model already assumes the fixity of sexual difference as a question of immobile and known "positions" to begin with. We should foreground sexual difference as a discourse, but one that is not wholly coterminous with the subject itself. If sexual difference were totally coterminous with the subject, we would never have sexual difference or feminism as subjects of this book since, if sexual difference "worked," there would be no opposition to it and thus it would not become visible through contention and conflict. Sexual difference is a struggle, emerging as such mostly within the discourses of feminism, and its complex hold on the subject guarantees nothing if not failure. It fails both for those who seek to validate its normativity as well as for feminism inasmuch as it neither "works" to divide the globe conveniently into "man" and "woman" without failure, abjection, and pain; nor does it guarantee for feminism that the female subject will turn away from it in heroic defiance. This failure makes feminism possible and cripples it from the outset, inasmuch as sexual difference cannot finally guarantee anything about political identification.

This last statement is one that feminism has known arguably forever insofar as the project of "consciousness raising," as a broad form of pedagogical and identificatory practice not entirely reducible to its 1970s connotations, has always been haunted by its limitations. Yet these limitations are ones that feminism might not lament, but rather exploit as they mark the moments at which sexual difference does not decide the subject's fate in politics. What I am proposing, then, is a pedagogical model in which feminism takes itself as a discourse of sexual difference, one that, though less popular, is nevertheless integral to the production of gendered subjects and the political identifications to which they might adhere. Feminism does not just answer to the discourse of sexual difference; indeed it inhabits it and remakes it to the extent that it determines what oppositional models of gender identification, embodiment, and political practice will look like.

Feminism has not always been so attuned to its own deployment of social categories and the foreclosures they might exact. More often, it has understood itself as responsive only to broader social institutions such as the family that produce specific kinds of genders and identifications. Instead of seeing feminism as the source of a collectively productive disidentification, feminism has more often understood itself within the logic of identity politics that, as Yingling (1995) draws out,

> fetishizes not only identity but also politics to the extent that it imagines social agency as a compulsion within the subject to implicitly obey and act out the power structures that define it *and* to the extent that it essentializes power as the content rather than the generative effect of social relations. (p. 163)

In this light, the fetishistic relation between identity and politics is one that takes compensatory refuge in identity as a kind of excuse, an alibi that can tell us what a person's politics will be and, conversely, how the "political" will shape her or his "identity." But as the opening critics suggested, feminism is ostensibly not about such a fetishization of the politics/identity dyad insofar as it encodes the possibility of disobedience and disidentification within the regulatory operations of sexual difference. Indeed, feminism would cease to be itself without the hope that the subject might disidentify with the apparatuses through which it is produced. But feminism lays bare its own compulsion to obey when it attempts to reconvene the possibilities and avenues in which such a gendered disidentification can occur.

As we move into a fuller articulation of the problems and promises of theorizing masculinity, I just hope we do not again characterize feminism only as a passive tool in the making of masculinity and femininity and instead see it as productive of forms of (oppositional) gendered embodiment. The hardest questions to ask may be: Will the education that feminism offers crack the complicitous relay between primary identification and politics, thus taking us somewhere we have not already been? Indeed, what kind of subjects will feminism make?

Notes

1. See Butler and Scott (1993) for a variety of takes, usually positive, on the uses of poststructuralist theory within feminism.

2. Indeed, the edition by Elam and Wiegman (1995) suggests that feminism never stands alone, but always beside something else, even itself.

3. See Wiegman (1995, pp. 179-202) for a deeper account of how this plurality of women's differences is still framed within a supposedly originary, binary structure of sexual difference.

4. In the foreword to the collection *The Making of Masculinities: The New Men's Studies,* Catharine R. Stimpson (1987) suggests that "as women's studies brought women into history, men's studies began to ask how men had experienced history as men, as carriers of masculinity" (p. xii). However, though I agree with Stimpson that bringing the category *men* into focus—particularizing it as a local and nonuniversal node of embodiment—is a crucial project, her suggestion that men are always already the "carriers of masculinity" seems to ride on a reduction of the category *men* to its most normative gendered articulation. Indeed, a feminist genealogy of the category *men* (which is not, it seems, the same thing as "men's studies") must take into account the disidentificatory relations men have had with masculinity as well as the relations between men that serve to render severe gradations in what we might recognize as "masculinity."

5. Butler (1993) argues, "This 'being a man' and this 'being a woman' are internally unstable affairs. They are always beset by ambivalence precisely because there is a cost in every identification, the loss of some other set of identifications, the forcible approximation of a norm one never chooses, a norm that chooses us, but which we occupy, reverse, resignify to the extent that the norm fails to determine us completely" (pp. 126-127).

6. As someone who works in film theory, I see this in the history of feminist film theory that understands all subordination in terms of a binary figuration of sexual difference. Film critic Dyer (1986) operates on precisely this problematic when he attempts to describe the filmic means by which black men are "feminized." He says, "The treatment of black men . . . constantly puts them into 'feminine' positions, that is, places them structurally . . . in the same positions as women typically occupy" (p. 116). However, this seems to reify sexual difference as the defining logic of race without qualifying the epistemological underpinnings of the production of sexual difference itself. Further, it does not account for the historical conditions in which this "feminization" has operated so as to displace the threatening possibility of masculine sameness.

7. On the question of what I have called locational politics, see Rich's (1986) formulation of a "politics of location" and Kaplan's (1994) take on the contemporary possibilities and limits of such a conception of the global and local for feminism.

8. Fuss is both working with and against Haraway's (1991b) polemic that a coalitional politics requires "affinity not identity" for its operation. Fuss (1996) develops the relations between affinity and politics more explicitly in terms of identification in her *Identification Papers.* There she argues that where Freud understands the political bond to be the effect of an identificatory sameness, "it may be more useful, and more accurate, to think of politics as originating not in proximity but in distance, not in similitude but in difference, or in the difference that makes a fantasy of similitude possible. . . . Politics thus emerges not out of sameness but out of the noncoincindence between self and other that gives rise to a desire for an illusory sameness" (p. 19, n27). This theorization of political identification as a con-

stituting force is crucial to the way in which I suggest that feminism must rethink the constitutive effects of its own identificatory discourses. It suggests that political identification retroactively produces the subjects it claims to represent and therefore it is at the level of discourses of identification that we might question feminism's regulatory production of identity categories.

References

Awkward, M. (1995). A black man's place in black feminist criticism. In M. Awkward, *Negotiating difference: Race, gender, and the politics of positionality* (pp. 42-57). Chicago: University of Chicago Press.

Boone, J. A. (1992). Of me(n) and feminism: Who(se) is the sex that writes? In J. Boone & M. Cadden (Eds.), *Engendering men: The question of male feminist criticism* (pp. 11-25). New York: Routledge.

Braidotti, R. (1990). *Nomadic subjects: Embodiment and sexual difference in contemporary feminist theory.* New York: Columbia University Press.

Butler, J. (1990). *Gender trouble: Feminism and the subversion of identity.* New York: Routledge.

Butler, J. (1993). *Bodies that matter: On the discursive limits of "sex."* New York: Routledge.

Butler, J., & Scott, J. W. (Eds.). (1993). *Feminists theorize the political.* New York: Routledge.

Califia, P. (1997). *Sex changes: The politics of transgenderism.* San Francisco: Cleis Press.

Dyer, R. (1986). *Heavenly bodies: Film stars and society.* London: Macmillan.

Elam, D. (1994). *Feminism and deconstruction.* New York: Routledge.

Elam, D., & Wiegman, R. (Eds.). (1995). *Feminism beside itself.* New York: Routledge.

Epstein, B. (1995). Why poststructuralism is a dead end for progressive thought. *Socialist Review, 25*(2), 83-119.

Fuss, D. (1989). *Essentially speaking: Feminism, nature, and difference.* New York: Routledge.

Fuss, D. (1996). *Identification papers.* New York: Routledge.

Grosz, E. (1991). Lesbian fetishism. *Differences: A Journal of Feminist Cultural Studies, 3*(2), 39-54.

Haraway, D. (1991a). Cyborgs at large: Interview with Donna Haraway. In C. Penley & A. Ross (Eds.), *Technoculture* (pp. 1-20). Minneapolis: University of Minnesota Press.

Haraway, D. (1991b). A manifesto for cyborgs: Science, technology, and socialist feminism in the 1980's. In L. Nicholson (Ed.), *Feminism/postmodernism* (pp. 190-223). New York: Routledge.

Harding, S. (1987). Is there a feminist method? In S. Harding, *Feminism and methodology* (pp. 1-14). Bloomington: Indiana University Press.

Jardine, A., & Smith, P. (Eds.). (1987). *Men and feminism.* New York: Routledge.

Juno, A., & Vale, V. (1991). Interview with Avital Ronell. In A. Juno & V. Vale, *Angry women* (pp. 127-153). San Francisco: Re/search Publications.

Kaplan, C. (1994). The politics of location as transnational feminist critical practice. In I. Grewal & C. Kaplan (Eds.), *Scattered hegemonies: Postmodernity and transnational feminist practices* (pp. 137-152). Minneapolis: University of Minnesota Press.

Modleski, T. (1991). *Feminism without women: Culture and criticism in a "postfeminist" age*. New York: Routledge.

Nelson, C. (1987). Men, feminism: The materiality of discourse. In A. Jardine & P. Smith (Eds.), *Men in feminism* (pp. 153-172). New York: Routledge.

Rich, A. (1986). *Blood, bread, and poetry: Selected prose, 1979-1985*. New York: Norton.

Silverman, K. (1996). *The threshold of the visible world*. New York: Routledge.

Stimpson, C. R. (1987). Foreword. In H. Brod (Ed.), *The making of masculinities: The new men's studies*. New York: Routledge.

Wiegman, R. (1995). *American anatomies: Theorizing race and gender*. Durham, NC: Duke University Press.

Yingling, T. (1995). Fetishism, identity, politics. In J. Roof & R. Wiegman (Eds.), *Who can speak? Authority and critical identity* (pp. 155-164). Urbana: University of Illinois Press.

Index

343

344   MASCULINITIES AT SCHOOL

About the Contributors

Brian Carr is a graduate student at the University of California, Irvine. His work has also appeared in *Cultural Critique.*

Diane Diamond is pursuing doctoral studies in Sociology at the State University of New York at Stony Brook.

Jackson Katz, Ed.M., is the founder and director of MVP Strategies, an organization that provides gender violence prevention training and materials to the U.S. military services, colleges, high schools, law enforcement agencies, community organizations, and small and large corporations. He is the cocreator of the multiracial, mixed gender Mentors in Violence Prevention (MVP) Program at Northeastern University's Center for the Study of Sport in Society. His film, *Tough Guise: Violence, Media, and the Crisis in Masculinity,* was released by the Media Education Foundation in the fall of 1999.

Michael S. Kimmel is Professor of Sociology at the State University of New York at Stony Brook. His books include *Changing Men* (1987), *Men Confront Pornography* (1990), *Men's Lives* (4th edition, 1997), *Against the Tide: Profeminist Men in the United States, 1776-1990* (1992), *The Politics of Manhood* (1996), and *Manhood: A Cultural History* (1996). He edits *Men and Masculinities,* an interdisciplinary scholarly journal, a book series on Men and Masculinity at the University of California Press, and the Sage Series on Men and Masculinities. He is Spokesperson for the National Organization for Men Against Sexism (NOMAS) and lectures extensively on campuses in the United States and abroad.

James R. King is Professor of Childhood/Language Arts/Reading at the University of South Florida in Tampa, where he teaches literacy and qualitative research. He has taught in a span of classrooms from first grade to graduate students. His studies with faculty at Western Michigan and West Virginia Universities resulted in two graduate degrees in reading and literacy. He has taught with colleagues at the University of Pittsburgh, Texas Woman's University, and the University of British Columbia. Currently, he is researching queer theory in education and the construction of error and accuracy in writing and reading pedagogy.

Jeffrey J. Kuzmic is an Assistant Professor of Social Education and teaches a range of courses in the undergraduate and graduate programs in the School of Education, DePaul University. His research and scholarship have examined the relationship between schooling, society, and the curriculum as a way of understanding educational practice, teacher education, and social and educational change. In particular, his work has focused on the relationship between societal values such as democracy, individual freedom, community, and the purpose of schooling within a democratic society. In his current research project, he and seven beginning teachers are working together in a qualitative study that seeks to explore the lives and work of beginning teachers and their collaborative efforts to conduct research in their classrooms.

Nancy Lesko teaches courses on curriculum, social theories, and gender in the Department of Curriculum and Teaching at Teachers College, Columbia University. She is completing a book that examines the construction of adolescence in psychology and policy, *Act Your Age! Developing the Modern, Scientific Adolescent*.

Máirtín Mac an Ghaill teaches in the Faculty of Social Sciences, University of Sheffield, England. He has research interests in questions of culture and educational arenas and emerging youth identities in a "postcolonial" society. He is the author of *The Making of Men: Masculinities, Sexualities and Schooling*. His most recent publication is *Contemporary Racisms and Ethnicities: Social and Cultural Transformations*.

Laurie Mandel, Ed.D., conducts teacher training workshops on resolving issues of teasing, gender disrespect, and social conflict in schools and teaches at Dowling College. Her current research focus examines the social context of gender relationships through the arts at the elementary school level. In addition, she is researching the relationship between the media, body image and identity.

Khaula Murtadha-Watts, Assistant Professor in the Department of Educational Leadership and Policy Studies, Indiana University, has published in the areas of African-centered pedagogy, cultural studies, and urban school teacher preparation. Her research interests include urban school leadership and women as leaders of organizational change. A mother of six sons and one daughter, she is acutely aware of the challenges facing those who are responsible for educating children in the urban context.

Jan Nespor is an Associate Professor in the Department of Teaching and Learning at Virginia Tech. His research examines curriculum processes in different kinds of educational organizations. In addition to articles in journals such as *Qualitative Studies in Education, Qualitative Inquiry,* and *Journal of Curriculum Studies,* he has written two books, *Knowledge in Motion* and *Tangled Up in School.*

Jeremy N. Price is Assistant Professor in the Department of Curriculum and Instruction at the University of Maryland, College Park. His teaching and research interests focus on understanding the lives of traditionally disenfranchised students and corresponding efforts to transform teaching and teacher education. His recent publications include articles in *Curriculum Inquiry, Journal of Curriculum Studies,* and *Theory Into Practice.*

Kirby Schroeder earned his M.A. in Sociology at SUNY Stony Brook, and is currently pursuing his Ph.D. at the University of Chicago. He intends to focus his dissertation research on women's experiences in military education.

Charol Shakeshaft, Ph.D., is Professor of Administration and Policy Studies at Hofstra University. Her primary research focus is gender and schools, and peer harassment. In addition, she has completed several studies that analyze the relationship between computer use and school achievement.

Melody J. Shank is a doctoral candidate in Curriculum Studies at Indiana University. She has been involved in the Coalition of Essential Schools initiative in Indiana for seven years as a state facilitator and a high school-based restructuring coordinator. In 1998-1999 she served as codirector of the Indiana Essential Schools Network, a regional center for the Coalition of Essential Schools. Her research interests include transforming high school curriculum, collegiality and inquiry among practicing teachers, and creating cultures of inquiry within schools.

John Willinsky is the Pacific Press Professor of Literacy and Technology at the University of British Columbia, and the author of *Learning to Divide the World: Education at Empire's End* (1998) and *Technologies of Knowing: A Proposal for the Human Sciences* (1999).

Lyn Yates teaches in the Graduate School of Education at La Trobe University, Australia. She is the author of many publications relating to inequality, public policy, and feminism and education, including *The Education of Girls: Policy, Research and the Question of Gender* (1993) and the edited collection *Feminism and Education* (1993). She has been Director of Women's Studies at La Trobe University, and is currently President of the Australian Association of Research in Education. Her current major research project, now nearing completion, is the *12 to 18 Project,* a qualitative, longitudinal study of young people, identities, and social and educational inequalities.